# THE JOHN HARVARD LIBRARY

Bernard Bailyn
*Editor-in-Chief*

THE JOHN HARVARD LIBRARY

# ESSAYS

## ON

# EDUCATION

## IN THE

# EARLY REPUBLIC

BENJAMIN RUSH • NOAH WEBSTER • ROBERT CORAM
SIMEON DOGGETT • SAMUEL HARRISON SMITH • AMABLE-
LOUIS-ROSE DE LAFITTE DU COURTEIL • SAMUEL KNOX

Edited by Frederick Rudolph

THE BELKNAP PRESS OF
HARVARD UNIVERSITY PRESS
Cambridge, Massachusetts
1965

Distributed in Great Britain by Oxford University Press, London

Library of Congress Catalog Card Number 65-19830

Printed in the United States of America

# CONTENTS

# 6

## SAMUEL HARRISON SMITH

# 7

## AMABLE-LOUIS-ROSE DE LAFITTE DU COURTEIL

# 8

## SAMUEL KNOX

# INTRODUCTION

Anyone who has been to California recently knows that he is in the presence of the future. He may not like everything that he finds there, but he cannot escape a deep sense that this is where we have been heading all along—a world where everyone is young, including the aged and retired, and where no one works, except teachers. Californians either play in the sun or go to school, and many of them do both at the same time. In the end, when affluence and automation have at last freed all men from the burden of physical labor so that all might pick up the burdens of mind and of heart, California will be indistinguishable from the University of California and all its many satellites. It almost is now, but the extent to which we are nearly everywhere becoming a nation of students and teachers has been hidden from us by our failure to recognize the sum of the parts that make this conclusion inescapable. Retirement comes earlier and lasts longer, vacations are longer and more frequent, marriage comes earlier and the child-rearing days come to an end earlier, and every year we push forward the terminal year of formal education for hundreds of thousands of young men and women.

How did we get here? With what philosophical foundations, and with what social intentions? What may have accelerated or slowed the process? What was the role played by the national government, by state and local government, by the institutions and practices of the economy, by natural and material abundance, by war and peace, by invention, by our history as a nation of immigrants, by measurable and unmeasurable qualities of the people themselves?

An instructive place to begin such an inquiry—and perhaps

the best—is in the company of a small number of men who first addressed themselves to the prospects, capabilities, and burdens of education in the United States. Theirs was not, and is not, the ultimate wisdom on such questions, but they had the decided advantage of not knowing how it all turned out, yet being convinced of what would have to happen if the Declaration of Independence and the American Revolution were to fulfill their promise. Writing in the last quarter of the eighteenth century, they spoke with the sometimes heady optimism of a world that believed in the inevitability of progress, but also with a hard-headed sense of many of the realities which educational undertakings would have to face in the United States. Native-born and foreign-born, ranging in age from twenty-four to forty-one, for the most part college-educated, they pursued careers in education, medicine, law, the church, and journalism. Their audiences were of varying size and description, their motives were not always the same, but all made a contribution to early republican educational thought.

"Early republican" as a style and a mood is not easily defined, but the phrase is intended to suggest what it means for these essays to have first appeared during the years when landmark documents of American national thought and practice were being written—the Declaration of Independence, the Constitution, the Bill of Rights, the Federalist Papers, Washington's Farewell Address. They were published, moreover, at a time when the nation was moving uncertainly and experimentally toward some new understanding of what republicanism could mean in the modern world. These eight essays by seven authors, published between 1786 and 1799, constitute a harvest of what was being said and thought about education during a period in our history when, as we all have known, much was being said and thought about small states and large states, interstate and foreign commerce, agriculture and manufacturing, debts and alliances. These are the major educational statements of the period, and as such they are as essential and

as useful as the familiar economic, political, and artistic documents in any effort to understand the American past.

Some of these essayists were of a more philosophical turn
of mind than others. One may have been more carried away
by the details of a plan or a system, another by the opportunity
to paint wide strokes on an even wider canvass. Some were more
cautious than others in launching into the great unknown of
the American future. Some backed away from a religious role
for the schools; others embraced religion freely. One author
avoided the question of female education as being altogether
too controversial; another devoted an essay to the subject.

Yet, there are words and expressions, touchstones of thought,
that reappear throughout these pages. Humanity is a common
point of departure; human happiness, a common goal. Even
the Calvinists among them, those who through learning or
experience had rubbed up against a less than sanguine view
of man, were optimists. The world can be shaped by men for
men; the very act of composition, the act of public address, the
bid for the attention of one's contemporaries—these are the
gestures of men seeking to be creative in an environment that
invites their creativity. It was a time of the new. There is cap-
tured in these essays a fluid and plastic temper, a deep sense of
a nation being formed, a people's character being shaped, the
destiny of man everywhere being changed for the better. Writing before the habits and practices of a federal polity had become either well understood or deeply ingrained, these essayists for the most part think nationally: sustained by a dream
of the nation that is to be, they leap beyond the provincial
loyalties of colony and state and even beyond the tug-of-war
and divided responsibility of state-and-federal practice. They
would not have understood how in 1964 there could be published under the title *Obstacle Course on Capitol Hill* an account of the repeated failure of Congress to think and act
nationally about education.[1]

1 Robert Bendiner, *Obstacle Course on Capitol Hill* (New York: McGraw-
Hill, 1964).

In their capacity to think nationally these men were informed by a generous view of mankind. Human capabilities, the possibilities of human improvement, the obligations of men to their fellows, the great power of nurture over nature—these articles of eighteenth-century English and French Enlightenment faith directed them to think broadly, to eschew the petty and the purely parochial. Even in Benjamin Rush's plans for Pennsylvania, with their uncharacteristic hostility to foreigners from other states and abroad, there is a magnificent vision of what a great state system of education might have been and of the national influence such a system might have had. "To make mankind better is a duty which every man owes to his posterity, to his country, and to his God," wrote Robert Coram of Wilmington, contemptuously dismissing that pessimistic view of human nature which in the past had held men in chains. "They first frame an hypothesis," he wrote, "by which they prove men to be wolves, and then treat them as if they really were such." The age refused, however, to be immobilized by the hypothesis of human depravity. As DuPont de Nemours noted in his memorandum to Thomas Jefferson, "God did not make bad ones and our education must prevent their becoming so!"[2] Samuel Harrison Smith of Philadelphia suggested how far down the road from the concept of depravity these sons of the American Revolution had traveled: "We should not even convey a suspicion of the honesty of him whom we wish to be virtuous."

The essayists therefore recognized the American Revolution as a dramatic moment in a revolutionary change in the human prospect. The Revolution and the years afterward were for them charged with an aura of urgency. At long last, man was freeing himself from the political, economic, and religious institutions and faiths that had all but held him in contempt: the Revolution opened up a great opportunity for human possibilities, those possibilities for good and for happiness that had

[2] Pierre Samuel DuPont de Nemours, *National Education in the United States of America*, ed. B. G. DuPont (Newark: University of Delaware Press, 1923), p. 82.

too long been denied or frustrated. "Americans, unshackle your minds and act like independent beings" was the summons of Noah Webster. In Massachusetts the Reverend Simeon Doggett catalogued the conditions of man from which Americans were to be spared: barbarism, paganism, Romanism, war, slavery, riot, license, poverty, and obscenity. Samuel Harrison Smith urged his fellowmen to embrace *"what ought to be,* instead of clinging to *what is* . . . Look upon the sentiments of the dead with distrust and oppose with intrepidity the prejudices of the living." Europe, concluded Lafitte du Courteil, is so well advanced toward barbarism that now is a most excellent time for the United States to siphon off all the best and most enlightened talents of the Old World.

Perhaps no one better understood the peculiar challenges of the mission thrust upon Americans by the Revolution than Robert Coram, the Delaware newspaper editor. Americans would have to abolish poverty, for "poverty makes mankind unnatural in their affections and behavior." Americans would not be able to leave the question of education "to the caprice or negligence of parents, to chance, or confined to the children of wealthy citizens; it is a shame, a scandal to civilized society, that part only of the citizens should be sent to colleges and universities to learn to cheat the rest of their liberties." Americans would have to reject "contemptible precedents from arbitrary and corrupt governments." Yet, Coram was not alone in specifying the nature of the demands upon America. All could agree with Webster in acknowledging "the superior advantages . . . [America] enjoys for augmenting the sum of social happiness."[3] All knew, with Smith, that "the era is at hand when America may hold the tables of justice in her hand and proclaim them to the unresisting observance of the civilized world."

The extent to which these essayists spoke a new language for a New World was revealed in the equalitarianism, not al-

---

[3] Noah Webster, *A Collection of Essays and Fugitiv Writings* (Boston: for the author by I. Thomas and E. T. Andrews, 1790), p. x.

ways recognized or acknowledged, that they found implicit in the American mission. They understood the democratic implications of what had been happening in America: the breakdown of social and political controls, the broad availability of careers to ambition and talent, the great imbalance of opportunity to the availability of men. When before had so much opportunity been offered to so few? When before had the possibilities of human life been so much within the power of men to perform? When before had the institutions and practices of society as it was been so inadequate to the needs and interests of society as it was becoming?

Only Lafitte du Courteil, the Frenchman, appears to have misunderstood the American prospect as he wrote in defense of a class- and status-oriented society, argued for the necessary functions of the lower orders, and warned against rearing up only pseudo-philosophers. Yet, his warnings have been repeated in the years since, and they did not actually make him hostile to widespread educational opportunity. Lafitte was an agrarian romantic, one with Jefferson in singing hymns to the simple freeholder, and he would have agreed with Samuel Harrison Smith that "though all men will never be philosophers, yet . . . all men may be enlightened."

And it was just this question of enlightenment that drew thinking men further toward some commitment to equality of opportunity and equality of condition. Smith, for instance, proposed that the hours of labor for everyone be reduced daily by two hours in order to free all men for contemplation and self-improvement. For Smith the leisure on which contemplation and, in the end, wisdom rested was to be universally available, although he respected those individual human differences which might or might not respond to education. Samuel Knox, a Maryland clergyman, appealed to the "rights of man" in his advocacy of an American system of education that would offer "instruction suitable to the offspring of free and independent citizens" in contrast to the great illiteracy and "two pompous universities" of England. For Robert Coram the challenge confronting the Americans was contained in the old problem of inequality which, he decided, was "artificial, not natural." Coram's goal, as of all these men, was a nation of free and independent men, supported by equality of access to education and, thereby, to property. "Are ye aware, legislators," he asked, "that in making knowledge necessary to the subsistence of your subjects, ye are in duty bound to secure to them the means of acquiring it?" And with a logic that joined a Jeffersonian commitment to widespread landholding with the stake-in-society theory held by Hamilton, he remarked, "It is said that men of property are the fittest persons to represent their country because they have least reason to betray it. If the observation is JUST, every man should have property that none be left to betray their country." Such logic paved the way toward equalitarian democracy in the United States, and no institutions were going to be more vital in achieving that democracy than the schools which this group of essayists considered central to the safety and progress of free government.

Free government placed extraordinary demands on ordinary men, and essentially what the Americans were proposing to do was to test the whole question of whether free men could govern successfully. For all the writers the success of the American experiment rested on the agencies of education that the Americans developed. In a society where so much depended on all men rather than on a few great men, Samuel Harrison Smith turned to the schools and colleges for the most widespread diffusion of knowledge. What were the conditions of a free society that argued for diffusion of education? Every man is a voter or a potential voter. Happiness is a commodity that must be available to all, and one great source of happiness is the kind of communication possible only to men of trained intelligence. Enlightenment is a better safeguard of human rights than ignorance. A free society, by being a society open to talent and ambition, encourages self-improvement of an intensity and extent that needs to be serviced by formal education. For Noah Webster the role of education was so central to the working of a free government that he flatly asserted it to be "the most important business in civil society." And like Coram, he stressed the necessity of universal accessibility to education and wealth as the fundamental support of republican government. Simeon Doggett equated tyranny and ignorance, liberty and knowledge. Samuel Knox joined him in recognizing ignorance as "the parent and stupid nurse of civil slavery." The thrust, therefore, that lay behind all these essays was an urgent recognition of the impossibility of a free society without universal formal education, an eagerness to abandon aristocratic notions of who needed to be educated for what roles, a readiness to launch out upon untried educational fields where all men might prove themselves, not only to their own glory but to the glory of man and of God.

If this larger goal inspired the essayists to their most purple prose, they in no sense were prepared to minimize the further burdens they expected the educational establishment to carry. For what was in the making in the United States was not only a republic, a great experiment in freedom. There was also a nation in the making, and education would of necessity play a central role in welding people of diverse backgrounds and conditions, conflicting loyalties, even of strange tongues, into one nation. Samuel Harrison Smith expected the educational system to achieve "harmony at home and respect abroad"; Lafitte du Courteil in effect suggested that the United States would achieve neither unless it did invigorate its educational institutions. Noah Webster would rewrite the textbooks in order to give them an American flavor, discourage the hiring of foreigners as teachers, and as an antidote to European influence and tradition he proposed that "a tour through the United States ought now to be considered as a necessary part of a liberal education."

Because they recognized themselves as being engaged in the making of a nation, the essayists thought readily about education as a national problem and as a national opportunity. Even Benjamin Rush, in designing his systematic plan for Pennsylvania, was writing for the benefit of enlightened statesmen beyond her borders. Simeon Doggett, addressing his little private academy in Massachusetts, was appealing to the universal interest of universal men. All the others wrote more specifically as nationalists, designing elaborate national systems of education, laying down ground rules that would apply in all states, or treating the inherited ills from the past with prescriptions of widespread applicability. Two of the essays, those by Samuel Harrison Smith and Samuel Knox, shared a $100 prize awarded by the American Philosophical Society in 1797 "for the best system of liberal education and literary instruction, adapted to the genius of the government of the United States; comprehending also a plan for instituting and conducting public schools in this country, on principles of the most extensive utility."[4]

These essayists revealed a bias toward "the good of society" rather than "the good of the individual." An orientation that gave highest priority to the needs of society, to the collective rather than the individual needs of men, of course did not neglect individuals. But there is an eighteenth-century quality in the great sense of social cohesiveness contained in Benjamin Rush's demand: "Let our pupil be taught that he does not belong to himself, but that he is public property." By the time that this view was being echoed by Horace Mann in Massa-

---

4 Merle M. Odgers, "Education and the American Philosophical Society," *Proceedings of the American Philosophical Society*, Vol. 87 (1944), pp. 12-24; William Edward Hershey, "A Study of Plans for a System of National Education as Submitted to the American Philosophical Society for Promoting Useful Knowledge—1797" MS, American Philosophical Society, Philadelphia. The contest, characteristic of the Society's expansive concern with institutions and social supports, was one of several authorized in 1795 at a meeting which also recorded interest in ship pumps, vegetable dyes, the longevity of peach trees, and domestic heating. Apparently only seven essays were submitted, and even the winners did not offer systems "so well adapted to the present state of society in this country as could be wished." Some of the unsuccessful essays remain in the manuscript collections of the Society, though the identities of their authors are lost. They varied little in inspiration and proposals from the essays here collected, with the exception of one that extended respect for Spartan models so far as to forbid a parental role in a child's educational and career plans.

chusetts in the 1830's, the industrial revolution, coupled with the great exploitive possibilities of untold natural wealth, was beginning to usher in a period of American history when the individual took precedence over society. There was no such foreshadow when these essays were written, and it was therefore fitting for Robert Coram to argue that the security of government and society depended on the education of the people to their obligations. "Society," insisted Samuel Harrison Smith, "must establish the right to educate, and acknowledge the duty of having educated, all children. A circumstance so momentously important must not be left to the negligence of individuals." Society essentially could not afford to leave the question of education up to parents. Either they are too poor or too incompetent, said Lafitte du Courteil. "Error is never more dangerous than in the mouth of a parent," warned Smith. And Samuel Knox, hostile to small private schools and domestic tutors, advocated putting all children into public schools where they might more readily learn something of the world and be taught a sense of humility.

They were, of course, to learn a great deal more, too, and these essays therefore are in one sense a commentary on the structure and pattern, or lack thereof, of organized education inherited from the colonial period. For while the broad philosophical purposes of the essayists were revealed in their oft-repeated commitments to mankind, to country, and to society, they spelled out these commitments in the many specific ways in which they would have the schools and colleges of the future differ from the schools and colleges of the past.

On the eve of the American Revolution, except in New England, there was no public provision for elementary education in the American colonies.[5] Charity schools conducted by

---

5 For colonial education, see Bernard Bailyn, *Education in the Forming of American Society* (Chapel Hill: University of North Carolina Press, 1960); Richard M. Gummere, *The American Colonial Mind and the Classical Tradition* (Cambridge: Harvard University Press, 1963); Robert Middlekauff, *Ancients and Axioms: Secondary Education in Eighteenth Century New England* (New Haven: Yale University Press, 1963).

the religious denominations were the common institutions of elementary learning in New York, Philadelphia, and other coastal towns. The responsibility for education rested largely with parents who, if they could manage a little instruction in reading, writing, and arithmetic, felt that they had done well by their children, as indeed they had. Itinerant free-lance teachers accounted for some of the formal training of the period, and in the South planters sometimes hired northern college graduates or employed indentured servants to tutor their children and run plantation schools. Characteristic of the American experience before the Revolution was Westchester County in New York, where but six families in 1704 could spare their children enough time to learn more than reading and writing.

Only a relatively few colonial Americans received any formal education beyond the elementary subjects. Secondary schools were rare. Private tutors and the local clergyman carried the main burden of college preparation. There were public secondary schools in New England, a few private schools in the middle colonies, and even fewer in the South—all of them concentrating on the Latin that led to college and a career in one of the learned professions.

Nine colleges of varying degrees of stability and age carried on in the New World the collegiate traditions of Oxford and Cambridge. Several of these institutions were barely able to prove their existence before the American Revolution gave a new twist to their fortunes. The colleges were in no sense popular; they were shaped by aristocratic traditions and they served the aristocratic elements of colonial society. A South Carolina newspaper took the position in 1770 that one of the worst things that could happen to South Carolina would be a college, not because the newspaper was hostile to education but because learning would become a cheap and common commodity, an open invitation to social and economic ambition.

If the purposes of the American Revolution were to be served, clearly the future would have to be different from the past. In turning to that unknown and uncertain future, the essayists registered a most apparent difference, of course, in the universality of the education they proposed and in the tax-based public support and responsibility that would nurture it. Only in colonial New England had any significant steps been made toward publicly supported education available to all; in these essays the New England experience served less as a model than as a reminder of how much yet needed to be done. Also among the challenges to be met was the clear necessity of developing a curriculum considerably more practical than that which characterized the colonial grammar schools and colleges. None of the essayists was as scathing in his denunciation of the standard classical studies as was DuPont de Nemours, who wrote: "All our great men have overcome the misfortune of having gone through these studies."[6] On the other hand, only Samuel Knox vigorously defended Latin and Greek, warning against too exclusive a vocational emphasis. Knox thought expansively and, therefore, while he was friendly to the encouragement of learning in the sciences and English and other practical studies, he envisioned a country with sufficient abundance and leisure to support a system of liberal and polite learning of no specific vocational utility. His contemporaries, less imaginative and therefore perhaps less able to leap into the twenty-first century, argued endlessly and convincingly for studies that would both get the nation's work done and underwrite large-scale social and economic mobility. Their outlook was best revealed in Samuel Harrison Smith's conclusion that "man may indulge himself in sublime reveries, but the world will forever remain uninterested in them. It is only when he applies the powers of his mind to objects of general use that he becomes their benefactor; until he does this he is neither entitled to their gratitude or applause." And their proposals went a long way in meeting the objection of Noah Webster "that what is now called a *liberal education* disqualifies a man for business."

[6] DuPont de Nemours, *National Education*, p. 124.

These authors would have had the greatest difficulty coming to some agreement on the proper role of religion in the schools. While they were certain that institutions of formal education were responsible for more than intellectual training, they differed on how virtue and morality might best be supported. Benjamin Rush, in preferring strongly denominational Christian schools but in allowing that any religious orientation was to be preferred to none, really proposed a system of state-supported parochial schools. His argument that "a Christian cannot fail of being a republican" was appealing if ingenuous, and it certainly would not have moved Robert Coram who wanted no religious instruction in the schools, Noah Webster who wanted no Bible reading, or Samuel Knox who was distressed by the great threat of denominationalism and religious bias to education. Wary of religious influence in the schools, sensitive to the desirability of moral instruction, Knox decided that "it would . . . appear to be no infringement of . . . [religious] liberty . . . for the public teacher to begin and end the business of the day with a short and suitable prayer and address to the great source of all knowledge and instruction." To these nondenominational prayers Knox would add a nondenominational catechism, courses in ethics, and various studies designed to make well-informed and responsible citizens.

Simeon Doggett warned that an excessive concern with skills in the arts and sciences would develop "angels in understanding, devils in conduct." We must "meliorate the heart," he urged. Samuel Harrison Smith agreed: "Is there anything in existence more interesting than an old man whose mind is stocked with wisdom and whose heart is full of sensibility?" "The heart," insisted Noah Webster, "should be cultivated with more assiduity than the *head.*" A bias in favor of the practical, therefore, did not lead these essayists to neglect the kind of men in whom practical skills were to be developed. Webster's contention that "the *virtues* of men are of more consequence to society than their *abilities*" may have been an especially strong statement of his own preference, but it is

doubtful if any of the essayists would have demurred. In assigning to the schools a major responsibility for the nation's
ethics and morals, however, they were greatly enlarging the
burdens of the educational enterprise and acknowledging the
extent to which society could no longer rely on family, church,
and community.

This enterprise, as seen in these essays, varied from author to
author, depending probably largely on the intended audience
and the original purpose of the essay. Samuel Harrison Smith
would have kept every American boy in school between the
ages of five and eighteen, with a national university available
thereafter for the most talented. Lafitte du Courteil's elaborate
institution, covering the years from six to twenty-five, provided
completely free education only for children whose families
accepted the task of rearing the nation's foundlings, but even
in his system tuition charges were to be only one form of support. Levies on the states, a national lottery, import duties,
and excise taxes were also intended to finance the great national
institution that he proposed.

As the United States increasingly moves toward some sense
of maturity and of the responsibility that goes with it, the
visions and the expectations of these eighteenth-century republicans can be instructive. They addressed themselves, after all,
to fundamental questions. When Benjamin Rush placed great
stress on the kind of teachers developed and employed in a
republic, he was confronting certain republican peculiarities—
not only the necessity that men somehow be better than they
had ever been before but also the possibility of their being so.
In assigning to his proposed national university the key role
of elevating and nurturing intellectual excellence in the republic, Samuel Knox was seeking an answer to a problem that
has weighed heavily on the minds of critics of mass culture.
Samuel Harrison Smith's argument that a republic is where
virtue pays, Benjamin Rush's recognition of commercial opportunity as security against the development of a landed

aristocracy, Simeon Doggett's warning that prayer must be supplemented by "spirited exertions"—these were the product of genuinely American voices.

Who best proposed what history adopted? Who best outguessed his contemporaries? Who was most wrong and why? Such questions offer one approach in reading these essays. And certainly in no other area of their interest do these writers provide the material of such questions so well as in their vision of a national university. For they grossly underestimated how long in the making the American nation would be, how long before Americans in truth would think and speak and act nationally. If, as sometimes now seems possible, we are beginning to think and act nationally in matters of education, these writers—Rush, Webster, Coram, Doggett, Smith, Lafitte du Courteil, and Knox—deserve our attention as the first Americans in any systematic way to turn their talents toward defining the American dream in education.

FREDERICK RUDOLPH

# A NOTE ON THIS EDITION

Candidates for inclusion in this volume had to meet very few tests:

(1) The essays were to have been published between the Declaration of Independence and the War of 1812. (Actually, those selected were written and published between 1786 and 1799.)

(2) Each essay was to be a substantial statement on education in the infant United States, essentially philosophical in orientation and somewhat extended and detailed in its consideration of the educational problems and prospects confronting the new republic.

(3) Each essay, in order to meet the not inflexible ground rules of the John Harvard Library, was to have been published originally as a separate title. (An exception has been made for Noah Webster's "On the Education of Youth in America.")

A survey of the writings of the period dictated the selection of the following essays as meeting these tests. Most of them were among those extensively quoted in Allen Oscar Hansen's study, *Liberalism and American Education in the Eighteenth Century* (New York: Macmillan, 1926). The omission here of some authors given extended treatment by Hansen means simply that the writings in question failed one of the three tests, usually the second.

A word may be in order on the omission from the collection of two names properly associated with the early republican era and the great educational questions it raised—Thomas Jefferson and Pierre Samuel DuPont de Nemours. As much as we might wish otherwise, Jefferson did not in fact write or publish an essay of comparable design and scope. While we know much about his educational views and while he deserves consideration as perhaps the most significant of our early educational philosophers, his views must be located in fragments among his correspondence, in his *Notes on Virginia*, and elsewhere. Jefferson's educational thought has been treated in

Adrienne Koch, *The Philosophy of Thomas Jefferson* (New York: Columbia University Press, 1943) and Roy J. Honeywell, *The Educational Work of Thomas Jefferson* (Cambridge: Harvard University Press, 1931). Julian P. Boyd, ed., *The Papers of Thomas Jefferson* (Princeton: Princeton University Press, 1950) is an admirable collection of the writings in which Jefferson's educational views are found.

DuPont de Nemours presents a different problem. His reputation as an American educational philosopher rests on an essay written in 1800 at Jefferson's request. This essay apparently did not appear in English translation until it was translated and edited by Bessie G. Dupont and published by the University of Delaware Press in 1923 as *National Education in the United States of America*. The 1923 edition was based on the second French edition of 1812—*Sur l'Education nationale dans les Etats-Unis d'Amerique* (Paris: Le Normant, 1812). Copies of a first edition (and there may not have been one) apparently have not survived, although what appears to be DuPont's original manuscript presented to Thomas Jefferson is among the Rare Book Room collections of the Library of Congress, bound with an 1805 Princeton catalogue. The essay itself, while fascinating in many ways, does not address itself in any fundamental way to the educational problems peculiar to the American republic; as an expression of enlightened thought on education it is of interest, but its tone and emphasis place it beyond the scope of the present volume.

In preparing the essays for publication, I have modernized spelling and brought capitalization, punctuation, and paragraphing into line with current practice. An occasional word or phrase, indicated by square brackets, has been inserted in the text for the sake of clarity. Some of the quotations in the essays contained insignificant errors of transcription, and have been restored to the original; any restorations involving a change in wording are mentioned in the editorial notes.

The original footnotes are indicated by stars and daggers;

some contain bracketed editorial supplements. The editor's notes, indicated by arabic superscripts, form a separate section at the end of the text.

The assistance of the following libraries, librarians, and scholars is gratefully acknowledged, the libraries for making available copies of the original editions of the essays and the librarians and scholars for assistance in the preparation of the notes:

Thomas R. Adams, librarian, John Carter Brown Library, Brown University; Professor Robert J. Allen, Williams College; Dr. H. Richard Archer, custodian, Chapin Library, Williams College; Professor Lawrence W. Beals, Williams College; Professor Dudley W. R. Bahlman, Williams College; Dr. Whitfield Bell, American Philosophical Society; Frederick C. Christie, Harvard University; Mrs. David B. Coghlan, the Historical Society of Delaware; Mrs. Wendell Garrett, Boston Athenaeum; Professor Frederick Charles Green, University of Edinburgh; Professor Charles W. Hendel, Yale University; Reverend William E. Hershey, University of Pennsylvania; Miss Gertrude D. Hess, American Philosophical Society; Professor Cornelius Kruse, Wesleyan University; Professor Sterling P. Lamprecht, East Peacham, Vt.; W. B. McDaniel, 2d, Library of the College of Physicians, Philadelphia; Professor Orville T. Murphy, Jr., State University of New York at Buffalo; Miss A. Adele Rudolph, Philadelphia; Professor Donald G. Rohr, Brown University; Dr. Richard H. Shryock, American Philosophical Society; Miss Juanita Terry, reference librarian, Williams College; Dr. Richmond D. Williams, Eleutherian Mills Historical Library, Wilmington.

Rare Book Room, Library of Congress; Library Company of Philadelphia; Widener Library, Harvard University; Williams College Library; Columbia University Library. The resources of the Library of Congress were especially useful, not only for the study of original editions in its possession but also for the identification of authors, books, and quotations referred to in the essays.

To my wife I am indebted for all of those qualities of encouragement, patience, and forbearance that scholars rely on but perhaps too often take for granted. And besides, much to my profit she read this manuscript.

F. R.

# BENJAMIN RUSH

*A Plan for the Establishment of Public Schools and the Diffusion of Knowledge in Pennsylvania; to Which Are Added, Thoughts upon the Mode of Education, Proper in a Republic. Addressed to the Legislature and Citizens of the State. (Philadelphia, 1786)*

[Benjamin Rush (1745 o.s.–1813) was the busiest of Philadelphians, the best-known American doctor of his day. He combined a career in medicine with a career in education, cementing the two with a deeply held patriotism. A 1760 graduate of the College of New Jersey (Princeton), he studied medicine at the College of Philadelphia (University of Pennsylvania) and at the University of Edinburgh. He taught at the college in Philadelphia, helped to found Dickinson College, and took an active interest in many movements intended to fulfill the promise of the American Revolution.

In this essay, published by Thomas Dobson at Philadelphia in 1786, Rush reveals himself as a self-confident if sometimes cautious republican dreamer. Alone among the essayists here collected, he was a signer of the Declaration of Independence, and he wrote always as if conscious of the peculiar responsibility which that action placed upon him.]

# P L A N
## FOR THE
## ESTABLISHMENT
## OF
## PUBLIC SCHOOLS

BEFORE I proceed to suggest a plan for the establishment of public schools in Pennsylvania, I shall point out, in a few words, the influence and advantages of learning upon mankind.

I. It is friendly to religion, inasmuch as it assists in removing prejudice, superstition, and enthusiasm, in promoting just notions of the Deity, and in enlarging our knowledge of his works.

II. It is favorable to liberty. A free government can only exist in an equal diffusion of literature. Without learning, men become savages or barbarians, and where learning is confined to a *few* people, we always find monarchy, aristocracy, and slavery.

III. It promotes just ideas of laws and government. "When the clouds of ignorance are dispelled," says the Marquis of Beccaria, "by the radiance of knowledge, power trembles but the authority of laws remains immovable."[1]

IV. It is friendly to manners. Learning in all countries promotes civilization and the pleasures of society and conversation.

V. It promotes agriculture, the great basis of national wealth and happiness. Agriculture is as much a science as hydraulics or optics and has been equally indebted to the experiments and researches of learned men. The highly cultivated state and the immense profits of the farms in England are derived wholly from the patronage which agriculture has received in that country from learned men and learned societies.

VI. Manufactures of all kinds owe their perfection chiefly to learning—hence the nations of Europe advance in manufactures and commerce only in proportion as they cultivate the arts and sciences.

For the purpose of diffusing knowledge through every part of the state, I beg leave to propose the following simple plan:

I. Let there be one university in the state, and let this be established in the capital. Let law, physic, divinity, the law of nature and nations, economy, etc. be taught in it by public lectures in the winter season, after the manner of the European universities, and let the professors receive such salaries from the state as will enable them to deliver their lectures at a moderate price.

II. Let there be four colleges. One in Philadelphia; one at Carlisle; a third, for the benefit of our German fellow citizens, at Manheim; and a fourth, some years hence, at Pittsburgh. In these colleges let young men be instructed in mathematics and in the higher branches of science, in the same manner that they are now taught in our American colleges. After they have taken a degree in one of these colleges, let them, if they can afford it, complete their studies by spending a season or two in attending the lectures in the university. I prefer four colleges in the state to one or two, for there is a certain size of colleges, as there is of towns and armies, that is most favorable to morals and good government. Oxford and Cambridge in England are the seats of dissipation, while the more numerous and less crowded universities and colleges in Scotland are remarkable for the order, diligence, and decent behavior of their students.

III. Let there be an academy established in each county for the purpose of instructing youth in the learned languages and thereby preparing them to enter college.[2]

IV. Let there be free schools established in every township or in districts consisting of one hundred families. In these schools, let children be taught to read and write the English and German languages and the use of figures. Such of them as have parents that can afford to send them from home and are disposed to extend their educations may remove their children from the free school to the county academy.

By this plan the whole state will be tied together by one system of education. The university will in time furnish masters for the colleges, and the colleges will furnish masters for the academies and free schools, while the free schools, in their turn, will supply the academies, the colleges, and the university with scholars, students, and pupils. The same systems of grammar, oratory, and philosophy will be taught in every part of the state, and the literary features of Pennsylvania will thus designate one great and equally enlightened family.

A question now rises, and that is, How shall this plan be carried into execution? I answer—

The funds of the University of Pennsylvania (if the English and other schools were separated from it) are nearly equal to the purpose of supporting able professors in all the arts and sciences that are taught in the European universities.[3]

A small addition to the funds of Dickinson College will enable it to exist without any further aid from government.[4]

Twenty thousand acres of good land in the late Indian purchase will probably afford a revenue large enough to support a college at Manheim and another on the banks of the Ohio in the course of twenty years.[5]

Five thousand acres of land, appropriated to each county academy, will probably afford a revenue sufficient to support them in twenty years. In the meanwhile let a tax from £ 200 to £ 400 a year be laid on each county for that purpose, according to the number and wealth of its inhabitants.

Let sixty thousand acres of land be set apart to be divided twenty years hence among the free schools. In the meanwhile let a tax from £ 30 to £ 60 a year be levied upon each district of one hundred families for the support of the schoolmaster, and to prompt him to industry in increasing his school, let each scholar pay him from 1s6 to 2s6 every quarter.

But, how shall we bear the expense of these literary institutions under the present weight of our taxes? I answer—These institutions are designed to *lessen* our taxes. They will enlighten us in the great business of finance. They will teach us to increase the ability of the state to support government by increasing the profits of agriculture and by promoting manufactures. They will teach us all the modern improvements and advantages of inland navigation. They will defend us from hasty and expensive experiments in government by unfolding to us the experience and folly of past ages, and thus, instead of adding to our taxes and debts, they will furnish us with the true secret of lessening and discharging both of them.

But, shall the estates of orphans, bachelors, and persons who have no children be taxed to pay for the support of schools from which they can derive no benefit? I answer in the affirmative to the first part of the objection, and I deny the truth of the latter part of it. Every member of the community is interested in the propagation of virtue and knowledge in the state. But I will go further and add [that] it will be true economy in individuals to support public schools. The bachelor will in time save his tax for this purpose by being able to sleep with fewer bolts and locks to his doors, the estates of orphans will in time be benefited by being protected from the ravages of unprincipled and idle boys, and the children of wealthy parents will be less tempted, by bad company, to extravagance. Fewer pillories and whipping posts and smaller jails, with their usual expenses and taxes, will be necessary when our youth are properly educated than at present. I believe it could be proved that the expenses of confining, trying, and executing criminals amount every year, in most of the counties, to more money than would be sufficient to maintain all the schools that would be necessary in each county. The confessions of these criminals generally show us that their vices and punishments are the fatal consequences of the want of a proper education in early life.

I submit these detached hints to the consideration of the legislature and of the citizens of Pennsylvania. The plan for the free schools is taken chiefly from the plans which have long been used with success in Scotland and in the eastern states* of America, where the influence of learning in promoting religion, morals, manners, government, etc. has never been exceeded in any country.

The manner in which these academies and schools should be supported and governed, the modes of determining the characters and qualifications of schoolmasters, and the arrangement of families in each district, so that children of the same religious sect and nation may be educated as much as possible together, will form a proper part of a LAW for the establishment of schools and, therefore, does not come within the limits of this plan.

I shall conclude this part of the plan by submitting it to the wisdom of the legislature whether in granting charters for colleges in future they should not confine them to giving degrees only in the *arts*, especially while they teach neither law, physic, nor divinity. It is a folly peculiar to our American colleges to confer literary honors in professions that are not taught by them and which, if not speedily checked, will render degrees so cheap that they will cease to be the honorable badges of industry and learning.

---

* There are 600 of these schools in the small state of Connecticut, which, at this time, have in them 25,000 scholars. Only two natives of this state have been executed in the course of the last 25 years. The German Lutherans in Pennsylvania take uncommon pains in the education of their youth. Not one of this society has submitted to the ignominy of a legal punishment, of any kind, in the course of the last 17 years.

I have said nothing of the utility of public libraries in each college, academy, and free school. Upon this subject I shall only remark that they will tend to diffuse knowledge more generally if the farmers and tradesmen in the neighborhood of them (upon paying a moderate sum yearly) are permitted to have access to them.

The establishment of newspapers in a few of the most populous county towns will contribute very much to diffuse knowledge of all kinds through the state. To accomplish this, the means of conveying the papers should be made easy, by the assistance of the legislature. The effects of a newspaper upon the state of knowledge and opinions appear already in several of the counties beyond the Susquehanna. The passion for this useful species of instruction is strongly marked in Pennsylvania by the great encouragement this paper has received in those counties. In the space of eight months the number of subscribers to the *Carlisle Gazette* have amounted to above 700.[6]

Henry the IVth of France used to say he hoped to live to see the time when every peasant in his kingdom would dine on a turkey every Sunday.[7] I have not a wish for the extension of literature in the state that would not be gratified by living to see a weekly newspaper in every farmhouse in Pennsylvania. Part of the effects of this universal diffusion of knowledge would probably be to produce turkies and poultry of all kinds on the tables of our farmers, not only on Sundays, but on every day of the week.

By multiplying villages and county towns, we increase the means of diffusing knowledge. Villages are favorable to schools and public worship, and county towns, besides possessing these two advantages, are favorable to the propagation of political and legal information. The public officers of the county, by being obliged to maintain a connection with the capital of the government, often become repositories and vehicles of news and useful publications, while the judges and lawyers who attend the courts that are held in these towns seldom fail of leaving a large portion of knowledge behind them.

# THOUGHTS

## UPON THE

# MODE OF EDUCATION

### PROPER IN A

# REPUBLIC.

THE business of education has acquired a new complexion by the independence of our country. The form of government we have assumed has created a new class of duties to every American. It becomes us, therefore, to examine our former habits upon this subject, and in laying the foundations for nurseries of wise and good men, to adapt our modes of teaching to the peculiar form of our government.

The first remark that I shall make upon this subject is that an education in our own is to be preferred to an education in a foreign country. The principle of patriotism stands in need of the reinforcement of *prejudice*, and it is well known that our strongest prejudices in favor of our country are formed in the first one and twenty years of our lives. The policy of the Lacedamonians is well worthy of our imitation. When Antipater demanded fifty of their children as hostages for the fulfillment of a distant engagement, those wise republicans refused to comply with his demand but readily offered him double the number of their adult citizens, whose habits and prejudices could not be shaken by residing in a foreign country.[8] Passing by, in this place, the advantages to the community from the early attachment of youth to the laws and constitution of their country, I shall only remark that young men who have trodden the paths of science together, or have joined in the same sports, whether of swimming, skating, fishing, or hunting, generally feel, through life, such ties to each other as add greatly to the obligations of mutual benevolence.

I conceive the education of our youth in this country to be peculiarly necessary in Pennsylvania while our citizens are composed of the natives of so many different kingdoms in Europe.[9] Our schools of learning, by producing one general and uniform system of education, will render the mass of the people more homogeneous and thereby fit them more easily for uniform and peaceable government.

I proceed, in the next place, to inquire what mode of education we shall adopt so as to secure to the state all the advantages that are to be derived from the proper instruction of youth; and here I beg leave to remark that the only foundation for a useful education in a republic is to be laid in RELIGION. Without this, there can be no virtue, and without virtue there can be no liberty, and liberty is the object and life of all republican governments.

Such is my veneration for every religion that reveals the attributes of the Deity, or a future state of rewards and punishments, that I had rather see the opinions of Confucius or Mohammed inculcated upon our youth than see them grow up wholly devoid of a system of religious principles. But the religion I mean to recommend in this place is the religion of JESUS CHRIST.

It is foreign to my purpose to hint at the arguments which establish the truth of the Christian revelation. My only business is to declare that all its doctrines and precepts are calculated to promote the happiness of society and the safety and well-being of civil government. A Christian cannot fail of being a republican. The history of the creation of man and of the relation of our species to each other by birth, which is recorded in the Old Testament, is the best refutation that can be given to the divine right of kings and the strongest argument that can be used in favor of the original and natural equality of all mankind. A Christian, I say again, cannot fail of being a republican, for every precept of the Gospel inculcates those degrees of humility, self-denial, and brotherly kindness which are directly opposed to the pride of monarchy and the pageantry of a court. A Christian cannot fail of being useful to the republic, for his religion teacheth him that no man "liveth to himself." And lastly, a Christian cannot fail of being wholly inoffensive, for his religion teacheth him in all things to do to others what he would wish, in like circumstances, they should do to him.

I am aware that I dissent from one of those paradoxical opinions with which modern times abound: that it is improper to fill the minds of youth with religious prejudices of any kind and that they should be left to choose their own principles after they have arrived at an age in which they are capable of judging for themselves. Could we preserve the mind in childhood and youth a perfect blank, this plan of education would have more to recommend it, but this we know to be impossible. The human mind runs as naturally into principles as it does after facts. It submits with difficulty to those restraints or partial discoveries which are imposed upon it in the infancy of reason. Hence the impatience of children to be informed upon all subjects that relate to the invisible world. But I beg leave to ask, Why should we pursue a different plan of education with respect to religion from that which we pursue in teaching the arts and sciences? Do we leave our youth to acquire systems of geography, philosophy, or politics till they have arrived at an age in which they are capable of judging for themselves? We do not. I claim no more, then, for religion than for the other sciences, and I add further that if our youth are disposed after they are of age to think for themselves, a knowledge of *one* system will be the best means of conducting them in a free inquiry into other systems of religion, just as an acquaintance with one system of philosophy is the best introduction to the study of all the other systems in the world.

I must beg leave upon this subject to go one step further. In order more effectually to secure to our youth the advantages of a religious education, it is necessary to impose upon them the doctrines and discipline of a particular church. Man is naturally an ungovernable animal, and observations on particular societies and countries will teach us that when we add the restraints of ecclesiastical to those of domestic and civil government, we produce in him the highest degrees of order and virtue. That fashionable liberality which refuses to associate with any one sect of Christians is seldom useful to itself or to society and may fitly be compared to the unprofitable bravery of a soldier who wastes his valor in solitary enterprises without the aid or effect of military associations. Far be it from me to recommend the doctrines or modes of worship of any one denomination of Christians. I only recommend to the persons entrusted with the education of youth to inculcate upon them a strict conformity to that mode of worship which is most agreeable to their consciences or the inclinations of their parents.

Under this head, I must be excused in not agreeing with those modern writers who have opposed the use of the Bible as a schoolbook. The only objection I know to it is its division into chapters and verses and its improper punctuation which render it a more difficult book to read *well* than many others, but these defects may easily be corrected, and the disadvantages of them are not to be mentioned with the immense advantages of making children early and intimately acquainted with the means of acquiring happiness both here and hereafter. How great is the difference between making young people acquainted with the interesting and entertaining truths contained in the Bible, and the fables of Moore and Croxall,[10] or the doubtful histories of antiquity! I maintain that there is no book of its size in the whole world that contains half so much useful knowledge for the government of states or the direction of the affairs of individuals as the Bible. To object to the practice of having it read in schools because it tends to destroy our veneration for it is an argument that applies with equal force against the frequency of public worship and all other religious exercises.

The first impressions upon the mind are the most durable. They survive the wreck of the memory and exist in old age after the ideas acquired in middle life have been obliterated. Of how much consequence then must it be to the human mind in the evening of life to be able to recall those ideas which are most essential to its happiness, and these are to be found chiefly in the Bible. The great delight which old people take in reading the Bible, I am persuaded, is derived chiefly from its histories and precepts being *associated* with the events of childhood and youth, the recollection of which forms a material part of their pleasures.

I do not mean to exclude books of history, poetry, or even fables from our schools. They may and should be read frequently by our young people, but if the Bible is made to give way to them altogether, I foresee that it will be read in a short time only in churches and in a few years will probably be found only in the offices of magistrates and in courts of justice.†

NEXT to the duty which young men owe to their Creator, I wish to see a SUPREME REGARD TO THEIR COUNTRY inculcated upon them. When the Duke of Sully became prime minister to Henry the IVth of France, the first thing he did, he tells us, "was to subdue and forget his own heart."[11] The same duty is incumbent upon every citizen of a republic. Our country in-

---

† In a republic where all votes for public officers are given by *ballot*, should not a knowledge of reading and writing be considered as essential qualifications for an elector? And when a man who is of a doubtful character offers his vote, would it not be more consistent with sound policy and wise government to oblige him to read a few verses in the Bible to prove his qualifications than simply to compel him to kiss the *outside* of it?

cludes family, friends, and property, and should be preferred to them all. Let our pupil be taught that he does not belong to himself, but that he is public property. Let him be taught to love his family, but let him be taught at the same time that he must forsake and even forget them when the welfare of his country requires it.

He must watch for the state as if its liberties depended upon his vigilance alone, but he must do this in such a manner as not to defraud his creditors or neglect his family. He must love private life, but he must decline no station, however public or responsible it may be, when called to it by the suffrages of his fellow citizens. He must love popularity, but he must despise it when set in competition with the dictates of his judgment or the real interest of his country. He must love character and have a due sense of injuries, but he must be taught to appeal only to the laws of the state, to defend the one and punish the other. He must love family honor, but he must be taught that neither the rank nor antiquity of his ancestors can command respect without personal merit. He must avoid neutrality in all questions that divide the state, but he must shun the rage and acrimony of party spirit. He must be taught to love his fellow creatures in every part of the world, but he must cherish with a more intense and peculiar affection the citizens of Pennsylvania and of the United States.

I do not wish to see our youth educated with a single prejudice against any nation or country, but we impose a task upon human nature repugnant alike to reason, revelation, and the ordinary dimensions of the human heart when we require him to embrace with equal affection the whole family of mankind. He must be taught to amass wealth, but it must be only to increase his power of contributing to the wants and demands of the state. He must be indulged occasionally in amusements, but he must be taught that study and business should be his principal pursuits in life. Above all he must love life and endeavor to acquire as many of its conveniences as possible by industry and economy, but he must be taught that this life "is not his own" when the safety of his country requires it. These are practicable lessons, and the history of the commonwealths of Greece and Rome show that human nature, without the aids of Christianity, has attained these degrees of perfection.

While we inculcate these republican duties upon our pupil, we must not neglect at the same time to inspire him with republican principles. He must be taught that there can be no durable liberty but in a republic and that government, like all other sciences, is of a progressive nature. The chains which have bound this science in Europe are happily unloosed in America. *Here* it is open to investigation and improvement. While philosophy has protected us by its discoveries from a thousand natural evils, government has unhappily followed with an unequal pace. It would be to dishonor human genius only to name the many defects which still exist in the best systems of legislation. We daily see matter of a perishable nature rendered durable by certain chemical operations. In like manner, I conceive that it is possible to analyze and combine power in such a manner as not only to increase the happiness but to promote the duration of republican forms of government far beyond the terms limited for them by history or the common opinions of mankind.

To assist in rendering religious, moral, and political instruction more effectual upon the minds of our youth, it will be necessary to subject their bodies to physical discipline. To obviate the inconveniences of their studious and sedentary mode of life, they should live upon a temperate diet, consisting chiefly of broths, milk, and vegetables. The black broth of Sparta and the barley broth of Scotland have been alike celebrated for their beneficial effects upon the minds of young people. They should avoid tasting spirituous liquors. They should also be accustomed occasionally to work with their hands in the intervals of study and in the busy seasons of the year in the country. Moderate sleep, silence, occasional solitude, and cleanliness should be inculcated upon them, and the utmost advantage should be taken of a proper direction of those great principles in human conduct—sensibility, habit, imitation, and association.

The influence [of] these physical causes will be powerful upon the intellects as well as upon the principles and morals of young people.

To those who have studied human nature, it will not appear paradoxical to recommend in this essay a particular attention to vocal music. Its mechanical effects in civilizing the mind and thereby preparing it for the influence of religion and government have been so often felt and recorded that it will be unnecessary to mention facts in favor of its usefulness in order to excite a proper attention to it.

In the education of youth, let the authority of our masters be as *absolute* as possible. The government of schools like the government of private families should be *arbitrary*, that it may not be *severe*. By this mode of education, we prepare our youth for the subordination of laws and thereby qualify them for becoming good citizens of the republic. I am satisfied that the most useful citizens have been formed from those youth who have never known or felt their own wills till they were one and twenty years of age, and I have often thought that society owes a great deal of its order and happiness to the deficiencies of parental government being supplied by those habits of obedience and subordination which are contracted at schools.

I cannot help bearing a testimony, in this place, against the custom which prevails in some parts of America (but which is daily falling into disuse in Europe) of crowding boys together under one roof for the purpose of education. The practice is the gloomy remains of monkish ignorance and is as unfavorable to the improvements of the mind in useful learning as monasteries are to the spirit of religion. I grant this mode of secluding boys from the intercourse of private families has a tendency to make them scholars, but our business is to make them men, citizens, and Christians. The vices of young people are generally learned from each other. The vices of adults seldom infect them. By separating them from each other, therefore, in their hours of relaxation from study, we secure their morals from a principal source of corruption, while we improve their manners by subjecting them to those restraints which the difference of age and sex naturally produce in private families.

I have hitherto said nothing of the AMUSEMENTS that are proper for young people in a republic. Those which promote health and good humor will have a happy effect upon morals and government. To increase this influence, let the persons who direct these amusements be admitted into good company and subjected by that means to restraints in behavior and moral conduct. Taverns, which in most countries are exposed to riot and vice, in Connecticut are places of business and innocent pleasure because the tavernkeepers in that country are generally men of sober and respectable characters.

The theater will never be perfectly reformed till players are treated with the same respect as persons of other ornamental professions. It is to no purpose to attempt to write or preach down an amusement which seizes so forcibly upon all the powers of the mind. Let ministers preach *to* players instead of *against* them; let them open their churches and the ordinances of religion to them and their families, and, I am persuaded, we shall soon see such a reformation in the theater as can never be effected by all the means that have hitherto been employed for that purpose. It is possible to render the stage, by these means, subsurvient to the purposes of virtue and even religion. Why should the minister of the gospel exclude the player from his visits or from his public or private instructions? The Author of Christianity knew no difference in the occupations of men. He ate and drank daily with the publicans and sinners.

From the observations that have been made it is plain that I consider it as possible to convert men into republican machines. This must be done if we expect them to perform their parts properly in the great machine of the government of the state. That republic is sophisticated with monarchy or aristocracy that does not revolve upon the wills of the people, and these must be fitted to each other by means of education before they can be made to produce regularity and unison in government.

Having pointed out those general principles which should be inculcated alike in all the schools of the state, I proceed now to make a few remarks upon the method of conducting what is commonly called a liberal or learned education in a republic.

I shall begin this part of my subject by bearing a testimony against the common practice of attempting to teach boys the learned languages and the arts and sciences too early in life. The first twelve years of life are barely sufficient to instruct a boy in reading, writing, and arithmetic. With these, he may be taught those modern languages which are necessary for him to *speak*. The state of the memory, in early life, is favorable to the acquisition of languages, especially when they are conveyed to the mind through the ear. It is, moreover, in early life only that the organs of speech yield in such a manner as to favor the just pronunciation of foreign languages.

I do not wish the LEARNED OR DEAD LANGUAGES, as they are commonly called, to be reduced below their present just rank in the universities of Europe, especially as I consider an acquaintance with them as the best foundation for a correct and extensive knowledge of the language of our country. Too much pains cannot be taken to teach our youth to read and write our American language with propriety and elegance. The study of the Greek language constituted a material part of the literature of the Athenians, hence the sublimity, purity, and immortality of so many of their writings. The advantages of a perfect knowledge of our language to young men intended for the professions of law, physic, or divinity are too obvious to be mentioned, but in a state which boasts of the first commercial city in America, I wish to see it cultivated by young men who are intended for the counting house, for many such, I hope, will be educated in our colleges. The time is past when an academical education was thought to be unnecessary to qualify a young man for merchandise. I conceive no profession is capable of receiving more embellishments from it.

Connected with the study of our own language is the study of ELOQUENCE. It is well known how great a part it constituted of the Roman education. It is the first accomplishment in a republic and often sets the whole machine of government in motion. Let our youth, therefore, be instructed in this art. We do not extol it too highly when we attribute as much to the power of eloquence as to the sword in bringing about the American Revolution.

With the usual arts and sciences that are taught in our American colleges, I wish to see a regular course of lectures given upon HISTORY and CHRONOLOGY. The science of government, whether it relates to constitutions or laws, can only be advanced by a careful selection of facts, and these are to be found chiefly in history. Above all, let our youth be instructed in the history of the ancient republics and the progress of liberty and tyranny in the different states of Europe.

I wish likewise to see the numerous facts that relate to the origin and present state of COMMERCE, together with the nature and principles of MONEY, reduced to such a system as to be intelligible and agreeable to a young man. If we consider the commerce of our metropolis only as the avenue of the wealth of the state, the study of it merits a place in a young man's education, but, I consider commerce in a much higher light when I recommend the study of it in republican seminaries. I view it as the best security against the influence of hereditary monopolies of land, and, therefore, the surest protection against aristocracy. I consider its effects as next to those of religion in humanizing mankind, and lastly, I view it as the means of uniting the different nations of the world together by the ties of mutual wants and obligations.

CHEMISTRY, by unfolding to us the effects of heat and mixture, enlarges our acquaintance with the wonders of nature and the mysteries of art; hence it has become in most of the universities of Europe a necessary branch of a gentleman's education. In a young country, where improvements in agriculture and manufactures are so much to be desired, the cultivation of this science, which explains the principles of both of them, should be considered as an object of the utmost importance.

In a state where every citizen is liable to be a soldier and a legislator, it will be necessary to have some regular instruction given upon the ART OF WAR and upon PRACTICAL LEGISLATION. These branches of knowledge are of too much importance in a republic to be trusted to solitary study or to a fortuitous acquaintance with books. Let mathematical learning, therefore, be carefully applied in our colleges to gunnery and fortification, and let philosophy be applied to the history of those compositions which have been made use of for the terrible purposes of destroying human life. These branches of knowledge will be indispensably necessary in our republic, if unfortunately war should continue hereafter to be the unchristian mode of arbitrating disputes between Christian nations.

Again, let our youth be instructed in all the means of promoting national prosperity and independence, whether they relate to improvements in agriculture, manufactures, or inland navigation. Let him be instructed further in the general principles of legislation, whether they relate to revenue or to the preservation of life, liberty, or property. Let him be directed frequently to attend the courts of justice, where he will have the best opportunities of acquiring habits of arranging and comparing his ideas by observing the secretion of truth in the examination of witnesses and where he will hear the laws of the state explained, with all the advantages of that species of eloquence which belongs to the bar. Of so much importance do I conceive it to be to a young man to attend occasionally to the decisions of our courts of law that I wish to see our colleges and academies established only in county towns.

But further, considering the nature of our connection with the United States, it will be necessary to make our pupil acquainted with all the prerogatives of the federal government.

He must be instructed in the nature and variety of treaties. He must know the difference in the powers and duties of the several species of ambassadors. He must be taught wherein the obligations of individuals and of states are the same and wherein they differ. In short, he must acquire a general knowledge of all those laws and forms which unite the sovereigns of the earth or separate them from each other.

I have only to add that it will be to no purpose to adopt this or any other mode of education unless we make choice of suitable masters to carry our plans into execution. Let our teachers be distinguished for their abilities and knowledge. Let them be grave in their manners, gentle in their tempers, exemplary in their morals, and of sound principles in religion and government. Let us not leave their support to the precarious resources to be derived from their pupils, but let such funds be provided for our schools and colleges as will enable us to allow them liberal salaries.

By these means we shall render the chairs—the professorships and rectorships of our colleges and academies—objects of competition among learned men. By conferring upon our masters that independence which is the companion of competency, we shall, moreover, strengthen their authority over the youth committed to their care. Let us remember that a great part of the divines, lawyers, physicians, legislators, soldiers, generals, delegates, counselors, and governors of the state will probably hereafter pass through their hands. How great then should be the wisdom, how honorable the rank, and how generous the reward of those men who are to form these necessary and leading members of the republic!

I beg pardon for having delayed so long, to say anything of the separate and peculiar mode of education proper for WOMEN in a republic. I am sensible that they must concur in all our plans of education for young men, or no laws will ever render them effectual. To qualify our women for this purpose, they should not only be instructed in the usual branches of female education but they should be instructed in the principles of liberty and government, and the obligations of patriotism should be inculcated upon them. The opinions and conduct of men are often regulated by the women in the most arduous enterprises of life, and their approbation is frequently the principal reward of the hero's dangers and the patriot's toils. Besides, the *first* impressions upon the minds of children are generally derived from the women. Of how much consequence, therefore, is it in a republic that they should think justly upon the great subjects of liberty and government!

The complaints that have been made against religion, liberty, and learning have been made against each of them in a *separate* state. Perhaps like certain liquors they should only be used in a state of mixture. They mutually assist in correcting the abuses and in improving the good effects of each other. From the combined and reciprocal influence of religion, liberty, and learning upon the morals, manners, and knowledge of individuals, of these upon government, and of government upon individuals, it is impossible to measure the degrees of happiness and perfection to which mankind may be raised. For my part, I can form no ideas of the golden age, so much celebrated by the poets, more delightful than the contemplation of that happiness which it is now in the power of the legislature of Pennsylvania to confer upon her citizens by establishing proper modes and places of education in every part of the state.

The *present time* is peculiarly favorable to the establishment of these benevolent and necessary institutions in Pennsylvania. The minds of our people have not as yet lost the yielding texture they acquired by the heat of the late Revolution. They will *now* receive more readily than five or even three years hence new impressions and habits of all kinds. The spirit of liberty *now* pervades every part of the state. The influence of error and deception are *now* of short duration. Seven years hence the affairs of our state may assume a new complexion. We may be riveted to a criminal indifference for the safety and happiness of ourselves and our posterity. An aristocratic or democratic junto may arise that shall find its despotic views connected with the prevalence of ignorance and vice in the state, or a few artful pedagogues who consider learning as useful only in proportion as it favors their pride or avarice may prevent all new literary establishments from taking place by raising a hue and cry against them, as the offspring of improper rivalship or the nurseries of party spirit.

But in vain shall we lavish pains and expense in establishing nurseries of virtue and knowledge in every part of the state, in vain shall we attempt to give the minds of our citizens a virtuous and uniform bias in early life, while the arms of our state are opened alike to receive into its bosom and to confer equal privileges upon the virtuous emigrant and the annual refuse of the jails of Britain, Ireland, and our sister states. Of the many criminals that have been executed within these seven years, four out of five of them have been foreigners who have arrived here during the war and since the peace. We are yet, perhaps, to see and deplore the tracks of the enormous vices and crimes these men have left behind them. Legislators of Pennsylvania!—Stewards of the justice and virtue of heaven!— Fathers of children who may be corrupted and disgraced by bad examples, say—can nothing be done to preserve our morals, manners, and government from the infection of European vices?

# 2

# BENJAMIN RUSH

*Thoughts upon Female Education, Accommodated to the Present State of Society, Manners, and Government in the United States of America. (Boston, 1787)*

[In this second essay, published at Philadelphia by Prichard and Hall in 1787 and at Boston by Samuel Hall in the same year, Rush invites his readers to acknowledge that the American woman is a new phenomenon requiring a new understanding of female education. The youthful spirit of these two essays and his sound sense of the country's future give to Rush's educational recommendations a refreshing quality. The present text is from the Boston edition. It was presented originally by Rush as an address to the visitors of the Young Ladies' Academy at Philadelphia, July 28, 1787, at the close of the quarterly examinations. Rush was an original trustee of the Young Ladies' Academy, which had opened May 1, 1786, and at the time he wrote this essay was a professor of chemistry at the University of Pennsylvania.]

I HAVE yielded with diffidence to the solicitations of the Principal of the Academy, in undertaking to express my regard for the prosperity of this seminary of learning by submitting to your candor a few thoughts upon female education.

The first remark that I shall make upon this subject is that female education should be accommodated to the state of society, manners, and government of the country in which it is conducted.

This remark leads me at once to add that the education of young ladies in this country should be conducted upon principles very different from what it is in Great Britain and in some respects different from what it was when we were a part of a monarchical empire.

There are several circumstances in the situation, employments, and duties of women in America which require a peculiar mode of education.

I. The early marriages of our women, by contracting the time allowed for education, renders it necessary to contract its plan and to confine it chiefly to the more useful branches of literature.

II. The state of property in America renders it necessary for the greatest part of our citizens to employ themselves in different occupations for the advancement of their fortunes. This cannot be done without the assistance of the female members of the community. They must be the stewards and guardians of their husbands' property. That education, therefore, will be most proper for our women which teaches them to discharge the duties of those offices with the most success and reputation.

III. From the numerous avocations to which a professional life exposes gentlemen in America from their families, a principal share of the instruction of children naturally devolves upon the women. It becomes us therefore to prepare them, by a suitable education, for the discharge of this most important duty of mothers.

IV. The equal share that every citizen has in the liberty and the possible share he may have in the government of our country make it necessary that our ladies should be qualified to a certain degree, by a peculiar and suitable education, to concur in instructing their sons in the principles of liberty and government.

V. In Great Britain the business of servants is a regular occupation, but in America this humble station is the usual retreat of unexpected indigence; hence the servants in this country possess less knowledge and subordination than are required from them; and hence our ladies are obliged to attend more to the private affairs of their families than ladies generally do of the same rank in Great Britain. "They are good servants," said an American lady of distinguished merit* in a letter to a favorite daughter, "who will do well with good looking after." This circumstance should have great influence upon the nature and extent of female education in America.

The branches of literature most essential for a young lady in this country appear to be:

I. A knowledge of the English language. She should not only read but speak and spell it correctly. And to enable her to do this, she should be taught the English grammar and be frequently examined in applying its rules in common conversation.

II. Pleasure and interest conspire to make the writing of a fair and legible hand a necessary branch of female education. For this purpose she should be taught not only to shape every letter properly but to pay the strictest regard to points and capitals.†

---

* Mrs. Graeme. [Rush was a frequent guest at the Philadelphia salons held at the home of Dr. and Mrs. Thomas Graeme. Ann Diggs Graeme (1700-1765) was a talented ornament of Philadelphia society. Thomas Allen Glenn, ed., "Graeme Park, near Philadelphia," *Some Colonial Mansions and Those Who Lived in Them* . . . (Philadelphia: H. T. Coates, 1898), pp. 367-398.]

† The present mode of writing among persons of taste is to use a capital letter only for the first word of a sentence, and for names of persons, places, and months, and for the first word of every line in poetry. The words should be so shaped that a straight line may be drawn between two lines without touching the extremities of the words in either of them.

I once heard of a man who professed to discover the temper and disposition of persons by looking at their handwriting. Without inquiring into the probability of this story, I shall only remark that there is one thing in which all mankind agree upon this subject, and that is in considering writing that is blotted, crooked, or illegible as a mark of a vulgar education. I know of few things more rude or illiberal than to obtrude a letter upon a person of rank or business which cannot be easily read. Peculiar care should be taken to avoid every kind of ambiguity and affectation in writing *names*.

I have now a letter in my possession upon business, from a gentleman of a liberal profession in a neighboring state, which I am unable to answer because I cannot discover the name which is subscribed to it. For obvious reasons I would recommend the writing of the first or Christian name at full length, where it does not consist of more than two syllables. Abbreviations of all kinds in letter writing, which always denote either haste or carelessness, should likewise be avoided. I have only to add under this head that the Italian and inverted hands, which are read with difficulty, are by no means accommodated to the active state of business in America or to the simplicity of the citizens of a republic.

III. Some knowledge of figures and bookkeeping is absolutely necessary to qualify a young lady for the duties which await her in this country. There are certain occupations in which she may assist her husband with this knowledge, and should she survive him and agreeably to the custom of our country be the executrix of his will, she cannot fail of deriving immense advantages from it.

IV. An acquaintance with geography and some instruction in chronology will enable a young lady to read history, biography, and travels, with advantage, and thereby qualify her not only for a general intercourse with the world but to be an agreeable companion for a sensible man. To these branches of knowledge may be added, in some instances, a general acquaintance with the first principles of astronomy and natural philosophy, particularly with such parts of them as are calculated to prevent superstition, by explaining the causes or obviating the effects of natural evil.

V. Vocal music should never be neglected in the education of a young lady in this country. Besides preparing her to join in that part of public worship which consists in psalmody, it will enable her to soothe the cares of domestic life. The distress and vexation of a husband, the noise of a nursery, and even the sorrows that will sometimes intrude into her own bosom may all be relieved by a song, where sound and sentiment unite to act upon the mind. I hope it will not be thought foreign to this part of our subject to introduce a fact here which has been suggested to me by my profession, and that is, that the exercise of the organs of the breast by singing contributes very much to defend them from those diseases to which our climate, and other causes have of late exposed them. Our German fellow citizens are seldom afflicted with consumptions, nor have I ever known but one instance of a spitting of blood among them. This, I believe, is in part occasioned by the strength which their lungs acquire by exercising them frequently in vocal music, for this constitutes an essential branch of their education. The music master of our academy‡ has furnished me with an observation still more in favor of this opinion. He informed me that he had known several instances of persons who were strongly disposed to the consumption who were restored to health by the moderate exercise of their lungs in singing.

VI. Dancing is by no means an improper branch of education for an American lady. It promotes health and renders the figure and motions of the body easy and agreeable. I anticipate the time when the resources of conversation shall be so far multiplied that the amusement of dancing shall be wholly confined to children. But in our present state of society and knowl-

‡ Mr. Adgate. [Andrew Adgate (?-1793), promoter of musical education in Philadelphia and author of *Rudiments of Music* (Philadelphia: John McCulloch, 1788); *The Philadelphia Songster* (Philadelphia: John McCulloch, 1789); *Philadelphia Harmony and Rudiments of Music* (Philadelphia: John McCulloch, 1789).]

edge, I conceive it to be an agreeable substitute for the ignoble pleasures of drinking and gaming in our assemblies of grown people.

VII. The attention of our young ladies should be directed as soon as they are prepared for it to the reading of history, travels, poetry, and moral essays. These studies are accommodated, in a peculiar manner, to the present state of society in America, and when a relish is excited for them in early life, they subdue that passion for reading novels which so generally prevails among the fair sex. I cannot dismiss this species of writing and reading without observing that the subjects of novels are by no means accommodated to our present manners. They hold up *life*, it is true, but it is not yet *life* in America. Our passions have not as yet "overstepped the modesty of nature," nor are they "torn to tatters," to use the expressions of the poet, by extravagant love, jealousy, ambition, or revenge.[1] As yet the intrigues of a British novel are as foreign to our manners as the refinements of Asiatic vice. Let it not be said that the tales of distress which fill modern novels have a tendency to soften the female heart into acts of humanity. The fact is the reverse of this. The abortive sympathy which is excited by the recital of imaginary distress blunts the heart to that which is real; and, hence, we sometimes see instances of young ladies who weep away a whole forenoon over the criminal sorrows of a fictitious Charlotte or Werter, turning with disdain at two o'clock from the sight of a beggar who solicits in feeble accents or signs a small portion only of the crumbs which fall from their fathers' tables.[2]

VIII. It will be necessary to connect all these branches of education with regular instruction in the Christian religion. For this purpose the principles of the different sects of Christians should be taught and explained, and our pupils should early be furnished with some of the most simple arguments in favor of the truth of Christianity.§ A portion of the Bible (of

§ Baron Haller's *Letters to his Daughter on the Truths of the Christian Religion* and Dr. Beatie's *Evidences of the Christian Religion Briefly and Plainly*

late improperly banished from our schools) should be read by them every day and such questions should be asked, after reading it, as are calculated to imprint upon their minds the interesting stories contained in it.[3]

Rousseau has asserted that the great secret of education consists in "wasting the time of children profitably."[4] There is some truth in this observation. I believe that we often impair their health and weaken their capacities by imposing studies upon them which are not proportioned to their years. But this objection does not apply to religious instruction. There are certain simple propositions in the Christian religion that are suited in a peculiar manner to the infant state of reason and moral sensibility. A clergyman of long experience in the instruction of youth|| informed me that he always found children acquired religious knowledge more easily than knowledge upon other subjects, and that young girls acquired this kind of knowledge more readily than boys. The female breast is the natural soil of Christianity, and while our women are taught to believe its doctrines and obey its precepts, the wit of Voltaire and the style of Bolingbroke will never be able to destroy its influence upon our citizens.[5]

I cannot help remarking in this place that Christianity exerts the most friendly influence upon science as well as upon the morals and manners of mankind. Whether this be occasioned by the unity of truth and the mutual assistance which truths upon different subjects afford each other, or whether the faculties of the mind be sharpened and corrected by embracing the truths of revelation and thereby prepared to investigate and

Stated are excellent little tracts and well adapted for this purpose. [Albrecht von Haller, *Letters from Baron Haller to His Daughter, on the Truths of the Christian Religion* (London, 1780); James Beattie, *Evidences of the Christian Religion; Briefly and Plainly Stated* (Philadelphia: Thomas Dobson, 1787).]

|| The Rev. Mr. Nicholas Collin, minister of the Swedish church in Wicaco. [Nicholas Collin (1746-1831) was the last Swedish minister of the Gloria Dei (Old Swede's) Church in Philadelphia. Early Swedish settlers named the area Wicaco (now Southwark), from an Indian phrase for "fir tree camp" or "pleasant place." Amandus Johnson, ed., *The Journal and Biography of Nicholas Collin, 1746-1831* (Philadelphia: New Jersey Society of Pennsylvania, 1936).]

perceive truths upon other subjects, I will not determine, but it is certain that the greatest discoveries in science have been made by Christian philosophers and that there is the most knowledge in those countries where there is the most Christianity.¶ By knowledge I mean truth only; and by truth I mean the perception of things as they appear to the divine mind. If this remark be well founded, then those philosophers who reject Christianity and those Christians, whether parents or schoolmasters, who neglect the religious instruction of their children and pupils *reject* and *neglect* the most effectual means of promoting knowledge in our country.

IX. If the measures that have been recommended for inspiring our pupils with a sense of religious and moral obligation be adopted, the government of them will be easy and agreeable. I shall only remark under this head that *strictness* of discipline will always render *severity* unnecessary and that there will be the most instruction in that school where there is the most order.

I have said nothing in favor of instrumental music as a branch of female education because I conceive it is by no means accommodated to the present state of society and manners in America. The price of musical instruments and the extravagant fees demanded by the teachers of instrumental music form but a small part of my objections to it.

To perform well upon a musical instrument requires much

---

¶ This is true in a peculiar manner in the science of medicine. A young Scotch physician of enterprising talents, who conceived a high idea of the state of medicine in the eastern countries, spent two years in inquiries after medical knowledge in Constantinople and Grand Cairo. On his return to Britain he confessed to an American physician whom he met at Naples that after all his researches and travels he "had discovered nothing except a single fact relative to the plague that he thought worth remembering or communicating." The science of medicine in China, according to the accounts of Du Halde, is in as imperfect a state as among the Indians of North America. [Jean Baptiste du Halde, *The General History of China* . . . , 4 vols. (London, 1736). In the 3d edition corrected, 4 vols. (London: J. Watts, 1741), Du Halde considers Chinese medical skills in III, 356-366, and provides translations of Chinese medical texts, 366-496. He gives a collection of Chinese medical prescriptions in IV, 1-56, and precepts on the care of health, IV, 57-85.]

time and long practice. From two to four hours in a day, for
three or four years, appropriated to music are an immense
deduction from that short period of time which is allowed by
the peculiar circumstances of our country for the acquisition
of the useful branches of literature that have been mentioned.
How many useful ideas might be picked up in these hours from
history, philosophy, poetry, and the numerous moral essays
with which our language abounds, and how much more would
the knowledge acquired upon these subjects add to the consequence of a lady with her husband and with society than the
best performed pieces of music upon a harpsichord or a guitar!
Of the many ladies whom we have known who have spent the
most important years of their lives in learning to play upon
instruments of music, how few of them do we see amuse themselves or their friends with them after they become mistresses
of families! Their harpsichords serve only as sideboards for
their parlors and prove by their silence that necessity and circumstances will always prevail over fashion and false maxims
of education.

Let it not be supposed from these observations that I am
insensible of the charms of instrumental music or that I wish
to exclude it from the education of a lady where a musical ear
irresistibly disposes to it, and affluence at the same time affords
a prospect of such an exemption from the usual cares and duties
of the mistress of a family as will enable her to practice it. These
circumstances form an exception to the general conduct that
should arise upon this subject, from the present state of society
and manners in America.

I beg leave further to bear a testimony against the practice
of making the French language a part of female education in
America. In Britain, where company and pleasure are the principal business of ladies, where the nursery and the kitchen form
no part of their care, and where a daily intercourse is maintained with Frenchmen and other foreigners who speak the
French language, a knowledge of it is absolutely necessary. But
the case is widely different in this country. Of the many ladies

who have applied to this language, how great a proportion of them have been hurried into the cares and duties of a family before they had acquired it; of those who have acquired it, how few have retained it after they were married; and of the few who have retained it, how seldom have they had occasion to speak it in the course of their lives! It certainly comports more with female delicacy, as well as the natural politeness of the French nation, to make it necessary for Frenchmen to learn to speak our language in order to converse with our ladies than for our ladies to learn their language in order to converse with them.

Let it not be said in defense of a knowledge of the French language that many elegant books are written in it. Those of them that are truly valuable are generally translated, but, if this were not the case, the English language certainly contains many more books of real utility and useful information than can be read without neglecting other duties by the daughter or wife of an American citizen.

It is with reluctance that I object to drawing as a branch of education for an American lady. To be the mistress of a family is one of the great ends of a woman's being, and while the peculiar state of society in America imposes this station so early and renders the duties of it so numerous and difficult, I conceive that little time can be spared for the acquisition of this elegant accomplishment.

It is agreeable to observe how differently modern writers and the inspired author of the *Proverbs* describe a fine woman. The former confine their praises chiefly to personal charms and ornamental accomplishments, while the latter celebrates only the virtues of a valuable mistress of a family and a useful member of society. The one is perfectly acquainted with all the fashionable languages of Europe; the other "opens her mouth with wisdom" and is perfectly acquainted with all the uses of the needle, the distaff, and the loom. The business of the one is pleasure; the pleasure of the other is business. The one is admired abroad; the other is honored and beloved at home.

"Her children arise up and call her blessed, her husband also, and he praiseth her."[6] There is no fame in the world equal to this, nor is there a note in music half so delightful as the respectful language with which a grateful son or daughter perpetuates the memory of a sensible and affectionate mother.

It should not surprise us that British customs with respect to female education have been transplanted into our American schools and families. We see marks of the same incongruity of time and place in many other things. We behold our houses accommodated to the climate of Great Britain by eastern and western directions. We behold our ladies panting in a heat of ninety degrees, under a hat and cushion which were calculated for the temperature of a British summer. We behold our citizens condemned and punished by a criminal law which was copied from a country where maturity in corruption renders public executions a part of the amusements of the nation. It is high time to awake from this servility—to study our own character—to examine the age of our country—and to adopt manners in everything that shall be accommodated to our state of society and to the forms of our government. In particular it is incumbent upon us to make ornamental accomplishments yield to principles and knowledge in the education of our women.

A philosopher once said, "let me make all the ballads of a country and I care not who makes its laws."[7] He might with more propriety have said, let the ladies of a country be educated properly, and they will not only make and administer its laws, but form its manners and character. It would require a lively imagination to describe, or even to comprehend, the happiness of a country where knowledge and virtue were generally diffused among the female sex. Our young men would then be restrained from vice by the terror of being banished from their company. The loud laugh and the malignant smile, at the expense of innocence or of personal infirmities—the feats of successful mimicry and the low priced wit which is borrowed from a misapplication of scripture phrases—would no more be considered as recommendations to the society of the ladies. A *double-entendre* in their presence would then exclude a gentleman forever from the company of both sexes and probably oblige him to seek an asylum from contempt in a foreign country.

The influence of female education would be still more extensive and useful in domestic life. The obligations of gentlemen to qualify themselves by knowledge and industry to discharge the duties of benevolence would be increased by marriage; and the patriot—the hero—and the legislator would find the sweetest reward of their toils in the approbation and applause of their wives. Children would discover the marks of maternal prudence and wisdom in every station of life, for it has been remarked that there have been few great or good men who have not been blessed with wife and prudent mothers. Cyrus was taught to revere the gods by his mother Mandane; Samuel was devoted to his prophetic office before he was born by his mother Hannah; Constantine was rescued from paganism by his mother Constantia; and Edward the Sixth inherited those great and excellent qualities which made him the delight of the age in which he lived from his mother, Lady Jane Seymour. Many other instances might be mentioned, if necessary, from ancient and modern history, to establish the truth of this proposition.

I am not enthusiastic upon the subject of education. In the ordinary course of human affairs we shall probably too soon follow the footsteps of the nations of Europe in manners and vices. The first marks we shall perceive of our declension will appear among our women. Their idleness, ignorance, and profligacy will be the harbingers of our ruin. Then will the character and performance of a buffoon on the theater be the subject of more conversation and praise than the patriot or the minister of the gospel; then will our language and pronunciation be enfeebled and corrupted by a flood of French and Italian words; then will the history of romantic amours be preferred to the immortal writings of Addison, Hawkesworth, and

Johnson; then will our churches be neglected and the name of the Supreme Being never be called upon but in profane exclamations; then will our Sundays be appropriated only to feasts and concerts; and then will begin all that train of domestic and political calamities.

But, I forbear. The prospect is so painful that I cannot help silently imploring the great Arbiter of human affairs to interpose his almighty goodness and to deliver us from these evils that, at least, one spot of the earth may be reserved as a monument of the effects of good education, in order to show in some degree what our species was before the fall and what it shall be after its restoration.

Thus, gentlemen, have I briefly finished what I proposed. If I am wrong in those opinions in which I have taken the liberty of departing from the general and fashionable habits of thinking, I am sure you will discover and pardon my mistakes. But, if I am right, I am equally sure you will adopt my opinions; for to enlightened minds truth is alike acceptable, whether it comes from the lips of age or the hand of antiquity or whether it be obtruded by a person who has no other claim to attention than a desire of adding to the stock of human happiness.

I cannot dismiss the subject of female education without remarking that the city of Philadelphia first saw a number of gentlemen associated for the purpose of directing the education of young ladies. By means of this plan the power of teachers is regulated and restrained and the objects of education are extended. By the separation of the sexes in the unformed state of their manners, female delicacy is cherished and preserved. Here the young ladies may enjoy all the literary advantages of a boarding school and at the same time live under the protection of their parents.* Here emulation may be excited without

---

\* "Unnatural confinement makes a young woman embrace with avidity every pleasure, when she is set free. To relish domestic life, one must be acquainted with it; for it is in the house of her parents a young woman acquires the relish." Lord Kames's *Thoughts upon Education, and the Culture of the Heart.* [Henry Home, Lord Kames, *Loose Hints upon Education, Chiefly Concerning the Culture of the Heart* (Edinburgh: John Bell, 1781), p. 139.]

jealousy, ambition without envy, and competition without strife.

The attempt to establish this new mode of education for young ladies was an experiment, and the success of it hath answered our expectations.† Too much praise cannot be given to our principal and his assistants, for the abilities and fidelity with which they have carried the plan into execution. The proficiency which the young ladies have discovered in reading, writing, spelling, arithmetic, grammar, geography, music, and their different catechisms since the last examination is a less equivocal mark of the merits of our teachers than anything I am able to express in their favor.

But the reputation of the academy must be suspended till the public are convinced by the future conduct and character of our pupils of the advantages of the institution. To you, therefore, YOUNG LADIES, an important problem is committed for solution; and that is, whether our present plan of education be a wise one and whether it be calculated to prepare you for the duties of social and domestic life. I know that the elevation of the female mind, by means of moral, physical, and religious truth, is considered by some men as unfriendly to the domestic character of a woman. But this is the prejudice of little minds and springs from the same spirit which opposes the general diffusion of knowledge among the citizens of our republics. If men believe that ignorance is favorable to the government of the female sex, they are certainly deceived, for a weak and ignorant woman will always be governed with the greatest difficulty.

I have sometimes been led to ascribe the invention of ridiculous and expensive fashions in female dress entirely to the gentlemen‡ in order to divert the ladies from improving their minds and thereby to secure a more arbitrary and unlimited authority over them. It will be in your power, LADIES, to correct

---

† The number of scholars in the academy at present amounts to upwards of one hundred.

‡ The very expensive prints of female dresses which are published annually in France are invented and executed wholly by GENTLEMEN.

the mistakes and practice of our sex upon these subjects by demonstrating that the female temper can only be governed by reason and that the cultivation of reason in women is alike friendly to the order of nature and to private as well as public happiness.

# NOAH WEBSTER

*On the Education of Youth in America. (Boston, 1790)*

[Noah Webster (1758-1843) was one of the great fathers of American nationality. As lexicographer and author of widely used spellers, he advanced the idea of a common American language and recorded its development. A 1778 graduate of Yale, he often addressed himself to educational questions. This essay, which appeared in Webster's *A Collection of Essays and Fugitiv Writings. On Moral, Historical, Political and Literary Subjects* (Boston: I. Thomas and E. T. Andrews for the author, 1790), pp. 1-37, was reprinted, with minor changes, from Webster's *American Magazine,* where it ran in six installments, 1787-1788. It was later reprinted in the *American Museum* and the *Hampshire Gazette,* and in part in the *American Journal of Education.* Here the 1790 text is used. In their disagreement on the role of the Bible in the public schools and in the suitability of instruction in French and the harpsichord for young ladies, Webster and Rush suggest that some educational questions may indeed be eternal.]

# On the EDUCATION of YOUTH in AMERICA

THE education of youth is, in all governments, an object of the first consequence. The impressions received in early life usually form the characters of individuals, a union of which forms the general character of a nation.

The mode of education and the arts taught to youth have in every nation been adapted to its particular stage of society or local circumstances.

In the martial ages of Greece the principal study of its legislators was to acquaint the young men with the use of arms, to inspire them with an undaunted courage, and to form in the hearts of both sexes an invincible attachment to their country. Such was the effect of their regulations for these purposes that the very women of Sparta and Athens would reproach their own sons for surviving their companions who fell in the field of battle.

Among the warlike Scythians every male was not only taught to use arms for attack and defense but was obliged to sleep in the field, to carry heavy burdens, and to climb rocks and precipices, in order to habituate himself to hardships, fatigue, and danger.

In Persia during the flourishing reign of the great Cyrus, the education of youth, according to Xenophon, formed a principal branch of the regulations of the empire. The young men were divided into classes, each of which had some particular duties to perform, for which they were qualified by previous instructions and exercise.

While nations are in a barbarous state, they have few wants and consequently few arts. Their principal objects are defense and subsistence; the education of a savage therefore extends little farther than to enable him to use with dexterity a bow and a tomahawk.

But in the progress of manners and of arts, war ceases to be the employment of whole nations; it becomes the business of a few who are paid for defending their country. Artificial wants multiply the number of occupations, and these require a great diversity in the mode of education. Every youth must be instructed in the business by which he is to procure subsistence. Even the civilities of behavior in polished society become a science; a bow and a curtsy are taught with as much care and precision as the elements of mathematics. Education proceeds therefore by gradual advances, from simplicity to corruption. Its first object, among rude nations, is safety; its next, utility; it afterwards extends to convenience; and among the opulent part of civilized nations it is directed principally to show and amusement.

In despotic states education, like religion, is made subservient to government. In some of the vast empires of Asia children are always instructed in the occupation of their parents; thus the same arts are always continued in the same families. Such an institution cramps genius and limits the progress of national improvement; at the same time it is an almost immovable barrier against the introduction of vice, luxury, faction, and changes in government. This is one of the principal causes which have operated in combining numerous millions of the human race under one form of government and preserving national tranquility for incredible periods of time. The empire of China, whose government was founded on the patriarchical discipline, has not suffered a revolution in laws, manners, or language for many thousand years.

In the complicated systems of government which are established among the civilized nations of Europe education has less influence in forming a national character; but there is no state in which it has not an inseparable connection with morals and a consequential influence upon the peace and happiness of society.

Education is a subject which has been exhausted by the ablest writers, both among the ancients and moderns. I am not vain enough to suppose I can suggest any new ideas upon so trite a theme as education in general; but perhaps the manner of conducting the youth in America may be capable of some improvement. Our constitutions of civil government are not yet firmly established; our national character is not yet formed; and it is an object of vast magnitude that systems of education should be adopted and pursued which may not only diffuse a knowledge of the sciences but may implant in the minds of the American youth the principles of virtue and of liberty and inspire them with just and liberal ideas of government and with an inviolable attachment to their own country. It now becomes every American to examine the modes of education in Europe, to see how far they are applicable in this country and whether it is not possible to make some valuable alterations, adapted to our local and political circumstances. Let us examine the subject in two views. First, as it respects arts and sciences. Secondly, as it is connected with morals and government. In each of these articles let us see what errors may be found and what improvements suggested in our present practice.

The first error that I would mention is a too general attention to the dead languages, with a neglect of our own.

This practice proceeds probably from the common use of the Greek and Roman tongues before the English was brought to perfection. There was a long period of time when these languages were almost the only repositories of science in Europe. Men who had a taste for learning were under a necessity of recurring to the sources, the Greek and Roman authors. These will ever be held in the highest estimation both for style and sentiment, but the most valuable of them have English translations, which, if they do not contain all the elegance, communicate all the ideas of the originals. The English language, perhaps, at this moment, is the repository of as much learning as one half the languages of Europe. In copiousness it exceeds all modern tongues, and though inferior to the Greek and French in softness and harmony, yet it exceeds the French in variety; it almost equals the Greek and Roman in energy and falls very little short of any language in the regularity of its construction.*

In deliberating upon any plan of instruction, we should be attentive to its future influence and probable advantages. What advantage does a mercant, a mechanic, a farmer, derive from an acquaintance with the Greek and Roman tongues? It is true, the etymology of words cannot be well understood without a knowledge of the original languages of which ours is composed. But a very accurate knowledge of the meaning of words and of the true construction of sentences may be obtained by the help of dictionaries and good English writers, and this is all that is necessary in the common occupations of life. But suppose there is some advantage to be derived from an acquaintance with the dead languages, will this compensate for the loss of five or perhaps seven years of valuable time? Life is short, and every hour should be employed to good purposes. If there are no studies of more consequence to boys than those of Latin and Greek, let these languages employ their time, for idleness is the bane of youth. But when we have an elegant and copious language of our own, with innumerable writers upon ethics, geography, history, commerce, and government—subjects immediately interesting to every man, how can a parent be justified in keeping his son several years over rules of syntax, which he forgets when he shuts his book, or which, if remembered, can be of little or no use in any branch of business? This absurdity is the subject of common complaint; men see and feel the impropriety of the usual practice, and yet no arguments that have hitherto been used have been sufficient to change the system or to place an English school on a footing with a Latin one in point of reputation.[1]

It is not my wish to discountenance totally the study of the dead languages. On the other hand, I should urge a more close attention to them among young men who are designed for the learned professions. The poets, the orators, the philosophers,

---

* This remark is confined solely to *its construction*; in point of orthography, our language is intolerably irregular.

and the historians of Greece and Rome furnish the most excellent models of style and the richest treasures of science. The slight attention given to a few of these authors in our usual course of education is rather calculated to make pedants than scholars, and the time employed in gaining superficial knowledge is really wasted.

> A little learning is a dangerous thing,
> Drink deep, or taste not the Pierian spring.[2]

But my meaning is that the dead languages are not necessary for men of business, merchants, mechanics, planters, etc., nor of utility sufficient to indemnify them for the expense of time and money which is requisite to acquire a tolerable acquaintance with the Greek and Roman authors. Merchants often have occasion for a knowledge of some foreign living language as the French, the Italian, the Spanish, or the German, but men whose business is wholly domestic have little or no use for any language but their own, much less for languages known only in books.†

There is one very necessary use of the Latin language which

---

† In our colleges and universities students read some of the ancient poets and orators, but the historians, which are perhaps more valuable, are generally neglected. The student just begins to read Latin and Greek to advantage, then quits the study. Where is the seminary in which the students read Herodotus, Thucydides, Xenophon, Polybius, Dionysius Halicarnasseus, Livy, Velleius Paterculus, and Tacitus? How superficial must be that learning which is acquired in four years! Severe experience has taught me the errors and defects of what is called a liberal education. I could not read the best Greek and Roman authors while in college without neglecting the established classical studies, and after I left college, I found time only to dip into books that every scholar should be master of, a circumstance that often fills me with the deepest regret. "Quis enim ignorat et eloquentiam et cæteras artes descivisse ab ista vetere gloria, non inopia hominum, sed desidia juventutis, et negligentia parentum, et inscientia præcipientium, et oblivione moris antiqui? ["Everybody is aware that it is not for lack of votaries that eloquence and the other arts as well have fallen from their former high estate, but because of the laziness of our young men, the carelessness of parents, the ignorance of teachers, and the decay of the old-fashioned virtue." William Peterson, trans., *The Dialogus of Publius Cornelius Tacitus* (Loeb Classical Library), pp. 86-89.] Nec in auctoribus cognoscendis, nec in evolvenda antiquitate, nec in notitia vel rerum, vel hominum, vel temporum satis operæ insumitur." *Tacitus, de Orat. Dial.* 28. 29. [". . . It is in the reading of authors, and in gaining a knowledge of the past, and in making acquaintance with things and persons and occasions that too little solid work is done." *Ibid.*, pp. 92-93.]

will always prevent it from falling into neglect; which is, that it serves as a common interpreter among the learned of all nations and ages. Epitaphs, inscriptions on monuments and medals, treaties, etc., designed for perpetuity, are written in Latin, which is everywhere understood by the learned and being a dead language is liable to no change.

But the high estimation in which the learned languages have been held has discouraged a due attention to our own. People find themselves able without much study to write and speak the English intelligibly and thus have been led to think rules of no utility. This opinion has produced various and arbitrary practices in the use of the language, even among men of the most information and accuracy; and this diversity has produced another opinion, both false and injurious to the language, that there are no rules or principles on which the pronunciation and construction can be settled.

This neglect is so general that there is scarcely an institution to be found in the country where the English tongue is taught regularly, from its elements to its true and elegant construction, in prose and verse. Perhaps in most schools boys are taught the definition of the parts of speech and a few hard names which they do not understand and which the teacher seldom attempts to explain; this is called *learning grammar*. This practice of learning questions and answers without acquiring any ideas has given rise to a common remark, *that grammar is a dry study*; and so is every other study which is prosecuted without improving the head or the heart. The study of geography is equally dry when the subject is not understood. But when grammar is taught by the help of visible objects, when children perceive that differences of words arise from differences in things, which they may learn at a very early period of life, the study becomes entertaining as well as improving. In general, when a study of any kind is tiresome to a person, it is a presumptive evidence that he does not make any proficiency in knowledge, and this is almost always the fault of the instructor.

In a few instances perhaps the study of English is thought an object of consequence, but here also there is a great error in the common practice, for the study of English is preceded by several years' attention to Latin and Greek. Nay, there are men who contend that the best way to become acquainted with English is to learn Latin first. Common sense may justly smile at such an opinion, but experience proves it to be false.

If language is to be taught mechanically or by rote, it is a matter of little consequence whether the rules are in English, Latin, or Greek, but if children are to acquire *ideas,* it is certainly easier to obtain them in a language which they understand than in a foreign tongue. The distinctions between the principal parts of speech are founded in nature and are within the capacity of a school boy. These distinctions should be explained in English, and when well understood will facilitate the acquisition of other languages. Without some preparation of this kind, boys will often find a foreign language extremely difficult and sometimes be discouraged. We often see young persons of both sexes puzzling their heads with French when they can hardly write two sentences of good English. They plod on for some months with much fatigue, little improvement, and less pleasure, and then relinquish the attempt.

The principles of any science afford pleasure to the student who comprehends them. In order to render the study of language agreeable, the distinctions between words should be illustrated by the differences in visible objects. Examples should be presented to the senses, which are the inlets of all our knowledge. That *nouns are the names of things and that adjectives express their qualities* are abstract definitions which a boy may repeat five years without comprehending the meaning. But that *table* is the name of an article and *hard* or *square* is its property is a distinction obvious to the senses and consequently within a child's capacity.

There is one general practice in schools which I censure with diffidence, not because I doubt the propriety of the censure, but because it is opposed to deep-rooted prejudices: this practice is the use of the Bible as a schoolbook. There are two reasons why this practice has so generally prevailed: the first is that families in the country are not generally supplied with any other book; the second, an opinion that the reading of the scriptures will impress upon the minds of youth the important truths of religion and morality. The first may be easily removed, and the purpose of the last is counteracted by the practice itself.

If people design the doctrines of the Bible as a system of religion, ought they to appropriate the book to purposes foreign to this design? Will not a familiarity, contracted by a careless disrespectful reading of the sacred volume, weaken the influence of its precepts upon the heart?

Let us attend to the effect of familiarity in other things.

The rigid Puritans who first settled the New England states often chose their burying ground in the center of their settlements. Convenience might have been a motive for the choice, but it is probable that a stronger reason was the influence which they supposed the frequent burials and constant sight of the tombs would have upon the lives of men. The choice, however, for the latter purpose was extremely injudicious, for it may be laid down as a general rule that those who live in a constant view of death will become hardened to its terrors.

No person has less sensibility than the surgeon who has been accustomed to the amputation of limbs. No person thinks less of death than the soldier who has frequently walked over the carcasses of his slain comrades or the sexton who lives among the tombs.

Objects that affect the mind strongly, whether the sensations they excite are painful or pleasurable, always lose their effect by a frequent repetition of their impressions.‡ Those parts of

‡ The veneration we have for a great character ceases with an intimate acquaintance with the man. The same principle is observable in the body. High seasoned food, without frequent intervals of abstinence, loses its relish. On the other hand, objects that make slight impressions at first acquire strength by repetition. An elegant simplicity in a building may not affect the mind with great pleasure at first sight, but the pleasure will always increase with repeated examinations of the structure. Thus by habit we become excessively fond of food which does not relish at first tasting, and strong attachments between the sexes often take place from indifference and even from aversion.

the scripture, therefore, which are calculated to strike terror to the mind lose their influence by being too frequently brought into view. The same objection will not apply to the history and morality of the Bible, select passages of which may be read in schools to great advantage. In some countries the common people are not permitted to read the Bible at all. In ours, it is as common as a newspaper and in schools is read with nearly the same degree of respect. Both these practices appear to be extremes. My wish is not to see the Bible excluded from schools but to see it is used as a system of religion and morality.

These remarks suggest another error which is often committed in our inferior schools: I mean that of putting boys into difficult sciences while they are too young to exercise their reason upon abstract subjects. For example, boys are often put to the study of mathematics at the age of eight or ten years and before they can either read or write. In order to show the impropriety of such a practice, it is necessary to repeat what was just now observed, that our senses are the avenues of knowledge. This fact proves that the most natural course of education is that which employs, first the senses or powers of the body or those faculties of the mind which first acquire strength, and then proceeds to those studies which depend on the power of comparing and combining ideas. The art of writing is mechanical and imitative; this may therefore employ boys as soon as their fingers have strength sufficient to command a pen. A knowledge of letters requires the exercise of a mental power, memory, but this is coeval almost with the first operations of the human mind, and with respect to objects of sense, is almost perfect even in childhood. Children may therefore be taught reading as soon as their organs of speech have acquired strength sufficient to articulate the sounds of words.§

§ Great caution should be observed in teaching children to pronounce the letters of the alphabet. The labials are easily pronounced; thus the first words a child can speak are *papa* and *mama*. But there are some letters, particularly *l* and *r*, which are of difficult pronunciation, and children should not be pressed to speak words in which they occur. The difficulty may produce a habit of stammering.

But those sciences a knowledge of which is acquired principally by the reasoning faculties should be postponed to a more advanced period of life. In the course of an English education, mathematics should be perhaps the last study of youth in schools. Years of valuable time are sometimes thrown away in a fruitless application to sciences, the principles of which are above the comprehension of the students.

There is no particular age at which every boy is qualified to enter upon mathematics to advantage. The proper time can be best determined by the instructors, who are acquainted with the different capacities of their pupils.

Another error which is frequent in America is that a master undertakes to teach many different branches in the same school. In new settlements, where people are poor and live in scattered situations, the practice is often unavoidable, but in populous towns it must be considered as a defective plan of education. For suppose the teacher to be equally master of all the branches which he attempts to teach, which seldom happens, yet his attention must be distracted with a multiplicity of objects and consequently painful to himself and not useful to the pupils. Add to this the continual interruptions which the students of one branch suffer from those of another, which must retard the progress of the whole school. It is a much more eligible plan to appropriate an apartment to each branch of education, with a teacher who makes that branch his sole employment. The principal academies in Europe and America are on this plan, which both reason and experience prove to be the most useful.

With respect to literary institutions of the first rank, it appears to me that their local situations are an object of importance. It is a subject of controversy whether a large city or a country village is the most eligible situation for a college or university. But the arguments in favor of the latter appear to me decisive. Large cities are always scenes of dissipation and amusement, which have a tendency to corrupt the hearts of youth and divert their minds from their literary pursuits.

Reason teaches this doctrine, and experience has uniformly confirmed the truth of it.

Strict discipline is essential to the prosperity of a public seminary of science, and this is established with more facility and supported with more uniformity in a small village where there are no great objects of curiosity to interrupt the studies of youth or to call their attention from the orders of the society.

That the morals of young men as well as their application to science depend much on retirement will be generally acknowledged, but it will be said also that the company in large towns will improve their manners. The question, then, is which shall be sacrificed—the advantage of an *uncorrupted heart* and an *improved head* or of polished manners. But this question supposes that the virtues of the heart and the polish of the gentleman are incompatible with each other, which is by no means true. The gentleman and the scholar are often united in the same person. But both are not formed by the same means. The improvement of the head requires close application to books; the refinement of manners rather attends some degree of dissipation or at least a relaxation of the mind. To preserve the purity of the heart, it is sometimes necessary, and always useful, to place a youth beyond the reach of bad examples, whereas a general knowledge of the world, of all kinds of company, is requisite to teach a universal propriety of behavior.

But youth is the time to form both the head and the heart. The understanding is indeed ever enlarging, but the seeds of knowledge should be planted in the mind while it is young and susceptible, and if the mind is not kept untainted in *youth,* there is little probability that the moral character of the *man* will be unblemished. A genteel address, on the other hand, *may* be acquired at any time of life and *must* be acquired, if ever, by mingling with good company. But were the cultivation of the understanding and of the heart inconsistent with genteel manners, still no rational person could hesitate which to prefer. The goodness of a heart is of infinitely more consequence to society than an elegance of manners; nor will any superficial accomplishments repair the want of principle in the mind. It is always better to be *vulgarly right* than *politely wrong*.

But if the amusements, dissipation, and vicious examples in populous cities render them improper places for seats of learning, the monkish mode of sequestering boys from other society and confining them to the apartments of a college appears to me another fault. The human mind is like a rich field, which, without constant care, will ever be covered with a luxuriant growth of weeds. It is extremely dangerous to suffer young men to pass the most critical period of life, when the passions are strong, the judgment weak, and the heart susceptible and unsuspecting, in a situation where there is not the least restraint upon their inclinations. My own observations lead me to draw the veil of silence over the ill effects of this practice. But it is to be wished that youth might always be kept under the inspection of age and superior wisdom; that literary institutions might be so situated, that the students might live in decent families, be subject in some measure to their discipline, and even under the control of those whom they respect.

Perhaps it may also be numbered among the errors in our systems of education that in all our universities and colleges the students are all restricted to the same course of study and, by being classed, limited to the same progress. Classing is necessary, but whether students should not be removable from the lower to the higher classes as a reward for their superior industry and improvements is submitted to those who know the effect of emulation upon the human mind.

But young gentlemen are not all designed for the same line of business, and why should they pursue the same studies? Why should a merchant trouble himself with the rules of Greek and Roman syntax or a planter puzzle his head with conic sections? Life is too short to acquire, and the mind of man too feeble to contain, the whole circle of sciences. The greatest genius on earth, not even a Bacon, can be a perfect master of *every* branch, but any moderate genius may, by suitable application, be perfect in any *one* branch. By attempting therefore to teach young gentlemen everything, we make the most of them mere smatterers in science. In order to qualify persons to figure in any profession, it is necessary that they should attend closely to those branches of learning which lead to it.

There are some arts and sciences which are necessary for every man. Every man should be able to speak and write his native tongue with correctness and have some knowledge of mathematics. The rules of arithmetic are indispensably requisite. But besides the learning which is of common utility, lads should be directed to pursue those branches which are connected more immediately with the business for which they are destined.

It would be very useful for the farming part of the community to furnish country schools with some easy system of practical husbandry. By repeatedly reading some book of this kind, the mind would be stored with ideas which might not indeed be understood in youth but which would be called into practice in some subsequent period of life. This would lead the mind to the subject of agriculture and pave the way for improvements.

Young gentlemen designed for the mercantile line, after having learned to write and speak English correctly, might attend to French, Italian, or such other living language as they will probably want in the course of business. These languages should be learned early in youth, while the organs are yet pliable; otherwise the pronunciation will probably be imperfect. These studies might be succeeded by some attention to chronology, and a regular application to geography, mathematics, history, the general regulations of commercial nations, principles of advance in trade, of insurance, and to the general principles of government.

It appears to me that such a course of education, which might be completed by the age of fifteen or sixteen, would have a tendency to make better merchants than the usual practice which confines boys to Lucian, Ovid, and Tully till they are fourteen and then turns them into a store, without an idea of their business or one article of education necessary for them, except perhaps a knowledge of writing and figures.

Such a system of English education is also much preferable to a university education, even with the usual honors, for it might be finished so early as to leave young persons time to serve a regular apprenticeship, without which no person should enter upon business. But by the time a university education is completed, young men commonly commence *gentlemen*; their age and their pride will not suffer them to go through the drudgery of a counting house, and they enter upon business without the requisite accomplishments. Indeed it appears to me that what is now called a *liberal education* disqualifies a man for business. Habits are formed in youth and by practice, and as business is in some measure mechanical, every person should be exercised in his employment in an early period of life, that his habits may be formed by the time his apprenticeship expires. An education in a university interferes with the forming of these habits and perhaps forms opposite habits; the mind may contract a fondness for ease, for pleasure or for books, which no efforts can overcome. An academic education, which should furnish the youth with some ideas of men and things and leave time for an apprenticeship before the age of twenty-one years would in my opinion be the most eligible for young men who are designed for active employments.

The method pursued in our colleges is better calculated to fit youth for the learned professions than for business. But perhaps the period of study required as the condition of receiving the usual degrees is too short. Four years, with the most assiduous application, are a short time to furnish the mind with the necessary knowledge of the languages and of the several sciences. It might perhaps have been a period sufficiently long for an infant settlement, as America was, at the time when most of our colleges were founded. But as the country becomes populous, wealthy, and respectable, it may be worthy of considera-

tion whether the period of academic life should not be extended
to six or seven years.

But the principal defect in our plan of education in America
is the want of good teachers in the academies and common
schools. By good teachers I mean men of unblemished reputation and possessed of abilities competent to their stations. That
a man should be master of what he undertakes to teach is a
point that will not be disputed, and yet it is certain that abilities
are often dispensed with, either through inattention or fear of
expense.

To those who employ ignorant men to instruct their children,
permit me to suggest one important idea: that it is better for
youth to have *no* education than to have a bad one, for it is
more difficult to eradicate habits than to impress new ideas. The
tender shrub is easily bent to any figure, but the tree which has
acquired its full growth resists all impressions.

Yet abilities are not the sole requisites. The instructors of
youth ought, of all men, to be the most prudent, accomplished,
agreeable, and respectable. What avail a man's parts, if, while
he is the "wisest and brightest," he is the "meanest of mankind?"[3] The pernicious effects of bad example on the *minds* of
youth will probably be acknowledged, but with a view to *improvement* it is indispensably necessary that the teachers should
possess good breeding and agreeable manners. In order to give
full effect to instructions, it is requisite that they should proceed
from a man who is loved and respected. But a low-bred clown or
morose tyrant can command neither love nor respect, and that
pupil who has no motive for application to books but the fear
of a rod will not make a scholar.

The rod is often necessary in school, especially after the children have been accustomed to disobedience and a licentious
behavior at home. All government originates in families, and if
neglected there, it will hardly exist in society, but the want of
it must be supplied by the rod in school, the penal laws of the
state, and the terrors of divine wrath from the pulpit. The gov-

ernment both of families and schools should be absolute. There should in families be no appeal from one parent to another, with the prospect of pardon for offenses. The one should always vindicate, at least apparently, the conduct of the other. In schools the matter should be absolute in command, for it is utterly impossible for any man to support order and discipline among children who are indulged with an appeal to their parents. A proper subordination in families would generally supersede the necessity of severity in schools, and a strict discipline in both is the best foundation of good order in political society.

If parents should say, "We cannot give the instructors of our children unlimited authority over them, for it may be abused and our children injured," I would answer, they must not place them under the direction of any man in whose temper, judgment, and abilities they do not repose perfect confidence. The teacher should be, if such can be found, as judicious and reasonable a man as the parent.

There can be little improvement in schools without strict subordination; there can be no subordination without principles of esteem and respect in the pupils; and the pupils cannot esteem and respect a man who is not in himself respectable and who is not treated with respect by their parents. It may be laid down as an invariable maxim that a person is not fit to superintend the education of children who has not the qualifications which will command the esteem and respect of his pupils. This maxim is founded on a truth which every person may have observed—that children always *love* an *amiable* man and always *esteem a respectable* one. Men and women have their passions, which often rule their judgment and their conduct. They have their caprices, their interests, and their prejudices, which at times incline them to treat the most meritorious characters with disrespect. But children, artless and unsuspecting, resign their hearts to any person whose manners are agreeable and whose conduct is respectable. Whenever, therefore, pupils cease to respect their teacher, he should be instantly dismissed.

Respect for an instructor will often supply the place of a rod of correction. The pupil's attachment will lead him to close attention to his studies; he fears not the *rod* so much as the *displeasure* of his teacher; he waits for a smile or dreads a frown; he receives his instructions and copies his manners. This generous principle, the fear of offending, will prompt youth to exertions, and instead of severity on the one hand and of slavish fear with reluctant obedience on the other, mutual esteem, respect, and confidence strew flowers in the road to knowledge.

With respect to morals and civil society, the other view in which I proposed to treat this subject, the effects of education are so certain and extensive that it behooves every parent and guardian to be particularly attentive to the characters of the men whose province it is to form the minds of youth.

From a strange inversion of the order of nature, the cause of which it is not necessary to unfold, the most important business in civil society is in many parts of America committed to the most worthless characters. The education of youth, an employment of more consequence than making laws and preaching the gospel, because it lays the foundation on which both law and gospel rest for success, this education is sunk to a level with the most menial services. In most instances we find the higher seminaries of learning entrusted to men of good characters and possessed of the moral virtues of social affections. But many of our inferior schools, which, so far as the heart is concerned, are as important as colleges, are kept by men of no breeding, and many of them, by men infamous for the most detestable vices.||

|| How different this practice from the manner of educating youth in Rome during the flourishing ages of the republic! There the attention to children commenced with their birth; an infant was not educated in the cottage of a hireling nurse, but in the very bosom of its mother, whose principal praise was that she superintended her family. Parents were careful to choose some aged matron to take care of their children, to form their first habits of speaking and acting, to watch their growing passions, and direct them to their proper objects, to guard them from all immodest sports, preserve their minds innocent, and direct their attention to liberal pursuits.

"—Filius . . . non in cellula emptæ nutricis sed gremio ac sinu matris educabatur, cujus præcipua laus, tueri domum, et inservire liberis. Eligebatur autem aliqua major natu propinqua, cujus probatis spectatisque moribus, omnis cujus-

Will this be denied? Will it be denied that before the war it was a frequent practice for gentlemen to purchase convicts who had been transported for their crimes and employ them as private tutors in their families?

Gracious Heavens! Must the wretches who have forfeited their lives and been pronounced unworthy to be inhabitants of a *foreign* country be entrusted with the education, the morals, the character of *American* youth?

Will it be denied that many of the instructors of youth, whose examples and precepts should form their minds for good men and useful citizens, are often found to sleep away in school the fumes of a debauch and to stun the ears of their pupils with frequent blasphemy? It is idle to suppress such truths; nay more, it is wicked. The practice of employing low and vicious

piam familiæ soboles committeretur, coram qua neque dicere fas erat quod turpe dictu, neque facere quod inhonestum factu videretur. Ac non studia modo curas-que, fed remissiones etiam lusus que puerorum, sanctitate quadam ac verecundia temperabat." ["In the good old days, every man's son, born in wedlock, was brought up not in the chamber of some hireling nurse, but in his mother's lap, and at her knee. And that mother could have no higher praise than that she managed the house and gave herself to her children. Again, some elderly relative would be selected in order that to her, as a person who had been tried and never found wanting, might be entrusted the care of all the youthful scions of the same home; in the presence of such an one no base word could be uttered without grave offence, and no wrong deed done. Religiously and with the utmost deli-cacy she regulated not only the serious tasks of her youthful charges, but their recreations also and their games." Peterson, trans., *Dialogus of Tacitus*, pp. 88-89.]

In this manner were educated the Gracchi, Cæsar, and other celebrated Romans. "Quæ disciplina ac severitas eo pertinebat, ut sincera et intergra et nullis pravitatibus detorta unius cujusque natura, toto statem pectore, arriperet artes honestas." *Tacitus, de Orat. Dial.* 28. ["The object of this rigorous system was that the natural disposition of every child, while still sound at the core and untainted, not warped as yet by any vicious tendencies, might at once lay hold with heart and soul on virtuous accomplishments . . . ." *Ibid.*, pp. 88-91.]

The historian then proceeds to mention the corruption of manners and the vicious mode of education in the later ages of Rome. He says, children were committed to some maid, with the vilest slaves, with whom they were initiated in their low conversation and manners. "Horum fabulis et erroribus teneri statim et rudes animi imbuuntur; nec quis quam in toto domo pensi habet, quid coram infante domino aut dicat aut faciat." *Ibm.* 29. ["It is from the foolish tittle-tattle of such persons that the children receive their earliest impressions, while their minds are still pliant and unformed; and there is not a soul in the whole house who cares a jot what he says or does in the presence of its lisping little lord." *Ibid.*, pp. 90-91.]

characters to direct the studies of youth is in a high degree criminal; it is destructive of the order and peace of society; it is treason against morals and of course against government; it ought to be arraigned before the tribunal of reason and condemned by all intelligent beings. The practice is so exceedingly absurd that it is surprising it could ever have prevailed among rational people. Parents wish their children to be *well-bred*, yet place them under the care of *clowns*. They wish to secure their hearts from *vicious principles* and *habits*, yet commit them to the care of men of the most *profligate lives*. They wish to have their children taught *obedience* and *respect* for superiors, yet give them a master that both parents and children *despise*. A practice so glaringly absurd and irrational has no name in any language! Parents themselves will not associate with the men whose company they *oblige* their children to keep, even in that most important period when habits are forming for life.¶

Are parents and guardians ignorant that children always imitate those with whom they live or associate? That a boy, bred in the woods, will be a savage? That another, bred in the army, will have the manners of a soldier? That a third, bred in a kitchen, will speak the language and possess the ideas of serv-

¶ The practice of employing low characters in schools is not novel. Ascham, preceptor to Queen Elizabeth, gives us the following account of the practice in his time. "Pity it is that commonly more care is had; yea and that among very wise men, to find out rather a cunning man for their horse, than a cunning man for their children. They say, nay, in word; but they do so, in deed. For to one they will give a stipend of two hundred crowns, and loth to offer the other two hundred shillings. God, that sitteth in the Heaven, laugheth their choice to scorn and rewardeth their liberality as it should: for he suffereth them to have *tame* and *well-ordered horses*; but *wild* and *unfortunate children*: and therefore in the end they find more pleasure in their horse, than comfort in their child." [Roger Ascham, *The Scholemaster* (2d ed., London: Iohn Daye, 1570), p. 7.]

This is *old language*, but the facts stated are *modern truths*. The barbarous Gothic practice has survived all the attacks of common sense, and in many parts of America a gentleman's groom is on a level with his schoolmaster in point of reputation. But hear another authority for the practice in England.

"As the case now stands, those of the first quality pay their *tutors* but little above half so much as they do their *footmen*." *Guardian*, No. 94. [*The [London] Guardian*, No. 94 (Monday, June 29, 1713), p. 1, col. 1.]

" 'Tis monstrous indeed that men of the best estates and families are more solicitous about the tutelage of a favorite *dog* or *horse*, than of their *heirs male*." *Ibm.*

ants? And that a fourth, bred in genteel company, will have the manners of a gentleman? We cannot believe that many people are ignorant of these truths. Their conduct therefore can be ascribed to nothing but inattention or fear of expense. It is perhaps literally true that a wild life among savages is preferable to an education in a kitchen or under a drunken tutor, for savages would leave the mind uncorrupted with the vices which reign among slaves and the depraved part of civilized nations. It is therefore a point of infinite importance to society that youth should not associate with persons whose manners they ought not to imitate; much less should they be doomed to pass the most susceptible period of life with clowns, profligates, and slaves.

There are people so ignorant of the constitution of our natures as to declare that young people should see vices and their consequences, that they may learn to detest and shun them. Such reasoning is like that of the novel writers, who attempt to defend their delineations of abandoned characters; and that of stage players, who would vindicate the obscene exhibitions of a theater; but the reasoning is totally false.* Vice always spreads by being published; young people are taught many vices by fiction, books, or public exhibitions, vices which they never would have known had they never read such books or attended such public places. Crimes of all kinds, vices, judicial trials necessarily obscene, and infamous punishments should, if possible, be concealed from the young. An examination in a court of justice may teach the tricks of a knave, the arts of a thief, and the evasions of hackneyed offenders to a dozen young culprits and even tempt those who have never committed a crime to make a trial of their skill. A newspaper may spread crimes by communicating to a nation the knowledge of an ingenious trick of villainy which, had it been suppressed,

---

* The fact related by Justin, of an ancient people, will apply universally. "Tanto plus in illis proficit vitiorum ignoratio, quam in his cognitio virtutis." An ignorance of vice has a better effect than a knowledge of virtue. [Justin, *De historiis Philippicis et totius mundi orginibus* II. ii. 24-25 (London, R. Clavel, 1701), p. 314.]

might have died with its first inventor. It is not true that the effects of vice and crimes deter others from the practice except when rarely seen. On the other hand, frequent exhibitions either cease to make any impressions on the minds of spectators or else reconcile them to a course of life which at first was disagreeable.

> Vice is a monster of so frightful mein,
> As to be hated, needs but to be seen;
> Yet seen too oft, familiar with her face,
> We first endure, then pity, then embrace.[4]

For these reasons children should keep the best of company that they might have before them the best manners, the best breeding, and the best conversation. Their minds should be kept untainted till their reasoning faculties have acquired strength and the good principles which may be planted in their minds have taken deep root. They will then be able to make a firm and probably a successful resistance against the attacks of secret corruption and brazen libertinism.

Our legislators frame laws for the suppression of vice and immorality; our divines thunder from the pulpit the terrors of infinite wrath against the vices that stain the characters of men. And do laws and preaching effect a reformation of manners? Experience would not give a very favorable answer to this inquiry. The reason is obvious: the attempts are directed to the wrong objects. Laws can only check the public effects of vicious principles but can never reach the principles themselves, and preaching is not very intelligible to people till they arrive at an age when their principles are rooted or their habits firmly established. An attempt to eradicate old habits is as absurd as to lop off the branches of a huge oak in order to root it out of a rich soil. The most that such clipping will effect is to prevent a further growth.

The only practicable method to reform mankind is to begin with children, to banish, if possible, from their company every low-bred, drunken, immoral character. Virtue and vice will not grow together in a great degree, but they will grow where they

are planted, and when one has taken root, it is not easily supplanted by the other. The great art of correcting mankind,
therefore, consists in prepossessing the mind with good principles.

For this reason society requires that the education of youth
should be watched with the most scrupulous attention. Education, in a great measure, forms the moral characters of men, and
morals are the basis of government.† Education should therefore be the first care of a legislature, not merely the institution
of schools but the furnishing of them with the best men for
teachers. A good system of education should be the first article
in the code of political regulations, for it is much easier to introduce and establish an effectual system for preserving morals
than to correct by penal statutes the ill effects of a bad system.
I am so fully persuaded of this that I shall almost adore that
great man who shall change our practice and opinions and make
it respectable for the first and best men to superintend the
education of youth.

Another defect in our schools, which, since the Revolution, is
become inexcusable, is the want of proper books. The collections which are now used consist of essays that respect foreign
and ancient nations. The minds of youth are perpetually led to
the history of Greece and Rome or to Great Britain; boys are
constantly repeating the declamations of Demosthenes and
Cicero or debates upon some political question in the British
Parliament. These are excellent specimens of good sense,
polished style and perfect oratory, but they are not interesting
to children. They cannot be very useful, except to young gentlemen who want them as models of reasoning and eloquence in
the pulpit or at the bar.

But every child in America should be acquainted with his
own country. He should read books that furnish him with ideas

---

† Plus ibi boni mores valent, quam alibi bonæ leges. Tac. de Mor. Germ. 19.
[". . . Good habits have more force with them than good laws elsewhere." Peterson, trans., *Dialogus of Tacitus*, pp. 292-293 ("Germania").]

that will be useful to him in life and practice. As soon as he opens his lips, he should rehearse the history of his own country; he should lisp the praise of liberty and of those illustrious heroes and statesmen who have wrought a revolution in her favor.

A selection of essays respecting the settlement and geography of America, the history of the late Revolution and of the most remarkable characters and events that distinguished it, and a compendium of the principles of the federal and provincial governments should be the principal schoolbook in the United States. These are interesting objects to every man; they call home the minds of youth and fix them upon the interests of their own country, and they assist in forming attachments to it, as well as in enlarging the understanding.

It is observed by the great Montesquieu that "the laws of education ought to be relative to the principles of the government."‡

In despotic governments the people should have little or no education, except what tends to inspire them with a servile fear. Information is fatal to despotism.

In monarchies education should be partial and adapted to the rank of each class of citizens. But "in a republican government," says the same writer, "the whole power of education is required."[5] Here every class of people should *know* and *love* the laws. This knowledge should be diffused by means of schools and newspapers, and an atttachment to the laws may be formed by early impressions upon the mind.

Two regulations are essential to the continuance of republican governments: 1. Such a distribution of lands and such principles of descent and alienation as shall give every citizen a power of acquiring what his industry merits.§ 2. Such a sys-

‡ Spirit of Laws. Book 4. [Charles Louis de Secondat, baron de la Brède et de Montesquieu, *The Spirit of Laws*, 2 vols. (London: J. Nourse and P. Vaillant, 1750), I, 42.]

§ The power of entailing real estates is repugnant to the spirit of our American governments.

tem of education as gives every citizen an opportunity of acquiring knowledge and fitting himself for places of trust. These are fundamental articles, the *sine qua non* of the existence of the American republics.

Hence the absurdity of our copying the manners and adopting the institutions of monarchies.

In several states we find laws passed establishing provision for colleges and academies where people of property may educate their sons, but no provision is made for instructing the poorer rank of people even in reading and writing. Yet in these same states every citizen who is worth a few shillings annually is entitled to vote for legislators.|| This appears to me a most glaring solecism in government. The constitutions are *republican* and the laws of education are *monarchical*. The *former* extend civil rights to every honest industrious man, the *latter* deprive a large proportion of the citizens of a most valuable privilege.

In our American republics, where government is in the hands of the people, knowledge should be universally diffused by means of public schools. Of such consequence is it to society that the people who make laws should be well informed that I conceive no legislature can be justified in neglecting proper establishments for this purpose.

When I speak of a diffusion of knowledge, I do not mean merely a knowledge of spelling books and the New Testament. An acquaintance with ethics and with the general principles of law, commerce, money, and government is necessary for the yeomanry of a republican state. This acquaintance they might obtain by means of books calculated for schools and read by the children during the winter months and by the circulation of public papers.

"In Rome it was the common exercise of boys at school to learn the laws of the twelve tables by heart, as they did their

---

|| I have known instructions from the inhabitants of a county, two thirds of whom could not write their names. How competent must such men be to decide an important point in legislation!

poets and classic authors."¶ What an excellent practice this in a free government!

It is said, indeed by many, that our common people are already too well informed. Strange paradox! The truth is, they have too much knowledge and spirit to resign their share in government and are not sufficiently informed to govern themselves in all cases of difficulty.

There are some acts of the American legislatures which astonish men of information, and blunders in legislation are frequently ascribed to bad intentions. But if we examine the men who compose these legislatures, we shall find that wrong measures generally proceed from ignorance either in the men themselves or in their constituents. They often mistake their own interest, because they do not foresee the remote consequences of a measure.

It may be true that all men cannot be legislators, but the more generally knowledge is diffused among the substantial yeomanry, the more perfect will be the laws of a republican state.

Every small district should be furnished with a school, at least four months in a year, when boys are not otherwise employed. This school should be kept by the most reputable and well informed man in the district. Here children should be taught the usual branches of learning, submission to superiors and to laws, the moral or social duties, the history and transactions of their own country, the principles of liberty and government. Here the rough manners of the wilderness should be softened and the principles of virtue and good behavior inculcated. The *virtues* of men are of more consequence to society than their *abilities*, and for this reason the *heart* should be cultivated with more assiduity than the *head*.

Such a general system of education is neither impracticable nor difficult, and excepting the formation of a federal govern-

¶ Middleton's *Life of Cicero*, volume 1, page 13. [Conyers Middleton, *The History of the Life of Marcus Tullius Cicero*, 2 vols. (London: The Author, 1741), I, 13.]

ment that shall be efficient and permanent, it demands the first attention of American patriots. Until such a system shall be adopted and pursued, until the statesman and divine shall unite their efforts in *forming* the human mind, rather than in loping its excrescences after it has been neglected, until legislators discover that the only way to make good citizens and subjects is to nourish them from infancy, and until parents shall be convinced that the *worst* of men are not the proper teachers to make the *best*, mankind cannot know to what a degree of perfection society and government may be carried. America affords the fairest opportunities for making the experiment and opens the most encouraging prospect of success.*

In a system of education that should embrace every part of the community the female sex claim no inconsiderable share of our attention.

The women in America (to their honor it is mentioned) are not generally above the care of educating their own children. Their own education should therefore enable them to implant in the tender mind such sentiments of virtue, propriety, and dignity as are suited to the freedom of our governments. Children should be treated as children, but as children that are in a future time to be men and women. By treating them as if

---

* It is worthy of remark that in proportion as laws are favorable to the equal rights of men, the number of crimes in a state is diminished, except where the human mind is debased by extreme servitude or by superstition. In France there are but few crimes; religion and the rigor of a military force prevent them; perhaps also ignorance in the peasantry may be assigned as another reason. But in England and Ireland the human mind is not so depressed, yet the distribution of property and honors is not equal; the lower classes of people, bold and independent as well as poor, feel the injuries which flow from the feudal system, even in its relaxed state; they become desperate and turn highwaymen. Hence those kingdoms produce more culprits than half Europe besides.

The character of the Jews, as sharpers, is derived from the cruel and villainous proscriptions which they have suffered from the bigotry of Christians in every part of Europe.

Most of the criminals condemned in America are foreigners. The execution of a native before the Revolution was a novelty. The distribution of property in America and the principles of government favor the rights of men, and but few men will commence enemies to society and government if they can receive the benefits of them. Unjust governments and tyrannical distinctions have made most of the villains that ever existed.

they were always to remain children, we very often see their childishness adhere to them, even in middle life. The silly language called *baby talk*, in which most persons are initiated in infancy, often breaks out in discourse at the age of forty and makes a man appear very ridiculous.† In the same manner, vulgar, obscene, and illiberal ideas imbibed in a nursery or a kitchen often give a tincture to the conduct through life. In order to prevent every evil bias, the ladies, whose province it is to direct the inclinations of children on their first appearance and to choose their nurses, should be possessed, not only of amiable manners, but of just sentiments and enlarged understandings.

But the influence of women in forming the dispositions of youth is not the sole reason why their education should be particularly guarded; their influence in controlling the manners of a nation is another powerful reason. Women, once abandoned, may be instrumental in corrupting society, but such is the delicacy of the sex and such the restraints which custom imposes upon them that they are generally the last to be corrupted. There are innumerable instances of men who have been restrained from a vicious life and even of very abandoned men who have been reclaimed by their attachment to ladies of virtue. A fondness for the company and conversation of ladies of character may be considered as a young man's best security against the attractives of a dissipated life. A man who is attached to *good* company seldom frequents that which is *bad*. For this reason, society requires that females should be well educated and extend their influence as far as possible over the other sex.

But a distinction is to be made between a *good* education and a *showy* one, for an education, merely superficial, is a proof of corruption of taste and has a mischievous influence on man-

† It has been already observed that a child always imitates what he sees and hears. For this reason he should hear no language which is not correct and decent. Every word spoken to a child should be pronounced with clearness and propriety. Banish from children all diminutive words, all whining, and all bad grammar. A boy of six years old may be taught to speak as correctly as Cicero did before the Roman Senate.

ners. The education of females, like that of males, should be adapted to the principles of the government and correspond with the stage of society. Education in Paris differs from that in Petersburg, and the education of females in London or Paris should not be a model for the Americans to copy.

In all nations a *good* education is that which renders the ladies correct in their manners, respectable in their families, and agreeable in society. That education is always *wrong* which raises a woman above the duties of her station.

In America female education should have for its object what is *useful*. Young ladies should be taught to speak and write their own language with purity and elegance, an article in which they are often deficient. The French language is not necessary for ladies. In some cases it is convenient, but, in general, it may be considered as an article of luxury. As an accomplishment, it may be studied by those whose attention is not employed about more important concerns.

Some knowledge of arithmetic is necessary for every lady. Geography should never be neglected. *Belles-lettres* learning seems to correspond with the dispositions of most females. A taste for poetry and fine writing should be cultivated, for we expect the most delicate sentiments from the pens of that sex which is possessed of the finest feelings.

A course of reading can hardly be prescribed for all ladies. But it should be remarked that this sex cannot be too well acquainted with the writers upon human life and manners. The *Spectator* should fill the first place in every lady's library. Other volumes of periodical papers, though inferior to the *Spectator,* should be read, and some of the best histories.

With respect to novels, so much admired by the young and so generally condemned by the old, what shall I say? Perhaps it may be said with truth that some of them are useful, many of them pernicious, and most of them trifling. A hundred volumes of modern novels may be read without acquiring a new idea. Some of them contain entertaining stories, and where the descriptions are drawn from nature and from characters and events in themselves innocent, the perusal of them may be harmless.

Were novels written with a view to exhibit only one side of human nature, to paint the social virtues, the world would condemn them as defective, but I should think them more perfect. Young people, especially females, should not see the vicious part of mankind. At best, novels may be considered as the toys of youth, the rattle boxes of sixteen. The mechanic gets his pence for his toys, and the novel writer, for his books, and it would be happy for society if the latter were in all cases as innocent playthings as the former.

In the large towns in America music, drawing, and dancing constitute a part of female education. They, however, hold a subordinate rank, for my fair friends will pardon me when I declare that no man ever marries a woman for her performance on a harpsichord or her figure in a minuet. However ambitious a woman may be to command admiration *abroad*, her real merit is known only at *home*. Admiration is useless when it is not supported by domestic worth. But real honor and permanent esteem are always secured by those who preside over their own families with dignity.‡

‡ Nothing can be more fatal to domestic happiness in America than a taste for copying the luxurious manners and amusements of England and France. Dancing, drawing, and music are principal articles of education in those kingdoms; therefore every girl in America must pass two or three years at a boarding school, though her father cannot give her a farthing when she marries. This ambition to educate females above their fortunes pervades every part of America. Hence the disproportion between the well-bred females and the males in our large towns. A mechanic or shopkeeper in town or a farmer in the country whose sons get their living by their father's employments will send their daughters to a boarding school, where their ideas are elevated and their views carried above a connection with men in those occupations. Such an education, without fortune or beauty, may possibly please a girl of fifteen but must prove her greatest misfortune. This fatal mistake is illustrated in every large town in America. In the country the number of males and females is nearly equal, but in towns the number of genteely bred women is greater than of men, and in some towns the proportion is as three to one.

The heads of young people of both sexes are often turned by reading descriptions of splendid living, of coaches, of plays, and other amusements. Such descriptions excite a desire to enjoy the same pleasures. A fortune becomes the principal object of pursuit; fortunes are scarce in America and not easily acquired; disappointment succeeds, and the youth who begins life with expecting

Before I quit this subject, I beg leave to make some remarks on a practice which appears to be attended with important consequences; I mean that of sending boys to Europe for an education or sending to Europe for teachers. This was right before the Revolution, at least so far as national attachments were concerned, but the propriety of it ceased with our political relation to Great Britain.

In the first place, our honor as an independent nation is concerned in the establishment of literary institutions adequate to all our own purposes, without sending our youth abroad or depending on other nations for books and instructors. It is very little to the reputation of America to have it said abroad that after the heroic achievements of the late war these independent people are obliged to send to Europe for men and books to teach their children A B C.

But in another point of view, a foreign education is directly opposite to our political interests and ought to be discountenanced, if not prohibited.

Every person of common observation will grant that most men prefer the manners and the government of that country where they are educated. Let ten American youths be sent, each to a different European kingdom, and live there from the age of twelve to twenty, and each will give the preference to the country where he has resided.

The period from twelve to twenty is the most important in life. The impressions made before that period are commonly effaced; those that are made during that period *always* remain for many years and *generally* through life.

Ninety-nine persons of a hundred who pass that period in England or France will prefer the people, their manners, their laws, and their government to those of their native country.

---

to enjoy a coach closes the prospect with a small living procured by labor and economy.

Thus a wrong education and a taste for pleasures which our fortune will not enable us to enjoy often plunge the Americans into distress or at least prevent early marriages. Too fond of show, of dress, and expense, the sexes wish to please each other; they mistake the means, and both are disappointed.

Such attachments are injurious, both to the happiness of the men and to the political interests of their own country. As to private happiness, it is universally known how much pain a man suffers by a change of habits in living. The customs of Europe are and ought to be different from ours, but when a man has been bred in one country, his attachments to its manners make them, in a great measure, necessary to his happiness. On changing his residence, he must therefore break his former habits, which is always a painful sacrifice; or the discordance between the manners of his own country and his habits must give him incessant uneasiness; or he must introduce into a circle of his friends the manners in which he was educated. These consequences may follow, and the last, which is inevitable, is a public injury. The refinement of manners in every country should keep pace exactly with the increase of its wealth, and perhaps the greatest evil America now feels is an improvement of taste and manners which its wealth cannot support.

A foreign education is the very source of this evil; it gives young gentlemen of fortune a relish for manners and amusements which are not suited to this country, which, however, when introduced by this class of people will always become fashionable.

But a corruption of manners is not the sole objection to a foreign education: an attachment to a *foreign* government, or rather a want of attachment to our *own*, is the natural effect of a residence abroad during the period of youth. It is recorded of one of the Greek cities that in a treaty with their conquerors it was required that they should give a certain number of *male children* as hostages for the fulfillment of their engagements. The Greeks absolutely refused, on the principle that these children would imbibe the ideas and embrace the manners of foreigners or lose their love for their own country, but they offered the same number of *old* men without hesitation. This anecdote is full of good sense. A man should always form his habits and attachments in the country where he is to reside for life. When these habits are formed, young men may travel without danger of losing their patriotism. A boy who lives in England from twelve to twenty will be an *Englishman* in his manners and his feelings, but let him remain at home till he is twenty and form his attachments, he may then be several years abroad and still be an *American*.§ There may be exceptions to this observation, but living examples may be mentioned to prove the truth of the general principle here advanced respecting the influence of habit.

It may be said that foreign universities furnish much better opportunities of improvement in the sciences than the American. This may be true and yet will not justify the practice of sending young lads from their own country. There are some branches of science which may be studied to much greater advantage in Europe than in America, particularly chemistry. When these are to be acquired, young gentlemen ought to spare no pains to attend the best professors. It may, therefore, be useful, in some cases, for students to cross the Atlantic to *complete* a course of studies, but it is not necessary for them to go early in life nor to continue a long time. Such instances need not be frequent even now, and the necessity for them

§ Cicero was twenty-eight years old when he left Italy to travel into Greece and Asia. "He did not stir abroad," says Dr. Middleton, "till he had completed his education at home, for nothing can be more pernicious to a nation than the necessity of a foreign one."—*Life of Cicero, vol.* 1. *p.* 45.

Dr. Moore makes a remark precisely in point. Speaking of a foreign education, proposed by a certain Lord who objected to the public schools in England, he says, "I have attended to his Lordship's objections, and after due consideration and weighing every circumstance, I remain of opinion that no country but Great Britain is proper for the education of a British subject who proposes to pass his life in his own country. The most important point, in my mind, to be secured in the education of a young man of rank of our country is to make him an Englishman, and this can be done nowhere so effectually as in England." See his *View of Society and Manners, etc.* vol. 1, page 197, where the reader will find many judicious remarks upon this subject. The following are too pertinent to be omitted.—"It is thought that by an early foreign education all ridiculous English prejudices will be avoided. This may be true, but other prejudices, perhaps as ridiculous and much more detrimental, will be formed. The first cannot be attended with many inconveniences; the second may render the young people unhappy in their own country when they return and disagreeable to their countrymen all the rest of their lives." These remarks, by a change of names, are applicable to America. [John Moore, *A View of Society and Manners in France, Switzerland, Germany, and Italy: With Anecdotes Relating to Some Eminent Characters* (Philadelphia: Robert Bell, 1783), I, 93.]

will diminish in proportion to the future advancement of literature in America.

It is, however, much questioned whether in the ordinary course of study a young man can enjoy greater advantages in Europe than in America. Experience inclines me to raise a doubt whether the danger to which a youth must be exposed among the sons of dissipation abroad will not turn the scale in favor of our American colleges. Certain it is that four fifths of the great literary characters in America never crossed the Atlantic.

But if our universities and schools are not so good as the English or Scotch, it is the business of our rulers to improve them, not to endow them merely; for endowments alone will never make a flourishing seminary; but to furnish them with professors of the first abilities and most assiduous application and with a complete apparatus for establishing theories by experiments. Nature has been profuse to the Americans, in genius and in the advantages of climate and soil. If this country, therefore, should long be indebted to Europe for opportunities of acquiring any branch of science in perfection, it must be by means of a criminal neglect of its inhabitants.

The difference in the nature of the American and European governments is another objection to a foreign education. Men form modes of reasoning or habits of thinking on political subjects in the country where they are bred; these modes of reasoning may be founded on fact in all countries, but the same principles will not apply in all governments because of the infinite variety of national opinions and habits. Before a man can be a good legislator, he must be intimately acquainted with the temper of the people to be governed. No man can be thus acquainted with a people without residing among them and mingling with all companies. For want of this acquaintance, a Turgot and a Price may reason most absurdly upon the constitutions of the American states; and when any person has been long accustomed to believe in the propriety or impropriety of certain maxims or regulations of government, it is very difficult to change his opinions or to persuade him to adapt his reasoning to new and different circumstances.[6]

One half the European Protestants will now contend that the Roman Catholic religion is subversive of civil government. Tradition, books, education have concurred to fix this belief in their minds, and they will not resign their opinions, even in America, where some of the highest civil offices are in the hands of Roman Catholics.

It is therefore of infinite importance that those who direct the councils of a nation should be educated in that nation. Not that they should restrict their personal acquaintance to their own country, but their first ideas, attachments, and habits should be acquired in the country which they are to govern and defend. When a knowledge of their own country is obtained and an attachment to its laws and interests deeply fixed in their hearts, then young gentlemen may travel with infinite advantage and perfect safety. I wish not therefore to discourage traveling, but, if possible, to render it more useful to individuals and to the community. My meaning is that *men* should travel and not *boys*.

It is time for the Americans to change their usual route and travel through a country which they never think of or think beneath their notice: I mean the United States.

While these states were a part of the British Empire, our interest, our feelings, were those of Englishmen; our dependence led us to respect and imitate their manners and to look up to them for our opinions. We little thought of any national interest in America, and while our commerce and governments were in the hands of our parent country and we had no common interest, we little thought of improving our acquaintance with each other or of removing prejudices and reconciling the discordant feelings of the inhabitants of different provinces. But independence and union render it necessary that the citizens of different states should know each others' characters and circumstances, that all jealousies should be removed, that mutual respect and confidence should succeed and a harmony of views and interests be cultivated by a friendly intercourse.

A tour through the United States ought now to be considered as a necessary part of a liberal education. Instead of sending young gentlemen to Europe to view curiosities and learn vices and follies, let them spend twelve or eighteen months in examining the local situation of the different states—the rivers, the soil, the population, the improvements and commercial advantages of the whole—with an attention to the spirit and manners of the inhabitants, their laws, local customs, and institutions. Such a tour should at least precede a tour to Europe, for nothing can be more ridiculous than a man traveling in a foreign country for information when he can give no account of his own. When, therefore, young gentlemen have finished an academic education, let them travel through America, and afterwards to Europe if their time and fortunes will permit. But if they cannot make a tour through both, that in America is certainly to be preferred, for the people of America, with all their information, are yet extremely ignorant of the geography, policy, and manners of their neighboring states. Except a few gentlemen whose public employments in the army and in Congress have extended their knowledge of America, the people in this country, even of the higher classes, have not so correct information respecting the United States as they have respecting England or France. Such ignorance is not only disgraceful but is materially prejudicial to our political friendship and federal operations.

Americans, unshackle your minds and act like independent beings. You have been children long enough, subject to the control and subservient to the interest of a haughty parent. You have now an interest of your own to augment and defend: you have an empire to raise and support by your exertions and a national character to establish and extend by your wisdom and virtues. To effect these great objects, it is necessary to frame a liberal plan of policy and build it on a broad system of education. Before this system can be formed and embraced, the Americans must *believe* and *act* from the belief that it is dishonorable to waste life in mimicking the follies of other nations and basking in the sunshine of foreign glory.

# 4

# ROBERT CORAM

*Political Inquiries: to Which Is Added, a Plan for the General Establishment of Schools throughout the United States. (Wilmington, 1791)*

[Robert Coram (1761-1796) was born at Bristol, England, and as a youngster emigrated with his family to South Carolina. Though he died just five years after the publication of this essay, he was the veteran of two wars—the American Revolution, in which he served on the *Bonhomme Richard* under John Paul Jones, and the journalistic war carried on between the friends and critics of the Washington administration. Coram, apparently without a college education but with a wide knowledge of the literary and political classics of his time, played an important role in the intellectual life of Wilmington, Delaware, where he established himself after the Revolution. As librarian of the Library Company of Wilmington, sometime proprietor of a night school providing instruction in Latin and French, but most significantly as editor and proprietor of the *Delaware Gazette*, he emerged as a strong antifederalist during the developing party battles of the period. His interest in elementary education and in the training of apprentices complements his neglect of higher education: both reveal Crèvecoeur's new man, the American, prescribing for new conditions, American conditions. His essay, published in 1791 by Andrews and Brynberg in Wilmington, makes a strong equalitarian case for free compulsory elementary education.]

*Above all, watch carefully over the education of your children. It is from public schools, be assured, that come the wise magistrates—the well trained and courageous soldiers—the good fathers—the good husbands—the good brothers—the good friends—the good men.*—RAYNAL.[1]

*This work is intended merely to introduce a better mode of education than that generally adopted in the country schools throughout the United States.*

# INTRODUCTION

IT is serious truth, whatever may have been advanced by European writers to the contrary, that the aborigines of the American continent have fewer vices, are less subject to diseases, and are a happier people than the subjects of any government in the Eastern world.

From the first of these facts may be drawn two important consequences—first, that the proneness to vice, with which mankind have always been charged and to check which is the ostensible purpose of government, is entirely chimerical; secondly, that vice in civilized nations is the effect of bad government. It is plain, if men are virtuous without laws, they may be virtuous with good laws, for no reason can be given why good laws should make men vicious. Government is, no doubt, a very complicated machine; but vice in the subject cannot be the mere consequence of complexity in the form of government: for if one good law would not necessarily produce vice, neither would one hundred. These truths are simple, but they are not the less useful.

Europeans have been taught to believe that mankind have something of the Devil ingrafted in their nature, that they are naturally ferocious, vicious, revengeful, and as void of reason as brutes, etc., etc. Hence their sanguinary laws, which string a man to a gibbet for the value of twenty pence. They first frame an hypothesis, by which they prove men to be wolves, and then treat them as if they really were such.

But notwithstanding the Europeans have proved men to be naturally wolves, yet they will assert that "men owe everything to education. The minds of children are like blank paper, upon which you may write any characters you please." Thus will they every day refute the fundamental principles upon which their laws are built, and yet not grow a jot the wiser.

Whoever surveys the history of nations with a philosophic eye will find that the civilized man in every stage of his civilization and under almost every form of government has always been a very miserable being. When we consider the very splendid advantages which the citizen seems to possess, the grand scheme of Christianity, the knowledge of sciences and of arts, the experience of all ages and nations recorded in his libraries for a guide, how mortifying must it be to him to reflect that with all his boasted science and philosophy he has made but a retrograde advance to happiness and that the savage, by superior instinct or natural reason, has attained what he, the citizen, by all his powers of refined and artificial intellect could never reach.

There must be some fundamental error, therefore, common to all civilized nations, and this error appears to me to be in education. In the savage state education is perfect. In the civilized state education is the most imperfect part of the whole scheme of government or civilization; or, rather, it is not immediately connected with either, for I know of no modern governments, except perhaps the New England states, in which education is incorporated with the government or regulated by it.[2]

In the savage state, as I said before, the system of education is perfect. To explain this, it will be necessary to define the word *education*, or at least what I mean by it. Education, then, means the instruction of youth in certain rules of conduct by which they will be enabled to support themselves when they come to age and to know the obligations they are under to that society of which they constitute a part. Nature, then, in the savage state is the unerring instructor of their youth in the first or principal part of education, for, when their bodily powers are complete, that part of education which relates to their support is complete also. When they can subdue the wild animals, they can procure subsistence. The second, or less essential part, is taught by their parents: their laws, or rather *customs*, being few and simple, are easily remembered and understood.

But the unfortunate civilized man, to obtain a livelihood, must be acquainted with some art or science, in which he is neither instructed by nature, by government, by his parents, or oftentimes by any means at all. He is then absolutely unable to procure himself subsistence without violating some law, and as to the obligations he is under to society, he knows indeed but very little if anything about them. In this state of the case, the situation of the civilized man is infinitely worse than that of the savage, nay, worse than that of the brute creation, for the birds have nests, the foxes have holes, and all animals in their wild state have permanent means of subsistence, but the civilized man has nowhere to lay his head: he has neither habitation nor food, but forlorn and outcast, he perishes for want and starves in the midst of universal plenty.

To alleviate, therefore, in some measure the miseries of this unhappy being is the intent of the following sheets. And in pursuit of an object of such importance the author shall not be afraid to follow truth wherever it may lead him. As an American, he asserts his claim to this privilege, and he hopes it may be allowed him, upon the double score of his birthright and the task he has undertaken, to plead the cause of humanity.

# CHAP. I

*Inquiry into the Origin of Government; and a Comparative View of the Subjects of European Governments with the Aborigines of America.*

No question has puzzled philosophers of all ages more than the origin of government. The wants and vices of mankind have been generally held out to be the causes of all the good and bad governments with which mankind have alternately been blessed or cursed from the earliest ages to the present day. But there is no satisfactory reason to believe that government originated from either of those causes. We can never believe it originated from his wants, considering the very small proportion of cultivated land in proportion to the uncultivated at this day in every part of the globe, some small islands excepted; nor will his vices afford a better solution of the question, since the savages of North America are infinitely more virtuous than the inhabitants of the most polished nations of Europe.

How the first government originated we are entirely in the dark. Scripture is silent on this head, and all that we know is that Cain founded a city and called it after the name of his son Enoch. As to the origin of modern governments, they seem chiefly to have been founded by conquest: their origin is, however, involved in much obscurity.

Since, then, we are unable to discover the origin of government from the impenetrable obscurity in which it is involved, let us consider its end as equally applicable to our purpose. The end of government, we are told, is public good, by which is to be understood the happiness of the community. The great body of the people in Europe are unhappy, not to say miserable: there needs no other argument to prove that all the European governments have been founded upon wrong principles, since the means used have not produced the end intended.

The following description from the Abbé Raynal may perhaps be with truth applied to the body of the people throughout Europe: "In our provinces the vassal or free mercenary digs and ploughs the whole year round lands that are not his own and whose produce does not belong to him, and he is even happy, if his labor procures him a share of the crops he has sown and reaped. Observed and harassed by a hard and restless landlord who grudges him the very straw on which he rests his weary limbs, the wretch is daily exposed to diseases which, joined to his poverty, make him wish for death rather than for an expensive cure followed by infirmities and toil. Whether tenant or subject, he is doubly a slave; if he has a few acres, his lord comes and gathers them where he has not sown; if he has but a yoke of oxen or a pair of horses, he must employ them in the public service; if he has nothing but his person, the prince takes him for a soldier. Everywhere he meets with masters and always with oppression."[3] Let us now consider the state of the American Indians.

This inquiry is attended with more difficulty than at first sight would appear. Indeed, if the present race of American Indians should shortly become extinct, it would be impossible for posterity to form any judgment of them, whether they were a species of orangutan or rational beings. The European libraries have been stuffed with such monstrous caricatures of the American that they have influenced their ablest philosophers, and Raynal and Buffon have both endeavored to account for the supposed defects in the man of the Western world.[4] Excepting Clavijero's *History of Mexico*, the short account given by Mr. Jefferson, Carver's *Travels*, *The History of the Five Nations*, and Bancroft's *History of Guiana*, I do not recollect an account of the American which deserves the name of history.[5] The translations from French and Spanish writers are generally full of the most glaring prejudice and absurdity. I once saw a history of Louisiana, translated from the French, in which some curious person had, in a fine hand in the margin, refuted almost the whole of the text.

And for a specimen of Spanish history, take the following from the *History of California* by Miguel Venegas: "The characteristics of the Californians as well as of all the other Indians are stupidity, an insensibility, want of knowledge and reflection, inconstancy, impetuosity, and blindness of appetite; an excessive sloth and abhorrence of all labor and fatigue, an incessant love of pleasure and amusement of every kind, however trifling or brutal; pusilanimity and relaxity; and, in fine, a most wretched want of everything which constitutes the real man and renders him rational, inventive, tractable, and useful to himself and society. It is not easy for Europeans who never were out of their own country to conceive an adequate idea of those people. For even in the least frequented corners of the globe there is not a nation so stupid, of such contracted ideas, and so wretched both in body and mind as the unhappy Californians."[6]

Some of the features of this miserable picture are of so heterogeneous a cast that one can hardly be induced to believe them copied from the same original. Stupidity, excessive sloth, and abhorrence of all labor and fatigue but ill agrees with impetuosity and incessant love of pleasure. I shall not be at the trouble of refuting this banter upon history, only to be equaled in absurdity by the philosophical researches of Mr. De Pauw,[7] but will content myself with quoting a little more from Mr. Miguel Venegas and leave the reader to judge for himself:

"However, in the Californians are seen few of those bad dispositions for which the other Americans are infamous; no inebriating liquors are used among them, and the several members of a rancheria live in great harmony among themselves and peaceably with others. What little everyone has is safe from theft. Quarrels are rarely known among them. All their malice and rage they reserve for their enemies, and so far are they from obstinacy, harshness, and cruelty that nothing could exceed their docility and gentleness; consequently they are easily persuaded to good or evil . . . They make their boats of the bark of trees, and every part of the workmanship, the shaping, joining, and covering them, is admired even by Europeans. The men likewise make nets for fishing, for gathering fruits, and for carrying the children, and even those worn by the women. But in this particular they show such exquisite skill, making them of so many different colors, sizes, and variety of workmanship, that it is not easy to describe them."[8]

Father Taraval says, "I can affirm that of all the nets I ever saw in Europe and New Spain none are comparable to these, either in whiteness, the mixture of the other colors, or the strength and workmanship in which they represent a vast variety of figures."[9] I hope the contradiction and absurdity are manifest.

The citizens of the United States differ as widely in their opinions and in many instances seem as much prejudiced against the Indians as the Europeans. Mutual jealousies among those who reside near the frontiers, the ferocity with which the Indians conduct their wars, but principally the numerous forged accounts published in our newspapers of horrid murders perpetrated by them have given the citizens of these states such an antipathy against the Indians as will not easily be removed. I traveled with one of Mr. McGillivray's men from Philadelphia to New York last summer and had the mortification to see him insulted in almost every public house at which we stopped on our route.[10] One of the landlords did not scruple to tell him that he, the landlord, would as leave shoot an Indian as a rattlesnake. And take the following account from the *Delaware Gazette*:

"Extract of a letter from Sunbury, Northumberland County, Pennsylvania, dated November 13, 1790.—

"One of the men who murdered the Indians at Pine Creek was tried on Saturday evening; and though a number of witnesses clearly proved the hand he had in perpetrating the horrible deed, and the confession of his counsel at the bar, which confirmed it; yet, notwithstanding an express charge from the judges to bring him in guilty, the jury, in a few minutes, returned with a verdict in his favor and a subscription to pay the costs of suit, that he might be set at liberty. And all this from a most absurd idea, which the Attorney General could not, with all his endeavors, beat out of them, that the crime was not the same to kill an Indian as a white man. For some minutes the Chief Justice was struck with astonishment. How the state can pacify the Indians now, Heaven knows; while at this moment the other murderers are at large in this country, and none will arrest them."[11]

It is said that the inhabitants of Canada and the other French settlements are very seldom troubled by the Indians. The French government has kept a watchful eye over the conduct of its subjects and never suffered any injury done to the Indians to pass unpunished. It is indeed in vain to expect peace with those people while the present rancor, too visible in the conduct of the citizens of those states, continues. But as this is rather foreign to my present purpose, I shall proceed with what I have to offer on the subject of the aborigines of America, from Carver's *Travels* and Bancroft's *History of Guiana*, as the least prejudiced testimony applicable to the present purpose which has fell under my observation.

"The Indians," says Mr. Carver, "in their common state are strangers to all distinction of property, except in the articles of domestic use, which everyone considers as his own and increases as circumstances may admit. They are extremely liberal to each other and supply the deficiency of their friends with any superfluity of their own. In dangers they readily give assistance to those of their band who stand in need of it, without any expectation of return, except of those just rewards which are always conferred by the Indians on merit. Governed by the plain and equitable laws of nature, everyone is rewarded solely according to his deserts, and their equality of condition, manners, and privileges, with that constant and sociable familiarity which prevails throughout every Indian nation, animates them with a pure and truly patriotic spirit which tends to the general good of the society to whom they belong.

"If any of their neighbors are bereaved by death or by an enemy of their children, those who are possessed of the greatest number of slaves supply the deficiency; and those are adopted by them and treated in every respect as if they really were the children of the person to whom they are presented.

"The Indians, except those who live adjoining to the European colonies, can form to themselves no idea of the value of money; they consider it, when they are made acquainted with the uses to which it is applied by other nations, as the source of innumerable evils. To it they attribute all the mischiefs which are prevalent among Europeans, such as treachery, plunderings, devastation, and murder. They esteem it irrational that one man should be possessed of a greater quantity than another and are amazed that any honor should be annexed to the possession of it. But that the want of this useless metal should be the cause of depriving persons of their liberty and that on account of this partial distribution of it great numbers should be immured within the dreary walls of a prison, cut off from the society of which they constitute a part, exceeds their belief. Nor do they fail, on hearing this part of the European system of government related, to charge the institutors of it with a total want of humanity and to brand them with the names of savages and brutes."[12]

The following character of the Caribbee Indians is taken from Bancroft's *Guiana*: "In reviewing the manners of these Indians, some few particulars excepted, I survey an amiable picture of primeval innocence and happiness, which arises chiefly from the fewness of their wants, and their universal equality. The latter destroys all distinctions among them, except those of age and personal merit, and promotes the ease, harmony and freedom of their mutual conversation and intercoursee [. .] The fewness and simplicity of their wants, with the abundance of means for their supply, and the ease with which they are acquired, renders all division of property useless. Each amicably participates [in] the ample blessings of an extensive country without rivaling his neighbor or interrupting his happiness. This renders all governments and all laws unnecessary, as in such a state there can be no temptations to dishonesty, fraud, injustice, or violence, or indeed any desires which may not be gratified with innocence; and that chimerical proneness to vice, which among civilized nations is thought to be a natural propensity, has no existence in a state of nature like this, where everyone perfectly enjoys the blessings of his native freedom and independence without any restraints or fears.

"To acquire the art of dispensing with all imaginary wants and contenting ourselves with the real conveniences of life is the noblest exertion of reason and a most useful acquisition, as it elevates the mind above the vicissitudes of fortune. Socrates justly observes 'that those who want least approach nearest to the gods, who want nothing.'[13] The simplicity, however, which is so apparent in the manners of those Indians is not the effect of a philosophical self-denial but of their ignorance of more refined enjoyments, which, however, produces effects equally happy with those which result from the most austere philosophy; and their manners present an emblem of the fabled Elysian fields where individuals need not the assistance of each other but yet preserve a constant intercourse of love and friendship.[14]

" 'O FORTUNATOS NIMIUM, SUA SI BONA NORINT. VIRO.' "[15]

"It is doubtless," says the immortal Raynal, "of great importance to posterity to record the manners of savages. From this source, perhaps, we have derived all our improvements in moral philosophy. Former metaphysicians sought for the origin of society in those very societies which had been long established. Supposing men guilty of crimes, in order that they may have the merit of giving them saviours; blinding their eyes, in order that they may become their guides and masters, they call *mysterious, supernatural,* and *divine* what is only the operation of time, ignorance, weakness, and chicane. But after perceiving that social institutions neither originated from natural wants nor from religious opinions—since many nations live independent without any worship—they discovered that all corruptions, both in morals and legislation, arose from society itself and that vice originally proceeded from legislators, who generally instituted laws more for their own emolument than public good, or whose views towards equity and right were perverted by the ambition of their successors or by the alteration of times and manners.

"This discovery has already thrown great light upon the subject, though it is still to mankind but as the dawn of a fine day. Its opposition to established opinions prevents it from suddenly producing those immense benefits which it will confer on posterity, and this latter circumstance ought to give consolation to the present generation. But however this may be we may assert with confidence that the ignorance of savages has contributed greatly to enlighten polished nations."

In the comparative view of the civilized man and the savage, the most striking contrast is the division of property. To the one, it is the source of all his happiness: to the other, the fountain of all his misery. By holy writ we are informed that God gave to man dominion over the earth, the living creatures, and the herbs; human laws have, however, limited this jurisdiction to certain orders or classes of men; the rest are to feed upon air if they can or fly to another world for subsistence. This parceling out to individuals what was intended for the general stock of society leads me to inquire farther into the nature and origin of property. I am not quite so visionary as to expect that the members of any civilized community will listen to an equal division of lands: had that been the object of this work, the author had infallibly lost his labor. But a substitute, and perhaps the only one, is highly practicable, as will hereafter appear.

## CHAP. II

*Inquiry into the Origin of Property; and a Refutation of Blackstone's Doctrine on That Subject.*

THERE is nothing which so generally strikes the imagination," says Dr. Blackstone, "and engages the affections of mankind as the right of property or that sole and despotic dominion which one man claims and exercises over the external things of this world, in total exclusion of the right of any other individual in the universe.[16] And yet there are very few that will give themselves the trouble to consider the origin and foundation of this right. Pleased as we are with the possession, we seem afraid to look back to the means by which it was acquired, as if fearful of some defect in our title; or at best we rest satisfied with the decisions of the laws in our favor, without examining the reason or authority upon which those laws have been built.

"We think it enough that our title is derived by the grant of the former proprietor, by descent from our ancestors, or by the last will and testament of the dying owner not caring to reflect that (accurately and strictly speaking) there is no foundation in nature, or in natural law, why a set of words upon parchment should convey the dominion of land, why the son should have a right to exclude his fellow creatures from a determinate spot of ground because his father had done so before him, or why the occupier of a particular field or of a jewel, when lying on his death bed and no longer able to maintain possession, should be entitled to tell the rest of the world which of them should enjoy it after him.

"These inquiries, it must be confessed, would be useless, and even troublesome, in common life. It is well, if the mass of mankind will obey the laws, when made, without scrutinizing too nicely into the reasons of making them. But when law is to be considered, not only as matter of practice but also as a rational science, it cannot be improper or useless to examine more deeply the rudiments and grounds of those positive constitutions of society."[17]

Doctor Blackstone seems to have been extremely cautious how he ventured upon his inquiry into the origin of property, as if fearful of some defect in his title; and his caution has, notwithstanding his profound sagacity, evidently run him into contradiction and absurdity. He tells us, in his chapter on the study of the law, that "every subject is interested in the preservation of the laws; it is therefore," says he, "incumbent upon every man to be acquainted with those at least with which he is immediately concerned, lest he incur the censure of living in society without knowing the obligations which it lays him under."[18]

And in the part we have just now quoted he obliquely censures the conduct of the generality of mankind, who, he says, will not give themselves the trouble to consider the origin and foundation of the right of property. But when he reflects upon the probable consequences of a rational investigation of this subject, he flies his ground. "These inquiries," says he, "it must be owned would be useless, and even troublesome, in common life. It is well, if the mass of mankind will obey the laws, when made, without scrutinizing too nicely into the reasons of making them."[19]

But though the mass of mankind are prohibited to scrutinize too nicely into the reasons of making laws, it seems that it is not improper for those who consider law as a matter of practice, and a rational science, to examine more deeply into their rudiments and grounds. That is, in plain English, lawyers may know the obligations of society, but the people not. Thus it was when corrupt priests despised the ordinances of a just God, defiled his altars with unhallowed sacrifices, and stained them with innocent blood, they hid their creed beneath the impenetrable veil of a dead language, that their iniquity might not be detected.

Thus it is, that those who should direct the opinions of mankind descend to contemptible sophistry and contradiction, turn traitors to their own principles, apostates to the sacred cause of truth, and while they pretend that their system of law is founded upon principles of equity tell us in plain terms that it will not bear investigation. The right to exclusive property is a question of great importance, and, of all others, perhaps, deserves the most candid and equitable solution. Such a solution will afford a foundation for laws which will totally eradicate from the civilized man a very large portion of those vices which such legislators as Dr. Blackstone pretend to be natural to the human race. One deplorable iniquity, at least, which has filled the earth with tears and the hearts of all good men with deep regret—I mean the slave trade—could never have existed among any people who had distinct ideas of property, but this subject has been treated of in such an obscure, vague, and contradictory manner by the European lawyers that it is impossible to determine by them what is property and what is not.

"In the beginning of the world," says Dr. Blackstone, "we are informed by holy writ the all bountiful Creator gave to man 'dominion over all the earth, and over the fish of the sea, and over the fowl of the air, and over every living thing that moveth upon the earth.' This is the only true and solid foundation of man's dominion over external things, whatever airy metaphysical notions may have been started by fanciful writers upon that subject."[20]

The Doctor, not the least fanciful of metaphysical writers, quotes the text in Genesis as a demonstration of his creed, to tell us that he believes in the Bible, which is in some measure necessary, as many of his arguments militate against such belief. If then the text in Genesis is the only true and solid foundation of man's dominion over external things, every son and daughter of Adam is co-heir to this paternal inheritance, for the gift was made in common to the whole race of Adam. How then have part of mankind forfeited their right to the bounties of Providence? Or from what source does the monopoly of lands originate, since it is plain it cannot be derived from the text in Genesis? The Doctor, indeed, tells us that "the earth, and all things thereon, are the general property of all mankind, exclusive of other beings from the immediate gift of the Creator. And while the earth continued bare of inhabitants, it is reasonable to suppose that all was in common among them and that everyone took from the public stock to his own use such things as his immediate necessities required."[21]

And why not take from the public stock, when men multiplied? The command from the Creator was, increase and multiply. And must men then forfeit their right to the bounties of Providence, by acting in obedience to this precept? Or does Dr. Blackstone suppose that the earth can support only a part of mankind, and that the rest live upon air, light, fire, or water, the only inheritance he has left them? It is plain, if the earth supports its inhabitants in the present unequal division of property, it will support them under an equal division. "These general notions of property," continues the Doctor, "were then sufficient to answer all the purposes of human life."[22] That is, the solid foundation of man's dominion over external things, is a notion: this notion was, however, sufficient to answer all the purposes of human life; "and might still have answered them," continues the Doctor, "had it been possible for mankind to have remained in a state of primeval simplicity, as may be collected from the manners of many American nations when first discovered by the Europeans."[23]

It is upwards of 5,000 years since the creation of the world. At the creation men were in a state of primeval simplicity; the American Indians are at this day in a state of primeval simplicity; ergo, it is not possible for men to remain in a state of primeval simplicity. Here is logic elegantly displayed! Thus it is that the sophistry of this English doctor flies before the test of investigation. It is therefore possible for men to remain in a state of primeval simplicity, since some of them are so at this day; unless indeed the Doctor supposes the Indians to be the offspring of a creation subsequent to Adam. This primeval simplicity, the Doctor supposes, was the case with the ancient Europeans, according to the memorials of the golden age.

"*Sed omnia communia et indivisa omnibus fuerint, veluti unum cunctis patrimonium esset.* Not," says the Doctor, "that this communion of goods seems ever to have been applicable, even in the earliest ages, to aught but the substance of the thing; nor could it be extended to the use of it."[24] Why not? Let us translate the passage. All things were common and undivided to all, even as one inheritance might be to all. The sense of this passage is so obvious and plain that a person could hardly think it possible to be misunderstood, but Dr. Blackstone is determined to understand it not as common sense but as unintelligible jargon. By a peculiar application of the participle *indivisa*, the Doctor infers that the community of goods could not be extended to the use of such goods, which is making downright nonsense of the sentence: it is making the patrimony left in such manner that not a single heir can enjoy the least use or benefit of it at all. Why should so much stress be laid on the participle *indivisa*, in the first part of the sentence, when the second part of the sentence is explanatory of the first?

The goods were left *communia & indivisa;* but in what manner? *Veluti unum cunctis patrimonium esset:* even as one
inheritance might be to all. The Doctor appears designedly
obscure in this very paragraph and seems rather desirous to
perplex his reader than to throw any light upon the subject.

"For by the law of nature and reason," continues the Doctor,
"he who first began to use a thing acquired therein a kind of
transient property that lasted so long as he was using it, and
no longer: or to speak with greater precision, the right of
possession continued for the same time only that the act of
possession lasted. Thus the ground was in common, and no
part of it was the permanent property of any man in particular; yet, whoever was in the occupation of any determinate
spot of it for rest, for shade, or the like, acquired, for the time,
a sort of ownership, from which it would have been unjust and
contrary to the law of nature to have driven him by force, but
the instant that he quitted the use or occupation of it another
might seize it without injustice."[25]

According to this vague account of natural law, it appears
that men had a right to that quantity of ground which happened to be in immediate contact with their feet, when standing up; with their backsides, when sitting; and with their body,
when lying down; and no more. No provision is made for agriculture; indeed it would not have suited the Doctor to have
allowed the existence of agriculture at that period of the world
for reasons which will hereafter appear.

Any person possessed of common sense and some erudition
who was not previously bent upon establishing a favorite system at the expense of truth might give us a rational account in
what manner property should be regulated under the law of
nature. Such a person would probably say all things subject to
the dominion of man may be included in two classes, land
and movables; the rational foundation of the tenure of each is
labor. Thus fruit growing on a tree was common, but when
collected it became the exclusive property of the collector; land
uncultivated was common, but when cultivated, it became the

exclusive possession of the cultivator. Men, then, according to the laws of nature, had an exclusive property in movables and an exclusive possession in lands, both which were founded on labor and bounded by it. For as labor employed in the collection of fruit could give an exclusive right only to the fruit so collected, so labor in the soil could give exclusive possession only to the spot so labored. But this kind of reasoning would by no means suit Dr. Blackstone.

"But," continues the Doctor, "when mankind increased in number, craft, and ambition, it became necessary to entertain conceptions of more permanent dominion and to appropriate to individuals, not the immediate use only, but the very substance of the thing to be used."[26] Query: could a man eat an apple without entertaining conceptions of permanent dominion over the substance? Those conceptions existed then anterior to the increase of men in number, craft, and ambition, and were not the consequence of it.

"Otherwise," continues the Doctor, "innumerable tumults must have arisen, and the good order of the world been continually broken and disturbed, while a variety of persons were striving who should get the first occupation of the same thing or disputing which of them had actually gained it."[27] From a system so vague as the Doctor's, and which he would pawn upon us for natural law, nothing but disputes could be expected, for nothing is determinate. His futile distinctions between the use of a thing and the substance of a thing and his motions of possession are truly ridiculous. But those contests for occupancy, this mighty bugbear so fatal to the good order of the world, we can easily prove to be a mere phantom of the Doctor's brain; like the raw head and bloody bones with which ignorant nurses scare their children, it has no existence in nature.

As labor constitutes the right of property in movables and the right of possession in lands, it is evident no disputes could arise merely from the nature of the right, for before labor was employed there could be no right to squabble about, and after labor was employed the right was completely vested. In fact, the whole of Blackstone's chapter on property was artfully contrived to countenance the monopoly of lands as held in Europe. "When men increased in number, craft, and ambition, it became necessary to entertain conceptions of more permanent dominion."[28] If the Doctor means anything he means that more permanent dominion was established as a check to craft and ambition; or, in other words, that the laws vested a permanent property in lands in some persons, to prevent their being dispossessed by unruly individuals. But this clearly demonstrates the Doctor to be as ignorant of the affections of the human heart as he is of natural law. For a community of lands is the most effectual check which human wisdom could devise against the ambition of individuals. What is the civilized man's ambition? To procure a property in the soil. But there is no such ambition among savages, for no man, civilized or savage, is ambitious of what is common to every man: land is common among savages; therefore they set no value upon it. In most civilized nations land is held only by a few and also made essential to the qualification of candidates for public offices: hence, to possess property in lands is the ambition of civilized nations.

But, continues the Doctor, "As human life also grew more and more refined, abundance of conveniences were contrived to render it more easy and agreeable, as habitations for shelter and safety and raiment for warmth and decency. But no man would be at the trouble to provide either, so long as he had only a *usufructuary* property in them, which was to cease the instant that he quitted possession, if, as soon as he walked out of his tent or pulled off his garment, the next stranger who came by would have a right to inhabit the one and wear the other."[29]

If his wise head would have suffered him to reason and not sophisticate, Dr. Blackstone would have found that there never was nor could be a *usufructuary* property in a garment or a house; the property in this case was from its nature always absolute. For a house or a garment in *statu quo* is no production of the earth and was certainly never considered as a part of the general stock of society. The materials of which the house or the garment was formed might have been common stock, but when by manual labor or dexterity the materials became converted into a house or a garment, it became the exclusive property of the maker. And this is not merely a scholastic or speculative distinction, but a distinction founded in nature and well known to the American Indians.

"The Indians," says Carver, "are strangers to all distinction of property, except in the articles of domestic use, which everyone considers as his own."[30] And this miserable sophist, Dr. Blackstone, knew better: he knew that a house or a garment could not be usufructuary property, for he establishes the position, which will hereafter appear, that "bodily labor bestowed upon any subject which before lay in common to all men gives the fairest and most reasonable title to exclusive property therein."[31]

It is a little surprising, if anything from Dr. Blackstone can surprise us, that he will not suffer men to have been so well provided for, under the law of nature, as the brute creation. "For," says he, "the brute creation, to whom everything else was in common, maintained a kind of permanent property in their dwellings, especially for the protection of their young; the birds of the air had nests and the beasts of the fields had caverns, the invasion of which they esteemed a very flagrant injustice and would sacrifice their lives to preserve."[32] The argument, therefore, of the necessity of more permanent dominion than was exercised under the law of nature, to secure a man's right to his house or garment, is totally false, seeing that not a usufructuary but an absolute and exclusive property was vested in him by the laws of nature.

"And there can be no doubt," continues the Doctor, "that movables of every kind became sooner appropriated than the permanent substantial soil, partly because they were susceptible of a long occupancy, which might be continued for months together, without any sensible interruption, and at length by usage ripen into an established right, but principally because few of them could be fit for use till improved and meliorated by the bodily labor of the occupant, which bodily labor bestowed upon any subject, which before lay in common to all men, is universally allowed to give the fairest and most reasonable title to an exclusive property therein."[33] But movables never were common stock, for by the very act by which they become movables, they become absolute and exclusive property. Thus fruit growing on a tree was not movable until collected, but when collected it became absolute and exclusive property. A tree standing was not movable, but when cut down it became exclusive property. Again, the animal creation could not be esteemed movables until they were caught; but when caught they became exclusive property.

"As the world by degrees grew more populous, it daily became more difficult to find out new spots to inhabit without encroaching upon former occupants; and by constantly occupying the same individual spot, the fruits of the earth were consumed and its spontaneous produce destroyed, without any provision for a future supply or succession. It therefore became necessary to pursue some regular method of providing a constant subsistence and this necessity produced, or at least promoted and encouraged, the art of agriculture."[34]

The Doctor had well nigh forgot his Bible. He should have recollected that the first man born was a tiller of the ground, and agriculture therefore nearly coeval with the creation. And although it may be objected that the art was lost in the deluge, yet we are certain that it was revived in the person of Noah, who, we are informed in the 9th Genesis, "began to be an husbandman, and he planted a vineyard."

The President Goguet, in his *Origin of Laws, Arts, and Sciences,* teaches much the same doctrine with Dr. Blackstone; it may therefore be necessary to attend to him also. "There was a time," says M. Goguet, "when mankind derived their whole subsistence from the fruits which the earth produced spontaneously, from their hunting, fishing, and their flocks. Such was the ancient manner of living till agriculture was introduced; in this manner several nations still live, as the Scythians, Tartars, Arabians, savages, etc."[35]

By savages, M. Goguet means the aborigines of America, and here he is clearly mistaken, for agriculture is known and practiced by every Indian tribe throughout the continent of America. Maize or Indian corn is a grain peculiar to this continent, and we have never heard of its growing wild; it must therefore have been cultivated by the aborigines of the continent. From the multitude of authorities which M. Goguet cites, when he treats of the savages, one would conclude that he had better information concerning them than of the Tartars, Arabians, and Scythians, and that if he is mistaken in regard to the savages, he may also be mistaken concerning the others.

But as the authors of false theories generally contradict themselves, so M. Goguet tells us that "Homer, in *Odyss.* L. vi. 10, says that in those remote ages it was one of the first cares of those who formed new establishments to divide the lands among the members of the colony . . . And the Chinese say that Gin Hoand, one of their first kings, who reigned 2,000 years before the vulgar era, divided the whole of his lands into nine parts, one of which was destined for dwelling, and the other eight for agriculture—" *Martini hist. de la Chine.*[36] "And by the history of Peru, we find that their first Incas took great pains in distributing their lands among their subjects—" *Accost hist. des Ind.*[37]

But further, M. Goguet tells us that agriculture introduced *landmarks*, the practice of which, he says, is very ancient: "We find it very plainly alluded to in Gen. xlix. 14."*[38] Now if landmarks be the consequence of agriculture (and landmarks existed

* In turning to the text which M. Goguet says alludes to landmarks, in the edition of the Bible dedicated to King James, I find the text, "Issachar is a strong ass, crouching down between two burdens." As I could perceive nothing here alluding to landmarks, I at first suspected the chapter or verse wrong quoted, but having recourse to the Vulgate edition, I found the text, "Issachar shall be a strong ass lying down between two borders," which borders, I presume, M. Goguet thought alluded to landmarks.

in the days of the patriarch Jacob), it follows that agriculture existed then also. But M. Goguet, had he believed or read his Bible, might have found texts enough to convince him that agriculture was known and practiced in the earliest ages. The example of Cain was surely pretty early, and although, as has before been observed, it might be said the art was lost in the deluge, yet we find frequent mention of it shortly after: Genesis xxx, 14—"And Reuben went in the days of wheat harvest and found mandrakes in the field," etc.

It seems difficult to account for the opinions of European authors, in denying agriculture to the first race of men, especially when the Bible which they all pretend to believe is so directly opposed to them. But as the Americans are always quoted to support this doctrine, it would seem that this opinion was founded upon the stupid productions, entitled Histories of America: inferences drawn from those relations, which bear every mark of prejudice and absurdity, are to be believed in preference to holy writ. Some of the Americans, say those authors, live on acorns: hence acorns were the original diet of mankind, for [that] men in early ages knew nothing of agriculture is plain from the practice of those savages. Here is first a false statement of fact and then a conclusion in opposition to holy writ.

M. Goguet, it is very plain, has fell into this error, for he says, "Travelers inform us that even at this day in some parts of the world they meet with men who are strangers to all social intercourse, of a character so cruel and ferocious that they live in perpetual war, destroying and devouring each other. Those wretched people, void of all the principles of humanity, without laws, polity, or government, live in dens and caverns, and differ but very little from the brute creation; their food consists of some roots and fruits, with which the woods supply them; for want of skill and industry, they can seldom procure more solid nourishment. In a word, not having the most common and obvious notions, they have nothing of humanity but the external figure."[39]

Here he quotes his authorities: *Voyage 5 le Blanc. Hist. nat. de Island. Hist. des Isles Marianes. Lettres edifiantes. N. Relat. de la France equinox. Hist. gen. des Voyages. Voyage de Frezier. Rec. des Voyages au Nordt.*[40] Many of them, no doubt, of equal authority with Robinson Crusoe. But, M. Goguet says, those savage people exactly answer the description given us by historians of the ancient state of mankind. Does M. Goguet believe that we are in possession of any history of the ancient primitive state of mankind except the Bible? But M. Goguet has established his opinion and will not flinch from it. He says, "But all the rest of mankind, except a few families of Noah's descendants who settled in Persia, Syria, and Egypt, I repeat it again, led the life of savages and barbarians."[41]

We will give up to M. Goguet's repetitions and his obstinacy, but we will think as we please; we know of no such orangutan as he has just described from ignorant voyages. So much for M. Goguet; let us hear what is said on the other side of the question: The editors of the *Encyclopedia* say, "Nor is there any solid reason for concluding that all nations were originally unskilled in agriculture." See article [on] "Agriculture," *Encyclopedia.*[42] Modern discoveries also prove that agriculture is everywhere known. For of all the rude and uncivilized inhabitants of our vast continent, of all the numerous islands in the Pacific Ocean,† of those under the equator, where reigns an

---

†CAROLINE ISLES.

Father Cantova, speaking of the Caroline Islands, says, "The principal occupation of the men is to make boats for fishing and to cultivate the earth." *Lettres edifiantes & curieuses. Tom. 15, p. 313.* [Juan Antonio Cantova (1697-1731), a Jesuit missionary in the Carolines, reported this in *Lettres edifiantes et curieuses, ecrites des missions etrangeres* (Paris: J. G. Merigot, 1781), XV, 313. Coram, however, translates this passage from an editorial note in James Cook, *A Voyage to the Pacific Ocean*, 3 vols. (London: W. and A. Strahan, 1784), I, 392, and goes on to quote the explorer extensively.]

FRIENDLY ISLES.

"The province allotted to the men is as might be expected far more laborious and extensive than that of the women: agriculture, architecture, boat building, fishing, and other things that relate to navigation are the objects of their care; cultivated roots and fruits being their principal support, this requires their constant attention to agriculture, which they pursue very diligently and seem

eternal spring—where a luxuriant soil and a vertical sun produce fruits in abundance and seem most to preclude the necessity of agriculture—it is notwithstanding universally known and practiced.

Dr. Blackstone's remarks on the origin of property are in many instances so similar to those of President Goguet that one would be apt to think that the Doctor did not come honestly by them but that he pilfered them from the *Origin of Laws, Arts, and Sciences.* "When husbandry was unknown," says the President, "all lands were common. There were no boundaries nor landmarks, everyone sought his subsistence where he thought fit. By turns they abandoned and repossessed the same

---

to have brought to almost as great perfection as circumstances will permit." [Cook, *Voyage*, I, 392.]

### OTAHEITE.

In the account of the agriculture of Otaheite, Captain Cook seems in some measure to contradict himself. He says, "It is doubtless the natural fertility of the country, combined with the mildness and serenity of the climate, that renders the natives so careless in their cultivation that in many places, though overflowing with the richest productions, the smallest traces cannot be observed. The cloth plant, which is raised by seeds brought from the mountains, and the ava or intoxicating pepper are almost the only things to which they pay any attention." Capt. Cook afterwards tells us that he supposes the inhabitant of Otaheite prevents the progress of the bread plant to make room for others, to afford him some variety in his food, the chief of which are the cocoanut and plantain, the first of which he says can give no trouble after it has raised itself a foot or two above the ground; but the plantain requires more care." Hence we may enumerate four species of vegetables cultivated at Otaheite, viz. the cloth plant, the ava, the cocoanut, and the plantain. But as the cocoanut and the plantain were the chief among other substitutes to the bread plant, here is a fair inference that some other species of vegetables were cultivated. [Cook, *Voyage*, II, 145.]

### SANDWICH ISLES.

"What we saw of their agriculture furnished sufficient proofs that they are not novices in that art. The vale ground is one continued plantation of taro and a few other things which have all the appearance of being well attended to. The potato fields and spots of sugar cane or plantains on the higher grounds are planted with the same regularity and always in the same determinate figure, generally as a square or oblong, but neither those nor the others are enclosed with any kind of fence, unless we reckon the ditches in the low grounds such, which, it is more probable, are intended to convey water to the taro. The great quantity and goodness of those articles may also perhaps be as much attributed to skillful culture as to natural fertility of soil." *Cook's last Voyage.* [*Voyage*, II, 244.]

districts, as they were more or less exhausted. But after agriculture, this was not practicable. It was necessary then to distinguish possessions and to take necessary measures that every member of society might enjoy the fruits of his labors."[43]

The President here supposes that vices which receive their existence with bad government are natural to the heart of man. The Indians pursue agriculture, but their land is in common; and they enjoy the fruits of their labor, without any boundaries, enclosures, or divisions of land. Theft is unknown among them; this is an incontrovertible fact, which totally overturns and demolishes the crazy theories of President Goguet and Doctor Blackstone.

"The art of agriculture," says the Doctor, "by regular connection and consequence, introduced the idea of more permanent property in the soil than had been hitherto received and adopted. It was clear that the earth could not produce her fruits in sufficient quantities without the assistance of tillage. But who would be at the pains of tilling it, if another might watch an opportunity to seize upon and enjoy the product of his industry, art, and labor. Had not, therefore, a separate property in lands, as well as movables, been vested in some individual, the world must have continued a forest and men have been mere animals of prey, which according to some philosophers is the genuine state of nature."[44] But we deny that by any connection or consequence the art of agriculture necessarily introduced more permanent property in the soil than was known in the days of Cain or than is now known by the American Indians. We deny that by the laws of nature any man could seize upon the product of the art, industry, or labor of another, and surely the Doctor forgets not only the Bible but his own words, for he has already established the position that bodily labor bestowed upon any subject which before lay in common gives the fairest and most reasonable title to exclusive property therein.

We deny that by any necessary consequence a community of lands would have detained the world a forest. A right to exclusive possession in lands, founded on the equitable and rational

principle of labor, would at all times have been sufficient for all
the purposes of men. What does the Doctor mean by *mere
animals of prey*? The savage, as we are pleased to call him, takes
his bow and repairs to some forest, to obtain subsistence by the
death of some animal: the polished citizen takes his pence and
repairs to some butcher; the brute creation are equally victims,
and men equally animals of prey.

Civilized or savage, bowels entombed in bowels is still his
delight; but the savage slays to satisfy his natural wants, the
citizen often murders for purposes of riot and ostentation; and
before he should upbraid the savage on this score, he should
have profited by the precepts which the poet puts into the
mouth of Pythagoras: *"Parcite mortales, dapibus temerare ne-
fandis corpora! sunt fruges, sunt deducentia ramos pondere
poma suo tumidæque in vitibus uvæ, sunt herbæ dulces, sunt
quæ mitescere flamma mollirique queant,"*‡ etc. Precepts which
were never conveyed to the savage, but which the citizen has
been in possession of for ages past.

The doctor's premises being therefore false, his conclusions
of the necessity of a separate property in lands being vested in
some individuals falls to the ground of course. But, continues
the Doctor, "Whereas now (so graciously has Providence interwoven our duty and our happiness together) the result of this
very necessity has been the ennobling of the human species, by

---

‡ Spare, O mortals! to pollute your bodies with horrid feasts. There are
fruits, there are apples, which bend the branches by their weight, and juicy
grapes on the vine. There are sweet herbs, and herbs which may be made
sweeter and softer by fire, etc. *Ov. Met. lib. 15.* [A more felicitous translation
may be found in Frank Justus Miller, trans., Ovid, *Metamorphoses* book 15, lines
75-79 (2 vols., Loeb Classical Library), II, 370-371.]

It may be indeed doubted whether butcher's meat is anywhere a necessary
of life. Grain and other vegetables, with the help of milk, cheese, and butter,
or oil where butter is not to be had, it is known from experience, can without any butcher's meat afford the most plentiful, the most wholesome, the most
nourishing, and the most invigorating diet. Decency nowhere requires that any
man should eat butcher's meat, as it in most places requires that he should
wear a linen shirt or a pair of leather shoes. *Smith's Wealth of Nations.* [Adam
Smith, *An Inquiry into the Nature and the Causes of the Wealth of Nations*,
3 vols. (Philadelphia: Thomas Dobson, 1789), III, 287.]

giving it opportunity of improving its rational faculties, as well as of exerting its natural [faculties], necessity begat property and order to insure that property, recourse was had to civil society, which brought with it a train of inseparable concomitants, states, governments, laws, punishments, and the public exercise of religious duties."[45]

That is to say, God created man imperfect and ignoble, a mere animal of prey, but when, with the sword of violence and the pen of sophistry, a few had plundered or cheated the bulk of their rights, the few became ennobled and the many were reduced from mere animals of prey to beasts of burden. But why not mention a few more concomitants of civil society, such as poverty, vices innumerable, and diseases unknown in the state of nature. Look around your cities, ye who boast of having established the civilization and happiness of man, see at every corner of your streets some wretched object with tattered garments, squalid look, and hopeless eye, publishing your lies, in folio to the world. Hedged in the narrow strait, between your sanguinary laws and the pressing calls of hunger, he has no retreat, but like an abortive being, created to no manner of purpose, his only wish is death. For of what use can life be but to augment his sufferings by a comparison of his desperate lot with yours?

But to continue, "The only question remaining," says the Doctor, "is how this property became actually vested, or what is it that gave a man an exclusive right to retain in a permanent manner that specific land which before belonged generally to everybody but particularly to nobody. And as we before observed that occupancy gave a right to the temporary use of the soil, so it is agreed upon all hands that occupancy gave also the original right to the permanent property in the substance of the earth itself, which excludes everyone else but the owner from the use of it.

"There is indeed some difference among the writers of natural law concerning the reason why occupancy should convey this right and invest one with this absolute property, Grotius and Pufendorf insisting that this right of occupancy is founded upon a tacit and implied assent of all mankind, that the first occupant should become the owner; and Barbeyrac, Titius, Mr. Locke, and others holding that there is no such implied assent, neither is it necessary that there should be, for that the very act of occupancy alone being a degree of bodily labor is from a principle of natural justice without any consent or compact sufficient of itself to gain a title . . ."[46] A dispute that favors too much of nice and scholastic refinement! However, both sides agree in this, that occupancy is the thing by which the title was in fact originally gained, every man seizing to his own continued use such spots of ground as he found most agreeable to his own convenience, provided he found them unoccupied by any man."[47]

But why this snarl at Barbeyrac, Titius, Mr. Locke, and others? It is plain that Dr. Blackstone had predetermined when he wrote his *Commentaries* to exclude the great body of mankind from any right to the bounties of Providence—light, air, and water excepted—or else why would he turn up his nose at a distinction absolutely necessary to set bounds to the quantum and prevent a monopoly of all the lands among a few? The position has been before established "that bodily labor bestowed on any subject before common gives the best title to exclusive property."[48]

But the act of occupancy is a degree of bodily labor; that is, the occupancy extends as far as the labor, or, in other words, a man has a right to as much land as he cultivates and no more, which is Mr. Locke's doctrine. This distinction is therefore absolutely necessary to determine the quantum of lands any individual could possess under the laws of nature. For shall we say a man can possess only the ground in immediate contact with his feet, or if he climbs to the top of a mountain, and exclaims, "Behold, I possess as far as I can see!," shall there be any magic in the words or the expression which shall convey the right of all that land, in fee simple, to him and his heirs forever?

No: as labor constitutes the right, so it sensibly defines the boundaries of possession.§

How then shall we detect the empty sophist who in order to establish his system of monopoly would fain persuade us that the Almighty did not know what he was about when he made man. That he made him an animal of prey and intended him for a polished citizen; that he gave his bounties in common to all and yet suffered a necessity to exist by which they could be enjoyed only by a few. Had Dr. Blackstone been disposed to give his readers a true account of the origin of landed property in Europe he might have said exclusive property in lands originated with government; but most of the governments that we have any knowledge of were founded by conquest: property therefore in its origin seems to have been arbitrary. He might then have expiated upon the difficulty and inconvenience of attempting any innovations upon the established rules of property. This would have sufficiently answered his purpose and saved him much sophistry and absurdity and not a little impiety: for it is surely blasphemy to say that there is a necessity of abrogating the divine law contained in the text of Genesis to make room for human laws which starve and degrade one half of mankind to pamper and intoxicate the rest.

"But after all," continues the Doctor, "there are some few things which must still unavoidably remain in common: such (among others) are the elements of light, air, and water."[49] Thank you for nothing, Doctor. It is very generous, indeed, to allow us the common right to the elements of light, air, and water, or even the blood which flows in our veins. Blackstone's *Commentaries* have been much celebrated, and this very chapter, so replete with malignant sophistry and absurdity, has been inserted in all the magazines, museums, registers, and other periodical publications in England and cried up as the most ingenious performance ever published. Dr. Priestley and Mr.

§ The Europeans have long supposed that the mere walking upon a piece of vacant ground gave them a right to it. Hence the Spaniards upon their first landing on this continent, set up a post, by which they claimed a right to it.

Furneaux both attacked Mr. Blackstone on the subject of some invectives against the dissenters and a mal-exposition of the toleration act, but no champion was to be found to take the part of poor forlorn Human Nature, and the Doctor was suffered, unmolested, to quibble away all the rights of the great brotherhood of mankind.[50]

Reduced to light, air, and water for an inheritance, one would have thought their situation could not be easily made worse, but it is not difficult to be mistaken. The bulk of mankind were not only cheated out of their right to the soil but were held ineligible to offices in the government because they were not freeholders. First cruelly to wrest from them the paternal inheritance of their universal Father, and then to make this outrageous act an excuse for denying them the rights of citizenship. This is the history of civil society in which our duty and happiness are so admirably interwoven together. We will, however, never believe that men originally entered into a compact by which they excluded themselves from all right to the bounties of Providence; and if they did, the contract could not be binding on their posterity, for although a man may give away his own right, he cannot give away the right of another.

"The only true and natural foundations of society," says Dr. Blackstone, "are the wants and fears of individuals."[51] The word *society* here is a vague term, by which we are at liberty to understand any government which has existed from the creation of the world to the present day. But if the European governments were erected to supply the wants and lessen the fears of individuals, we may venture to assert that the first projectors of them were errant blockheads. The wants of man, instead of having been lessened, have been multiplied, and that in proportion to his boasted civilization; and the fear of poverty alone is more than sufficient to counterbalance all the fears to which he was subject in the rudest stage of natural liberty.

From this source arise almost all the disorders in the body politic. The fear of poverty has given a double spring to avarice, the deadliest passion in the human breast; it has erected a golden image to which all mankind, with reverence, bend the knee regardless of their idolatry. Merit is but an abortive useless gift to the possessor, unless accompanied with wealth; he might choose which tree whereon to hang himself, did not his virtuous mind tell him to "dig, beg, rot, and perish well content, so he but wrap himself in honest rags at his last gasp and die in peace."

It is a melancholy reflection that in almost all ages and countries men have been cruelly butchered for crimes occasioned by the laws and which they never would have committed, had they not been deprived of their natural means of subsistence. But the governors of mankind seem never to have made any allowance for poverty, but like the stupid physician who prescribed bleeding for every disorder, they seem ever to have been distinguished by an insatiable thirst for human blood. The altars of a merciful God have been washed to their foundation from the veins of miserable men; and the double-edged sword of Justice, with all its formality and parade, seems calculated to cut off equally the innocent and guilty. Between religion and law, man has had literally no rest for the sole of his foot.

In the dark ages of Gothic barbarity ignorance was some excuse for the framing of absurd systems, but in the age in which Dr. Blackstone lived, he should have known better, he should have known that the unequal distribution of property was the parent of almost all the disorders of government; nay, he did know it, for he had read Beccaria, who treating upon the crime of robbery, says, "But this crime, alas!, is commonly the effect of misery and despair, the crime of that unhappy part of mankind to whom the right of exclusive property (a terrible and perhaps unnecessary right) has left but a bare subsistence."[52] There is no necessity for concealing this important truth, but much benefit may be expected from its promulgation —It offers a foundation whereon to erect a system, which like the sun in the universe, will transmit light, life, and harmony to all under its influence—I mean—A SYSTEM OF EQUAL EDUCATION.

# CHAP. III

*Consequences Drawn from the Preceding Chapters, by Which It Is Proved that All Governments Are Bound To Secure to Their Subjects the Means of Acquiring Knowledge in Sciences and in Arts.*

I N the first part of this work, we have shown that the most obvious difference between the situation of the savage and the civilized man is the division of property. We have shown also that this difference is the origin of all the miseries and vices of the one and of all the innocence and happiness of the other. We have also demonstrated that the civilized man has been unjustly deprived of his right to the bounties of Providence and that he has been rendered, as much as human laws could do it, an abortive creation.

We will now inquire the best mode of alleviating his miseries, without disturbing the established rules of property. In the savage state, as there is no learning, so there is no need of it. Meum & tuum, which principally receives existence with civil society, is but little known in the rude stages of natural liberty; and where all property is unknown, or rather, where all property is in common, there is no necessity of learning to acquire or defend it. If in adverting from a state of nature to a state of civil society, men gave up their natural liberty and their common right to property, it is but just that they should be protected in their civil liberty and furnished with means of gaining exclusive property, in lieu of that natural liberty and common right of property which they had given up in exchange for the supposed advantages of civil society; otherwise the change is for the worse, and the general happiness is sacrificed for the benefit of a few.

In all contracts, say civilians, there should be a *quid pro quo.* If civil society therefore deprives a man of his natural means of subsistence, it should find him other means; otherwise civil society is not a contract, but a self-robbery, a robbery of the basest kind: "It represents a madman, who tears his body with his arms, and Saturn, who cruelly devours his own children." Society should then furnish the people with means of subsistence, and those means should be an inherent quality in the nature of the government, universal, permanent, and uniform, because their natural means were so. The means I allude to are the means of acquiring knowledge, as it is by the knowledge of some art or science that man is to provide for subsistence in civil society. These means of acquiring knowledge, as I said before, should be an inherent quality in the nature of the government: that is, the education of children should be provided for in the constitution of every state.

By education I mean instruction in arts as well as sciences. Education, then, ought to be secured by government to every class of citizens, to every child in the state. The citizens should be instructed in sciences by public schools, and in arts by laws enacted for that purpose, by which parents and others, having authority over children, should be compelled to bind them out to certain trades or professions, that they may be enabled to support themselves with becoming independency when they shall arrive to years of maturity.

Education should not be left to the caprice or negligence of parents, to chance, or confined to the children of wealthy citizens; it is a shame, a scandal to civilized society, that part only of the citizens should be sent to colleges and universities to learn to cheat the rest of their liberties. Are ye aware, legislators, that in making knowledge necessary to the subsistence of your subjects, ye are in duty bound to secure to them the means of acquiring it? Else what is the bond of society but a rope of sand, incapable of supporting its own weight? A heterogenous jumble of contradiction and absurdity, from which the subject knows not how to extricate himself, but often falls a victim to his natural wants or to cruel and inexorable laws—starves or is hanged.

In the single reign of Henry VIII, we are informed by Harrison that seventy-two thousand thieves and rogues were hanged in England.[53] How shall we account for this number of executions? Shall we suppose that the English nation at this period were a pack of thieves and that everyone of this number richly deserved his fate? Or shall we say that the lives of so many citizens were sacrificed to a wretched and barbarous policy? The latter seems to be the fact.

The lands in England, at this time, were held under the feudal system, in large tracts, by lords; the people were called vassals; but the conditions of their servitude were so hard, their yoke so grievous to be borne, that numbers left the service of their lords. But where could they fly or how were they to provide for subsistence? The cultivation of the soil was denied them, except upon terms too vile and degrading to be accepted, and arts and commerce, which at this day maintain the bulk of the people, were then in their infancy and probably employed but a small proportion of the people.

We despise thieves, not caring to reflect that human nature is always the same; that when it is a man's interest to be a thief he becomes one, but when it is his interest to support a good character he becomes an honest man; that even thieves are honest among each other, because it is their interest to be so. We seldom hear of a man in independent circumstances being indicted for petit felony: the man would be an idiot indeed who would stake a fair character for a few shillings which he did not need, but the greatest part of those indicted for petit felonies are men who have no characters to lose, that is—no substance, which the world always takes for good character.

If a man has no fortune and through poverty or neglect of his parents he has had no education and learned no trade, in such a forlorn situation, which demands our charity and our tears, the equitable and humane laws of England spurn him from their protection, under the harsh term of a vagrant or a vagabond, and he is cruelly ordered to be whipped out of the county.

From newspapers we often gather important and curious information. In the *Baltimore Advertiser*[54] of the 16 Nov. 1790 is the following extract from an English newspaper: "The French exult in having been the first nation who made their King confess himself a citizen. With all due deference to the French, we manage those things as well in England. In the last reign there was a good deal of dispute between the parish of St. Martin and the Board of Green Cloth about the payment of poor rates for the houses in Scotland Yard. The Board would not pay, because they belonged to the King! 'And if they do belong to the King, is not the King a parishioner?,' was the reply; *'but if the thing is at all doubtful, we will put it beyond dispute;'* and they accordingly elected his majesty to the office of church warden. The King served the office by deputy and was thankful they had not made him a constable. They might have made him an overseer of the poor, which every King is, or ought to be, in right of his office, but in that case, by the old constitution of St. Martin, he might have had the flogging of vagrants to perform with his own hands, for there is in the books of the parish a curious item of expense: *'To furnishing the Overseer of the poore with one cloke, maske and cappe, to whippe the beggars out of the parish.'* "

So much for English parish law, a remnant of which, says a writer in the *Delaware Gazette*, has more than once been put in execution in this state. Strangers suspected of being poor have been imprisoned because they could produce no pass from the place they last left. Unfortunate civilized man! Too much reason had Raynal to say, "Everywhere you meet with masters and always with oppression." How often, says this venerable philosopher, have we heard the poor man expostulating with heaven and asking what he had done, that he should deserve to be born in an indigent and dependent station.[55]

How can those English vagrant acts be reconciled to that law which pretends to protect every man in his just rights? Or have poor men no rights? How will they square with the doctrines of the Christian religion which preach poverty, charity, meekness, and disinterestedness, after the example of their humble founder. "Let us dwell no longer," says a French writer, "upon those miseries, the detail of which will only grieve and tire you; believe that the ornaments of your churches would better cover the nakedness of Jesus Christ in the sacred and miserable persons of your poor: yes, you would have more merit to cover his terrestrial members than to entertain a pomp foreign to his laws and the charity of his heart. The Church, the spouse of a God, poor and humble, hath always had a terrible fear of poverty: she has preserved wisely, and in good time, resources against this terrifying sin. The immense wealth she has amassed by preaching poverty hath put her at her ease, until the consummation of ages."

Is it any wonder that poverty should be such a formidable terror to civilized nations, when it never meets with quarter, but always with persecution, when both religion and law declare it to be the object of their most implacable hatred and disgust. English vagrant acts, although they are a manifest abuse of civilization, have been hitherto impregnable to the attacks of sound reason and elegant satire. Many English authors have honestly reprobated them; Mr. Fielding in several of his novels has highly ridiculed them; and Doctor Goldsmith has exposed them in a vein of inimitable satire, in his history of a poor soldier.[56] Pity such philosophers were not magistrates!

"In vain," says Raynal, "does custom, prejudice, ignorance, and hard labor stupify the lower class of mankind, so as to render them insensible of their degradation; neither religion nor morality can hinder them from seeing, and feeling, the injustice of the arrangements of policy in the distribution of good and evil."[57]

But how comes this injustice in the arrangements of policy? Is it not evident that it is all the work of men's hands? Thus it is that the sins of the fathers are visited upon the children unto the third and fourth generation. A tyrant, a madman, or a fool forms a society; to aggrandize his own family and his dependants, he creates absurd and unnatural distinctions; to make one part of the people fools, he makes the other part slaves. His posterity in a few generations mix with the mass of the people, and they then suffer for the despotism, the folly, or the ignorance of their ancestor. The distinctions, however, which are the root of their misery, still exist, although their author is extinct; thus it is that the folly of man outlives himself and persecutes his posterity.

"To live and to propagate," says the before-mentioned author, "being the destination of every living species, it should seem that society, if it be one of the first principles of man, should concur in assisting this double end of nature."[58] We should be cautious how we unite the words *society* and *government,* they being essentially different. Society promotes but bad governments check population. In bad governments, only, is celibacy known, and it is of little consequence what class of subjects practice it, whether the clergy, as in France, or the servants, as in England—it is always baneful. It estranges the affections of the human heart from its proper object and gives the passions an unnatural direction. Poverty, the great scourge of civilized nations, is the immediate cause of celibacy in the lower class of people.

Celibacy in the higher ranks proceed from the same cause, though not so immediately. The fear of poverty has made the love of gain the ruling passion: hence parents to secure an estate to their children marry them in their infancy: hence money is always title good enough to procure a husband or wife: hence those preposterous matches which unite beauty and deformity, youth and old age, mildness and ferocity, virtue and vice. In Europe the inclination of a girl is seldom consulted in regard to a husband: hence the infidelity to the marriage bed so common in those countries and the matrimonial strife so frequent, which deter many from entering into that state who have both ability and inclination.

It has been observed that the attraction of the sexes is in many circumstances similar to gravity, the spring of motion in the universe, that it always acts in the same degree in the same climate. If the design of Providence in the creation of man was that he should multiply and replenish the earth, why endeavour to destroy this natural propensity? Why encourage celibacy repugnant to nature and death to society? Men do not, in fact, practice celibacy through inclination but necessity: in short, nothing is wanting to induce men to marry, but [what is wanting is what is required] to enable every man to maintain a wife, and should the care of government extend to the proper education of the subject, every man would be enabled to do it.

We have already demonstrated that government should furnish the subject with some substitute in lieu of his natural means of subsistence, which he gave up to government when he submitted to exclusive property in lands. An education is also necessary in order that the subject may know the obligations he is under to government.

The following observations of a celebrated English historian are very applicable: "Every law," says Mrs. Macaulay in her *History of England*, "relating to public or private property and in particular penal statutes ought to be rendered so clear and plain and promulgated in such a manner to the public as to give a full information of its nature and extent to every citizen. Ignorance of laws, if not wilful, is a just excuse for their transgression, and if the care of government does not extend to the proper education of the subject and to their proper information on the nature of moral turpitude and legal crimes and to the encouragement of virtue, with what face of justice can they punish delinquency? But if, on the contrary, the citizens, by the oppression of heavy taxes, are rendered incapable, by the utmost exertion of honest industry, of bringing up or providing for a numerous family, if every encouragement is given to licentiousness for the purpose of amusing and debasing the minds of the people or for raising a revenue on the vices of the subject, is punishment in this case better than legal murder? Or, to use a strong yet adequate expression, is it better than infernal tyranny?"[59]

Time was when the laws were written in a language which

the people did not understand, and it seemed the policy of government that the people should not understand them, contrary to every principle of sound policy in legislation. If the system of English law was simplified and reduced to the standard of the common sense of the people, or were the understandings of the people cultivated so as to comprehend the system, many absurdities which exist at this day would have been rejected.

We are told by Sir William Blackstone that it is a settled rule at common law that no counsel shall be allowed a prisoner upon his trial upon the general issue in any capital crime unless some point of law shall arise proper to be debated.[60] This is without doubt a barbarous law, and it is a little surprising that while every other art and science is daily improving, such inconsistencies should have been suffered to continue to this time of day in a science on which our lives depend. Men are every day liable to suffer in their property by their ignorance of the forms of legal writings adopted by lawyers. But although a man should be under the necessity of suffering in his property by not knowing which form of writing would best secure his debts or preserve his estate, yet certainly he might be allowed to know some little of the statute law in which his life is concerned. Those governments, therefore, which think the instruction of youth worthy [of] their attention, would do well to cause an abridgement of their statute law to be read in their schools at stated times, as often as convenient.

Mankind, ever inclined to the marvelous, run astray in search of a phantom, an *ignis fatuus,* while they neglect those simple and palpable truths which could only conduct them to that happiness they are so eagerly in search of. How many volumes have been wrote upon predestination, free will, liberty, and necessity, topics which are not properly the objects of the human understanding and of which after we have wrote a thousand volumes we are not a whit wiser than when we began, while the economy of society is but little understood and the first and simplest principles of legislation entirely neglected.

Nothing is more obvious than that every person in a civilized society should contribute towards the support of government. How stupid, then, is the economy of that society conducted, which keeps one half of the citizens in a state of abject poverty, saddling the other half with the whole weight of government and the maintenance of all the poor beside? Every citizen ought to contribute to the support of government, but all obligations should bind within the limits of possibility; a man, at least, should be able to pay a tax before he is compelled to do it as a duty. But the pauper who cannot procure even the vilest food to spin out a miserable existence may indeed burden but can never support the government.

The English, whose absurdities we are at all times proud to imitate, in this respect seem justly to have deserved the keen satire of Dr. Swift, who says the sage professors of Laputa were employed in extracting sunbeams out of cucumbers, calcining ice into gunpowder, and making fire malleable.[61] The policy of the English government appears to have been to make the mass of people poor and then to persecute them for their poverty, as their vagrant acts abundantly testify; those acts, as has been said before, are a manifest abuse of civilization—they are impolitic, barbarous, inhuman, and unjust, and would disgrace even a society of satyrs.

In an essay on trade, written in the reign of George II, are the following paragraphs:

"The *Spectator* calculates 7 parts in 8 of the people to be without property and get their bread by daily labor.[62] If so, will trade pretend to employ all hands equally and constantly? If not, it will be worth considering how they live in the present situation of things. Mr. Gee, a very intelligent author, computes three millions unemployed in the three kingdoms: the truth of which appears by divers particulars.[63] Prisons, workhouses, transports, and beggars are so many instances to confirm the truth of this observation. Some preposterously complain that in any labor or business that requires expedition a sufficiency of hands is wanting.

"But what numbers are there continually traveling from one country to another, from nation to nation, who would work day and night for a little more pay—which argues that the choice is to live by honest means, and if they are hurried into others less justifiable, it is for want of employment. And as such men must eat and drink whether they work or no, they are put to many shifts for a subsistence; no wonder, then, if the empty stomach fills the head with dangerous projects. It is unnatural to think that many of those poor wretches who are doomed to death or exile would have run the hazard of their lives, or liberty, in such trifles as it is frequently forfeited for (the 10d. or 12d. convicts) were they not compelled to it by griping necessity; for it is well known that many of those who are sent abroad alter their sentiments with their circumstances, and this is a principal argument to recommend the christianity of transportation.

"Rapin, in his history of Edward VI, thus speaks of the people's complaints—for they were so early that they were not able to gain their livelihoods—1st, because business was fallen into more hands, meaning the vagabond monks; 2d., by inclosures; 3d., by breeding sheep, which took fewer hands and lessened the wages.[64] Dean Swift gives much the same reasons for the miserable poverty of Ireland.[65]

"Philips, Esq., argues thus—If, says he, there were full employment, labor would rise to its just value, as everything else does when the demand is equal to the quantity; and therefore [he] denies that there is work enough, or that property is reasonably and sufficiently diffused, till necessaries are rendered so plentiful and thereby so cheap that the wages of the laboring man will purchase a comfortable support.[66]

"Vanderlint's late pamphlet adjusts every article of expense and at the lowest computation supposes a laborer cannot support himself, a wife, and four children at less than £.50 a year.[67] Now if he works daily as a laborer, the top wages he can get exceeds not 18d. a day. Masons, carpenters, etc. have half a crown, but both fall short of the sum, though in full employ, so that beggary and thievery from this account seem their inevitable destiny; and while one part of the world condemns and punishes the delinquents, the other ought to rejoice, for the greater the numbers that go into idle and unwarrantable ways of living, the better and securer state it makes for those behind.

"Dr. Garth has ingeniously described the use of such contingencies in higher life:

> *For sickly seasons the physicians wait,*
> *And politicians thrive in broils of state;*
> *In sessions the poor lay all their stress,*
> *And hope each month their crowds will be the less.*[68]

"Poverty makes mankind unnatural in their affections and behavior. The child secretly wishes the death of the parent, and the parent thinks his children an incumbrance and has sometimes robbed their bellies to fill his own. Many yield themselves up to the unnatural lusts of others for a trifling gratuity, and the most scandalous practices are often the effects of necessitous poverty. Is it not therefore of consequence to provide for the growing evil, and worthy a legislative inquiry how the poor people are brought up? Men else come to renounce their generative faculty or destroy that fruit whose misery they cannot prevent.

"The difficulty of getting money to purchase food is the same thing now which dearths were formerly, with this little difference, that as famine might vex them once in an age or two, this sticks close every year for the lifetime of laborers who are at low wages and at an uncertainty even in that, numbers of them being driven to great straits, sitting in the market place till the eleventh hour, and then called perhaps a servant to the plantations; some through a meekness of disposition starve quietly and in private; others associate in crimes and are hanged or in fear of that, hang themselves. It is in vain to argue against fact, no nation on earth, nor perhaps all the absolute kingdoms together, affording so many instances of suicides and executions as England, and plainly for a care in most of them about this mortal body how it shall subsist."

But if such has been the situation of the poor, in the nation whose government has been so much boasted of, how have they fared in the rest of Europe? Take the following description of the galley slaves of Italy, from the Sieur Dupaty. "All sorts of wretches are fastened indiscriminately to the same chain; malefactors, smugglers, dealers, Turks taken by the corsairs, and volunteers, galley slaves. Voluntary galley slaves! Yes—These are poor men, whom government get hold of between hunger and death. It is in this narrow passage they wait and watch for them. Those wretched beings, dazzled with a little money, do not perceive the galleys and are enlisted. Poverty and guilt are bound in the same chain! The citizen who serves the republic suffers the same punishment with him who betrays it!

"The Genoese carry their barbarity still further; when the term of their enlisting is near expiring, they propose to lend a little money to those miserable creatures. Unhappy men are eager for enjoyment; the present moment alone exists for them; they accept—but at a week's end nothing remains to them but slavery and regret, insomuch that at the expiration of that time they are compelled to enlist again, to discharge their debt, and sell eight years' more of their existence. Thus do the greatest part of them consume, from enlistments to loans, and from loans to enlistments, their whole lives at the galleys in the last degree of wretchedness and infamy: there they expire . . . Let us add one more trait to this picture of the galleys. I saw the wretches selling from bench to bench, coveting, disputing, stealing even the fragments of aliment which the dogs of the street had refused—Genoa! thy palaces are not sufficiently lofty, spacious, numerous, nor brilliant, we still perceive thy galleys!"[69]

We may apostrophize more generally. Civilization, thy benefits are not sufficiently solid, numerous, nor splendid; we everywhere perceive that degradation and distress which thy daughter poverty has entailed upon our race.

Finally, the security of all governments must in a great measure depend upon the people. Should a savage be introduced into a civilized society and denied all means of improving himself, could it be expected that he could form any accurate notions of the policy, economy, or obligations of that society? And yet among the great body of the people in polished Europe, among the laboring poor, how rare is it to find a man possessed of anything equal to the general knowledge of an ingenious savage?

The European artist is expert in the particular article of his trade or art. Thus a pin maker is dexterous at making pins, but in everything else he is as grossly stupid, his understanding is as benumbed and torpid, as it is possible for any intellectual faculty to be. The number of executions in England has been already observed to be occasioned more by the wretched policy of the government than by any innate depravity of the people, who, generally speaking, are ignorant to a proverb. They have, it is true, universities and colleges, with a few charity schools, but the former receive none but the sons of wealthy subjects and the latter are very circumscribed; few poor children have even the chance of balloting for admittance. Hence the body of the people are ignorant.

And in France, if one hundredth part of the money expended in the maintenance of legions [of] fat, lazy, lubberly ecclesiastics had been employed in instructing the people in public schools, the nation would be a nation of men instead of a rude and ignorant rabble, utterly incapable of profiting by the golden opportunity which now offers and which, were it not for the exertions of their leaders, would, instead of emancipating them, only serve more strongly to rivet their fetters. Humanity is wounded by the outrages of the mob in France, but what better can be expected from *ignorance,* the natural parent of all enormity?

The actions of mobs are always characteristic of the people who compose them, and we will find the most ignorant always guilty of the greatest outrages: hence the striking difference between American and European mobs. The mob that burnt the tea at Boston, and even that under Shays, was a regular and orderly body, when compared with that of Lord George Gordon or any of the late mobs in France.[70] We know of no such outrages committed in America.

But as there will be sometimes disorders in the very best of governments, such as keep the mass of people in profound ignorance must abide by the consequences when the body politic is convulsed. Mr. Noah Webster is the only American author, indeed the only author of any nation, if we except perhaps Montesquieu, who has taken up the subject of education upon that liberal and equitable scale which it justly deserves. I had the present work in idea some time before Mr. Webster's essays made their appearance and was not a little pleased to think he had anticipated my idea.

Although I am sensible that I have dealt pretty freely with quotations in this work already, yet I think it a debt due to Mr. Webster to introduce part of his sentiments on this subject —"A good system of education," says this author, "should be the first article in the code of political regulations, for it is much easier to introduce and establish an effectual system for preserving morals than to correct by penal statutes the ill effects of a bad system. I am so fully persuaded of this that I shall almost adore that great man who shall change our practice and opinions and make it respectable for the first and best men to superintend the education of youth.[71]

"It is observed by the great Montesquieu that 'the laws of education ought to be relative to the principles of the government.' In despotic governments the people should have little or no education, except what tends to inspire them with a servile fear. Information is fatal to despotism. In monarchies education should be partial and adapted to each class of citizens. But 'in a republican government,' says the same writer, 'the whole power of education is required.' Here every class of people should *know* and *love* the laws. This knowledge should be diffused by means of schools and newspapers, and an attachment to the laws may be formed by early impressions upon the mind.

"Two regulations are essential to the continuance of republican governments: 1. Such a distribution of lands and such principles of descent and alienation as shall give every citizen a power of acquiring what his industry merits. 2. Such a system of education as gives every citizen an opportunity of acquiring knowledge and fitting himself for places of trust. These are fundamental articles, the *sine qua non* of the existence of the American republics."[72]

"Hence the absurdity of our copying the manners and adopting the institutions of monarchies. In several states we find laws passed establishing provisions for colleges and academies where people of property may educate their sons, but no provision is made for instructing the poorer rank of people even in reading and writing. Yet in these same states every citizen who is worth a few shillings annually is entitled to vote for legislators. This appears to me a most glaring solecism in government. The constitutions are *republican* and the laws of education are *monarchical*. The *former* extend civil rights to every honest industrious man, the *latter* deprive a large proportion of the citizens of a most valuable privilege.

"In our American republics, where government is in the hands of the people, knowledge should be universally diffused by means of public schools. Of such consequence is it to society that the people who make laws should be well informed that I conceive no legislature can be justified in neglecting proper establishments for this purpose.

"Such a general system of education is neither impracticable nor difficult, and excepting the formation of a federal government that shall be efficient and permanent, it demands the first attention of American patriots. Until such a system shall be adopted and pursued, until the statesman and divine shall unite their efforts in *forming* the human mind, rather than in lopping its excrescences after it has been neglected, until legislators discover that the only way to make good citizens and subjects is to nourish them from infancy, and until parents shall be convinced that the *worst* of men are not the proper teachers to make the *best,* mankind cannot know to what degree of perfection society and government may be carried. America affords the fairest opportunities for making the experiment and opens the most encouraging prospect of success."[73]

Suffer me then, Americans, to arrest, to command your attention to this important subject. To make mankind better is a duty which every man owes to his posterity, to his country, and to his God; and remember, my friends, there is but one way to effect this important purpose—which is—by incorporating education with government.—*This is the rock on which you must build your political salvation!*

# C H A P.   IV

*The System of Education Should Be Equal. Equality of Men Considered. Raynal Mistaken in His Notions of Equality.*

THAT the system of education should be equal is evident, since the rights given up in the state of nature and for which education is the substitute were equal. But as I know it will be objected by some that the natural inequality of the human intellect will obviate any attempt to diffuse knowledge equally, it seems necessary to make some inquiry concerning the natural equality of men.

That all men are by nature equal was once the fashionable phrase of the times, and men gloried in this equality and really believed it, or else they acted their parts to the life! Latterly, however, this notion is laughed out of countenance, and some very grave personages have not scrupled to assert that as we have copied the English in our form of federal government, we ought to imitate them in the establishment of a nobility also.

For my part, I do believe that if there was any necessity for two distinct hereditary orders of men in a society that men would have been created subordinate to such necessity and would at their birth be possessed of certain characteristic marks by which each class would be distinguished. However, as much has been said of late upon grades and gradations in the human species, I will endeavor to add my mite to the public stock.

In the dark ages of the world it was necessary that the people should believe their rulers to be a superior race of beings to themselves, in order that they should obey the absurd laws of their tyrants without "scrutinizing too nicely into the reasons of making them." As neither the governors nor governed understood any other principle of legislation than that of fear, it was necessary in order that the people should fear their rulers to believe them of a superior race to themselves.

Hence in the Jewish theocracy their rulers came in under a *jure divino* title, consecrated and anointed by the Deity himself. Hence the Mexican emperors were descended in a direct line from the sun, and in order to conduct the farce completely the descendants of the female line only inherited, in order that the blood line of the sun might never be lost. This was a master stroke of policy, perhaps never equalled in the eastern world, but it sufficiently shows that the emperors were apprehensive that if the people suspected an extinction of the blood line that they would conclude they were governed by men like themselves, which would be subversive of the principle of fear on which their government was erected.

But until the light of letters be again extinct, vain will be the attempt to erect a government on the single principle of fear or to introduce a nobility in America. If the Americans could be brought seriously to believe that by giving a few hereditary titles to some of their people, such people would immediately upon their being invested with such titles become metamorphosed into a superior race of beings, an attempt for a nobility might succeed.

But to return to our inquiry—If an elegant silver vase and some ore of the same metal were shown to a person ignorant of metals, it would not require much argument to convince him that the vase could never be produced from the ore. Such is the mode of reasoning upon the inequality of the human species. Effects purely artificial have been ascribed to nature, and the man of letters who from his cradle to his grave has trod the paths of art is compared with the untutored Indian and the wretched African in whom slavery has deadened all the springs of the soul.

And the result of this impartial and charitable investigation is that there is an evident gradation in the intellectual faculties of the human species. There are various grades in the human mind [—this] is the fashionable phrase of the times. Scarce a superficial blockhead is to be met with but stuns you with a string of trite commonplace observations upon gradation, and no doubt thinks himself *in primo gradu* or at the top of the ladder.

Nature is always various in different species, and except in cases of *lusus naturæ*, always uniform in the same species. In all animals, from the most trifling insect to the whale and elephant, there is an evident uniformity and equality through every species. Where this equality is not to be found in the human species it is to be attributed either to climate, habit, or education, or perhaps to all. It must be obvious to every intelligent person the effect which habit alone has upon men. Awkward boobies have been taken from the ploughtail into the Continental army in the late war and after a few campaigns have returned home, to the surprise and admiration of their acquaintances, elegant, ornamental, and dignified characters. Such astonishing metamorphoses have been produced by the army that to habit alone may be ascribed all the inequality to be found in the human species.

If then education alone (for in this sense, the army may be properly called a school) is capable of producing such astonishing effects, what may not be ascribed to it when united with climate? Indeed we have numberless commonplace observations which have been always read as true and which are entirely founded upon this idea of equality in the intellectual faculties of the human race. Take the following—The minds of children are like blank paper, upon which you may write any characters you please. But what tends most to establish this idea of natural equality [is that] we find it always uniform in the savage state.

Now if there was a natural inequality in the human mind, would it not be as conspicuous in the savage as in the civilized state? The contrary of which is evident to every observer acquainted with the American Indians. Among those people all the gifts of Providence are in common. We do not see, as in civilized nations, part of the citizens sent to colleges to learn to cheat the rest of their liberties who are condemned to be hewers of wood and drawers of water. The mode of acquiring information, which is common to one, is common to all; hence we find a striking equality in form, size, and intellectual faculties nowhere to be found in civilized nations.

It is only in civilized nations where extremes are to be found in the human species—it is here where wealthy and dignified mortals roll along the streets in all the parade and trappings of royalty, while the lower class are not half so well fed as the horses of the former. It is this cruel inequality which has given rise to the epithets of nobility, vulgar, mob, canaille, etc. and the degrading, but common observation—Man differs more from man, than man from beast—The difference is purely artificial. Thus do men create an artificial inequality among themselves and then cry out it is all natural.

If we would give ourselves time to consider, we would find an idea of natural intellectual equality everywhere predominant but more particularly in free countries. The trial by jury is a strong proof of this idea in that nation; otherwise would they have suffered the unlettered peasant to decide against lawyers and judges?[74] Is it not here taken for granted that the generality of men, although they are ignorant of the phrases and technical terms of the law, have notwithstanding sufficient mother wit to distinguish between right and wrong, which is all the lawyer with his long string of cases and reports is able to do? From whence also arises our notion of common sense? Is it not from an idea that the bulk of mankind possess what is called common understanding?

This common understanding must be supposed equal, or why should we apply the term common which implies equality? But it will perhaps be objected that the minds of some men are capable of greater improvement than others, which daily experience testifies: to which I answer that there is perhaps as great a variety in the texture of the human mind as in the countenances of men. If this be admitted, the absurdity of judging of the genius of boys by the advances they make in any particular science will be evident. But a variety is by no means inconsistent with an equality in the human intellect. And although there are instances of men who by mere dint of unassisted genius have arose to excellence, while others have been so deficient in mental powers as not to be capable of improvement from the combined efforts of art, yet when we enumerate all the idiots and sublime geniuses in the world, they will be found too few in number when compared with the rest of mankind to invalidate the general rule that all men are by nature equal.

But why should a strict mathematical equality be thought necessary among men, when no such thing is to be found in nature? In the vegetable creation, the generality of plants arrive to perfection, some reach only half way, and some are blights, yet the vegetable creation is perfect. The soil is to plants what government is to man. Different soils will produce the same species of vegetables in different degrees of perfection, but there will be an equality in the perfection of vegetables produced by the same soil in the same degree of cultivation. Thus governments which afford equal rights to the subjects will produce men naturally equal; that is, there will be the same equality in such men as is to be found in all the productions of nature. As one soil, by manuring it in patches, will produce vegetables in different degrees of perfection, so governments, which afford different privileges to different classes of people will produce men as effectually unequal as if the original germ of stamina of production was essentially different.

The notion of a natural inequality among men has been so generally adopted that it has created numerous obstacles to the investigation of their rights and biased the most discerning of modern writers. The Abbé Raynal, whose philanthropy I revere and of whose works I am far from being a willing critic, seems to have adopted this erroneous opinion.

"It has been said," says the Abbé, in his *Revolution of America*, "that we are all born equal; that is not so—that we had all the same rights; I am ignorant of what are rights, where there is an inequality of talents, of strength, and no security or sanction—that nature offered to us all the same dwelling, and the same resources; that is not so—that we were all endowed indiscriminately with the same means of defense; that is not so; and I know not in what sense it can be true that we all enjoy the same qualities of mind and body. There is amongst men an original inequality for which there is no remedy. It must last forever, and all that can be obtained by the best legislation is not to destroy it but to prevent the abuse of it.

"But in making distinctions among her children like a stepmother, in creating some children strong and others weak, has not nature herself formed the germ or principal of tyranny? I do not think it can be denied, especially if we look back to a time anterior to all legislation, a time in which man will be seen as passionate and as void of reason as a brute."[75]

But how is it that we are not all born equal? There may be a difference between the child of a nobleman and that of a peasant, but will there not also be an inequality between the produce of seeds collected from the same plant and sown in different soils? Yes, but the inequality is artificial, not natural. It has been already observed that there is a striking equality in form, size, and intellectual faculties among the American Indians nowhere to be found in what we call civilized nations. Men are equal where they enjoy equal rights. Even a mathematical equality in powers among men would not necessarily secure their rights.

It had escaped the Abbé's reflection that nature, when she formed more men than two, formed the germ or principle of tyranny as effectually as when she created one man of double powers to another, for among three men of equal powers two could as effectually overpower the third as one man of six feet could overcome one of three. But although a mathematical equality among men neither exists nor is necessary, yet the generality of men educated under equal circumstances possess equal powers. This is the equality to be found in all the productions of nature, the equality and the only equality necessary to the happiness of man.

The inhabitants of the United States are more upon an equality in stature and powers of body and mind than the subjects of any government in Europe. And of the United States, the states of New England, whose governments by charter verged nearest to democracies, enjoy the most perfect equality. Those who live ashore are all legislators and politicians;‖ and those who follow the sea are all captains and owners; yet their governments are orderly and their ships navigated with as much success as if they were commanded with all the etiquette and subordination of royal navies. But though the constitution of the New England states were democratical, yet their laws were chiefly borrowed from the British code, many of which were unequal, such as vagrant acts, acts which confer rights of residence and citizenship, and the like—hence the equality of the citizens of New England, though striking when compared with any of the European governments, is not strictly natural. But among the American Indians, where no vestige of European absurity is found interwoven in their laws, where they are governed by the plain and equitable code of nature, here is perfect natural equality.

The Abbé Raynal seems to be mistaken in his opinion con-

‖ See Morse's Geography. [Jedidiah Morse: *The American Geography* . . . (Elizabethtown: Shepard Kollock for the author, 1789, p. 146.]

cerning the origin of government. Speaking of the miseries to which man is subject in his civilized state, he says, "In this point of view, man appears more miserable and more wicked than a beast. Different species of beasts subsist on different species, but societies of men have never ceased to attack each other. Even in the same society, there is no condition but devours and is devoured, whatever may have been or are the forms of government or artificial equality which have been opposed to the primitive and natural inequality."[76]

Men educated under bad governments, who see nothing but vice and infamy around them, who behold hardened wretches falling victims to the laws daily, are apt to conclude that man is naturally wicked—that in a state of nature, he is a stranger to morality, he is barbarous and savage, the weak always falling a prey to the strong—that government was instituted to protect the weak and to restrain the bold and to bring them more upon an equality.

But this is all a mistake—the man of America is a living proof to the contrary. He is innocent and spotless when compared with the inhabitants of civilized nations. He has not yet learned the art to cheat, although the traders have imposed upon him by every base and dirty fraud which civilized ingenuity could invent, selling him guns which are more likely to kill the person who fires them than the object at which they are presented; and hatchets without a particle of steel—incapable of bearing an edge or answering any use. I have seen whole invoices of goods, to a very considerable amount imported for the Indian trade, in which there was not an article which was not a palpable cheat.

Some excuse indeed seems necessary to those who have brought men under the yoke of cruel and arbitrary governments, and nothing is more easy than to say, it is all their own faults; that is, the faults of the people. They had given themselves up to the full possession of their unruly passions, appetites, and desires, every man tyrannizing over his neighbor. Government, therefore, arose out of necessity. This they will assert with as much confidence and maintain with as much obstinacy as if, forsooth, they had been personally present at the first conventions of men in a state of nature—and although no vestige is to be found of the foundation of any of the governments now existing being laid in any such convention, and although the conduct of individuals in those societies which approach nearest to the state of nature are so very far from supporting this opinion that they rather teach us to believe that men excel in wickedness in proportion to their civilization.

Therefore, instead of supposing with Abbé Raynal a primitive inequality which was found necessary to be lessened by the artificial equality opposed to it in different forms of government, we will suppose a primitive equality, and this equality to be disturbed and broken by an external force, not by members of the same society opposed to each other, but by the conquest of one society by another, when the conquering society became the governors and the conquered society the governed.

This is clearly the case in regard to the English government, which we know was founded by conquest, and which Mr. Blackstone, with much eloquence but more sophistry, would fain persuade us had a much more equitable origin. The English, indeed, seem in their theory of the gradation of the human species to have forgotten the state of their ancestors when conquered by the Romans—a rude and barbarous people, dwelling in caverns, feeding on roots, their only clothing the uncouth representation of the sun, moon, and stars, daubed in barbarous characters on their skins; yet the descendants of these wretched savages pretend that there is an evident gradation in the intellectual faculties of the human species. Since, therefore, men are naturally equal, it follows that the mode of education should be equal also.

It is generally observed that most of the American legislatures are composed of lawyers and merchants. What is the reason? Because the farmer has no opportunity of getting his son instructed without sending him to a college, the expense of which is more than the profits of his farm. An equal representation is absolutely necessary to the preservation of liberty. But there can never be an equal representation until there is an equal mode of education for all citizens. For although a rich farmer may, by the credit of his possessions, help himself into the legislature, yet if through a deficiency in his education he is unable to speak with propriety, he may see the dearest interest of his country basely bartered away and be unable to make any effort except his single vote against it. Education, therefore, to be generally useful should be brought home to every man's door.

## CHAP. V

*Wretched State of the Country Schools throughout the United States, and the Absolute Necessity of a Reformation.*

THE country schools through most of the United States, whether we consider the buildings, the teachers, or the regulations, are in every respect completely despicable, wretched, and contemptible. The buildings are in general sorry hovels, neither windtight nor watertight, a few stools serving in the double capacity of bench and desk and the old leaves of copy books making a miserable substitute for glass windows.

The teachers are generally foreigners, shamefully deficient in every qualification necessary to convey instruction to youth and not seldom addicted to gross vices. Absolute in his own opinion and proud of introducing what he calls his European method, one calls the first letter of the alphabet *aw*. The school is modified upon this plan, and the children who are advanced are beat and cuffed to forget the former mode they have been taught, which irritates their minds and retards their progress. The quarter being finished, the children lie idle until another master offers, few remaining in one place more than a quarter. When the next schoolmaster is introduced, he calls the first letter *a*, as in *mat*—the school undergoes another reform and is equally vexed and retarded. At his removal, a third is introduced, who calls the first letter *hay*. All these blockheads are equally absolute in their own notions and will by no means suffer the children to pronounce the letter as they were first taught, but every three months the school goes through a reform—error succeeds error—and dunce the second reigns like dunce the first.

The general ignorance of schoolmasters has long been the subject of complaint in England as well as America. Dr. Goldsmith says, "It is hardly possible to conceive the ignorance of many of those who take upon them the important trust of education. Is a man unfit for any profession, he finds his last resource in commencing schoolmaster—Do any become bankrupts, they set up a boarding school and drive a trade this way when all others fail—nay, I have been told of butchers and barbers who have turned schoolmasters, and more surprising still, made fortunes in their new profession."[77] And I will venture to pronounce that however seaport towns, from local circumstances, may have good schools, the country schools will remain in their present state of despicable wretchedness unless incorporated with government.

> *Now, blame we most the nurslings or the nurse?*
> *The children crook'd, and twisted, and deform'd*
> *Through want of care, or her whose winking eye*
> *And slumb'ring oscitancy mars the brood?*
> *The nurse, no doubt. Regardless of her charge,*
> *She needs herself correction. Needs to learn*
> *That it is dang'rous sporting with the world,*
> *With things so sacred as a nation's trust,*
> *The nurture of her youth, her dearest pledge.*[78]

If education is necessary for one man, my religion tells me it is equally necessary for another, and I know no reason why the country should not have as good schools as the seaport towns, unless indeed the policy of this country is always to be directed, as it has been, by merchants. I am no enemy to any class of men, but he that runs may read.

A blind adherence to British policy seems to have pervaded both the general and state governments, notwithstanding there is no analogy between the two countries; and this will be the case until we can raise men in the country who will think for themselves and be able to arrange and communicate their ideas. Towns have the advantages of libraries, the country of retirement—the youth of the former may become elegant imitators; those of the latter, bold originals; being out of the sphere of vice so attractive in cities, their productions will bear the stamp of virtuous energy.

When I say that the policy of this country, has been hitherto directed by merchants, etc., I mean that the inhabitants of seaport towns have a very considerable influence in all our public proceedings and that from education and local circumstances such inhabitants appear to me to have an improper bias in favor of commercial and mercantile habits and interests, habits and interests which do not appear to me to be congenial with the true interest of the United States.

The necessity of a reformation in the country schools is too obvious to be insisted on, and the first step to such reformation will be by turning private schools into public ones. The schools should be public, for several reasons—1st. Because, as has been before said, every citizen has an equal right to subsistence and ought to have an equal opportunity of acquiring knowledge. 2d. Because public schools are easiest maintained, as the burden falls upon all the citizens.

The man who is too squeamish or lazy to get married contributes to the support of public schools as well as the man who is burdened with a large family. But private schools are supported only by heads of families, and by those only while they are interested, for as soon as the children are grown up their support is withdrawn, which makes the employment so precarious that men of ability and merit will not submit to the trifling salaries allowed in most country schools and which, by their partial support, cannot afford a better.

Let public schools then be established in every county of

the United States, at least as many as are necessary for the present population; and let those schools be supported by a general tax. Let the objects of those schools be to teach the rudiments of the English language, writing, bookkeeping, mathematics, natural history, mechanics, and husbandry—and let every scholar be admitted gratis and kept in a state of subordination without respect to persons.

The other branch of education, I mean, instruction in arts, ought also to be secured to every individual by laws enacted for that purpose, by which parents and others having authority over youth should be compelled to bind them out at certain ages and for a limited time to persons professing mechanical or other branches, and the treatment of apprentices during their apprenticeship should be regulated by laws expressly provided, without having recourse to the common or statute law of England. I mention this because, independent of the difference of circumstances between these United States and England, I think a more humane and liberal policy might be established than that now in usage in England and better adapted to the present circumstances of America; and indeed it is high time to check that blind adherence to transatlantic policy which has so generally prevailed.

It would be superfluous to insist on the necessity of trades—their use is obvious. I shall only remark that, considering the transitory nature of all human advantages, how soon a man may be dispossessed of a very considerable property—how many avenues there are to misfortunes; a good trade seems to be the only sheet anchor on which we may firmly rely for safety in the general storms of human adversity. How much then is it to be lamented that ever the tyranny of fashion or pride of birth gave an idea of disgrace to those virtuous and useful occupations.

To demonstrate the practicability of establishing public schools throughout the United States, let us suppose the states to be divided into districts according to the population, and let every district support one school by a tax on the acre on all lands within the district. Let us suppose, for argument's sake, six miles square, which will be 36 square miles—sufficient for a district for the mean population of the United States. The schoolhouse should be built of brick and in the center of the district; it would be then three miles from the schoolhouse door to the boundary of the district. The building might be two stories, with a large hall on the lower floor for the schoolroom; the rest of the house should be for the master's family and might consist of two rooms on the lower floor and three or four in the second story, with perhaps an acre of ground adjoining.

We will suppose the ground to cost £10, the building £800, the master's salary £150 per annum, and £50 for an assistant, with £50 for mathematical instruments; in all £1060, of which £800 is for building the schoolhouse; and as people enough will be willing to contract for building the house, to wait a year for half the money, we will suppose £400 to be paid the first year. Now in 36 square miles are 23,040 acres, which is little better than 4d. per acre; the next year's payment will be £660, which will be about 7d.; then the succeeding years there will be the teacher's salary, £150, the assistant £50, and £50 for contingent expenses, books, etc. will be £250. per annum, which will not amount to 3d. per acre.

Now when we consider that such a trifling tax, by being applied to this best of purposes, may be productive of consequences amazingly glorious, can any man make a serious objection against public schools? "It is unjust," says one, "that I should pay for the schooling of other people's children." But, my good sir, it is more unjust that your posterity should go without any education at all. And public schools is the only method I know of to secure an education to your posterity forever. Besides, I will suppose you to be the father of four children—Now, sir, how can you educate these four children so cheap, even in your present paltry method? The common rate at present is 8s. 4d. per quarter, which is 33s. 4d. per year, which for 4 children is £6 13 4. Now if you hold 300 acres of land, you will pay towards the support of decent public schools, at 3d. per acre, 900d. or £3 15 per annum.

Perhaps no plan of private education can ever be so cheap as public. In the instances of public schools a considerable part of the master's salary would be spent in the district. The farmer might supply him with provisions, and the receipts might be tendered as a part of his tax to the collector. Thus the farmer would scarcely feel the tax.

No modes of faith, systems of manners, or foreign or dead languages should be taught in those schools. As none of them are necessary to obtain a knowledge of the obligations of society, the government is not bound to instruct the citizens in any thing of the kind.—No medals or premiums of any kind should be given under the mistaken notion of exciting emulation. Like titles of nobility, they are not productive of a single good effect but of many very bad ones: my objections are founded on reason and experience. In republican governments the praises of good men, and not medals, should be esteemed the proper reward of merit, but by substituting a bauble instead of such rational applause, do we not teach youth to make a false estimate of things and to value them for their glitter, parade, and finery? This single objection ought to banish medals from schools forever.

I once knew a schoolmaster who besides being an arithmetician was a man of observation: this person had a school of upwards of 90 scholars and at every quarterly examination a gold medal was given to the best writer and a silver one to the best cipherer. I requested him one day candidly to inform me of the effects produced by those medals; he ingenuously told me that they had produced but one good effect, which was [that] they had drawn a few more scholars to his school than he otherwise would have had, but that they had produced many bad effects.

When the first medal was offered, it produced rather a general contention than an emulation and diffused a spirit of envy, jealousy, and discord through the whole school; boys who were bosom friends before became fierce contentious rivals, and when the prize was adjudged became implacable enemies. Those who were advanced decried the weaker performances; each wished his opponent's abilities less than his own, and they used all their little arts to misrepresent and abuse each other's performances. And of the girls' side, where perhaps a more modest and more amiable train never graced a school, harmony and love, which hitherto presided, were banished, and discord reigned triumphant—jealousy and envy, under the specious semblance of emulation, put to flight all the tender, modest, amiable virtues, and left none but malignant passions in their stead. But the second quarter, things changed their faces.

There must indeed be almost a mathematical equality in the human intellect, if in a school of nearly 100 scholars, one or two do not, by superior genius, take the lead of the rest. The children soon found that all of them could not obtain the medal, and the contention continued sometimes among three, but seldom with more than two. But although the contention was generally confined to two, yet the ill effects produced by the general contention of the first quarter still remained and discord as generally prevailed. But more, the medal never failed to ruin the one who gained it and who was never worth a farthing afterwards; having gained the object of his ambition, he conceived there was no need of further exertion or even of showing a decent respect either to his tutor or his schoolmates; and if the losing competitor happened to be a girl, she sometimes left the school in tears and could never be prevailed upon to enter it afterwards.

Those are the effects of medals as they operated on the school, but they extended their mischief still further. The flame of jealousy was kindled in the breasts of the mothers, who charged the master with partiality in the distribution of the medals, although they were adjudged by four or five indifferent persons of merit in the town, and although the tutor uniformly refused to give his opinion on the merit of any performance, and care was taken that the authors of none of the performances were known by the persons who adjudged the prize.

To conclude, to make men happy, the first step is to make them independent. For if they are dependent, they can neither manage their private concerns properly, retain their own dignity, or vote impartially for their country: they can be but tools at best. And to make them independent, to repeat Mr. Webster's words, two regulations are essentially necessary. First, such a distribution of lands and principles of descent and alienation as shall give every citizen a power of acquiring what his industry merits. Secondly, such a system of education as gives every citizen an opportunity of acquiring knowledge and fitting himself for places of trust. It is said that men of property are the fittest persons to represent their country because they have least reason to betray it. If the observation is just, every man should have property, that none be left to betray their country.

"It has been observed that the inhabitants in mountains are strongly attached to their country, which probably arises from the division of lands, in which, generally speaking, all have an interest. In this, the Biscayners exceed all other states, looking with fondness on their hills as the most delightful scenes in the world and their people as the most respectable, descended from the aborigines of Spain. This prepossession excites them to the most extraordinary labor, and to execute things far beyond what could be expected in so small and rugged a country, where they have few branches of commerce. I cannot give a greater proof of their industry than those fine roads they have now made from Bilboa to Castile, as well as in Guypuscoa and Alaba. When one sees the passage over the tremendous mountains of Orduna, one cannot behold it without the utmost surprise and admiration."¶

It is with infinite satisfaction that I have seen a similar sentiment adopted by the Court of Errors and Appeals, in the Dela-

¶ Dillon's Travels in Spain. [John Talbot Dillon, *Travels Through Spain, With a View To Illustrate the Natural History and Physical Geography of That Kingdom, in a Series of Letters* (London: R. Baldwin, 1782), p. 167.]

ware state, in the case of Benjamin Robinson and William Robinson appellants, against the lessee of John Adams, respondent. "Estates in fee tail," say the court, "are not liable to division by will, or upon intestacy, as estates in fee simple are; & those distributions are very beneficial.* It is much to be wished that *every citizen could possess a freehold*, though some of them might happen to be small. Such a disposition of property cherishes domestic happiness, endears a country to its inhabitants, and promotes the general welfare. But what ever influence such reflections might have upon us, on other occasions they can have but little if any on the present for reasons that will hereafter appear."

From the last sentence in the foregoing paragraph, and the note beneath, it would appear that this republican sentiment was introduced by the court, not from any immediate relation, reference, or application, which it had to the cause under consideration, but merely that it might be generally diffused.

And now, my fellow citizens, having thus, though in an indigested manner, shown you the great cause of all the evils attendant on an abuse of civilization, it remains with you to apply the remedy. Let it not be said, when we shall be no more, that the descendants of an Eastern nation, landed in this Western world, attacked the defenseless natives and "divorced them in anguish, from the bosom of their country," only to establish narrow and unequitable policies, such as the governments of our forefathers were.[79]

But let us, since so much evil has been done, endeavor that

---

* "It is greatly to be desired that the persons appointed by our courts, for viewing and dividing lands among the children of intestates, would not suffer themselves so easily to be prevailed upon to report that the lands will not bear a division. Thus, very often an estate is adjudged as incapable of division, to one of the children that might well be divided into five or six, if not more farms, as large as many in the Eastern states; upon which the industrious and prudent owners live happily. By the usual way of proceeding among us, one of the children is involved in a heavy debt that frequently proves ruinous to him; or if the debt of valuation is paid to the other children, it is in a number of such trifling sums and at such distances of time, one from another, that they are of very little use to those who receive them. This matter deserves very serious consideration."

some good may come of it. Let us keep nature in view and form our policy rather by the fitness of things than by a blind adherence to contemptible precedents from arbitrary and corrupt governments. Let us begin by perfecting the system of education as the proper foundation whereon to erect a temple to liberty and to establish a wise, equitable, and durable policy, that our country may become *indeed* an asylum to the distressed of every clime—the abode of liberty, peace, virtue, and happiness—a land on which the Deity may deign to look down with approbation—and whose government may last till time shall be no more!

# 5

# SIMEON DOGGETT

*A Discourse on Education, Delivered at the
Dedication and Opening of Bristol Academy, the
18th Day of July, A.D. 1796. (New Bedford,
1797)*

[Simeon Doggett (1765-1852) was a New England Unitarian minister, the only American-trained clergyman represented in this
collection of essays. A graduate of the College of Rhode Island
(Brown) in the class of 1788, he taught there as a tutor 1791-1796. In
1796 he left Brown to become the principal of the Bristol Academy
at Taunton, Massachusetts, a position that he held until 1813, when
he accepted a call from the church at Mendon. This essay, published at New Bedford by J. Spooner in 1797, is Doggett's statement
of the role and responsibilities of the American secondary school as
it was then developing in New England. It was, as its title states,
delivered as a dedicatory address on the opening of the Bristol
Academy, July 18, 1796.]

'TIS EDUCATION FORMS THE COMMON MIND;
JUST AS THE TWIG IS BENT THE TREE'S INCLIN'D.

*POPE.*[1]

---

CITIZENS & FRIENDS,

THE abundant diffidence and anxiety which at all times so justly belong to me are at the present partly lost in the flow of sympathetic joy and gratitude which animate my heart to felicitate you on this happy meeting. While some of our fellow creatures are roaming in the gloomy forest as beasts of prey; or, in wild enthusiasm and dark superstition, celebrating the rites of idol and unknown gods; or exulting, with barbarous pleasure, in the excruciating torture of captive enemies: while millions are dragging out a miserable existence in the dreary countries of ignorance and despotism, or more awfully bleeding under the cursed lash of slavery; and others, with unfeeling hearts, wantonly rioting upon these sufferings of their brother creatures and the bounties of Heaven: while thousands are armed with the implements of death in order to cut and mangle the bodies of their fellow men and to shed each other's blood, and whole nations are experiencing all the horrors of war: we, my friends, in the ample enjoyment of national liberty, prosperity, and peace, are this day convened by an occasion connected with everything great and valuable to man.

This day, by the munificence of an all-wise and directing Providence, we celebrate the dedication of a literary institution: an institution which, by the grace of God, we would sacredly consecrate to literature, virtue, and the true dignity of man. Every circumstance of the occasion is calculated to touch the most noble feelings of our nature, to sublime our hearts to the throne of God on the swift wings of gratitude and love. And while the occasion irresistibly claims a tribute of gratitude to the Father of lights and God of all grace, at the same time it claims more irresistibly, if possible, our most ardent prayers that the God of science, order, and virtue would enable and dispose us ever to hold in view the sublime objects to which our institution is this day solemnly consecrated; and that those who are more immediately concerned may be endowed from on high with all that wisdom and fortitude which from time to time may be necessary to direct the institution in the ways of truth and virtue. Neither can those who are intimately concerned in the prosperity of the Academy rest its consecration to knowledge and virtue on thanksgiving and prayer alone; they will be constrained, from the powerful voice of duty and interest, to co-operate with the all-bountiful hand of Providence by their most ardent resolutions and spirited exertions.

Thus congratulating each other on the opening of our promising seminary and, together with thanksgiving by prayer and pious resolutions, sacredly dedicating it to literature and morality, our minds are naturally arrested by the great, the all-interesting subject of education. Here the importance of education, at once, opens upon our view a wide field, rich with many of the most interesting particulars.

Expatiating in this delightful field, the objects which education ought to embrace first catch our attention. These objects, I conceive, are, principally, literature and morality: by the former to inform and direct the understanding; by the latter to meliorate the heart, to conform the affections, will, and conduct to the rules of rectitude or will of our Maker and great Moral Governor.

Whatever might have been the reason, either some deficiency in those who have been employed in conducting youth or an idea that the heart is unalterable otherwise than by an immediate miracle of the Divine hand, or some other reason, it is a melancholy truth that the morality of youth has not been considered, so much as their literature, the province of the instructor. While unwearied pains have been taken to give learning to youth, to give them skill in the arts and knowledge in the sciences, the habitudes of the heart, their dispositions, tastes, and sentiments, on which moral character is grafted, have been too much neglected. There is doubtless great connection between truth and virtue, between the understanding and the moral habitudes of the soul, so that by informing the understanding there is strong probability that the morality will be improved. Yet it must be confessed that this connection is not an inseparable one, since we have the unhappiness sometimes to see gentlemen of the first learning and abilities the lowest sunk in depravity and vice. We have the unhappiness sometimes to see souls widely expanded in knowledge awfully maculated with the dark shades of vice: angels in understanding, devils in conduct.

Hence we see education, which is designed to prepare youth for the sequel of life, to render them useful, respectable, and happy, will be immensely deficient, unless it be professedly extended to their morality as well as their literature. The constitution of human nature proves the propriety and importance of doing this. The prominent principles of our nature are those of imitation and habit. Youth are ever learning to do what they see others around them doing, and these imitations grow into habits. Fact and experience prove to us that every function of the body, every faculty and capacity of the mind, are more or less affected and directed by imitation and habit. How infinitely important then is it in early youth, when every power and capacity is pliable and susceptible of any direction or impression, so to manage education that imitation may turn the young mind to virtue as well as knowledge, and habit confirm him in both. Not only then are we to educate our youth in arts and sciences, but also, as saith the Apostle, *in the nurture and admonition of the Lord.*[2]

Being so convinced of its consequence, I cannot forbear adding manner as another object which education ought to embrace. Though the head be filled with science and the heart with sentiment, though knowledge and virtue mark every trait of the character, constraint and awkwardness of manner will in a measure render the person forbidding and repulsive, lessen his influence, and detract from his usefulness. Hence while education strives to form the mind to learning and virtue, it will not fail to embellish both with the ornaments of ease and grace of manner. One blessed with such an education will command that influence which his substantial acquirements justly challenge and will diffuse, wherever he goes, light, virtue, love, and joy.

Having pointed at the great objects which education ought to embrace, the importance of it will more fully appear by opening our eyes upon that dignity and happiness which the Creator designed for the human race. When we analyze man, raptures of solemn joy and gratitude must fill our hearts to see what greatness, sublimity, glory, and happiness our faithful Creator designed for him! The erect posture, the curious and wonderful structure, and the commanding countenance of man all indicate the superior powers of his soul. As an intellectual being, how wonderful is man! Through his senses, as so many windows to his dark body, the knowledge of the material world is beamed upon his mind. By reflecting on the powers and operations of his own mind, he rises to a knowledge of the spiritual world, of angels, of God. By discernment and reasoning he sees the agreement and disagreement of his ideas; the broad effulgence of knowledge and truth illumine and expand his soul. Curiosity urges his ardent pursuits of knowledge, and, through an exquisite sense of truth, his feelings are enraptured with her view. By memory he calls from oblivion scenes that are past; from experience corrects his errors and re-enjoys the delights of life. His imagination wings his soul with fire, traverses all that is grand and sublime in the universe, ascends the skies, surveys the shining orbs and bright intelligences of immensity, and, from nature, rises to nature's God.

As an active and moral being, still more wonderful is man! His body, formed to a variety of operation, is pliable and energetic; his mind is quick and powerful as the electric spark. His soul is winged with the most animating passions. Desire of happiness and aversion to misery, love and hatred, hope and fear, rouse all the faculties of man and command his greatest, noblest exertions. Implanted in the heart is conscience, the monitor of Heaven, as by the hand of God, diffusing peace and joy through the virtuous soul and punishing vice by the torture of remorse and the awful forebodings of guilt. Thus endowed, man has the honor of being made capable of religion, of rising to a knowledge of the invisible God, the Creator and Governor of the universe, of his attributes and will; capable of the sublime affections of piety, of gratitude and love, adoration and obedience. To complete the dignity and happiness of man, God hath constituted him a free and moral agent, while supporting [him], [having] delegated to his mind an ample, an unembarrassed power to direct all his active faculties. So exalted is the human race in the scale of beings that while the Creator, of his other works said, They were very good; of man He saith, In the image of God created He him!

If we, for a moment, look without us, we shall be still farther convinced of the dignity and happiness designed for our race. Man is constituted king of earth. Hence the revolving seasons, the air and souls of heaven, the vast ocean and its inhabitants, and the cattle upon a thousand hills all bespeak his glory. But if we just glance an eye of faith into our holy religion, what has hitherto been said of human greatness dwindles to a point. Here we find *life and immortality*, beyond the grave, *brought to light*.[3] Here we find, *Eye hath not seen, nor ear heard, neither have entered into the heart of man, the things,* the dignity and happiness, *which God hath prepared*[4] *for* the virtuous. And, what is more than all, that all the human race might be raised to this invisible height of perfection, the blessed Emmanuel, the only Son and image of God, left his throne in heaven for a humble residence on earth, assumed humanity, and even died to disembarrass us from those depravities which might sully our glory.

Such are the greatness and value of human nature, and such her powers and capacities. But where in this world is much of all this known or realized and enjoyed? The experience of fact replies, only there where have been enjoyed the blessings of education. All these intellectual, active, and moral powers and capacities, experience shows us, are under the influence of the great principles of IMITATION and HABIT, which Deity, for the wisest purposes, implanted in our nature; and hence, by the powerful hand of a well-directed education, and due attention, may be vastly heightened and improved; or, by neglect and vicious indulgence depressed, enervated, if not finally destroyed.

Let us, for a moment, look at the savage of the wilderness natively possessed of all this dignity and value of nature but untouched by the moulding hand of education. Destitute of all the arts of civilized life, he roves a naked animal in the uncultivated forest. His intellectual powers lying unexercised and undirected, his ideas, his language, and his knowledge are confined within the small compass of his chase. His passions undisciplined are ungovernable, impetuous, and awful. Ignorant of his own origin and value, of God and religion, he adores the sun and stars and bends his knee to the rude image formed by his own unskillful hand. And not only is the heart, which embraces the whole family of man, constrained to weep over millions of the human race who through the deficiency of education are low sunk in barbarity, but even in civilized life where the means of education and the light of religion are enjoyed, even among the highly privileged Americans, the tear of humanity is frequently started to see many of our brethren, some of whom the most excellent of nature's works, through the neglect of education and by bad example in a situation almost as pitiable as that of the roving Tartar.

How infinitely different is the character of him whom a well-conducted education and due attention and the grace of God have brought upon the stage of action! In him all the noble powers and capacities of human nature are improved and exalted and still progressing. Truth and knowledge illumine and expand his mind. His understanding is broad as the heavens. Swayed by reason, his imagination and his passions are calm and regular as the heavenly orbs. Unshackled by superstition, his candor is diffusive as the light. His conscience, unhurt by the torpedo of vice, is tender and delicate as the sensitive plant. Freed from prejudice, his faith, founded on evidence, is firm as the everlasting mountains. Flowing from conviction, his morality is steady as the sun in his course. His zeal and devotion, being according to knowledge, are without enthusiasm, uniform, rational, sublime. Such a one is dignified and happy in himself, honorable to his connections, useful to the world, loved and respected by all, blessed of Heaven, and preparing for the society of angels in the city of God.

But the field of the importance of education is not yet fully explored. Widening our view upon nations, still greater objects arrest our attention. What but the blessings of education raise the improved and civilized nations of Europe so far above the roving tribes of Africa? Though the arts of civilized life may originate from necessity, yet it is by the improvements of knowledge that their principles are investigated, without which they never will be carried to any considerable perfection. The principles unfolded by mechanical philosophy have given birth to all that variety of machinery by which labor is abridged and the arts of life improved. Commerce very much owes her existence to the advancement of science. By this means the vast ocean is navigated, the most distant nations which it flows between made acquainted with each other, and their various productions exchanged to the advantage of both. In short, "in civilized life everything is effected by art and skill," both which, in a great measure, are the gifts of education—"Whence a person who is provided with neither (and neither can be acquired without exercise and instruction) will be useless; and he that is useless will generally be, at the same time, mischievous to the community. So that to send an uneducated child into the world is injurious to the rest of mankind; it is little better than to turn out a mad dog or a wild beast into the streets."[5]

But the infinite importance of education, in a national view, appears in still brighter colors from this eternal truth, that the mode of government in any nation will always be moulded by the state of education. The throne of tyranny is founded on ignorance. Literature and liberty go hand in hand. Every ray of knowledge which darts through the dark cloud of ignorance that rests on an inslaved nation threatens death to the despot. The dark ages of gothecism opened an ample field for ecclesiastical tyranny. While the Pope of Rome and his satellites established in the ignorant minds of Europe the doctrine of the Pope's infallibility, that he was Peter's successor, vicegerent of Christ, and held the keys of heaven, the kings of Europe trembled before him and laid their treasures at his feet. As the sun of science has been rising upon Europe, the papal throne has been melting; and the prospect now is that his holiness will soon be no more. In those dark ages also the ridiculous doctrine of the divine right of kings being instilled into the ignorant mind, the authority of despots became the authority of God, and their subjects prepared tamely to suffer every indignity. But as the increase of knowledge has gradually given those nations better notions of the equal rights of men, tyranny has been proportionally declining. Let general information and a just knowledge of the rights of man be diffused through the great bulk of the people in any nation, and it will not be in the power of all the combined despots on earth to enslave them.

Of this truth France may be an example. Of the influence of education on government, the history of our own nation affords us a most happy specimen. Convinced of the vast consequence of literature, our pious ancestors gave the earliest attention to the education of their youth. By this means, information was generally diffused through the colonies, and many of our citizens were profound in science, the rights of man, the histories of nations, and political wisdom. Thus guarded, vain were the attempts of Britain to oppress us. Separation was the consequence; independence the issue. Guided by the same potent hand of literature, our lives are crowned with a government which secures to us all the blessings of society and civil liberty.

That we may transmit to posterity our happy government pure and uncorrupted, let the glories of education ever be our theme.

Were it not unnecessary to say more on this head, the inestimable value of education would still vastly magnify by viewing its connection with our holy religion.

Though at first Christianity was miraculously sent from heaven to earth by the hand of a glorious mediator, the continuation and propagation of it in the world depends, under Providence, almost entirely on education. "Christianity is a historical religion, founded on facts which are related to have passed, upon discourses which were held, and letters which were written in a remote age and distant country. The records of these things are preserved in languages which have long ceased to be spoken in any part of the world." Obvious it is then that education, and most probably the clergy, are necessary to perpetuate the evidences of our holy religion and to interpret those ancient writings in which this religion is contained.

Not to dwell longer on this most copious head, filled with the infinite consequence of education to man, the mind is naturally turned and most powerfully excited to consider the way and means by which it may be most successfully advanced. One of the most important particulars is that the great work of education be begun in early life. As soon as the powers and capacities of the mind begin to unfold, the directing and fostering hand of education should be applied. The time of human life is too short and valuable to suffer a moment of it to pass away without improvement. Beside, the work of acquiring a good education, filling the mind with knowledge, and moulding it into virtuous habits is a work of vast labor. Life is short; science and improvement infinite.

Not only so, but such is the constitution of nature, the young mind cannot be stationary. The great principles of imitation and habit will operate. Hence, if the skillful hand of education does not, as its faculties unfold, turn the mind right, by directing these principles, they will, through bad example and indulgence, turn it wrong. And, what is more, the turn which the young mind receives while it is tender and pliable and its powers and capacities are unfolding and maturing is very stubborn and probably will in a measure continue until and—awful thought!—beyond death. Perhaps under five years of age some impressions and principles are set upon the mind and manners of the child which he will carry through life. Experience has long since drawn this observation into a decided maxim. A great poet expresses thus:

> 'Tis education forms the common mind;
> Just as the twig is bent the tree's inclin'd.

And one, who for almost three thousand years has been renowned for his superior wisdom, has left us this all-interesting maxim in still more decisive terms. *Train up a child in the way he should go; and when he is old, he will not depart from it.*[6] Upon these principles it is that we so urgently recommend early education. Upon these principles it also is that a late education is encumbered with many embarrassments. Entering late upon education, the scholar not only has his learning to obtain but bad habits and erroneous prejudices to correct. Very few have abilities adequate to the arduous task. Though such a one may become accurate in theory, it is lucky if his old habits do not cause him to blunder in practice. Though his knowledge may be fine, he is very liable to have his manner constrained and his execution bad.

Female education is another particular very essential as a means to its general and far advancement.

We have seen [that] education ought to begin with the beginnings of understanding. At this eventful period of life the little folks are in the arms of their mothers. Has the mother been well-educated, is the tender parent a good preceptress, the fortunate child is at the best school in the universe while in its mother's lap. As the faculties of the young mind expand, she will with a delicate and skillful hand nurture and direct it to knowledge and virtue. The pupil, being constantly with and strongly attached to the mother, will assume her as an example of perfection and imitate her every look, word, and gesture. These imitations will soon grow into habits and probably fix traits upon the child's mind, speech, and manners which will be durable as life. Hence the maxim, as is the parent so is the child; and hence the inconceivable consequences of female education.

Beside, such is the happy constitution of nature that wherever ladies are highly improved by a well-directed and refined education, there the gentlemen will soon become so. It is an aphorism, which it must be confessed carries much truth with it, that the fair part of creation rule the world. Would they, guided by the wise dictates of a virtuous education, give their approbation only to those who were (considering their circumstances) duly informed and virtuous, we might venture to affirm [that] scarcely an uneducated, irregular man would be seen in society. Permit me, then, ladies, to say, on you it very much rests to fix the boundaries of human improvement. The Creator hath put it in your power to reform the world. Let not the idle, dissipated character share your caresses, and the work is done. Doing this, you will have the honor of doing more than all the magistrates, moralists, and preachers in the world.

When we consider the dignity, value, and happiness a good education adds to the human mind, how surprising it is that, in this, one half of the human race have been so basely neglected—especially when we consider how a refined education in them reforms the world. This doubtless is a trait of barbarity. In the savage state, where strength is honor, the delicate female is depressed far below the dignity of her rank. As civilization and improvement advance in families or nations, female education gains ground, ladies assume their proper rank and command respect. Happy am I to observe this trait of barbarity in our country rapidly wearing away. May that glorious era soon commence when a virtuous and refined education shall adorn the fair daughters of America—then dissipated gallantry shall be banished [from] society and modest virtue be triumphant.

It is obvious to observe that good instruction is another very essential particular in the means of advancing education.

It is as easy for the scholar to learn right as wrong. Let him be taught right, and his learning will be so of course. Whether he be so or not, the scholar, as he ought, thinks his teacher is right, follows his precepts, and copies his example. On these truths the following general rule is erected for the election of instructors: Such a character as you would wish your child to be, choose for his instructor. Would you wish your child to be a blunderer and a guesser in learning, without points or accuracy, thus let his instructor be, and the work is done. Would you wish him vulgar in his diction, horrid in his pronunciation, and awkward in his manners, then choose an instructor of such a mould. But, as better suited to this enlightened age in which we have the happiness of living, do you wish, as I am persuaded you do, to have your children right and accurate in their learning, easy and graceful in their manners, and sentimental and regular in their morals, then choose for their instructor a scholar and gentleman and a Christian, and your ardent and noble wishes, by the blessings of Heaven, will be gratified.

It is most painful and gloomy to the patriot and philanthropist to observe that the instruction of our youth has, through mistake or deficiency of patronage, too generally fallen into inadequate hands. But we are animated, happy in the consideration that the good sense of the people is now rapidly correcting this mistake. Raptures of enthusiasm fill our hearts in anticipating the golden era when Socrateses shall again be schoolmasters.

But in addition to good instruction, there must be great attention and exertion on the part of the scholar.

Where the work to be performed is great, the time to perform it is short, and the reward ample, every possible exertion is naturally called into act. This, my young friends, is your situation who are making the first advances in education. Your object, as you have already seen, is most great and noble: it is the improvement of your natures in everything amiable, virtuous, and praiseworthy, that you may be satisfied with and happy in yourselves, joy to your parents, honor to your instructors, useful in this world, and happy in the next. To obtain that good education which secures these great objects is an amazing work: a work which calls for your greatest attention, care, resolution, industry, and most ardent prayers. Many difficulties are to be encountered, many self-denials assumed. The hill of a literary and virtuous education is, in some parts, steep, craggy, and laborious. But be not discouraged; its assent is more easy as you advance, and its sublime summit is irradiated with a broad effulgence of glory. On this summit fix your eyes, and no exertions will seem too great, no attention tedious.

Especially will this laborious attention be urged upon you by the consideration of the shortness of youth. When the age of manhood arrives, as it soon will, the great objects of life, profession, domestic establishment and cares, duties to your country, and extended connections will crowd upon you and command your attention. The age of youth, when the mind is free from all these cares, is the time which God hath appointed to obtain education and prepare for manhood. This time is too short and precious to squander a moment of it in useless trifles and amusements. It is a mistake that youth is the age for idleness and diversion: it is the age for education, on which depend your future prosperity and greatness.

I have reserved for the last place one of the most essential means to the promotion of literature, I mean, that of the encouragement and patronage of government and gentlemen of distinction and ability.

Honor and profit are objects which have a very commanding influence on the minds of men. Let the government of a nation and its able characters who have these to bestow amply confer them on teachers and virtuous literary merit, and that nation will soon become distinguished in education. Gentlemen of the first character and abilities will aspire to the noble profession of instructing youth. Youth will be animated, enthusiastic in their attention, and thousands of citizens emulous in the course of improvement. The golden ages of literature, which are immortalized on the page of history, in Greece, Rome, Florence, France, and England, all are replete with facts which testify to us the vast consequence of this encouragement and patronage. But we need not go to distant ages and nations for the proof of this; our own prosperous country affords us a sufficient one.

Those states in the union are the most distinguished for the general diffusion of information where the legislature of the state and able individuals have been the most active and liberal in their encouragement and patronage. I presume we shall not injure our sister states if we say Massachusetts justly claims a rank among those of this description. Numerous, noble, and distinguished are the monuments of her exertion in the glorious cause of education. On these we might exhaust the language of panegyric, but the recent instance of the liberal patronage of literature which ornaments Bristol County and felicitates our present meeting more immediately commands our gratitude and claims a tribute of acknowledgment. The voice of duty is, let the magnanimous sentiments of patriotism be a grateful return. The voice of duty also calls for a grateful tribute to the noble patronage of individuals, with whom the government have entrusted their character and liberal deposit. And, I presume, with my own, I shall gratify the feelings of my audience if I add as another claim of our gratitude the spirited but disinterested exertions of a distinguished character* who now blesses another clime.

Permit me to say, gentlemen, by accepting the honorable appointment of trustees to our infant seminary, you accept a great and solemn trust. The expectations of the community are justly upon you. On you it rests to manage the institution, that it may under your auspices effect the all-important objects for

---

* General DAVID COBB, *who removed from* Taunton *to* Gouldsbury, *in the* Province of Maine, *a few weeks before the Academy was opened.*

which God and our legislature designed it: the diffusion of knowledge and virtue among our fellow citizens. Your talk is arduous, your responsibility is great, but the dignity of the object will not fail to animate the generous heart with resolution, zeal, and unremitting perseverance. With such an object in view, you have on your side the good wishes and ardent prayers of all the virtuous; you have on your side the Providence of that God who is the great Father of Lights and Conductor of the Universe. Persevere then with the same spirited, noble exertions with which you have begun, that Bristol Academy may, in the diffusion of literature and morality, be a great and permanent blessing to the county and community and hold an honorable rank among the flourishing seminaries which adorn and bless our country.

Impressed with grateful sentiments for the attention and candor of this large and respectable audience and convinced of the infinite consequence of education to us all, I cannot but beg leave, in the close of our subject, again to call your attention to it. It is from the want of education that, notwithstanding the native dignity of human nature, millions of our race are now low sunk in barbarity, clothed with the unwrought skins of animals, subsisting as beasts of prey by the precarious events of the chase, covered with little else than the canopy of heaven, exposed to all the elements of nature, hostile, and awfully cruel in their dispositions, ignorant of their origin or destination, of the one only living and true God, and the Lord Jesus Christ, worshiping idols, and living and dying but a little exalted above the beasts of the forest. It is from the want of education, and so of a just knowledge of the rights of man, that almost the whole of the human race have, from their first creation to the present day, been dragging out existence under the iron sceptres of tyrants and despots, and bleeding under the cursed lash of slavery. It is from the want of education, or from an erroneous one, that the pure religion of Jesus has been so basely maculated and debased with superstition and absurdity.

The kingdom of antichrist was laid in ignorance; and by this the Pope of Rome, for more than a thousand years, swayed the horrid sceptre of ecclesiastical tyranny over all the nations of Christendom. It is from the want of a right education that we have the humiliation and great unhappiness to see many of our fellow citizens enveloped in darkness and prejudice; many wretched between the demands of idleness and poverty; many, most shockingly debased in the corruptions of obscenity; many, for their outrages on society, dragging the chain in the horrid dungeon or suspended on the shameful gallows; many devoted to dissipation and the gratification of ungovernable appetites and passions. In short, it seems not too much to say that almost all the vices and evils of life may be traced back either to the want of an education or an erroneous one.

But how refulgent is the contrast of a right education! By this all the dignified faculties of man are improved and directed towards that exalted state of perfection and happiness for which the Creator designed him. By this he becomes conscious of his own dignity and rises into self-satisfaction and enjoyment. By this he becomes useful to the world, a crown of glory to his friends, and respected and loved by all. By this he becomes acquainted with the wonderful works of God which are everywhere spread around him—and by this he becomes acquainted with our holy religion, is impressed with its precepts, and directed to heaven. By education nations enjoy all the blessings of society. Agriculture, manufactures, and commerce, which bless mankind with all the necessaries and conveniences of life, are perfected by the all-powerful hand of education. By this also the government of a nation is moulded, and its citizens rise to a knowledge of the rights of man and the enjoyment of civil liberty. In short, by this only, a nation is made happy at home and respectable abroad.

Such then, my friends, being the immense value of education, let all embark in its cause. Let government and able individuals offer their patronage and encouragement. Let parents exhaust their tenderest affections in this glorious work. Let teachers realize and carefully discharge the amazing responsibility which lies upon them. Let both sexes equally share in those exertions; let them be begun early and no time be lost. Let youth be impressed with the value of a good education and the laborious attention necessary to acquire it. Let their exertions be measured by the greatness and value of the work and the brevity and value of the morning of life and correspondent to the anxious wishes, prayers, and exertions of their parents and instructors. As all of us are equally interested in the great and common cause; let us, in heart and hand, unite to advance it, and the blessings of God will attend us.

AMEN.

# 6

# SAMUEL HARRISON SMITH

*Remarks on Education: Illustrating the Close Connection Between Virtue and Wisdom. To Which Is Annexed a System of Liberal Education. Which, Having Received the Premium Awarded by the American Philosophical Society, December 15th, 1797, Is Now Published by Their Order. (Philadelphia, 1798)*

[Samuel Harrison Smith (1772-1845) shared with Samuel Knox the prize offered by the American Philosophical Society in 1797 for the best essay on a national system of education. The youngest of the essayists in this collection, Smith was graduated from the University of Pennsylvania in 1787, at the age of fifteen. In 1796 he launched a long career as a party journalist by publishing a Jeffersonian newspaper in Philadelphia; under his editorship the *National Intelligencer* became the official organ of the Jefferson administration. This essay, written in 1796, was published at Philadelphia by John Ormrod in 1798. Smith's stress upon the mutual dependence of a climate of freedom, economic and social opportunity, and education makes him an authentic prophet of the American experience. His recognition of the probable role of applied intelligence in significantly reducing the demands of physical labor in America make him a remarkable guide to the American future.]

# PREFACE

THE following pages were written in the summer of 1796. They are presented to the public, with only a few verbal alterations, as they were then written. New ideas have since occurred to the author, and those which are contained in the essay might, in many instances, have been better expressed. But as the production, as it now appears, received the premium, it was thought improper to make any substantial additions.

As this performance may be read by some persons unacquainted with the author, it may be proper to state that he neither claims the reverence due to age nor the respect attached to established reputation. The fewness of his years preclude the former, while his moderate attainments withhold the latter. If the efforts which he has made shall excite the genius of his fellow citizens and he shall prove, in a degree however limited, the instrument of attracting the public attention to a subject of all others the most momentous, he will be rewarded to the extent of his wishes.

# REMARKS ON EDUCATION

THE man who aspires to the honor of forming a system of education adapted to a republic should either possess the capacity of original reflection or that of improving, without adopting the ideas of others. His hatred to vice and aversion to error should be as strong as his attachment to virtue and love of truth. He should look upon the sentiments of the dead with distrust and oppose with intrepidity the prejudices of the living. As the tribunal to which he appeals may be shrouded in delusion, he must have the courage to rend the veil that intercepts the light of truth. He must consider the first suggestions of his own mind as treacherous, nor suffer them to form a link in his chain of reasoning till they shall have passed the ordeal of re-iterated investigation. Having undergone this trial unimpaired, he will dare to hold them forth to truth, as her legitimate off-spring, and to prejudice, as her merited scourge. No motive can bear him through this arduous performance but a supreme sense of duty, which, feeling ample retribution from the con-sciousness of doing good, neither solicits nor despises general applause.

The two great objects of a correct education are to make men virtuous and wise.

The terms virtuous and wise do not seem susceptible of absolute definition. Accordingly, as applied to different persons and varying circumstances, they present different aspects, though it be possible, nay probable, that the elements or first principles of each, however modified by endless combination, are the same. This hypothesis derives some confirmation from the great affinity of one virtue to another and the close alliance between the several departments of science and literature.

Without attempting precise definition, it may be sufficiently correct, so far as it regards the objects of this essay, to style VIRTUE that active exertion of our faculties which in the highest degree promotes our own happiness and that of our fellow men; and WISDOM, that intelligent principle which improves our faculties, affords them the means of useful exertion, and deter-mines the objects on which they are exercised.

While wisdom and virtue have united, time immemorial, to panegyrise each other in reference to the general good they produce in the world, two questions of great importance have remained undecided, viz.

I. Whether wisdom and virtue are in any degree necessarily connected; and if they are, whether universally or partially.

II. Whether wisdom, in its greatest practical extension, would, if universally diffused, produce the greatest portion of general happiness.

It will be acknowledged that these points deserve a patient

discussion, as their decision will determine the definite objects of education and as it is absolutely necessary that man should know the *objects* he desires to accomplish before he can apply, with the prospect of a successful result, the *means* adapted to secure them.

I. The first inquiry is, "Whether wisdom and virtue are, in any degree, necessarily connected; and if they are, whether universally or partially."

It has been the opinion of some distinguished philosophers that virtue and instinct are the same and that a wise providence has not left the direction of the moral principle under the capricious and feeble influence of reason, while others have contended that although man be by nature ignorant and entirely destitute of moral principle, yet that he possesses faculties capable of high improvement, if not of perfection itself. Both these systems, notwithstanding their numerous votaries, are probably founded in error.

If instinct and virtue be synonymous, it is clear that where there is most instinct there should be most virtue and that, as the brute creation possess instinct in a much higher degree than man, they must likewise possess virtue in a higher degree. This result will not be seriously contended for by anyone. For, however ferocious and ignorant man may be, he is infinitely surpassed in these qualities by every animal that has the capacity of being ferocious. In this contrast too, it is proper to observe that, however the instinct of the brute may withhold him from doing injury, it seldom, if ever, inspires him with the ardor of doing good.

Were instinct and virtue the same, it would be clear that the infant would be more virtuous than his sire and the savage inhabitant of the forest more virtuous than the offspring of civilization and science. For the ears of the infant are open to the voice of nature alone, while those of its parent are not altogether regardless of the dictates of reason. A precise analogy exists between the infant and its parent and the savage and civilized man; the mind of the savage is still in its infancy,

while civilization, if the expression be allowed, imparts manhood to the mind. If this point remain still undecided in the
mind of any, let it be asked if the idiot or the lunatic are ever
esteemed virtuous? It will then be seen that virtue without
reason is a phantom which never existed.

Those who would ascribe everything to reason and nothing
to nature probably adopted their ideas more from a conviction
that the rival system was false than from any distinct conviction
of the truth of their own and from that disposition of the mind
which makes us readily, if not eagerly, embrace the reverse of
that which we have found to be erroneous.

To affirm that because education does much, it can therefore
accomplish everything, is to pronounce a maxim refuted by
universal experience. Every circumstance in this life partakes
of a finite nature, and the power of education, however great,
has doubtless its limits.

However difficult, if not impossible, it might be to gain the
assent of some philosophers to the system of natural inequality
in reference to virtue or capacity, they will, without hesitation,
agree that the physical part of man is infinitely modified by
nature; they will also grant that an infinite variety seems to be
delighted in by the author of nature, and that this variety is
most displayed in those works which abound in the highest
degree with qualities that excite our admiration or regard. Both
these instances, borrowed from material objects, furnish striking analogies, illustrative of the existence of variety of morality
and intellect in different minds uninfluenced by education. Is it
to be believed that an object so important as variety appears
to be in the estimation of the author of nature should be left to
the control of causes operating so unequally and in so contracted a sphere as reason and civilization? Were it to depend
entirely on these accidental circumstances, might it not be
highly endangered? Might it not be lost?

There are some things which, however controverted by the
refinements of philosophy, will always continue to be held in
secure belief by the good sense of mankind. Such is the con-

viction of natural bias—of one person possessing genius; another, fancy; a third, memory; etc.—

The deductions from this concise and necessarily superficial view of a subject in some respects intricate are that nature is neither so liberal nor education so omnipotent as the rival systems affirm; that man is indebted to both; that certain passions are born with him which he cannot exterminate but may control; that a varied capacity is imparted to him which by education he can weaken or improve; but that still the traces of nature are visible in his thoughts and actions; and that her voice never ceases to be heard amidst all the refinements of art.

But even granting what is far from being the truth, that man, unenlightened by education, has engraven upon his heart certain great principles of duty and is possessed of the means necessary for their discharge, it yet remains uncontested that these principles are few and undefined and that they do not comprehend half the relations in which men stand towards each other. If follows, of course, that they must be extended and improved before they can answer the great purposes for which they were originally implanted in man and submitted to his guidance, modification, and extension.

Besides, it should never be forgotten in discussions similar to this that man is already in a great degree civilized and that though it may be possible for the savage to resist the force of improvement and remain unshaken in his attachment to his original state, yet that man, once civilized, has it not in his power to return to his natural condition. He may overturn all the trophies of the arts, he may consign to the flames every vestige of science, he may extinguish every spark of genius, but he is still unable to reduce himself to the savage state. We behold him more debased, perhaps, than the barbarian, but without his ferocity. The world abounds with scenes in which the triumphs of science have been succeeded by the most brutal ignorance, over which fear, meanness, and indolence have spread their gloomy features, features the very opposite of those which characterize the savage life.

We cannot, therefore, err in assuming it as a fact that virtue and wisdom are in some degree necessarily connected, that the crude wisdom which nature bestows is unequal to the production and government of virtue such as man in his pursuit of happiness discovers it to be his interest to practice, and that to insure this desirable object it is necessary that the original faculties of the mind should be vigorously exercised, extended, and strengthened.

It still remains to be considered whether wisdom and virtue are partially or universally connected.

It is generally agreed that no being can be perfectly good without being perfectly wise. Such is the sublime idea we form of deity. It will be observed that perfect goodness is not here made to depend solely on the *intention* of the agent but also on the *good effected,* as we now consider virtue an efficient principle exerting all the energies of its nature.

The assertion that the man who, without equaling this character, approaches it the nearest, would partake in the highest degree of the divine excellence, might be deemed correct were not the world full of examples of men who, though possessed of comprehensive powers of mind, are not only deficient in the exercise of virtue but actually famed for the most profligate indulgence in vice. This enigma, however, admits of easy solution. Great endowments of mind are so rare that they are seldom displayed without exciting more envy than attachment. He who not only admires but esteems another for his talents must possess no inconsiderable portion of talent himself, just as the best evidence of a supreme love of virtue is a high regard for the source of all virtue. The class of men possessed of these qualities being small and that possessed of different, if not hostile qualities, being very numerous, it is not surprising that resentment and malice should be active in their efforts to crush so formidable an adversary. Thus the most unworthy means are used to nip in the bud talents qualified to enlarge the sphere of human happiness.

Human virtue has its limits. To be the object of unceasing

calumny and detraction, without fighting for vengeance, would argue an apathy of heart by no means mortal. The subject of oppression has now in his turn recourse to those means which had been so successfully applied to his ruin, and finding them successful, he throws away the crutch of truth for the staff of deception. Ceasing to feel an interest in that virtue which he had just seen so much despised, his ambition grasps objects which bring with them immediate gratification and lull the conscience to a dangerous repose. Wealth, power, and pleasure throw out their gay and splendid solicitations, and virtue is exiled from the heart in which it lately delighted to dwell.

This would not be the case if virtue and talents were as common as vice and ignorance. The moment a majority enlist themselves on the side of the former marks the era of their eternal reign. This era is that which all good and great men should unite to hasten.

From a review of history, it will appear that just in proportion to the cultivation of science and the arts has the happiness of man advanced in the nation which cultivated them. And this arose in a great measure from this consideration. The wants of nature are few in its unimproved state. Man of course is exempt from the necessity of making any great efforts for his support. He is therefore indolent. Not dependent on another for anything which his heart holds dear, he is reserved, distant, unaccommodating in his deportment. He scarcely merits the epithet of a social being. Of course, if his vices are not numerous, his virtues are still less so.

The very reverse of this takes place as society improves. The dearest part of man's happiness in this stage of his existence is connected with a supply of articles which depend on the industry of one who is alike dependent on him. Hence a reciprocity of wants! Hence the origin of new and permanent regards, the parents of a thousand new virtues! From what source do these proceed, but from the development of reason, suggesting to man the improvement of his situation? This improvement seems susceptible of endless extension. Hence the conclusion that reason in alliance with virtue admits of progression without termination and that the purity of the last is best secured by the strength of the first.

We proceed to consider,

II. Whether wisdom itself, in its greatest extension, would, if universally diffused, produce the greatest portion of general happiness.

The affirmative side of this question will be illustrated by considering:

That the diffusion of knowledge actually produces some virtues, which without it would have no existence, and that it strengthens and extends all such virtues as are generally deemed to have, in a limited degree, an existence independent of uncommon attainments. And that,

The exercise of these virtues is the only certain means of securing real happiness.

The virtues, which are the exclusive and appropriate offspring of an enlightened understanding, are those which are disconnected with any particular time, person, or place. Existing without reference to these, a spirit of universal philanthropy is inspired that views the whole world as a single family and transfers to it the feelings of regard which are indulged towards the most amiable of our acquaintance. This sentiment, free from the alloy of personal consideration or national attachment, lifts the mind to an elevation infinitely superior to the sensation of individual regard, superior to the ardent feelings of patriotism and rivals, in a measure, the enjoyment of the sublime ideas we connect with the apprehension of the divine mind. This tone of mind must acknowledge congeniality with the noblest virtues. The mind is full and yet tranquil. The turbulence of passion is subdued into a reverence of reason. Man feels himself too ennobled to do a base or a mean thing. He yields to an irresistible enthusiasm to achieve whatever unites the highest portion of greatness with the largest portion of goodness. Language is inadequate to the description of the feelings of a man thus inspired; it hastens to his actions, which can receive only a feeble delineation.

It will be found still more unequivocally that a diffusion of knowledge strengthens and extends all such virtues as have in a limited degree an existence independent of uncommon attainments. This class of virtues comprehends those which are created by the relation in which one man stands to another and which are the basis of what may be denominated common duty.

The discretion with which man is vested implies the necessity of some knowledge. Were it not for this possession, he would be the sport of casualty and accident. He would nominally be his own master, but really a slave to some unknown power.

Nature appears to have been liberal in its endowments to most of her offspring, as far as respects the preservation of each species, but to have been least liberal in this respect to man, doubtless because she has lavished her bounty in imparting to him alone the capacity of gradual and large improvement.

The doctrine of original depravity here affords a forcible illustration. It is not material to decide whether this belief be correctly true in the extent to which some writers have carried it or whether the alleged depravity be a crime or only a defect. It is sufficient that such a belief almost universally prevails and that all mankind acknowledge the vast intermediate space that lies between the barrenness of the state of nature and the improvement effected by a liberal education. This general opinion of mankind is alike authoritative in regard to virtue as well as reason. If it has any superior application, it tends more to establish, in the natural state, the absence of virtue than of intellect.

All agree that virtue can never be carried too far. But does not the truth of this remark depend entirely upon the manner in which virtue is directed or more properly, perhaps, on an accurate definition of it? If this be true, will not the greatest portion of virtue be ascribed to the man who, with given means, accomplishes the most good? And is not this the same with saying that virtue in its highest exercise requires the greatest attainments? If it be inquired what these attainments should be, it may be replied that, as all knowledge is susceptible of practical application and is abused when it does not receive such application, it is improper to fix any limits to the improvement of the mind which in proportion to its extension is qualified to effect general good.

"In general and in sum," says Lord Bacon,* "certain it is that *veritas* and *bonitas* differ but as the seal and the print, for truth prints goodness, and they be the clouds of error which descend in the storms of passion and perturbation."

The duties of men are precisely co-extensive with their knowledge. If that be granted, which cannot be denied, that every man is bound to do all the good he can, then follows clearly the obligation of everyone to enlarge the powers of his mind as the only means of extending the sphere of his usefulness.

It has been observed, in refutation of these remarks, that half the knowledge of which philosophy boasts withdraws the mind from useful employment by occupying it with considerations of idle curiosity and unproductive speculation. But if it be inquired by whom this observation has been made, it will appear that literature and science disclaim it, that it has generally arisen from the indolence and envy of ignorance or sprung from the malice of blasted pretensions. It is true that he whose years revolve in acquiring, without using, learning, is even more selfish and criminal than the miser, as he hoards from society a greater good; and, in this view of the subject, what Bacon says is strictly just:

"As for the philosophers, they make imaginary laws for imaginary commonwealths, and their discoveries are as the stars, which give little light, because they are so high."†

But has that science been ever named, the prosecution of

---

* Bacon, vol. 2, p. 447. [*The Works of Francis Bacon* . . . , 4 vols. (London: A. Millar, 1740), II, 447.]

† Bacon, vol. 2, p. 537. [*Works*, II, 537-538.]

which is entirely unconnected with the general good? Has not astronomy, now acknowledged to be the most sublime of studies, which unites whatever is great and astonishing both on the moral and physical scale, been the theme of unconscious ignorance and folly? Has not chemistry been assailed by the too successful satire of illiterate wit? That satire which now fastens on the departments of natural history and botany? Has not superstition attempted to identify astronomy and profanity and for a time succeeded? And yet astronomy‡ now holds, by an undissenting voice, an elevated rank among the sciences, and chemistry, notwithstanding the philosopher's stone, unfolds, every day its high practical importance, and discoveries which at first promised only cold speculative truth have produced the greatest practical good.§

It is worthy of remark that all kinds of knowledge are intimately allied and that the perfection of one department of science depends as much on the advancement of other departments as it does on the accurate development of its own peculiar principles.‖ An exclusive devotedness of the mind to one branch of knowledge, instead of enlarging, will impair it. Instead of furnishing it with truth, it will burden it with error. Of this tendency Locke relates several whimsical instances.

‡ "Astronomy is not merely a speculative science: its use is as extensive as its researches are profound. To it navigation owes its safety; to it commerce is indebted for its extension and geography for its improvement. But what above all speaks its praise is that it has led the way to the diffusion of knowledge and to the civilization of mankind." Sullivan, vol. II, p. 426. [Richard Joseph Sullivan, *A View of Nature, in Letters to a Traveller among the Alps. With Reflections on Atheistical Philosophy, Now Exemplified in France*, 6 vols. (London: T. Becket, 1794), II, 426.]

§ "What benefit do we receive from the celebrated deeds of an Alexander or a Cæsar? But Pythagoras gave us our commerce and our riches: if it be true that he invented the 47th proposition of the first book of Euclid, which is the foundation of trigonometry and consequently of navigation." Sullivan, vol. 6, p. 303. [*View of Nature*, VI, 303.]

‖ "Generally let this be a rule that all partitions of knowledge be accepted rather for lines and veins than for sections and separations and that the continuance and entireness of knowledge be preserved. For the contrary hereof hath made particular sciences to become barren, shallow, and erroneous, while they have not been nourished and maintained from the common fountain." Bacon, vol. 2, p. 478. [*Works*, II, 478.]

"A metaphysician," he says, "will bring plowing and gardening immediately to abstract notions; an alchemist will reduce divinity to the maxims of his laboratory and allegorize the scriptures into the philosopher's stone. And I heard once a man who had more than ordinary excellence in music seriously accommodate Moses's seven days of the first week to the seven notes of music, as if from thence had been taken the measure and method of the creation."[1] He, therefore, who grants it to be necessary that one science should be deeply explored yields more than the superficial observer imagines. He acknowledges the propriety of applying all the necessary means, and these will be found to embrace a considerable acquaintance with almost every branch of knowledge.

Were a specification to be made of those circumstances most closely connected with the happiness of man, it would appear in how eminent a degree they are promoted by a cultivated understanding.

Under the head of morals, it would appear that the virtues appropriate to a family would be secured as well as rendered more captivating, secured by the enlightened conviction of the intimate convection between duty and interest, rendered more captivating by their borrowing a new character from the liberal spirit inspired by reason. To the natural tie of parental regard would be added the grateful sensation excited in the mind of a child from the communication of new ideas and the production, of course, of new pleasures. To the magic of instinct would be superadded the charm of reflection.

The sense of justice and honesty would be confirmed by the folly of injustice and dishonesty. Supposing a general illumination of mind to prevail, the means of detecting and the consequences of exposing dishonesty would be so easy and serious that every rational being would see his interest inseparably connected with justice and honesty.

Patriotism, a virtue which has fertilized the barren rock and given the greatest expansion to the mind and the heart, would become a steady and a rational principle. Founded on an unprejudiced attachment to country, we should cease to glory in error, solely because it proceeded from our ancestors. Love of country would impel us to transfuse into our own system of economy every improvement offered by other countries. In this case, we should not be attached so much to the soil as to the institutions and manners of our country.

In physics, it would appear that in proportion to the extension of philosophical research new connections and relations are discovered between natural objects, which result in discoveries of high practical use, promoting whatever tends to the convenience and comfort of social life, enlarging the sphere of harmless gratification, and giving birth to new and frequently ingenious occupations.

It remains to be considered whether the exercise of enumerated virtues be not the only means of securing real happiness.

No necessity is believed to exist to prove that a system of pure selfishness is hostile in the highest degree to happiness. If this system should find any advocates but those whose object it is to dazzle by ingenuity and wit, instead of convincing by argument, I would appeal to the universal odium attached to an indulgence of those passions which center entirely in selfish enjoyment. Avarice, drunkenness, monastic seclusion are all now the objects of impartial execration, while the practicer of these selfish indulgences holds in as great contempt the world which despises him and feels himself independent only in wretchedness.

I shall not dwell longer on this subject, but assume from what has been already said and from that which must obviously suggest itself to every mind that the exercise of feelings which lead to beneficent actions is the surest pledge of internal happiness.

Whether reason itself would be fertile in the production of virtue need not be decided. It is probable that reason is only that power which directs the passions to their fit objects and determines the force with which they ought to be applied. Rousseau says, "It is by the activity of our passions that our reason improves; we covet knowledge merely because we court enjoyment, and it is impossible to conceive why a man exempt from fears and desires should take the trouble to reason. The passions, in their turn, owe their origin to our wants."¶

The passions, as imparted by nature, are few but impetuous. The whole energy of the soul here speaks in every word and action. The conduct of one individual to another, in proportion as man obtains a more correct knowledge of duty, becomes the subject of a certain portion, often a moderate one, of praise or blame, of reward or punishment. And, accordingly, civilized man is as cautious in pronouncing an opinion on the conduct of the person who invites his strictures, as unbridled passion is impetuous and rash. The last knows no gradations between virtue and vice and of course loves or hates in the extremest degree. The consequence is that man is miserable, as miserable perhaps from the consciousness of ill-directed vengeance or misapplied regard as from the sense of undeserved resentment.

In proportion to the advancement of the arts and sciences, the passions are increased in number and abridged in force by the diversity of objects which solicit their exercise. Man, reduced from a sullen state of independence, becomes the subject of innumerable wants, the center of innumerable pleasures. Avarice, so congenial to ignorance and indolence, is robbed of more than half its violence by the love of pleasure and a regard to popular opinion. It never fails to be as much weakened in the vortex of activity as it is cherished in the listlessness of seclusion. In large commercial towns there are few misers. In monasteries they abound. Besides, the ambition of acquiring more keeps afloat immense riches, which circulate till they become the inheritance of an heir, who seldom feels a disposition to hoard them.

¶ Rousseau, *On Inequality of Mankind*, 8 vo. edit., p. 40. [Jean Jacques Rousseau, *A Discourse upon the Origin and Foundation of the Inequality among Mankind* (London: R. and J. Dodsley, 1761), p. 40.]

Pity is said by some writers to be the strongest passion of nature. But how does it operate? Upon every object it meets. Accident accomplishes everything. Entirely mechanical, it as frequently encourages vice as it relieves virtue, whereas knowledge produces discernment and discrimination. The benevolence of an improved mind is virtue, because it aids merit in distress; natural pity is often vice, because it is blind and as frequently assists the wicked as the good, perhaps oftener, as virtue is more averse to solicitation than vice.

Let us consider the different effects of pity and benevolence, as here distinguished, on the person who exercises them. Pity is a mere natural impulse; there is no merit in obeying its voice; the good which it does is forgotten as soon as accomplished; all the happiness it affords is confined to a moment, and this is an unreflecting happiness; it is the happiness of an infant. Benevolence, on the contrary, is never practiced without reflection. It chooses its objects with care, which, when chosen, it is liberal in rewarding. It does not give to depravity the debt due to virtue and thereby generate self-reproach. Virtue and merit are its creditors, to whom it ever struggles to be just. Gratitude, almost unknown to the dispenser of pity, is the offspring of benevolence. Remembrance recalls, perhaps heightens, the pleasures excited by the good effected, and he who is actuated by enlightened benevolence is amply rewarded by his own feelings, independently of the treatment he may receive from the object of his bounty or the propitious influence of his actions on his future peace.

The same remarks, illustrating the difference between the passions of the ignorant and the wise, might be extensively applied with but little variation. Suffice it in addition to say that, with the wise, inclination is supplanted by duty, caprice by consistency. Emulation and competition too come in with all their forces and, perhaps, produce more virtue in the world than they found in it.*

---

* "And it is without all controversy that learning doth make the minds of men gentle, generous, amiable, and pliant to government, whereas ignorance

He who has been accustomed to feel within himself the resource of reflection and the capacity of improvement delights in abstracting his attention from grovelling pursuits and in disengaging himself from the sordid cares of low occupation. However impossible it be for him entirely to withdraw himself from these engagements, yet he always possesses an unexhausted treasure on which he may draw when oppressed with them. Neither the mind nor the body seem designed for one uniform employment. The more extensive the objects, therefore, within the reach of man, the larger is his circle of enjoyment. History enforces the truth of this remark. Who more happy as well as distinguished than they who alternately exchanged the plough for the closet, who now procured food for the body and now sought food for the mind? Who more unrivalled in tranquil pleasure, in unambitious retirement, in splendid consideration than Cincinnatus?[2]

That man seems, on the whole, to be the most happy, who, possessed of a large stock of ideas, is in the constant habit of increasing them and whom every hour of his existence renders more informed. The energy of such a mind is almost without limits; it admits of constant activity, for when fatigued with one train of ideas, it finds repose in another. A rich variety of enjoyment is ever before it, the bare consciousness of possessing which is sufficient of itself to make it happy.

Some notice is due to the objections to the connection between knowledge and happiness. It is said that a refinement of ideas disinclines the mind to an attention to common objects, to which a very moderate degree of reflection is equal. This objection, if it has any present force at all, would be wholly removed by that knowledge becoming common which is now rare. We now find it to be the general exclamation that prosperity is altogether owing to accident, and this remark is sanc-

---

makes them churlish, thwarting, and mutinous. And the evidence of time doth clear this assertion, considering that the most barbarous, rude, and unlearned times have been most subject to tumults, seditions, and changes." Bacon, vol. 2, p. 421. [*Works*, II, 421.]

tioned, in some measure, by the concurrence of the wise as well as the uninformed. This arises from the imperfection of human knowledge, whereby men obtain a good desired, not through the fit means as discovered by reason, but as suggested by accident. Hence the inclination is so often repugnant to availing itself of the means of acquiring a desirable object that it is frequently coerced into them, contrary to its wishes. Hence the affairs of the world are called a lottery, where fortune presides and reason is blind.

As, however, every effect is inseparable from its cause, and as the events of this life, which men most covet, depend upon causes which the improved mind without doubt possesses the power of discovering, the time may and probably will arrive in which by far the greater part, if not the whole, of those things at present the gift of accident will be the reward of virtue and reflection. It will then be as great a phenomenon for wisdom not to be succeeded by prosperity, as it is now to be connected with it, even in reference to those objects which it ever will deem subordinate.

One philosopher of great distinction, it is granted, has said that were man to consult his real happiness, he would never reflect;[3] intimating that the act of reflection is injurious to health. This aspersion on science can be traced, as it regards Rousseau, to no better origin than that of a mind inconsistent with itself and discontented with every present enjoyment. The mind of Rousseau was, without doubt, a great one; it emitted as copiously as genius or fancy could desire the sparks of a noble intellect, which dared to disdain the shackles of prejudice and break the chains of ignorance. But it must be allowed that in those cases which admitted of personal application he grossly erred and generally suffered his strong sense to be overruled by his inexplicable feelings.

Complete refutation, however, will be the portion of this injurious remark, by considering the persevering zeal which has characterized the conduct of the cultivators of science, by considering their unanimous opinion that the moment which gives birth to a new thought is a period of unrivaled enjoyment, which has been compared to the feelings of deity at the creation;† and lastly, by considering that longevity has, in a remarkable degree, been the reward of those who have cultivated science. Let anyone who doubts this fact consult a biographical dictionary, and all the prejudices he ever possessed on the subject must vanish; he will grant that as the mind depends on the exercise of the body for its vigor, so the health of the body, in its turn, is promoted by the active employment of the faculties of the mind.

One great objection cannot be here overlooked; its discussion is highly important from its connection with numerous prejudices and particularly with the passion of avarice. It will be said that though refined happiness be intimately connected with virtue and knowledge, yet that this kind of happiness was never designed for the mass of any nation, as their subsistence depends entirely on labor and the productiveness of labor depends on the time devoted to it.

It only requires a zealous disposition to embrace *what ought to be,* instead of clinging to *what is,* to disarm this objection of all its force. It is granted that a small portion of that time which is at present occupied by the labor of the body, will, should these ideas be adopted, be absorbed in the exercise of the mind. But it should be observed:

1. That it is not true, as implied in the objection, that the mind and body are incapable of contemporaneous employment. So far is this from being a fact that some activity of body is absolutely necessary to vigorous reflection. The more severe the reflection, the more likely is the student to be involved in even involuntary exercise. Viewing this objection with the greatest partiality, it can only apply to those studies that require the highest abstraction of mind, which will forever be confined to a few. Those trains of thought which are connected with practi-

† "Is not such the delight of mental superiority that none on whom nature or study have conferred it would purchase the gifts of fortune by its loss." Sullivan, vol. 6, p. 102. [*View of Nature,* VI, 110].

cal improvement will be aided rather than impaired by labor, if it be not uncommonly severe.

2. The actual labor necessary to subsist man is much less than that which occupies the whole of his time. The hours at present devoted to labor are about twelve. Let us suppose these to be abridged by bringing them down to ten. A question occurs whether this diminution of time will lessen the mass of articles of necessity or convenience fabricated. The solution of this question either affirmatively or negatively is of little consequence, though from the first suggestions of the mind it would seem important. It is not probable it would produce the diminution supposed, because ten hours of active labor may in their result be equal to twelve, as there is a protraction of labor destructive of all energy.

This is so abundantly illustrated in the case of slaves, compared with freemen, that the fact needs only to be mentioned to be decisive, but yielding for a moment that ten hours of manual labor will not produce so much as twelve, will not more be gained by improved modes of labor than is lost by this dereliction of two hours? Will not the habit of reflection and progressive improvement continually devise new means of accomplishing a given object? Have not the powers of machinery already given a new creation to manufactures? And is not agriculture equally susceptible of improvement?

But granting that this abridgment of labor would diminish the articles of use, is it unequivocal that this effect would be an evil? The necessaries of life would still be produced in abundance. The conveniencies of life produced would be fully equal to a moderate indulgence of its pleasures. The only deficiency existing would apply to articles of luxury. And whether these ought to be encouraged or repressed cannot be a question in a state of society in which every man is a candidate for equal happiness. An indulgence in luxury is a selfish enjoyment, which may be said to seduce everyone from his duty. The less, therefore, it prevails, the better for virtue and general happiness.

3. The relative wealth of individuals, under this arrangement, would remain the same with that under the old one, as far as it applied to the citizens of the United States. Some small difference might be produced between the relative wealth of the United States and that of foreign nations, but its effects seem too unimportant to be dwelt on.

Let us, then, consider a moderate increase of the hours of reflection and a small decrease of those of labor as a leading feature in a system of republican education. He who thinks frequently imbibes a habit of independence and of self-esteem which are perhaps the great and the only preservatives of virtue. Let us consider this feature as new and as one which would be happily distinctive. Let us consider it as the prerogative of political virtue to ennoble man as much as it is the assumption of political vice to degrade him.

A review of what I have written convinces me that I have entered a field which seems to acknowledge no limits. Points of morality and expedience occur in profusion whose elucidation still demands the highest talents, after having employed, for ages, the deepest powers of research.

In the subsequent part of my remarks, I shall, to avoid prolixity, aim at the most rigid conciseness and trust almost entirely to the reader for an examination of what I state.

The diffusion of knowledge, co-extensive with that of virtue, would seem to apply with close precision to a republican system of education, because:

1. An enlightened nation is always most tenacious of its rights.

2. It is not the interest of such a society to perpetuate error, as it undoubtedly is the interest of many societies differently organized.

3. In a republic the sources of happiness are open to all without injuring any.

4. If happiness be made at all to depend on the improvement of the mind and the collision of mind with mind, the happiness of an individual will greatly depend upon the general

diffusion of knowledge and a capacity to think and speak correctly.

5. Under a republic, duly constructed, man feels as strong a bias to improvement as under a despotism he feels an impulse to ignorance and depression.

We have now reached the goal of the preceding speculations. The necessary limits to an essay of this nature have prohibited minute illustration, but it has, we hope, been made to appear with sufficient perspicacity that human happiness depends upon the possession of virtue and wisdom, that virtue cannot be too highly cultivated, that it is only secure when allied with knowledge, and of consequence that knowledge itself cannot possibly be too extensively diffused. It follows that the great object of a liberal plan of education should be the almost universal diffusion of knowledge.

But as knowledge is infinite and as its complete attainment requires more time than man has at his command, it becomes interesting to assign:

I.   The time fit to be devoted to education.

II.   The objects proper to be accomplished; and

III.   The manner of accomplishing them.

I.  *The time fit to be devoted to education.*

Philosophy, which is but another word for experience, has decided the happiness of man to depend upon the labor of the body and the exercise of the mind. It had been well for mankind, had the human race in its earliest age been under the control of principles of legislation which by a judicious apportionment of the hours of reflection to those of labor had produced in infancy and youth habits destined from their strength to remain unimpaired in advanced age. Had the voice of philosophy dictated such a system, it would have been established on these principles. Bare subsistence requires certain articles which are the product of labor. These are necessaries of life and must be obtained by labor. Convenience demands a further supply, the furnishing of which would occupy an additional period of labor. This convenience is essentially connected with happiness, mental as well as corporeal. Labor would, therefore, have been called upon to satisfy the claims of necessity and convenience; it would have been unseduced by the allurements of luxury.

Unfortunately for mankind no such system has been adopted. It has scarcely even been thought of. The novelty of the plan forms no objection to its truth. If it possess decided advantages, let us dare to believe human virtue equal to its accomplishment.

We have seen that in a nation in which the hours of labor should be abridged and those of reflection increased, no injury would be sustained by individuals and little, if any, by the nation itself.

It were a vain attempt, however, instantaneously to inspire with a love of science men from whose minds reflection has long been alienated. The improvement proposed must be the effect of a system of education gradually and cautiously developed.

Previously to any prospect of success, one principle must prevail. Society must establish the right to educate, and acknowledge the duty of having educated, all children. A circumstance so momentously important must not be left to the negligence of individuals. It is believed that this principle is recognized in almost all our state constitutions. If so, the exercise of it would not be contested. Indeed, whether at present acknowledged or not, it would produce such beneficial effects, as well in reference to the parent as the child, that a general acquiescence might be relied on.‡

Having contemplated in reference to man an abatement of two hours of labor, the next object of inquiry is what time should be devoted to the education of youth. It should unques-

‡ "It is proper to remind parents that their children belong to the state and that in their education they ought to conform to the rules which it prescribes." Preliminary speech of Cambaceres, on a plan of a Civil Code for France. [Jean Jacques Regis de Cambaceres (1753-1824), French statesman and legal expert, played an important role in drafting the Napoleonic civil code. His "Discours Preliminaire" supporting a projected code appears in *Corps Legislatif: Projet de Code Civil, présenté au Conseil des Cinq-Cents* . . . (Paris: Imprimerie Nationale, 1796). The section here translated by Smith is on p. 8.

tionably be much larger, as during this period the mind is un-improved, as impressions of the greatest strength are rapidly made, and as the future bias of the mind entirely depends upon the improvement of these impressions. The period, however, should have its limits. Study should never be continued after it becomes oppressive. The preceptor should be as cautious in using every means necessary to prevent disgust as he ought to be zealous in exciting a thirst of knowledge. Without aiming at rigid precision, in considering the claims of labor and study, we shall not, perhaps, materially err in assigning four hours each day to education.

II. *The objects proper to be accomplished.*

It is necessary that the principle of a universal diffusion of knowledge should be in the highest degree energetic. This is a principle which cannot be too extensively embraced, for it is too true that all the efforts of an enlightened zeal will never make a whole nation as well informed as its interests would prescribe.

But this necessary limit forms no objection to every practicable extension of it. We shall be furnished with irrefragable evidence of its beneficial tendency, on considering that knowledge has only produced injurious effects when it has been the subject of monopoly. The efforts of ignorance to oppress science have excited a spirit of retaliation, which we must not be surprised at beholding, in its turn, its own avenger. The moment, however, which marks the universal diffusion of science, by withdrawing the temptation to, as well as the means of, injury, will restore knowledge to its original purity and luster. It is with knowledge as with every other thing which influences the human mind. It acts precisely in proportion to the force of the object acted upon. As the beggar cannot corrupt by gold the beggar, so neither can opulence corrupt opulence. In the same manner, equality of intellectual attainments is a foe to oppression, and just as mankind shall advance in its possession, the means as well as the inducement to oppress will be annihilated.

We are correct, therefore, in declaring a diffusion of knowledge, the best, perhaps the only, pledge of virtue, of equality, and of independence.

Let us, then, with mental inflexibility, believe that though all men will never be philosophers, yet that all men may be enlightened, and that folly, unless arising from physical origin, may be banished from the society of men.§

The ideas already expressed, and those which succeed, must be understood as applicable to a system of general education. They only prescribe what it is necessary every man should know. They do not attempt to limit his acquisitions. Wealth and genius will always possess great advantages. It will be their prerogatives, if properly directed, to carry improvement to its highest eminences.

In forming a system of liberal education, it is necessary to avoid ideas of too general a character as well as those which involve too minute a specification. Considerable latitude must be allowed for the different degrees of natural capacity and the varying shades of temper and bias. It seems, therefore, fit to lay down principles which possess properties common to every mind and which will, of course, in their application, admit of few, if any, exceptions.

The first great object of a liberal system of education should be the admission into the young mind of such ideas only as are either absolutely true or in the highest degree probable; and the cautious exclusion of all error.

Were man able to trace every effect to its cause, he would probably find that the virtue or the vice of an individual, the happiness or the misery of a family, the glory or the infamy of a nation, have had their sources in the cradle, over which the prejudices of a nurse or a mother have presided. The years of infancy are those in which the chains of virtue or of vice are

§ "Let no man, upon a weak conceit of sobriety, or an ill applied moderation, think or maintain that a man can search too far, or be too well studied in the books of God's word, or in the book of God's work; divinity or philosophy; but rather let men endeavor an endless progress or proficience in truth." Bacon's *Works*, vol. 2, p. 417. [I, 417.]

generally forged. First impressions are almost omnipotent. Their reign is silent, but not on that account the less secure. The mind no sooner begins to unfold itself than it grasps with eagerness every new idea. Intoxicated, as it were, with pleasure at its reception, it surrenders itself more to enjoyment than reflection. Indeed, it has now the capacity to enjoy but not to reflect. In proportion to the length of time any idea occupies the mind does it acquire strength and produce conviction. And no sooner have these ends been accomplished than it constitutes itself the judge of every other resembling or opposing idea. Hence it tyrannizes with despotic authority.

If this view be correct, should it not be thought treason against truth and virtue to instill prejudice and error into the young mind? If this be treason against truth and virtue, what shall we say of those who inculcate principles which they know to be false and attempt in this way to establish systems that only exist in the midst of human carnage and destruction?

Whether we consider man's existence as terminated by the grave or view him, as he doubtless is, the heir of a future life, we must consider his happiness as altogether dependent on the observance of certain moral principles. The universality with which these have been received may be considered as the test of their truth. These principles are few and simple. As the mind expands they should be explained. They require no other aid than clear illustration. The unperverted understanding acknowledges their truth as it were by intuition.‖

Let then those truths in which all men agree be firmly impressed, let those which are probable be inculcated with caution, and let doubt always hang over those respecting which the

‖ "The savage receives divine truths carelessly, hears them with indifference, apprehends them confusedly, and suffers them soon to be obliterated from his memory. But a *Newton* listens to them attentively, weighs them deliberately, comprehends them accurately, and keeps them in careful remembrance. *In short nothing can secure the mind from error and imposture but the precision arising from a candid philosophical spirit, which admits no terms that are not clear, no premises that are not evident, and no conclusions that do not intuitively follow premises well ascertained.*" Sullivan's *View of Nature*, vol. 2, p. 231.

good and the wise disagree. Above all things let the infant mind be protected from conviction without proof.

But it will be said that in almost all the departments of a general plan of education, the perusal of approved books must be chiefly relied on. The indispensable economy of arrangements which are to pervade a whole society will prohibit the employment of preceptors of either great or original talents. It will therefore be fit that the preceptor, instead of inculcating his own immature ideas, should be guided by prescribed works. It is asked where performances explaining and enforcing plain and undeniable truths and avoiding prejudices or falsehoods are to be found. Such productions are acknowledged to be rare. It is also granted that this difficulty presents one of the most serious obstacles to successful education. But it is not insurmountable. It is attempted to be removed, as will appear hereafter, by offering large rewards for books of this nature and by inciting the learned by other inducements to embark in so noble a service. At present we must be satisfied in giving the preference to those works which abound most with truth and are the most exempt from error.

The elements of education, viz. reading and writing, are so obviously necessary that it is useless to do more than enumerate them.

Of nearly equal importance are the first principles of mathematics, as at present almost universally taught.

A tolerably correct idea of geography would seem, in a republic especially, to involve great advantages. The interest of the mercantile part of the community is closely connected with correct geographical knowledge. Many important departments of science include an accurate knowledge of it. But the most important consideration is that which contemplates the United States as either allied in friendship or arrayed in hostility with the other nations of the earth. In both which cases it becomes the duty of the citizen to have just ideas of the position, size, and strength of nations, that he may as much as possible confide in his own judgment in forming an opinion of our foreign relations, instead of yielding his mind to a dangerous credulity. A most interesting part of geography relates to a knowledge of our own country. Correct information on this subject will always conduce to strengthen the bands of friendship and to dissipate the misrepresentations of party prejudice.

The cultivation of natural philosophy, particularly so far as it relates to agriculture and manufactures, has been heretofore almost entirely neglected. The benefits, however, which it would produce are great, both as they regard the happiness of the individual and as they regard national wealth. Many of the labors of the farmer and the mechanic, so far from forbidding reflection, invite it. Thus the constant development of new beauties in nature and the almost as constant production of new wonders in art extort admiration from the most ignorant and even impress their minds with considerable delight. And yet how little do they know of the energies of nature or art? Lost in the contemplation of effects, the tribute of a grateful mind finds vent in simple wonder.

If we reverse the scene and behold the farmer enlightened by the knowledge of chemistry, how wide a field of reflection and pleasure, as well as profit, would acknowledge his empire?

The ingenuity of the mechanic would not long remain passive. Repeated efforts at improvement would often prove successful and be the source of new and rapid wealth. At any rate, in all these cases, whether prospered with the expected success or not, an adequate compensation would be conferred on the mind thus employed whose thoughts generally bring with them their own reward.

The circumscribed advantages, attending geographical knowledge, will be greatly enlarged by a liberal acquaintance with history. In proportion as this branch of education shall be cultivated, men will see the mighty influence of moral principle, as well on the private individuals of a community as on those who are called to preside over its public concerns. It will be distinctly seen that ambition has generally risen on a destruction of every sentiment of virtue and that it much oftener merits execration than applause. Power, long enjoyed, will appear to be hostile to the happiness and subversive of the integrity of the individual in whom it centers. Fanaticism and superstition will appear surrounded with blood and torture. War will stand forth with the boldest prominence of vice and folly and make it, for a while, doubtful whether man is most a villain or a fool. In short the mirror which history presents will manifest to man what it is probable he will become, should he surrender himself up to those selfish pursuits, which centering in his own fame alone have enabled him without horror to wade through the blood and tears of millions.

This horrid truth, confirmed by every page of history, will restrain, as it undoubted has restrained, the indulgence of furious passion. The immortal admiration attached to great and disinterested virtue, the immortal detestation inseparable from great and selfish vice, will furnish the mind at once with the strongest incentives to the one and the liveliest abhorrence of the other.

The second leading object of education should be to inspire the mind with a strong disposition to improvement.

It is acknowledged that science is still in its infancy. The combination of ideas is infinite. As this combination advances, the circle of knowledge is enlarged and of course the sphere of happiness extended. At present science is only cultivated by a few recluse students, too apt to mingle the illusions of imagination with the results of indistinct observation. Hence the reproach that theory and practice oppose each other. But no sooner shall a whole nation be tributary to science than it will dawn with new luster. To adopt a physical illustration, its rays may be expected to meet with little absorption from ignorance but to be reflected with additional luster from every object they strike.

The most splendid discoveries have not been made by philosophers of profound erudition and abstracted reflection but by men of moderate attainments and correct observation. They have proceeded from steady and patient observation.

Were the progress of a mind to improvement attended with no other effects than internal delight, it would still deserve the highest rank among those objects which produce happiness. Banishing from the mind all those sensations of indifference, ennui, and vacancy which produce effects the more cruel from their being almost wholly without remedy, it would give to existence a thousand new charms, not fleeting, but constant and always at command. The periods of youth and of active life would be invigorated, the close of existence would become a blessing instead of a burden. Is there anything in existence more interesting than an old man whose mind is stored with wisdom and whose heart is full of sensibility?

Were it supposed probable that any objection would be made to a vigorous spirit of research, an appeal might be made to the words of Dr. Clarke, alike eminent for distinction in virtue and science: "A free and impartial inquiry into truth is far from being reprehensible. On the contrary, it is a disposition which every man ought in himself to labor after and to the utmost of his power encourage in others. It is the great foundation of all our knowledge, of all true virtue, and of all sincere religion."[4]

This progressive improvement would be promoted, in the third place, by inspiring youth with a taste for and an attachment to science, so firm that it should be almost impossible to eradicate it in the subsequent periods of life.

For this purpose studies which address themselves to the heart, as well as those which require strong mental attention, should invite the exercise of their thoughts. Rewards should be liberally bestowed, as well those which furnish the means of moderate pleasure as those which confer distinction. Coercion should be seldom if ever applied.¶

¶ "The end of masters in the long course of their studies is to habituate their scholars to serious application, to make them love and value the sciences, and to cultivate such a taste as shall make them thirst after them when they are gone from school." Rollin. [Charles Rollin, *The Method of Teaching and Studying the Belles Lettres* . . . , 4 vols. (2d ed., London: A. Bettesworth and C. Hitch, 1737), IV, 263.]

But this great object would be assisted more than by any other consideration by—

Rendering, in the fourth place, knowledge as highly practical as possible.

This idea has been already noticed. But it merits a more extensive discussion. Next to the first object it claims the greatest notice.

All science ought to derive its rank from its utility. The real good which it actually does, or is capable of doing, is the only genuine criterion of its value. Man may indulge himself in sublime reveries, but the world will forever remain uninterested in them. It is only when he applies the powers of his mind to objects of general use that he becomes their benefactor; until he does this he is neither entitled to their gratitude or applause.

He is the best friend of man who makes discoveries involving effects which benefit mankind the most extensively. Moral truths are therefore of importance but little short of infinite. For they apply to numbers which almost evade enumeration and to time which loses itself in eternity. These truths, all agree, are not to be sought in the cloister. They are only acquired by uniting the calm and patient reflection of retirement with the bold and penetrating observation of active life.

In physics the happiness of mankind is in the highest degree increased by discoveries and improvements connected with agriculture and manufactures. These two occupations employ nine-tenths of most communities and a much larger proportion of others. Does it not then become an interesting inquiry whether it be not expedient in infancy and youth to communicate to the mind the leading principles of nature and art in these departments of labor, not only by a theoretical exposition of them but also by their practical development.

If almost the whole community be destined to pursue one or other of these avocations from necessity, and if it be the duty of an individual to support himself, whenever he can, by an exertion of his own powers, and if these can only yield a sure support from an ability to be acquired in youth to prosecute a particular branch of agriculture or mechanics, does it not seem to be the duty of society to control education in such a way as to secure to every individual this ability? If this ability existed, how much misery would be annihilated, how much crime would be destroyed? Even under a government,* in which the happiness of men does not appear to have been the leading object, the nobility were obliged to be instructed fully in the principles and partially in the practice of a particular trade.

Should, however, the justice of abridging natural right in these cases be doubted and its expedience denied, the propriety of a union of practical with theoretic instruction will not be contested in reference to those who are designed for agriculture or mechanics.

Naked speculation is either unintelligible or uninteresting to the young mind, while it delights in examining external appearances and often in searching after their causes. Those objects which have engaged our earliest, and surely in some respects our happiest days, are cherished and pursued by the mind with increasing delight in advanced and old age. From this plain view of the subject, it appears that in youth the addition of practical to theoretical knowledge would add to its charms; while in maturer age the blending theoretic with practical knowledge would render labor more agreeable and engaging.

As the period of education will, it is probable, in most instances be protracted till the child shall be engaged in preparing himself for some employment in life, it would be important to confine his attention in a considerable degree to the acquisition of that kind of knowledge which would be of the greatest practical use in the profession for which he is destined. Give the mind an object worthy of its efforts and you may rely upon their being made. In this case the child would realize the connection between its present pursuits and its future prosperity, and this impression could not fail to kindle new ardor in its youthful breast.

* In France.

The fifth object should be the inspiring youth with an ardent love for mankind. To accomplish this end, the preceptor should cautiously avoid instilling into the mind of his pupil a mean idea of human nature. The pages of the moralist by debasing man have aided that degeneracy which they deprecate. We should not even convey a suspicion of the honesty of him whom we wish to be virtuous. Those who have led the public mind, so far from attending to this maxim, have almost universally portrayed the heart and conduct of man as infinitely depraved, and we have often beheld the gloomy spectacle of a misanthropic infant. If we examine the tendency of the unperverted principles of nature, we must acknowledge their hostility to that suspicion and jealousy which have proceeded from the force of education.

The delight which we all feel on contemplating the absence of suspicion is an evidence of the triumph of virtue and nature. The child has no doubt of the honesty of those about him until his mind has received an artificial bias. Having received this unfortunate bias and looking upon his fellow beings as hostile, as he enters on life he treats them with suspicion and perhaps, on the supposition that they would pursue their own interest even to his injury, he hesitates not to pursue his to theirs. This aggression, on his part, cannot fail to produce from them that conduct which he has been taught to expect, and thus irrationally is strengthened a conviction dictated by prejudice.

We know, in our intercourse with the world, that confidence is the parent of friendship, which forbids its subject to do an act base or dishonorable. On the other hand, it is alike evident that distrust produces enmity and that enmity will often dictate, in the paroxysm of resentment, a mean and disgraceful action.

In whatever light this subject is viewed by reason, it will appear that men are the creatures of sentiment and that their virtue is often greatly, sometimes altogether, dependent on the opinion entertained of them by others. Let us then embrace the sentiment so forcibly expressed by Sullivan. "It is not possible," says he, "for a sane mind, for any continuance, to look upon mankind, either as emmets below his serious attention or as monsters more worthy of his hatred than his regard."[5]

III.  *The manner of accomplishing the objects of education.*

This branch of the subject may, in many respects, claim superior importance to the other branches. It involves a more detailed statement and more minute and specific ideas than those which have been already discussed.

It is to be feared, however, that the necessary specification of small objects which it requires to render it clear or useful may lessen, in the minds of some, the dignity of the subject and expose it to the edge of ridicule. But it should be considered that as education itself altogether consists in a vigilant attention to small objects and would be wholly defeated without such attention, so that system of education, other considerations being equal, must be the best which in these small objects leaves the least to error, negligence, and caprice. As in the natural world the boundless ocean takes its source in innumerable petty springs, so the mind, invigorated with extensive acquisitions, acknowledges its dependence on the humblest ideas.

Before we proceed to adjust the several parts of the system, two interesting inquiries present themselves for solution.

I.  At what age education should commence?

II.  Should education be public or private?

I.  Every correct view of human nature shows the young mind, though tender, to be capable of great improvement. The injury it so often sustains from yielding to superstitious notions, by being sacrificed to unmanly fear and by being wedded to numerous prejudices, abundantly attests the influence of certain ideas on the mind, which had it been honestly directed would have embraced truth instead of delusion and courage instead of pusillanimity. Mark the first dawnings of the mind and say if the infant exhibit any evidence of attachment to falsehood? On the contrary, with the most engaging simplicity, you behold it giving expression to truths the most obvious. Regard the interesting credulity with which the child hears a marvelous story, until its mind labor under the oppressive burden of a tissue of supernatural incidents. We may then assume it as an undeniable fact that an attachment to truth is the property of the unperverted mind.

While this principle is in its vigor, it is infinitely important that the mind should be as highly exercised as possible. But it is said that it should not be fatigued, much less oppressed. Granted. But, let it in reply be remarked that at no period of our life, as at the earliest, are we in some respects so capable of a constant exercise of our faculties. Every object around, every idea within, is then new. Novelty is the source of our highest enjoyment; of course not an object impresses the senses, not an idea is formed in the mind, which does not yield the most exquisite delight. Why is the remembrance of the scenes of childhood so dear to us, but from the interesting recollection of scenes

Forever varying, and forever new.

On this branch of the subject we may gather correct ideas by attending to the remarks of a writer of antiquity who has for the most part united with masterly skill philosophy and a knowledge of human nature. Quintilian says, "Some have thought that none should be instructed in letters who are under seven years of age, because that early period can neither comprehend learning nor endure labor.

"But what can they do better from the time at which they are able to talk? For something they must do. Or why should we slight the gain, little as it is, which occurs before the age of seven? For certainly, however little that may be which the preceding age shall have contributed, yet the boy will be learning greater things in that very year in which he would otherwise have been learning smaller. This, extended to several years, amounts to a sum, and whatever is anticipated in infancy is an acquisition to the period of youth.

"Let us not then throw away even the very first period, and the less so as the elements of learning require memory alone, which is not only found in little boys but is very tenacious in them."[6]

It is true that the measure of knowledge which infancy will receive is small. But in most systems of education it has been injudiciously restricted. The mind has lost half its vigor by being oppressed with the nomenclature of science. Languages have been exclusively forced upon it, and it has been compelled to believe legitimate science to be as unmeaning and as barren as the words which it has acquired.

Had a different plan been pursued, had our native language only occupied the attention until well understood, had the simple elements of morals and physics received concurrent inculcation, intellectual strength might have been secured instead of being spent. The mind, engaged in objects intimately connected with its own happiness and the happiness of those around it, would have imbibed a love of knowledge which would probably never have been lost.†

These remarks are forcibly illustrated by a luminous observation of Montesquieu. "Another advantage," says he, "their (the ancients) education had over ours; it never was effaced by

† "There is nothing to hinder a child from acquiring every useful branch of knowledge and every elegant accomplishment suited to his age without impairing his constitution, but then the greatest attention must be paid to the powers of the body and the mind, that they neither be allowed to languish for want of exercise nor be exerted beyond what they can bear." Dr. Gregory. [John Gregory, *A Comparative View of the State and Faculties of Man with Those of the Animal World* (3d ed., London: J. Dodsley, 1766), p. 55. Gregory (1724-1773) was a professor of medicine at the University of Edinburgh; his works were widely reprinted in colonial America.]
Further,
"He who in his early age has been taught to study and revere the characters of the sages, heroes, statesmen, and philosophers, who adorn the annals of Greece and Rome, will necessarily imbibe the most liberal notions. He will catch a portion of that generous enthusiasm which has warmed the hearts and directed the conduct of the benefactors and ornaments of the human race." Knox, p. 172. [Vicesimus Knox, *Liberal Education: Or a Practical Treatise on the Methods of Acquiring Useful and Polite Learning* (6th ed., London: C. Dilly, 1783), p. 172. Knox (1752-1821) was a fellow of St. John's College, Oxford, and master of Turnbridge School.]

contrary impressions. Epaminondas the last year of his life, said, heard, saw, and performed the very same things as at the age in which he received the first principles of his education."[7]

One consideration may deserve some attention, though it is not known hitherto to have received any; and as it flows from a general law of nature, its truth is confided in. All animals excepting man are submitted almost wholly to their own efforts as to subsistence and welfare as soon as they have acquired physical strength sufficient to protect them from the invasion of force. No animal is known to exist which does not require a certain portion of sagacity to guide it. This sagacity it may therefore be fairly supposed to possess as soon as it attains its physical manhood. Man alone, in his present state, passes a course of years in corporeal manhood and mental infancy. May not the idea be hazarded that this has arisen from false education, which has retarded the progress of the mind and protracted the period of mental infancy beyond the limits assigned it by nature.

From these considerations it appears that the earlier the mind is placed under a proper regimen, the greater is the probability of producing the desired effects. Some years must be surrendered to the claims of maternal regard; some will elapse before the child is able to attend to anything but those external objects which irresistibly force themselves on its notice.

Making an allowance of five years for these unavoidable sacrifices and for the acquisition of those elements of knowledge which are with facility acquired in any situation, we arrive at the period of life most proper for commencing a system of general education.

It is acknowledged that there is something arbitrary in fixing the period of commencing the education of youth, as the mind varies in different persons. Still, however, it seems necessary that age should decide the time fit for beginning education, which on the whole, with perhaps few variations, will be found the least exceptionable mode of giving to this part of the system a feature definite and certain, a feature which shall not be under the control of parental weakness or ignorant caprice. If at the age of five the mind in some children be too tender to receive much, an intelligent instructor will be satisfied with imparting little. No danger need be apprehended from intense application at this period of life. Every idea formed in the mind will be simple, and it is only in the combination of ideas that much mental vigor is required.

II. *Should education be public or private?*

The most distinguished talents have been engaged in the discussion of this subject, and here, as in most controversies of a speculative cast, we find a great diversity of sentiment. Quintilian and Milton are warm in their eulogium on a public, while Locke is equally animated in his praise of a private system of education.[8] The great argument which may be called the center of all others urged is the production of emulation by a public education, while the great objection made to public education is the sacrifice, alleged to be produced, of morality and honesty.

As there is, undoubtedly, truth on both sides, it becomes necessary to consider what weight the alleged advantages and disadvantages ought to possess in determining the preference of the judgment to one over the other system. It will, perhaps, be possible to reconcile the apparently conflicting ideas in such a way as to make the result of benefit produced infinitely larger than the risk of injury sustained.

The early period of life is under parental and especially maternal control. The solicitude of a mother is now the best, the only protection, which the child can receive. Some years elapse before the mind seems capable of being impressed with true or false knowledge in a degree sufficient to influence its future expansion, and during this period it is fortunate that we have not occasion to regret the unenlightened state of the female mind. But though these years do not mark much strength of mind, yet they rapidly unfold and form the disposition which seldom fails to receive a virtuous bias from a mother who, however vicious herself, feels deeply interested in the virtue of her offspring. Hence those amiable affections are excited which are the ornament of human nature. Before the age of five the child seldom feels a disposition to do an immoral thing, and even if it should exhibit such a symptom, the temper is so flexible that it easily yields to a more virtuous direction.

The young mind, having passed five years of its existence free from much corruption, and a plan of education being now commenced, it becomes an object of consideration whether the child should remain with its parents or be separated from them.

As a large portion of parental solicitude still exists which alone seems capable of securing a vigilant attention to those little indications of temper and mind which now so profusely appear, it seems highly important that the child should still remain under the immediate control of parental authority. That affection which on the part of the child is but half formed will have time and opportunity to gain strength, a love of domestic tranquillity will be produced, and both these principles will form a firm shield to virtue.

On the other hand, the daily attendance at school will withdraw the mind of the child from an *entire* dependence on its parents, will place it in situations demanding the exercise of its faculties, and will strengthen, instead of weakening, its attachment to domestic scenes. To be deprived of that which we love is in some degree painful to us all; to children it is painful in the highest degree. Yet a habit of voluntary or compulsory abstinence from pleasure is absolutely necessary to human happiness.

The child, in this situation, having its time divided between school, the hours of diversion, and those spent in the house of its parents, will, perhaps, remain as free from a prostration of morals as can be expected in infancy. This, indeed, is the plan which universally prevails in the civilized world, and its universality is certainly some argument in its favor.

Let this plan, partly domestic and partly public, be pursued till the mind begins boldly to expand itself and to indicate an ability and an inclination to think for itself. The commencement of this capacity of combining ideas takes place about the age of ten. We have now reached the period which claims the closest attention. The mind now feels its vigor and delights in displaying it. Ambition is kindled, emulation burns, a desire of superiority and distinction are roused.

This, then, appears to be the era, if ever, of public education. The indulgence of parental tenderness should now be exchanged for the patient and unobstructed exercise of the mental powers. Let us attend to the advantages of the two rival systems at this period.

With regard to the plan of public education:

1. Emulation is excited. Without numbers there can be no emulation. It is founded on the love of distinction. In a private family this distinction cannot be acquired.

2. An attention to study, when the child is removed from the house of its parent, may be uninterrupted, whereas while it resides with him a thousand trifling, menial avocations will always take precedence. From this results the conviction in the mind of the child that study is altogether subordinate to the objects to which it is compelled to attend.

3. But, above every other consideration, the system of public education inspires a spirit of independent reflection and conduct. Removed from a scene where it has little occasion to think and less to act, the child now finds itself placed in a situation free from rigid parental authority.‡ Placed in the midst of objects of pursuit, its preference of one object to another is often determined by its own volition. Hence reflection is excited; and with children there is certainly no danger

---

‡ "Too long have we been accustomed to consider as an authority a duty of protection engraved by nature in our hearts. Contrary to the eternal order of things, a power of administration has been turned to the exclusive advantage of those by whom it was exercised. This mistaken idea originated in the opinion long implicitly received that man can belong to man, an atrocious system which the Romans modified in the days of their refinement, and which we propose totally to overthrow, by reducing the relations between father and child to kindness and benefits on the one side and to respect and gratitude on the other." Preliminary speech of Cambaceres, on a plan of a civil Code for France. ["Discourse Preliminaire," pp. 7-8. Translated by Smith.]

of too much thought, the only apprehension is that there being too little.

Let a spirit of independent reflection animate a large number of even youthful minds and the acquisition of useful truths will soon be rapid. This spirit, aided by the instruction of enlightened precepts, must give an undeniable ascendancy to the public over the private plan.

Error is never more dangerous than in the mouth of a parent. The child, from the dawn of its existence, accustomed to receive as undoubted every idea from this quarter, seldom, if ever, questions the truth of what it is told. Hence prejudices are as hereditary as titles, and you may almost universally know the sentiments of the son by those of the father.§ Now by education remote from parental influence, the errors of the father cease to be entailed upon the child. Still farther the child, having acquired true ideas, very often, from the superior force of truth, dissipates the errors of his parent by the remonstrances of reason.

As education professes to improve the state and character of men and not barely to oppose their declension, it must follow that domestic education is improper, as it does no more, even if successful, than secure the last at the expense of the first.

When we consider the argument urged against public education (for only one is urged with any tenacity), we shall find that the evil it deprecates arises from the imperfection of human nature more than from any appropriate and exclusive property of public education.

§ These are the sentiments of Juvenal, whom justice forbids us solely to regard as a poet. His character is only duly appreciated by considering him as one of the most enlightened and inflexible moralists of antiquity.
"There are many reprehensible things which the parents themselves point out and hand down to their children—So nature orders it; the examples of vice which we see at home corrupt us sooner than any other—One or two, whose hearts Titan has formed of better clay, and with a partial hand, may, indeed escape the influence of such example; but the rest are led into those footsteps of their fathers which ought to be shunned; and the path of some habitual vice pointed out for a long time, by a parent, draws them into it." [*Juvenal and Persius*, trans. G. G. Ramsay (Loeb Classical Library), pp. 264-267. Smith has paraphrased and condensed lines 1-40 of Juvenal's satire XIV.]

"Wherever there are numbers of children assembled together, there will be mischief and immorality." This is true, but is it so extensively true as to countervail the numerous advantages which have been partially stated? Is it equal to the injury sustained by the mechanical adoption of parental error or vice? More mischief, more immorality, have sprung from this source than from the one complained of. On the other hand does not the conduct of children in a public institution in a considerable degree resemble the actions of men in the world? The knowledge therefore thus acquired, though sometimes at the expense of honesty and truth, must be deemed of some importance.

It is probable that it arose from the spirit of their plans of education that Sparta was the last nation that fell a prey to the Macedonians, and Crete to the Romans. The Samnites, Montesquieu observes, had the same institutions which furnished those very Romans with the subject of four and twenty triumphs.[9] Indeed, though it be probable that no plan can ever be devised which shall admit all the advantages of an honorable and zealous competition and exclude all the injuries heretofore so closely allied as to be deemed inseparable, yet some improvement ought not to be despaired of amidst the universal tendency of everything to amelioration.

The discussion of this subject appears in some measure superseded and the preference unequivocally established of the public over the private plan by the small expense of the first compared with the impracticable expense of the last. If parents educated their children, the hours withdrawn from business would alone impoverish them.

Before a detail is given of the course of education proposed, it may be proper concisely to state the points which it has been the object of the preceding remarks to establish.

In the first place, virtue and wisdom have been deemed to possess an inseparable connection, and the degree and efficiency of the one has been decided to depend on the measure and vigor of the other. From this proposition the inference is deduced that a nation cannot possibly be too enlightened and that the most energetic zeal is necessary to make it sufficiently so for the great interests of virtue and happiness.

Secondly. That it is the duty of a nation to superintend and even to coerce the education of children and that high considerations of expediency not only justify but dictate the establishment of a system which shall place under a control, independent of and superior to parental authority, the education of children.

Thirdly. The preference has been given at a certain age to public education over domestic education.

Fourthly. The period of education recommended has been fixed at an age so early as to anticipate the reign of prejudice and to render the first impressions made on the mind subservient to virtue and truth.

Guided by these principles it is proposed:

I.  That the period of education be from 5 to 18.

II.  That every male child, without exception, be educated.

III.  That the instructor in every district be directed to attend to the faithful execution of this injunction. That it be made punishable by law in a parent to neglect offering his child to the preceptor for instruction.

IV.  That every parent who wishes to deviate in the education of his children from the established system be made responsible for devoting to the education of his children as much time as the established system prescribes.

V.  That a fund be raised from the citizens in the ratio of their property.

VI.  That the system be composed of primary schools, of colleges, and of a *University*.

VII.  That the primary schools be divided into two classes, the first consisting of boys from 5 to 10 years old, the second consisting of boys from 10 to 18, and that these classes be subdivided, if necessary, into smaller ones.

VIII.  That the instruction given to the first class be the rudiments of the English language, writing, arithmetic, the commission to memory and delivery of select pieces, inculcating moral duties, describing natural phenomena, or displaying correct fancy.

IX. Though this class is formed of boys between the age of 5 and 10 years, yet should rapid acquisitions be made in the above branches of knowledge at an earlier age than that of 10, the boy is to be promoted into the second class.

X. The most solemn attention must be paid to avoid instilling into the young mind any ideas or sentiments whose truth is not unequivocally established by the undissenting suffrage of the enlightened and virtuous part of mankind.

XI. That the instruction given to the second class be an extended and more correct knowledge of arithmetic; of the English language, comprising plain rules of criticism and composition; the concise study of general history and a more detailed acquaintance with the history of our own country; of geography; of the laws of nature, practically illustrated. That this practical illustration consist in an actual devotion of a portion of time to agriculture and mechanics, under the superintendence of the preceptor. That it be the duty of this class to commit to memory and frequently to repeat the Constitution and the fundamental laws of the United States.

XII. That each primary school consist of 50 boys.

XIII. That such boys be admitted into the college as shall be deemed by the preceptor to be worthy, from a manifestation of industry and talents, of a more extended education. That one boy be annually chosen out of the second class of each primary school for this preferment.

XIV. That the students at college so promoted be supported at the public expense, but that such other students may be received as shall be maintained by their parents.

XV. That the studies of the college consist in a still more extended acquaintance with the above stated branches of knowledge, together with the cultivation of polite literature.

XVI. That each college admit 200 students.

XVII. That an opportunity be furnished to those who have

the ability, without interfering with the established studies, of acquiring a knowledge of the modern languages, music, drawing, dancing, and fencing, and that the permission to cultivate these accomplishments be held forth as the reward of diligence and talents.

XVIII. That a National University be established in which the highest branches of science and literature shall be taught. That it consist of students promoted from the colleges. That one student out of ten be annually chosen for this promotion by a majority of the suffrages of the professors of the college to which he may belong.

XIX. That the student so promoted be supported at the public expense and be lodged within the walls of the university, remaining so long as he please on a salary, in consideration of his devoting his time to the cultivation of science or literature, in which last case he shall become a fellow of the university.

XX. The number of professors in the college and the university is not fixed, but it is proposed that the last contain a professor of every branch of useful knowledge.

XXI. It is proposed that the professors be in the first instance designated by law; that afterwards, in all cases of vacancy, the professors of the college choose the preceptors of the primary schools and that the professors of the university choose the professors of the colleges.

XXII. For the promotion of literature and science, it is proposed that a board of literature and science be established on the following principles:

It shall consist of fourteen persons skilled in the several branches of, 1. Languages. 2. Mathematics. 3. Geography and history. 4. Natural philosophy in general. 5. Moral philosophy. 6. English language, belle-lettres, and criticism. 7. Agriculture. 8. Manufactures. 9. Government and laws. 10. Medicine. 11. Theology. 12. Elements of taste, including principles of music, architecture, gardening, drawing, etc. 13. Military tactics. And in addition, 14. A person eminently skilled in science, who shall be president of the board.

The persons forming the board shall, in the first instance, be determined by law, and in case of vacancy, a new election shall be held by the remaining members of the board.

Twenty years subsequent to the commencement of the established system, all vacancies shall be supplied by a choice made in the first instance by the professors of the university, which shall be then approved by a majority of colleges, the professors of each college voting by themselves, and finally sanctioned by a majority of the fellows of the university voting. No person under 30 years of age shall be eligible.

The persons so elected shall hold their offices during life and receive a liberal salary, which shall render them independent in their circumstances. No removal shall take place unless approved by the suffrages of three-fourths of the colleges, three-fourths of the professors of the university, and three-fourths of the fellows of the university.

It shall be the duty of this board to form a system of national education to be observed in the university, the colleges, and the primary schools; to choose the professors of the university; to fix the salaries of the several officers; and to superintend the general interests of the institution.

As merit and talents are best secured by liberal rewards, a fund shall be established and placed under the control of this board, out of which premiums shall be paid to such persons as shall, by their writings, excel in the treatment of the subjects proposed by the board for discussion or such as shall make any valuable discovery.

It shall further be the duty of this board to peruse all literary or scientific productions submitted to them by any citizen, and in case they shall pronounce any such work worthy of general perusal and calculated to extend the sphere of useful knowledge, it shall be printed at the public expense and the author rewarded.

It shall be the especial duty of the board to determine what authors shall be read or studied in the several institutions and at any time to substitute one author for another.

As the extensive diffusion of knowledge is admirably promoted by libraries, it shall be in the power of the board to establish them wherever it shall see fit and to direct all original productions of merit to be introduced into them.

It is not concealed that on the establishment of this board the utility, the energy, and the dignity of the proposed system are deemed greatly to depend. It will therefore be proper to exhibit with some minuteness the reasons which render such an institution expedient, or in other words to state the advantages which may be expected to be derived from it.

Our seminaries of learning have heretofore been under the management of men either incompetent to their superintendence or not interested in a sufficient degree in their welfare. Voluntary and disinterested services, however honorable, are but rarely to be obtained. The zeal which embarks a man of talents in the promotion of any object will cool unless sustained by some substantial benefits, either received or expected. It is almost impossible in this country for the case to be different. Affluence is so uncommon that few are to be found who possess it in union with intellectual attainments. Independent of this consideration, it is generally conceded that more knowledge is to be expected from men in a subordinate sphere of life who are constrained to cultivate their minds, than from those who can live, without such cultivation, in ease and affluence. From this combination of acknowledged facts, it must clearly appear that every advantage will flow from the institution of the proposed board, which either does or can proceed from those formed on the existing plans, and that great and exclusive additional benefits may be expected.

The high responsibility of this board will ensure its fidelity. Every member of it, being distinguished by eminent attainments in some department of learning, will be constrained by the powerful obligations due to character to superintend with zeal and honesty those concerns specially delegated to him. No branch of science or literature will flourish at the expense of another, as they will all be represented at this board. This board being the source from which all inferior appointments proceed, if it be governed in its choice of persons by incorrupt and intelligent motives, the several stations of professors and preceptors will probably be filled with men equally eminent for knowledge and industry.

So far the advantages connected with the establishment of such a board have been contemplated in their immediate relation to the education of youth. Benefits, equally great and more splendid, will flow to society from the security given to morals and the impulse given to science. To this board, if liberally endowed with funds, talents will look for sure protection and encouragement. Not only talents previously existing will be rewarded and animated to the noblest efforts but talents which had never otherwise existed will trace their creation to this institution. The reliance on having publicity given to their discoveries and researches and the being rewarded by fame and some share of pecuniary assistance will encourage all those who feel conscious of possessing great powers of mind to give them activity and expansion.

As it may be relied upon that a body of men, well-known and possessing a full sense of the value of character, will guard with peculiar circumspection the interests of virtue and will only reward talents when exerted in its cause, we may expect that authors, as they regard the approbation of this board, will be careful to promote and not attack morals. Hence it may be inferred that fewer vicious productions will issue from the press than at present disgrace it.

When it is considered how slow literary merit is at present in receiving its reward and that posthumous is more frequent than living fame, when it is considered how detrimental this circumstance is to the acquisition of knowledge, when it is further considered that poverty is almost always the sure lot of devotion to science, it becomes difficult to assign limits to the advantages which science would derive from always knowing where to meet with protection and receive both reputations and pecuniary reward. Every work recommended to general acceptance by this board would surely go into a rapid circulation, which of itself will generally amply recompense the author.

If any one circumstance be more connected with the virtue and happiness of the United States than another it is the substitution of works defining correctly political, moral, and religious duty in the place of those which are at present in use. The radical ideas we have already established and which are in a great measure peculiar to us claim a new and entirely different exposition from that which they have yet received. Every new work, therefore, which comes from the pen of a citizen may be deemed an important acquisition, a stay to our virtue and a shield to our happiness.

Exclusively of the enumerated advantages which science may derive from this board, great advances in knowledge may be expected from the individual contributions of its several members. Inured in the early period of their lives to close application, having acquired the habits of patient and persevering study, and at length being placed in independent and easy circumstances, we need not fear disappointment in expecting from them performances and discoveries of the first order.

In considering the objections likely to be urged against embracing the plan of education here proposed, only two of much importance are foreseen. The first is its extensiveness, the second its expense.

As the extensiveness can only be objectionable in reference to the expense, this alone seems to require examination.

To give a fair trial to this system, liberal compensation should be allowed to the preceptors and professors. Their offices should be esteemed as honorable as any employments, either public or private, in the community; and one sure way of rendering them so is to attach to them independence. Without this appendage we shall in vain expect that exclusive attention to science and professional duty which can alone accomplish the ends desired.

The necessary expense must, then, be submitted to without reluctance. On an inquiry into the sources of taxation we shall find more encouragement than discouragement. When it is stated that the wealth of the state of Pennsylvania alone may be estimated at more than 400 million of dollars, it will at once be seen how little the most liberal sum raised for the purpose of education would partake of burden or oppression. When on the other hand the greatness of the object is correctly estimated and truly felt, all prejudices ought at once to be annihilated, and it is only doing justice to the patriotism of our citizens to believe that they would be annihilated.

Two subjects connected with a general system of education, viz. female instruction and that which has been called ornamental, have been avoided. Both of these certainly involve very important considerations. But in the existing diversity of opinion respecting the nature and extent of the first, such coincidence and agreement as to produce a system must absolutely be despaired of. It is sufficient, perhaps, for the present that the improvement of women is marked by a rapid progress and that a prospect opens equal to their most ambitious desires.

With regard to ornamental instruction, it would seem to rest more on principles of expediency than of necessity. It may, also, be considered as a kind of mental luxury, which like that of a grosser nature, will imperceptibly, but surely, by the allurements and pleasures which its cultivation holds forth, insinuate itself into general acceptance. But as it is of some consequence that a plan of instruction in the polite arts should be devised, which so far from being incompatible with, might aid the promotion of branches of knowledge more immediately necessary, it is proposed that a limited opportunity be offered in the colleges and a full one in the university to become acquainted with the principles as well as execution of every polite art. The effects of these elegant pursuits on the mind and temper are of the most beneficial nature.|| They may be emphatically denominated the finished offspring of civilization and refinement. Besides, a system of sufficient comprehensiveness should contain a department for every species of genius. Every spark of mental energy should be cherished. The mind should be left free to choose its favorite object and when chosen should find the means of prosecuting it with ardor.

Such is the system proposed. Its imperfections are beyond doubt numerous. Of this fact, no man can be more sensible than their author. In the discussion of a subject which has ably employed the pens of the most distinguished writers without producing a general conviction of the preference of one plan over another, it became the writer to exercise as much diffidence as consists with the exposition of truth. If he has manifested in any part of the preceding speculations the appearance of arrogant confidence in his own sentiments, he trusts it will be ascribed to his impressions of the importance of the subject and not to a vain attachment to his peculiar ideas. He who is solemnly impressed with interesting truths will think with energy and express his thoughts with decision.

Notwithstanding the universal agreement of all men in this

---

|| "A just taste in the fine arts, by sweetening and harmonizing the temper, is a strong antidote to the turbulence of passion. Elegance of taste procures to a man so much enjoyment at home, or easily within reach, that, in order to be occupied, he is, in youth, under no temptation to precipitate into hunting, gaming, drinking; nor, in middle age, to avarice. A just relish of what is beautiful, proper, elegant, and ornamental, in writing or painting, in architecture or gardening, is a fine preparation for discerning what is beautiful, just, elegant, or magnanimous in character or behavior." Lord Kames's *Elements of Criticism.* [Henry Home, Lord Kames, *Elements of Criticism*, 2 vols., (3d ed., Edinburgh: A. Millard and A. Kincaid and J. Bell, 1765), I, 8-10. Smith fashioned this statement out of quotation, misquotation, excision, and paraphrase. It does no great violence to Kames's original, although on p. 9 Kames counted on a taste in the fine arts to strengthen a man of middle age from delivering himself "over to ambition" and a man of old age "to avarice."]

"The truth is that polite learning is found by experience to be friendly to all that is amiable and laudable in social intercourse, friendly to morality. It has a secret but powerful influence in softening and meliorating the disposition. True and correct taste directly tends to restrain the extravagances of passion by regulating that nurse of passion, a disordered imagination." Knox's *Plan of a Liberal Education*, p. 8. [*Liberal Education*, pp. 8-9.]

country as to the necessity of a reform in education, so essentially do their professions disagree with their actions that nothing short of the commanding eloquence of truth, without cessation thundered on their ears, can produce that concurrence of action, that unity of effort, which shall give efficiency to a wise system of education. Let then the voice of the good man mingle with that of the wise in announcing the necessity of speedily adopting such a measure. Instead of one party denouncing another for equivocal political crimes, let all parties unite in attesting their patriotism by their co-operating efforts in so great a cause. Is it a question with any man whether our liberties are secure? Let him know that they depend upon the knowledge of the people and that this knowledge depends upon a comprehensive and energetic system of education. It is true that some nations have been free without possessing a large portion of illumination, but their freedom has been precarious and accidental, and it has fallen as it rose.

The two things which we are most interested in securing are harmony at home and respect abroad. By calling into active operation the mental resources of a nation, our political institutions will be rendered more perfect, ideas of justice will be diffused, the advantages of the undisturbed enjoyment of tranquillity and industry will be perceived by everyone, and our mutual dependence on each other will be rendered conspicuous. The great result will be harmony. Discord and strife have always proceeded from, or risen upon, ignorance and passion. When the first has ceased to exist and the last shall be virtuously directed, we shall be deprived of every source of misunderstanding. The sword would not need a scabbard, were all men enlightened by a conviction of their true interests.

Harmony at home must produce respect abroad. For the era is at hand when America may hold the tables of justice in her hand and proclaim them to the unresisting observance of the civilized world. Her numbers and her wealth vie with each other in the rapidity of their increase. But the immutable wisdom of her institutions will have a more efficient moral influence than her physical strength. Possessed of both she cannot fail to assume, without competition, the station assigned her by an overruling power.

Such is the bright prospect of national dignity and happiness, if America give to her youth the advantages of a liberal and just education. On the other hand, should avarice, prejudice, or malice frustrate this great object, and should a declension of knowledge, gradually, but not the less decisively as to a future period, be suffered to triumph, the prospect is gloomy and dreadful. Gigantic power misapplied, towering ambition unsatiated with criminal gratification, avarice trampling poverty underfoot, mark but a few of the dark shades which will, in all probability, envelop our political horizon. On such an event, we must expect the miseries of oppression at home and conquest abroad.

It may interest the attention, as it certainly will amuse the fancy, to trace the effects of the preceding principles of education on a future age. It has been observed that however virtuous, enlightened, and vigorous our first efforts to aggrandize the human character, it were, notwithstanding, folly to expect the celerity of preternatural agency. A system founded on true principles must gradually and cautiously eradicate error and substitute truth. The period, will, therefore, be remote before the world is benefited by its complete development.

Let us contemplate the effects of a just system,

    I.  ON THE INDIVIDUAL CITIZEN.

    II.  ON THE UNITED STATES.

    III.  ON THE WORLD.

    I.  The citizen, enlightened, will be a free man in its truest sense. He will know his rights, and he will understand the rights of others; discerning the connection of his interest with the preservation of these rights, he will as firmly support those of his fellow men as his own. Too well informed to be misled, too virtuous to be corrupted, we shall behold man consistent and inflexible. Not at one moment the child of patriotism, and at another the slave of despotism, we shall see him in principle forever the same. Immutable in his character, inflexible in his honesty, he will feel the dignity of his nature and cheerfully obey the claims of duty. He will look upon danger without dismay, so he will feel within himself the power of averting or the faculty of disarming it. With Lucretius, he may say,

It is a view of delight to stand or walk on the shore side and to see a ship tossed with tempest upon the sea or to be in a forti-fied tower and to see two battles joined upon a plain. But it is a pleasure incomparable for the mind of man to be settled, landed, and fortified in the certainty of truth, and from thence to descry and behold the errors, perturbations, labors and wan-derings up and down of other men.[10]

The love of knowledge, which even a moderate portion of information never fails to inspire would at the same time shut up many sources of misery and open more sources of happiness. The love of wealth would cease to be predominant passion of the heart; other objects would divide the attention and perhaps challenge and receive a more constant regard.

The acquisition of knowledge is open to all. It injures no one. Its object is disinterested. It delights in distinction only so far as it increases the mass of public good. Here then is an object which all may pursue without the interference of one with another. So far from producing interference, it will con-stantly tend to destroy it; for the more men think, the more they will resemble each other, and the more they resemble each other, the stronger will their mutual attachment be.

II.  Viewing the effects of such a system on the United States, the first result would be the giving perpetuity to those political principles so closely connected with our present happiness. In addition to these might be expected numerous improvements in our political economy.

By these means government without oppression and protec-tion without danger will exist in their necessary strength.

Politics are acknowledged to be still in their infancy. No circumstance could so rapidly promote the growth of this science as a universal illumination of mind. The minds of millions centering in one point could not fail to produce the sublimest discoveries. Hence the prospect that our political institutions would quickly mature into plans as perfect as human happiness would require.

If all the genius of a nation could be impelled into active exertion, philosophy, both moral and physical, would soon present a new face. Every new discovery would probably tend to abridge the labor of the body and to allow opportunity, as well as inspire inclination, to cherish reflection. Man would feel himself in possession of two extensive sources of enjoyment, the exercise of the body and the reflection of the mind; and he would soon find the last as submissive as the first.

This state of things could not fail to elevate the United States far above other nations. Possessed of every source of happiness under the guardianship of all necessary power, she would soon become a model for the nations of the earth. This leads in the third place to,

III. The consideration of the effects of such a system on the world.

Nation is influenced as powerfully by nation as one individual is influenced by another. Hence no sooner shall any one nation demonstrate by practical illustration the goodness of her political institutions than other nations will imperceptibly introduce corresponding features into their systems. No truth is more certain than that man will be happy if he can. He only wants a complete conviction of the means to pursue them with energy and success. This conviction the United States may be destined to flash on the world.

Independent of this necessary effect, other effects will be produced. Many of the most enlightened of our citizens will traverse the globe with the spirit of philosophical research. They will carry with them valuable information and an ardent enthusiasm to diffuse it. Its diffusion will be the era of reform wherever it goes.

But more important, still, will be the example of the most

powerful nation on earth, if that example exhibit dignity, humility, and intelligence. Scarcely a century can elapse before the population of America will be equal and her power superior to that of Europe. Should the principles be then established, which have been contemplated, and the connection be demonstrated between human happiness and the peaceable enjoyment of industry and the indulgence of reflection, we may expect to see America too enlightened and virtuous to spread the horrors of war over the face of any country and too magnanimous and powerful to suffer its existence where she can prevent it. Let us, then, with rapture anticipate the era when the triumph of peace and the prevalence of virtue shall be rendered secure by the diffusion of useful knowledge.

# 7

# AMABLE-LOUIS-ROSE de LAFITTE du COURTEIL

*Proposal To Demonstrate the Necessity of a National Institution in the United States of America, for the Education of Children of Both Sexes. To Which Is Joined, a Project of Organization, etc. (Philadelphia, 1797)*

[Amable-Louis-Rose de Lafitte du Courteil has escaped the attention of students of French immigration and of French influence in American life. The essay appears to have been a lone literary effort, undertaken by this apparent refugee from the French Revolution while he was "professor of the French Language, Mathematics, Geography, History, etc.," and "master of drawing" at an academy for boys at Bordentown, New Jersey. Founded by the Reverend Burgess Allison in 1778, the school was under the direction of the Reverend William Staughton during Lafitte's "professorship." Educated in Paris at the royal military school, Lafitte came to the United States in 1796 and after a period of travel accepted the position at Bordentown. While there is a military bias and an even stronger agrarian bias in his outlook, this essay reveals a sensitive understanding of American conditions and needs. Lafitte du Courteil is sometimes obscure: he is not a master of English. Occasional phrases and words have been inserted, as indicated, in an effort to increase clarity, but further liberties with his text have not been taken. Lafitte's essay was published at Philadelphia by G. Decombaz in 1797.]

### To the Citizens of the United States of America.

CITIZENS,

The love of humanity, the acknowledgment of the peaceable existence which I enjoy in your country, has rendered it my duty to present you with some remarks by writing. Occupied with the instruction of some of your children, I every day form wishes for their happiness and that of their posterity. My intentions are then pure. If I have been mistaken, if my plan is not agreeable to you, in favor of my zeal, be indulgent for my errors. But if there is a single idea of mine which may contribute to your happiness, I shall be too happy; my recompense is in this hope.

### To the Assemblies of the states; to the municipal officers, governors, and all who are in public offices.

And you, gentlemen, who enjoy the confidence of your fellow patriots and who consecrate your cares and talent: to consolidate the more and more the edifice of their happiness; in your precious quality of citizens of this republic, I have just expressed to you my wishes and my hope; as magistrates, permit me to address more particularly to you my profession of faith, to have no other intention than that of seconding your activity. Sometimes a useful thing springs from a weak ray, even of error. Let not then the imperfections of this little writing determine you to condemn it without examination. From the trunk of a deformed tree, the hand of the careful man may extract honey.

### To the President, the Senate, and the House of Representatives of the United States of America.

GENTLEMEN,

Permit me to refer myself to what I have just said to you as Citizens of the United States of America; and after having addressed to you the same solicitations as to others, who are in the public office of every state; I, and by assuring you of my entire devotion, [shall be happy] if my weak knowledge can be of any service to your country.

DE LAFITTE DU COURTEIL.

# GENERAL EXAMINATION

The United States of America afford an observer afflicting contrasts. If he first visits the principal cities, from Boston to Charleston, he is astonished at the extent of these cities, their luxury, their commerce, and their population. It does not appear to him that he has left Europe [when he visits] these states which have seen superb cities progressively increase in proportion as the population of their neighboring countries has need of more artificers, more staples for the exchange of the superfluity of their fields, more merchants for the necessary supplies of this laboring people, etc. [The observer is further astonished,] as this population has [also] engendered idle people, calling themselves livers on their revenues, and under the protection of the latter, some people who do nothing, and libertines who conceal themselves in the multitude of the population of great cities, and by that means escape the eye of the good man, who only loves the man who is occupied in some manner or other and who with his look alone would overwhelm them with scorn.

They there escape also very often the watchfulness of the magistrates, who would have little to do for the maintenance of good order if these last individuals were not tolerated. I say individuals, for I cannot call them citizens, the perfection of their existence being not to infringe upon the laws of their country; like drones they devour the fruit of the bee's precious labor, stung with their hoarse buzzing, and so much the more as they aspire to engage our attention. Too happy should we be if by this means we would know that it is only venom they can diffuse.

If after this first examination of the cities, this observer travels through the country, then his heart will be truly wounded. What! says he to himself, agriculture is here in his birth; the country is without population, and I have seen the citizens in every part priding themselves on the plans of their cities' aggrandizement: I have seen that indeed they are incessantly raising new magazines, houses, edifices, etc.

Does he look for public establishments such as announce an organized nation? Not an arsenal, no stocks whereon to build ships, not a casting house, very few manufactures, and all the first stuffs are to be found in the country; no national institution for the education of subjects.

I shall limit this introduction to these first observations: they are sufficient for those who wish to understand me. I am going to name some of the causes of these defects, and show the remedies briefly. It may be perceived that their development would demand a long work, probably beyond my abilities; and which would be a digression from my principal object (the necessity of a public national institution for the education of children of both sexes).

In naming the causes, there are some very peremptory [causes] which prudence commands me not to mention. Not that cowardly prudence which causes a too faithful mirror to err for fear of displeasing someone, and even to curry the general favor by an interested flattery more or less ingeniously disguised but that prudence which enjoins me to temper austerity, in some sort of stoical and metaphysical, in order not to miss my design by a misplaced obstinacy which has relation either to the ridicule of misanthropy, or to the effects of a peevish humor, which is insulting and which consequently ought to produce either pity or ridicule, or what is worse, revolting and hardening, instead of improving and rectifying.

> *Sincerum est nisi vas, quadcumque infundis*
> *acescit.*
> HORACE[1]

Truth, which a trifle disgraces, disfigures, alters, or even destroys, commanded me to represent these causes and their primitive effects with the features and colors which are peculiar to them. Prudence, less delicate, dissuaded me from it, observing that the colors and features would be too strong not to cause any person to be revolted and that too much truth would spoil all. But what do I say, Prudence? If I make a severe examination of my secret sentiments, am I sure that this virtue which I boast of would not be here in my mouth what it is under the pen of some writers in philosophy, reputed wise men; an honorable word which they impose, under any pretext whatever, to their weak courage, or to the weakness of their conceptions, always faint, when they do not appear gigantic and foolish to the multitude. The fear of displeasing, founded upon pure love, always speaks well and never does evil. But if this fear bears ever so little upon self-love, it speaks so much the worst as its locutions would be more applauded; and then it becomes a vile rhetorician who flatters, emboldens, fortifies, multiplies, perpetuates, and produces vices and error.

Let the emphatic predictions of G. T. Raynal on the difficulty of making the inhabitants of America a sociable people be put aside; but let us agree with him that their population is an assemblage of elements, sprung from all the European nations: then it will not be so astonishing to see that population, concentered in the cities, contract itself upon the coasts, the inhabitants always being turned towards their native country, where they have left so many cherished objects.[2] A magnetic attraction exists in us for the places where we were born; it also exists in our children, produced by the correspondence which we keep with foreign countries, by what they learn of the charms and enjoyments which they lavish on their inhabitants.

If to these primitive causes are joined those of our interest by a continual commerce and first cause of our fortune, [if it is so] that we are only clothed and surrounded in our houses with objects manufactured in Europe, can we be astonished if this tendency towards our native countries is transmitted from generation to generation? Certainly after this sketch we shall no more be surprised of the resemblance which is seen between the cities of the United States of America and those of the different states of Europe, nor at the state of languor in which the countries are. The desertion of the country naturally flows from this commercial existence: [it derives from] the application of the greatest part of the individuals to professions relative to this exterior commerce, such as carpenters who find a double means of existing by building ships or magazines in cities, where they grow lazy, attracted by a thousand vices whose poison is there multiplied without number and under seducing forms, for it is oftenest flowers which conceal the serpent.

It is easy to remark that in that part of the country which is nearest to cities almost all the men exercise trades in preference to agriculture, which they very often abandon to their wives and children: these weak beings confine it to the unformed cultivation of some vegetables or the crop of some fruits. Most of the trees are not taken care of, either through the defect of their knowledge or because these peasants are not for the most part the proprietors of the land and their lease is for only one year; consequently they have no emulation to cultivate trees without enjoying their fruit, unless to submit themselves to the avarice of the proprietors, who would then augment the price of the lease every year.

It was this consideration which made them adopt in Europe the letting of a lease for nine years. If the proprietor during the time does not enjoy an annual augmentation of revenues, his fund acquires more, and the progressive profits during the nine years, being for the benefit of the cultivator, excite his emulation. He considers himself as the patron of the ground he cultivates; he augments the price of his lease without repugnance, at every renewal of the nine years, and in France it was very common to see the son succeed the father in the farms, as one proprietor succeeds another in the possession. There certainly results very constant and very advantageous relations from it, between these two classes of true patriots. But from considering to considering, I have digressed from what I wished singly to declare, which is that men who are not determined by motives powerful enough to be farmers work at trades and abandon agriculture, such as we have mentioned, with rural economy. The care of cattle, dairies, food, and poultry [is left] to women and children who take as much care of them as they are able, induced to that [occupation] by the daily sale of these objects in the cities. But those families live miserably upon those estates.

Frugality, they will say, renders these objects sufficient. I shall answer, without dwelling upon any comparison of the frugality of the table with luxury of the other part, I shall answer that what they here call by the fine name of frugality is truly the greatest principle of maladies and, above all, the cause of the mortality which is observed upon infancy. I here speak more particularly of the country, although it may be easy to appropriate almost everything to the cities; but the country is more particularly the object of my solicitude, because it is through it that a state has a positive consistency.

But in the country the children are entirely left to themselves, and they eat the most unwholesome food. (In Europe the police punishes those merchants who expose in the markets unwholesome fruits; they are effectively poisoners.) If the countrymen are sick, there is no help at hand; the difficulty of procuring physicians who reside in the cities and the excessive prices they demand for their care cause them not to be often applied to. The unhappy men who are dispersed through the country are commonly surrounded only with other men as unhappy as themselves. If there were here and there some great proprietors living upon their plantations, some pastors, they would find at both their houses physical and moral aid—remedies for their maladies and counsels how to employ them, and advices for their conduct both with regard to agriculture and social existence. These pastors and great proprietors would teach them agriculture by their example. The success which they would obtain by the lopping of trees, the cultivating the land in the proper seasons, and employing the manures to enrich it would excite their emulation; ease would be manifest, and the country would be abundantly populated with true American patriots.

For I cannot conceive the idea of a true patriot in the person of a merchant whose interest consists much more in his correspondence with foreign countries than in that which he inhabits, there being a possibility of his factory existing the same if he dwelt in any other. A merchant is essentially a cosmopolite and citizen in the city he inhabits, I grant it, but assuredly he cannot be a patriot. I could by the analysis of this question deduce in the result a demonstration as precise as in a geometrical theorem, but that would lead me too far—I shall finish this declaration by two comparisons which will give it extension and which will show its justice.

A country is a circle of which every proprietor of a manor, which I call a *Patriot* especially when he has a wife and children, is a *Diameter*, for he touches the two extremities of the circumference and passes through the center. Every *Merchant* is a *Tangent*, for he touches the circumference by his exterior correspondences; and a man who lives in a state of celibacy is a *Secant*, for he deforms the circle. And a *Patriot* being the hypotenuse of a rectangled scalene triangle, a *Merchant* in a trading republic is the greatest of the other sides, and the workman the least.

I shall here observe that the opinion so much credited at the present time that every individual should learn a trade is produced by irreflection, unless they consider agriculture as a trade and every kind of labor relative to it. Which being not at all what they mean by the word trade, I affirm that it is the right way of making men free from all attachment and of breaking the ties of society, that it causes agriculture to be rejected with disdain and stifles population. Trades are resources for ramblers; trades for the most part call those who work at them to the city. The apprenticeship of trades makes

young libertines and very often conducts to an old age which
decency forbids me to name, but which far from frightening
youth serves them as an excuse. A tradesman says that with his
trade he can get a living anywhere; thencefrom he has no particular country. If he is without work, he employs his time in
libertinism. A husbandman is attached to the ground. The
desire of running from country to country scarcely ever enters
his mind. He is a stranger to libertinism in his youth; he is yet
farther from it as he advances in age, by the habit which he
has contracted; when old his example is a lesson for youth, for
he labors still, and what young man would dare not to imitate
him? Certainly work is never wanting in rural life. In order
to be assisted in the care of his little family, he must have a
wife; he is a father. Ah! this is the character of a true patriot.

The spirit of exterior commercial existence, which is seen
in the United States of America, always gives them the air of
a colony more or less immediately dependent on some power
of Europe, as that which is peculiar to the isles of St. Chris-
topher, Barbados, Jamaica, St. Domingo, etc. Commerce may
be in great recommendation in some republics such as Venice,
Genoa, Geneva, whose territories are very narrow. It may also
be the principal occupation of England, on account of her
present power, as this island is fortunately the capital of Britan-
nic states, and the same reason subsists for Holland. But an
organization of this kind must be very defective in every republic which, like the United States has land sufficient to
receive fifty millions of inhabitants, of which forty millions
ought to be tillers of the ground.

Certainly if the people of America had been more addicted
to agriculture from the formation of their first establishments,
it would now be infinitely more populous, flourishing, and
more happy. Nothing weakens the national character that the
people ought to have so much as that kind of dependency under
which they are to the powers of Europe, by always seeking their
prosperity and aggrandizement from exterior correspondence.
Without this predominant tendency to foreign correspondence,

would the Americans so much fear the fleets and corsairs? What would they be in need of if they would turn their attention towards their land, if they would attach themselves to their country by rural habitations, which, in a little time, after having been their consolation and resources for what they would have abandoned of commerce, would constitute their happiness?

Abundance would grow in their country, manufactures would be raised in every part, and the belligerent nations would first come to purchase the superfluity of their fields, and in a little time after, the work of their manufactures. For a long time after general peace, all nations would come to the United States for the necessary supplies of a thousand objects; this republic, thus made populous and fertile, under the shade of the olive tree and the shepherd's crook, would in all ages be admired by the universe.

A word more concerning the divergency of propensities to exterior commerce, from a character, manners, and a national organization—It is that this propensity makes many men determine upon celibacy, and by a great many secondary causes, then the loving, tender, lively sex made to weave the bands of a polite society is abandoned, is——But whether the sex be considered in the legitimate, honest, and virtuous light which forms social relations and the charms of life, or whether it be considered in a light which disorganizes and afflicts the civil existence, nothing ought to be offered but essays upon the amiableness of modesty, and

> C'est une beauté simple une vierge ingénue,
> Qui hait d'être parée et rougit d'être nue.*

Magistrates of the people, you whom the interest of society ought incessantly to animate, your families, your daughters also solicit you, take the flambeau of interest and seek the truth. Here I stop, for

---

* Modesty is
a simple beauty, an ingenuous maid
Pomp she abhors, and blushes unarray'd.

La vérité plait moins quand elle est toute nue;
Et c'est la seule vierge en ce vaste univers,
Qu'en aime à voir un peu vétue.†

In peace with all the nations of the world, the United States of America have been since the beginning of the French Revolution the asylum of an immense number of individuals of every sex, of every age, of every profession: they would have a still greater number of the unfortunate in their country if cupidity did not intercept many in their course (the excessive price of passages). They might have fixed a great many of them here for life if they had offered to these unhappy victims the means of making it their country. In good policy, the United States ought to have granted to every captain who would have brought passengers without having made them pay for their passage (specially women and children) a gratification, not only capable of indemnifying him but also of exciting others to do the same, so that when those passengers would be arrived, they ought to have settled them in the country at a distance from the city and seacoasts, where it would have been easy to furnish them with occupations proportionable to their abilities, which would have indemnified the expense; or to have distributed land among them, making the necessary advances in order to establish them on any condition whatever.

In fine, they ought to have given the same advantages to everyone who would have been willing to settle himself in the country. These advances might have produced a real good both to the country and to individuals, who would now gather the fruits of their labor, would have caused habitations to be raised for them, to which they would be attached. Instead of the distributions of succor which pity, beneficence, and even generosity have distributed upon the refugees, have lodged them in the cities, kept them in idleness, which has drawn a great number of them into dreadful misconduct, at present their misery

---

†                                    Truth
  She, far the loveliest virgin, stands confest
  Whom all delight to view a little drest.

has increased by the scorn they have fallen into and the habit they have contracted of leading a life of idleness which produces their discouragement. And perhaps most part of them have become incapable of displaying a remainder of energy, if the government or some particular persons offered them the advantages that I have just hinted at.

I say *or particular persons*, because there is a number of particular persons who are proprietors of immense plantations which they keep uncultivated, for want of hands to cultivate them, or by speculation, in order to sell them at any price which their imagination conceives. To those last, I shall willingly call to mind the fable of the avaricious man who found a stone in the place of the treasure which he had buried. But it is better to show to both that hands who would cultivate well this land would cause these hidden treasures to be fruitful; it must be observed to these proprietors that such a one who would cultivate his own property would not easily dispose himself to do that of another; one might have a good capacity for cultivating the ground well and no money to buy a plantation; and that, in fine, good farmers ought to find a real recompense for their labor, specially that of assuring themselves an asylum and ease for old age.

But let these great proprietors of uncultivated lands grant some of it to persons with a good intention to cultivate them; let them join to it, if it is necessary, the necessary funds to procure instruments, with the wants of a little family for the first year; and taking an account of the whole, the grantee will be obliged to pay the 10, 12, or 15th part of the fruits, obliging himself further to put a certain part every year in a state of cultivation till it is all grubbed; the said obligations of the grantee observed till he pays the sum at which the lands and the advances shall be esteemed, a reimbursement which ought always to remain at his option with the condition, if they will, to be advertised of it three, six months, or a year beforehand. By this means the uncultivated land will produce annually to the speculative proprietor not only the partial retribution of the produce, which I have just mentioned, but also secondary benefit by the furnitures that he will make for the cultivators of the land of things necessary for their daily wants, and in selling again the productions of the earth which the farmers shall have given to him in payment for these things. The period of time will come when he will receive the great price which constitutes the object of his ambition.

I have known many unhappy fathers of families, full of courage and knowledge and having good hands, who might have accepted such arrangements and would have settled themselves in the United States, probably for life; tormented with chagrin and misery, despair has forced them to return to the colonies. They have there perished by poignards, victims of too many sentiments . . .[3] But I am digressing from my subject; let us return to it, but let us observe lastly that such new cultivators divided in the country would cause an emulation and perfection in agriculture, which I have already observed how much it is in need of.

I have had occasion to say a few words concerning officers of health relatively to the country and the great price these gentlemen demand for their care; I shall add nothing to this last consideration; but I shall remark that in the cities one sees with astonishment that everyone there exercises, as he pleases, physic, surgery, and that apothecary shops are excessively multiplied. Would it then be against the Constitution of the United States to have a police who should watch for the public, so that when some person goes to seek help for his health, he might do it with security? But, they will say it is his part who has need of such an help to address himself to persons capable of giving it. But I shall answer in my turn that I have been many times witness that French apothecaries have refused medicines because they knew them to be contrary to the ends which such people proposed themselves; I have had the curiosity sometimes to follow persons thus dismissed; and I have seen them go to other apothecaries and there buy the same medicines. The most often in the class of common people the choice is determined either by the nearness or by the appearance of the shops. Let everyone be, if he pleases, a merchant of cloths, of candles, or of iron; even master of language, of dancing, or other arts or sciences, it is very simple. But not to be obliged in society to make a trial of any capacity for exercising medicine, surgery, or pharmacy, it is a fatal indifference to the vital principles of a number of individuals and I think it to be in the first rank of homicides.

I return to the consideration of the elements which have concurred and yet concur in forming the population of the United States of America. And after the incontestable observation that we have already made with M. G. T. Raynal that they have sprung from all the nations of Europe, I must also add to that of being transplanted in the country, either by views of interest or on account of any reasons whatever that have made them abandon their original country, it is certain that there is to be remarked first, the essential difference in the habit of almost every family and, secondly, the same tendency in all and everyone towards fortune. From the first of these two remarks results evidently a perpetual and constant estrangement for the reasons that we have already exposed from a national character, and consequently a diminution of the patriotic sentiments which it produces.

From the second, and which is produced by the absence of a national character, an indifference for every public establishment, a kind of negligence for the education of children, to whom they content themselves by giving information concerning a few commercial calculations and tables.

With regard to this consideration concerning the education of youth, it is essential to observe that whether because parents are occupied with their affairs or through apathy or a mistaken tenderness, all the youth of both sexes is absolutely neglected. From one extremity of America to the other, the children are seen running about the streets alone, and dispersing themselves in the country without their parents ever knowing or informing themselves where they have been. It is from the cradle that good as well as bad habits are contracted—and the latter, unless a disposition or circumstances singularly fortunate take possession of the first steps of children.

If one wishes then to instruct these children, everything is troublesome to them. They have never experienced a sedentary life. Work is yet more disagreeable to them, and as every beginning is rough with thorns, they see the roots of all them in the character of their institutor; they decide that, not for this reason only, they will no more study under him, but also because he is not capable of teaching them. This institutor wishes to master them, and at their father's houses they did just what they pleased; they went out of the house when it seemed good to them and did not come in again until it suits their fancies. How would they support the requisite rules under a stranger whom they look upon in some manner as their servant, because he is paid by their parents for his cares and lessons and because they have seen their father's clerks have attention and condescendence for their caprices. The domestics who receive wages wait upon them. The children make all their complaints to their parents who condescend to put them in other hands.

The same thing is repeated till at last they find an institutor, by *name,* mercenary in fact, who lets them act just as they please, in order to attract to himself a great number of boarders, make himself a fortune by the collection of his treasures, which the great number renders easy to accomplish. The institutors are heard saying, "I cannot execute my business well; and besides the parents do not wish their children to be troubled: I am not then obliged to do any better." It is not uncommon for many students to agree among themselves to suddenly quit a boarding house, in order to ruin the master; if they perceive that he is sensible of his interest, this menace is made to him. I leave to everyone to conclude what can be expected from an institutor who undertakes for the number, what ought to be hoped from his pupils.

One vice more, and of the greatest consequence, in the American seminaries of learning is the not having an uniform and durable rule to which all the students should be subject without any other preface. The method which is in practice of proposing every article of the rules to the youth in order to collect the majority of the voters for those articles which are agreeable to them and reject the others; this method is more than ridiculous; for those rules are puerile objects adapted to the age of children; if they had judgment enough to discuss and pronounce upon their validity or invalidity, their utility or inutility, assuredly they would not only be useless but of an unwarrantable ridiculousness. If this method has for its origin a principle of republicanism (such as the kind of liberty to which the children are abandoned at their parents' houses and in the houses of education), it must be agreed that those who introduce such customs only know the puerility and the imperfections of the republican government and by no means its essence.

In truth, this pretended liberty to which children are abandoned might form itself into a kind of animal independence which knows no father, when the physical organs are sufficient for the use of this animality; neither order nor master; if the collar did not force the dog to obey, the iron and spur the horses, the goad the oxen, and the stick for the ass: and which still presents to us every animal that is not tamed, ravaging everywhere he passes, and forces us to employ the sword to guard ourselves against his invincible ferocity, such are the tiger, the leopard, the bear, etc. Is it with this first state of nature that they wish us push up their children? They are approaching to it at a great rate. If they wish to inoculate them early with the social order, that is to say, the reunion of several individuals to concur to the ends which are useful to all and agreeable to the wants of everyone—that is, in the schools the one of teaching, the other of learning—it is necessary to have such statutes or rules that no one shall infringe upon.

This habit of living under laws, of seeing their institutors conform to them, would give them the first notions of what is truly denominated social liberty. They would learn that there are recompenses for those who distinguish themselves in the observations of the laws and punishments for those who violate them. Certainly one would teach them what ought to direct their first steps in the world; for they would be obliged to conform themselves to laws established before they are in the condition of voting for the formation of any. After this knowledge, immediately comes that of making distinguish the liberty which belongs to everyone in the social state.

I shall finish by observing that though some vestiges of punishment may be remarked in their seminaries of learning, yet it does not appear that they have ever thought of establishing the least reward. It is a considerable vice. They ought not only to have recompense, but also a great many of them, well adjusted and very distinct: in a word, they must be in some sort prodigal of recompenses and avaricious of punishments. I absolutely think like him who said he found nothing in children but men viewed through the convex side of a microscope, and in men, children viewed through the concave side. Therefore by expressions adapted to the organs of the understanding of the one as well as of the other we must employ exactly the same language. The same method must be practiced. But to multiply the laws is to furnish a man with many opportunities of being culpable of transgressing them; to multiply the punishments is the means of degrading him; and on the contrary, to multiply the recompenses is the means of enabling his soul; to adjust them with propriety is to push them with an adroit hand on the way of the noblest enthusiasm. But I shall have occasion to show how much the institutions of a state ought to be rather continual invitations than positive laws.

The summary of what I have just said is that there is not a true national character in the United States of America, nor any of those public establishments which announce a nation, and that the education of the youth of each sex is almost nothing and the houses of instruction very defective.

To say to fathers and mothers that their children are subjects of the state and were born to become members of the republic is what they know and what nobody pretends to deny. But to tell them that the consequence of this principle is that the direction and immediate inspection of the education of children belongs to the jurisdiction of government will not be perhaps so generally avowed. "It is my child" and all the cries of nature which command attention even in their weakness, especially when a mother manifests them by the impulsion of a truly alarmed tenderness, are considerations to which it is not permitted to answer with the stoical coldness of a presentation of principles.

But is there no means of calming these too sensible mothers? Let the advantages which would occur to their children from a careful education be represented to them under their divers aspects, the utility of which they will be to their country when they shall put in practice the lessons which they have received, their particular fortune and advancement marching with a step equal to that of the aggrandizement of their country. I shall say to these unquiet mothers, you have conceived them, carried them in your womb, nourished them with your milk; they owe you life and the development of their infancy; you have fulfilled towards them the duties of nature; employ yourself now with those of the social state in which you live and for which they are destined; be careful of their fortunes whilst we are going to implant in their young hearts sentiments of the respectful acknowledgments which they owe you, and sow in their souls the seeds of talents which will make you cherish them doubly when become the honor of their country; all their contemporaries will dispute with your tender and lively sentiments the right of loving them; with posterity, that of admiring them.

The evidence in this question is entirely established, and the show of an erudition which would here retrace the laws of ancient republics, such as Athens, Lacedemonae, etc., with regard to the pains taken by the country for the education of youth, such a show must be tiresome; nevertheless, it ought to be permitted to observe that on account of the difference of the elements which form the population of the United States of

America an institution of national education is there evidently more necessary to form a proper character than it was in the republics of antiquity.

This institution is absolutely necessary to make and cause principles of patriotism to be inoculated in the heart of infancy; to strengthen the bans of a union which needs to be incessantly solicited in an immense republic composed of divers particular states; nothing cements intimacies for life like the habit of a friendship contracted in the correspondences and plays of infancy, in schools; the experience of every age has taught it. If then the republic of which we preserve a remembrance bordering on admiration concentered in narrow bounds believed it their duty to assure themselves by the laws and under the eyes of their representative magistrates of the education and instruction of their youth, though their fathers were in every generation citizens of the same respective republics, if notwithstanding these primitive advantages, they hold their glory and their posterity only by public institutions, by how much stronger reasons ought the United States of America to be busy in organizing a like establishment, specially as they present a mixture of elements sprung from all parts of the world, united in an immense country and classed in states which have each particular laws.

After these first considerations which certainly are the most important, I ought to declare this. That it is impossible for any establishment, except a *national institution,* to be able to unite the different branches of instruction and the objects which it renders necessary; specially to form great subjects.—This is easy to conceive at first on account of the expenses; but a thousand other reasons less striking concur, some of which relate to energy, to the noble enthusiasm of patriotic mind. What difference (to indicate it with only one dash of the pen), what difference between a schoolmaster who instructs in the obscurity of his retreat some children who hardly will remember him when they enter the world and the institutor, a professor, who is the man of the nation, seen by every member in the lessons he gives: the consideration by which his cares are applauded and recompensed elevates him to the height of his subject. Nature creates beings organized mechanically with the union of the faculties of animal instinct and the propensity to the most sublime transports of reason; an institutor forms men, and his glory here seems the same as that of the Supreme Being. The schoolmaster is always contracted with the view of gaining a present livelihood and amassing something for old age; a public institution leaves those who consecrate their time to it nothing to desire. Let us add that if emulation exists for the institutors, it will also diffuse its happy influence into his pupils; the greatest progress results from both.

In Europe, in ancient France, for example, there was seen in all parts seminaries of learning, kept either by laymen or monks (Paris alone offered multitudes of these houses); in these latter times (in 1751) Louis XV instituted the royal military school (the emperor Joseph II formed, in his states, establishments in imitation of this, at Maline; the empress Catherine formed one at Petersburg). This establishment, although it was not finished, has proved what I have just said. The minister St. Germain[4] under Louis XVI in 1776 having by little prospects of economy changed its organization, it has done nothing since but to stagger under the direction of every new minister, till the moment it was annihilated by the revolution. But it has given to know that it would have produced the greatest subjects if the views of the institutor had been followed progressively.

This establishment seen by the eye of Louis XV had the college of La Fleche for its nursery. The students there made their low classes; and high latinity for the subjects who were destined to the robe or the church, till the first of these were of an age suitable to go and make their course of *juris* in the universities, and the others, finish their studies in the house and royal society of Sorbonne.

The subjects who were destined for the military profession were conducted at 14 years of age to the military royal school near Paris, where they had all the masters relative to the different kinds of arms to which they were destined. Those destined to the navy, after examinations at the assembly, were sent to the king's ports, either at Brest, at Rochefort, or at Toulon, where they then received the instructions absolutely necessary to that station and began to navigate. Those who were destined for the royal corps of engineers, after examination at the assembly, were sent to the royal school of Mezieres, where they were entirely occupied with the knowledges useful to an engineer.

Those destined to the royal corps of artillery, after the examinations, were sent to the schools of La Fere or of Bapeaume, where they were entirely occupied with the studies of knowledge relative to that state: they then passed to one of the brigades, which all of them had in the places of their residence, schoolrooms, casting houses, and arsenal. While they were lieutenants, they were obliged to keep in the rooms, at least till they were judged by the masters to be sufficiently instructed in the theory. Those destined to the cavalry, after having finished their courses of horsemanship, osteology, riding at the royal military school, were placed in the corps of cavalry. And those destined for the infantry were equally placed in the regiments. All learned both by theory and practice the military laws, the exercise, the evolutions; in general the elements of tactic and those of the fortifications of the country.

The horse doctor schools of Charenton, near Paris, and of Lyon furnished subjects not only to all the regiments of cavalry but also in every province, distributed according to the wants of the country.

Independently of the particular courses of physic, surgery, pharmacy, etc., which were made under the different masters, of those which were made under the direction of officers of health placed by the king in the hospitals, or public courses in the universities, particularly at Paris and at Montpellier, the king kept in every generality under the immediate inspection of his commissary a course of midwifery which had for its object the instruction of matrons in a sufficient number, to the end that they might be divided into the country at the reach of all the inhabitants.

In order to excite a greater emulation and diffuse knowledge more generally, besides the colleges and universities there was in many cities of province academies or societies of men of letters patented by the king, a number of which received a maintenance: premiums were there annually distributed to the most authentic assembly. Most generally, these premiums turned towards the perfection of subjects in the arts and sciences which they cultivated and consequently to that of these said arts and sciences; for example, as a premium in the academy of drawing, painting, and architecture, a subject made a tour to Rome at the expense of the king, in order to take notice of the masterpieces this city possesses and to perfect his talents at that school.

It would be misplaced here to speak with more particulars of those different establishments: it suffices to name them as well as those of the *Observatory* of Paris, *Garden of Plants and Cabinet of Natural History,* vulgarly *the Garden* of the king; the *Academy of Music and Dancing, Libraries of the King, Royal Manufacture of Gobelins, of Chinaware at Sevres, of Crystals and Enamels.*

The young persons of the fair sex were educated in the royal houses of St. Cyr and the Enfant Jesus.

After this representation of the principal national establishment that France offered to her children (where they were educated gratis), it is easily perceived that the creation of such institutions belongs only to the beneficent and paternal hand of government. If we have a little expatiated upon the enumeration of the different establishment in France, it has been only in order to indicate with a distinctive precision those which ought to be formed in the republic of the United States of America: but as, I repeat it, from the whole there result innumerable advantages, specially that of going more directly towards the formation of a national character and union; secondly, that of creating that institution in a manner the least expensive. It is proper that there be at first only one establishment: in other respects, when the population shall be augmented so that one house cannot suffice, the first of these considerations will be less pressing; and with regard to the second, I observe that the foundation ought then to be in a condition of making establishments of seminaries in the divers states, which will always depend on it, to which it will then belong to finish education.

I am going to expose in what manner I conceive the organization and foundation of such an establishment. If my ideas are judged of some utility, I shall give them all the explanation that they are susceptible of. I declare in consequence that I have conceived the plan wholly and meditated on its subdivisions, both for the edification of the house, with its distributions adapted to the different courses and customs; and for its police, either in that which results from the jurisdiction of the administration or for any other object. Having been educated at the royal military school, I have known so much the more particularly the secret ways of that establishment; as I have been obliged to analyze it in 1776 and 1787, when I addressed a petition to the ministers for its defense and for that of the royal hotel of invalids. The same reason has made me observe with the most particular attention the other establishments which I have spoken of.

I shall still add in favor of the establishment of a public national institution that it is probable that many fathers, specially those who inhabit the country, have neither the convenience nor the necessary means of giving their children a good education, and that many others (experience proves it), by a prejudice more or less mistaken, restrain the instruction of their children, refuse to make them learn certain things that would be useful to them, either for their development or for a thousand other considerations. These children are then educated with views and particular motives, and not uniformly for the good harmony of their common country or society in which they are to live; other causes which dispel the establishment of a national character—some refuse to their children the exercise of horse, dance, fencing, drawing, music, etc., all of which are agreeable and often useful arts.

The exercise of the body is conducive to health, unfolds youth, and gives it graces. To imagine that fencing gives a propensity to dueling is an extreme error. A man is a quarreler either by character or by a series of trouble which makes everything appear dark to him. When education does not correct a quarrelsome disposition or has not given power to support contrarieties and troubles, whether they have learned to fence or not they are not less exposed to quarrel; those which are terminated by the sword, when thoroughly considered, are less frequent and less brutally disgusting than those which are terminated by fists; in deforming their figure or tearing out their eyes, the latter way of deciding seems to be relative to the impulsion of animality. It is so that two dogs are seen tearing one another with their teeth in their brutal rage. It has been observed in all times that persons who were the most expert at fencing were more reserved, more honest, and less addicted to dueling, for which good education generally inspires them with horror. But in a republic, where every man ought to be a soldier for the defense of his country, ought they to be frightened at these exercises which learn them to make use of arms?

It will not be digressing from my subject to solicit here that the education of children be begun at the earliest age; as well by the consideration that it is essential in the formation of a national character as to make appear what we have observed concerning the differences belonging to the origin of every family; and yet by this other, no less important, [consideration] and with which the children's souls must be penetrated, if it is wished to render them capable of great things; it is to make them know that money (money is here understood to be material fortune of any kind whatever) ought to be considered only as a good servant, but as the worst of masters, to make them very sensible of the danger of abandoning themselves to the love of riches, which contracts, degrades, the soul, and always holds it ready to commit the vilest and most criminal actions—it is then essential to teach children that merit alone ought to excite the homage of men, and there is a thousand means of comparisons which present themselves in the course of a public education to inculcate this truth in an indelible manner.

There are also surely others to make them sensible that real fortune is only in the love of working, and that the possessor of this, in augmenting it, far from hurting others, does them good, in the same time that he does good to himself. But it is by being occupied in their infancy that man contracts this love of business, the surest way and with it the advantage of amassing materials to make it easy, agreeable, and profitable, as well for themselves as for others. It is not useless to observe that children born with what is vulgarly called fortune ought to be the most applied to those knowledges which are the immediate resort of the understanding: truly, if any revolution in their private affairs or in their country deprives them of their material fortune, their learning is independent of that reverse— were they maimed, that is to say deprived of the use of any of their limbs, their real fortune abandons them only with life, which it causes to pass with a thousand sweetnesses. In so rapid an examination as this little writing contains, I can but so indicate, and I think, I have said enough concerning it.

People of the UNITED STATES OF AMERICA, will you form a national character and naturalize the arts and sciences in your own country as a source of happiness to your future generations and of glory to a polished nation? Possess yourselves of the earliest infancy; as Nature has placed in the breasts of women the precious and salutary milk which nourishes, unfolds, and fortifies the child who owes her life, so let the children of America, when they have eyes and ears, find in their country the milk of the arts and sciences in a national source, and you will have numbers of children who will assure the glory of their country and raise it to the place which the extent of its dominions and its topographic position assign it in the political harmony of the known worlds.

After this explanation of the reasons which urge for what is relative to the education, to profit of the earliest infancy, I ought to show that the part of instruction has a number of peremptory reasons to authorize the same demand. Indeed, it is at this age that the soul's organs seize perfectly the proper pronunciation of every language, and as the head is not yet furnished with anything, there is room for all—languages, which are knowledges purely dependent on the remembrance of words, do not require maturity of judgment—in a more advanced age, not only the pronunciation is incontestably more difficult to acquire, but it is also much more difficult for this reason to silence the thinking and commemorative faculties, to apply oneself only to the learning of words.

I have observed that persons arrived to a certain age learn languages with a readiness proportionate to their minds being more or less occupied; that those of an active imagination, then always more or less inclined towards things which affect their morals, were continually diversed from the study of languages, [and] found it insipid; so that in spite of themselves, they shut their grammars, abandoning themselves to their ideas, loathed with this study of words. The least number of these, by an effort of mind and urged by want, have succeeded in learning foreign languages; others abandon them entirely, but no one learns them so well as a child, however unsteady he may be.

It is enough to show the necessity of teaching the languages to children at the earliest age; all other parts of instruction must also be given before the memory and the understanding be occupied and before anything has taken possession of the first intellectual faculties. Mathematics must be taught early, because they have the advantage of impressing rectitude on the mind and method in the development of what is uttered and in inquiries. Beginning in every undertaking is loathsome, say they incessantly; but it is no less true that the elements are more painful to him who has already ideas in his head than to chil-

dren who may only be diverted from them by the puerility of
their plays; it is easy to remark in this the absence of combined
ideas. They do not yet occupy the place designed for those elements.

When they wait for adolescence to begin the study of subjects,
the abandonment in which their infancy was spent adds new
difficulties to their learning; and one commonly thinks to make
them repair the time lost by making them apply themselves to
many things at once, a practice absolutely vicious, specially in
the study of languages, which ought to be learned one after
another, consecrating one day in a week in revising what they
have already learned in order that they may not forget it.

In fine, youth must learn words only from 6 to 12 years; that
is, to read and write; languages and music; drawing and dancing. Adolescence must receive ideas from 12 to 16 years, that is,
to be taught mathematics, geography, history, and be otherwise
occupied with the exercises of infancy; adding to these, those of
fencing and military discipline, etc.; from 16 to 18, to make application of the two first courses, to the study of things necessary
and useful to society: whether the studies of navigation, en-
ginery, artillery, natural philosophy, botany, public and civil
laws, etc.; after that, youth must apply itself (from 18 to 25
years) to the grand studies relative to the different professions
they are going to embrace, that they may be able to display the
knowledges of it in manhood and amuse their old age by trans-
mitting the result of the observations of their life to society.

I have declared that the institutors, professors, and masters
employed in a national institution ought always to be vested
with the cloak of the public consideration, and indeed, without
this consideration, the best lessons for his pupils, would they
have any, for the things which should be taught them? And
would they not lose a great deal of emulation? Children seeing
no more in the national institution, their professors and masters
as hirelings, will have a greater propensity towards the sentiments which are to be desired in them; and persons of knowledge and merit of all kinds will consecrate with a noble ardor

their watch and cares to an establishment which must constitute the glory of a nation.

Certainly there are many persons of understanding and merit
in the United States of America; either citizens of the country
or those who are there accidentally. It is not permitted to doubt
of the eagerness of the former to concur with all their capacity
in the formation of such an establishment; and it cannot be
difficult to make the second determine upon it. But it requests a
great soaring to lead this establishment rapidly towards a certain
degree of perfection. Let a prospectus of its creation be spread
all over the different states of Europe: let it call upon all
persons skilled in any art or science whatever, assuring them a
comfortable existence, not only for themselves but for their
widows and children, if any of them happen to die in their
functions; and there will presently come from all parts a
number of subjects of the greatest merit.

The circumstance is the most favorable; the misfortune of a
general war in Europe, the end of which is beyond human cal-
culation, renders the arts and sciences wandering and fugitive—
Being friends to humanity, they are only pleased with peace
and do not prosper without it. What do I say?—If I abandon my
pen to the impulsion of grief, with which my heart is torn,
would I not be obliged to present the cruel foresight of the
extinction of the arts and sciences in Europe? This vast part of
the universe, traveling with giant's steps towards the condition
of prime animality peculiar to savages. This superb Europe,
after having been during ages the seat of the world, whose sov-
ereign she pretended to be, become too vain of her knowledges
falling in oblivion. Our descendants will have the same notions
of it as we have now of ancient Egypt, of ancient Greece, of the
Alexanders, the Dariuses, of their power; and as to the time,
will be what America was in the XV century. No, it is not the
nervous and wholesome love of the arts and sciences which has
caused the masterpieces of every part of Europe to be carried
away to decorate the museum of Paris. It is the agony of this
love, which is manifested by convulsive motions, or it is—for—

But I return and conclude that if the United States of America wish to become the country of arts and sciences, everything concurs to offer her every means to do it.

## Plan *of* Situation *and* Organization

I. In order to arrive at the ends proposed in the preceding survey, I think it convenient that the house of national institution be under the immediate direction of Congress, who for this effect will appoint three, five, or seven of their members at every session to the inspection of it, to repress abuses, if any should be introduced; to order provisionally all what will be judged necessary after the report and advice of the particular council of that house, in which they shall always have the right of sitting in the first places, the oldest of their commissaries being in the chair and the governor [of the national institution] in the second place, whatever might be the number of these commissaries.

II. To determine where to build the house of the national institution. This house ought to be situated as near the center of the United States as possible, far from the seacoasts. It is farther to be desired that it be removed from any great cities; the reason of this situation may be perceived after what has been said in the preceding introduction.

There must be a very spacious tract of ground, because independent of the buildings, which will be in a great number, there ought to be an esplanade or Champs-de-Mars adjacent, convenient for the evolutions of infantry and cavalry and a school of artillery. This Champs-de-Mars must also present some models of fortifications.

Besides this piece of ground for a Champs-de-Mars, there must be another one, to plant a garden in, in order to obtain the knowledge of culinary vegetables and fruit trees, so that their cultivation may become an object of their instruction; at the same time their product will be a daily resource for the house. This knowledge is very necessary and very interesting to be propagated in the countries of the United States.

In fine, another piece of ground for a botanic garden; the utility of this knowledge is too generally known to need a demonstration.

The house of the national institution must also have at hand a river dependent on it, large enough for a little navigation: the establishment of little stocks. This is as an elementary introduction to navigation. There must be established a reservoir of water, commodious for a school of swimming, for it is useful that men learn to swim.

With regard to the plan of distributing the buildings and various other objects, if my work obtains any attention or if thought worthy of execution, when the place where it is to be situated be decided upon, after having taken notice of this place, I shall furnish the plan of it, such as I conceive it at present. Then it will only be a question to adapt it to this place.

III. It is necessary to settle upon every person attached to the said establishment a provision which may procure him a comfortable existence and proportionate to the employment which he there holds: classing for this object all those persons in five principal orders, to wit:

1. The institutors. That is to say, the governor, two assistants, the general director of studies, the intendant of policy and finances.

2. The professors, masters, and officers of health, and the minister of holy worship.

3. The guardians, tutors, library-keeper, the secretary-keeper of the archives, the gardener master, keepers of the magazines of artillery, of fortifications, and of the stocks.

4. The chiefs of the infirmary, of the cloths, dormitories, of the kitchen, of the pantry, and of the cellar.

5. The servants.

N.B. As the national institution ought to comprehend the youth of both sexes, it is understood that in these three last orders there shall be subjects of both sexes.

It is to be wished that all the persons employed in this house be married, and of preference the women whose husbands would be employed should be employed also.

Besides these provisions, it is necessary to determine that the widows of persons employed, who till the death of their husband had not been employed in any business, if they then wish to devote themselves to it, they should be preferred to all others and kept in the house till there shall be a vacancy; (surely it will always be possible to occupy them relatively to their stations) if they wish to retire, a living shall be granted them equal to that which is going to be stipulated for those who are employed before the decease of their husbands.

With regard to the widows who shall have been employed during the life of their husbands, they shall be there maintained and shall receive as an annual gratification one quarter, third, half, three quarters, or the whole of the allowances which their husbands enjoyed, in proportion to the time they shall have exercised, that is to say, one quarter for ten years, one third for fifteen, and a half for twenty, three quarters for twenty-five, and the whole for thirty. This proportion is that which ought to be observed in granting retreats to the man as well as to the women employed in the said house; and the half of this same progressive gratification ought to be granted to both above their provisions at the said epochs of 10, 15, 20, 25 and 30 years of exercise. There ought also to be a favor for those who should become infirm, to be taken care of, in every point gratis, in premises contiguous to the infirmary, with the enjoyment of half the annual gratification for each sex, there not being any more appointments for them.

The children of each sex, of persons attached to the house, will be there educated at the expense of the said house and according to the condition of their respective parents. Education comprehends always the maintenance, as well in health as in sickness. But if some parents wish to make their children change their station, they shall pay half the price which shall have been fixed upon, for the board of the children of the inhabitants of the country. And those children whose fathers shall have died after having left their functions shall be placed in the same kind of condition as their fathers by the care of the administrators of the house, and they shall there be sustained by a portion at the rate that shall be judged sufficient for their maintenance till 25 years of age, this establishment being to them in that case a father and tutor till the age of majority, at which time they must be able to shift for themselves. The orphans whose fathers shall have died in their offices must be settled and endowed by this establishment: Their dowry shall be the furniture and garnishment of a farm tillable by two ploughs, or its value.

It has undoubtedly been remarked that I indicate precautions for children being maintained as much as possible in the condition of their father. It is on a very positive purpose that I say so. The end of the institution which I propose being to develop a growing nation and not to produce a source of half-learned men, of pseudo-philosophers who with systems of a foolish imagination wish to substitute a metaphysical existence, and always reasoning from the part of every individual to the active and useful, which is commanded by all the necessities of nature, and at every instant. Besides, should we then be so far from seeing that in a republic all the professions are useful, and for that reason man is estimable and merits the consideration of every individual of society when he well fulfills all the duties of the station which he has chosen? That he who devotes himself to professions which prejudices have imagined to regard with an eye of disdain, because they only suppose the action of the physical organs, merits as much more as he renounces both the present luster and a fame to transmit to posterity, to be more useful to his contemporaries?

I speak here principally of all the professions relative to agriculture, of all the mechanic arts, of all trades, and of all kinds of service. And by this word service are expressed all the possible functions of society. But more particularly it is equally understood of a man in the military character, or another in being a servant; surely because both impose an absolute silence to their own wills, to the development of their judgment and diverse motions of their soul, to render their actions dependent, the use that they can make of their physical faculties, to the orders which they receive from his overseers. These reflections, which I have often made in the course of my military career, never made me behold my station as a degradation of my being, suppressing social considerations which are justly granted to it, though generally without seeing the motives of it.

In the metaphysical meditations of the man who shuts himself up in his closet, abandons society in order to create his own world, to people it, and organize its relations; in such meditations, without doubt, the case is not the same and very different to the unreflecting man who exists in the vortex of the world, enjoys the established regards, and exacts so much the more as he does neither suspect to what title they are granted to him nor what he himself owes to others. But if one will pause a moment upon this idea, I am persuaded he will perceive that social existence being the negation of pure nature, one must be in the world a tiger, a bear, a wolf, a fox, a sheep, etc., or making use of reason, which gives us a superiority over beasts makes us sociable, by the submission of the transports of our animality (which are no others than our being abandoned to passions) to the want of other men, to have a right to their regard and a reciprocity of help and good offices.

Between people of different trades this is very easy to perceive; for a tailor says to a shoemaker, make me a pair of shoes and I will make you a coat. And just so the physician says to the workman, to his domestic, serve me in your different lines and I shall have time to study to help you in your sicknesses. The surgeon and the apothecary use the very same language. The lawyer says that he studies and watches incessantly to assure the fortune and the repose of everyone and to preserve them from assassins and thieves; the mechanic, that he constructs machines to lighten hardships, etc. And saying these truths, everyone acknowledges his dependence on other professions.

Therefore in a society we serve one another reciprocally, the manner alone in which we do it differs. And like Dominick the vinegar merchant dragging along his wheelbarrow says to a rich merchant, *"You sell by wholesale, and I by retail, but it is always to sell in order to gain."*

Upon the theater of the world the merchant flourishes in a manner very different from that of his interlocutor. However, what is the end of their respective situation? It is that the merchant being ruined by immense losses and not being able to support his station in society would have died perhaps for grief, had not the good Dominick, always sober, according to his condition been able to bring him the produce of his economy, to re-establish his affairs. *"Money, pernicious metal,"* says the vinegar merchant, *"thou hast done so much mischief in the world,* do thou good *for once, if thou canst."* The union of his son (an honest fellow) with the daughter of the merchant, whom he loved with a sweet return, finished to seal the axiom of equality: *it is always selling in order to gain.*

But after what I have said concerning the relation which there is between military and domestic service, some persons might believe I was discharging my passion or any other sentiment equally unworthy of being listened to. I declare, then, that I have nothing to retract, that it is long since I have perceived these relations, that I am a soldier from extraction, from condition, that in a word I glory in it; for, if the extent of sacrifices ought to be of any consideration, must it not be granted that there is no profession which exacts so many as that of arms? How many illustrious magistrates, people of letters, philosophers of every class, to a few warriors whose names are transmitted to posterity? The multitude of the children of Bellona[5] do not leave after them any trace of their existence, as much because they profess a state, almost in every case, passively submitted to laws, which permitted little ground for the development of their knowledge and their particular character; and that above all, the law of subordination causes a single one to shine by the courage, the talents, and the virtues of thousands.

Instead then of the melancholy envy tormenting itself with the degrees of consideration granted to this profession, let everyone rather be impressed to acknowledge that the pains and sacrifices are in progression more by a hundredfold than the considerations and recompenses! The sacrifice of a comfortable life, of health, of fortune, and above all that, the sacrifice of self-love, on account of subordination, which compress it continually, opposes with fetters at every step, to display one's talents, to acquire a reputation and the advantages which accompany it, a transcendent reputation to leave to posterity, both for the satisfaction and patrimony to his latest posterity. Who has ever seriously reflected upon all these considerations? He who has fixed them with an eye free from prejudices and who shall know a term for his acknowledgment towards the defenders of his country will never dare to name himself.

But by educating children in the same condition as their fathers, it cannot be here understood, literally, that the son of a geometer shall be a geometer; that of a grammarian, a grammarian; that of a cook, a cook; that of a domestic, a domestic, etc., but only a relation of condition which may be called, if they please, after the name of the class or order. And it ought to be nevertheless very precisely understood that a pupil who should show a disposition and a determined inclination for any state or profession whatever should be educated according to that state, the principal object being to make subjects capable of being serviceable to their country.

For this purpose they will be, as much as possible, placed in the interior part of the republic, either attached to manufactures or other public establishments, in order to improve and naturalize the arts, sciences, and a national character—for it is in this manner a wise government ought to direct a nation towards its aim, to inoculate the children of every generation with its plants. It gently unfolds itself without convulsions, without trouble, without those abominable rentings which produce divided minds, maintained by hotheads calling themselves philosophers, in the very instant they display more of that ferocious character which distinguishes the sect.

The sect would overturn and destroy spontaneously everything which does not at first submit to their wills and to create as by a magic effect all the dreams of their exasperated imaginations. The blood which it causes to flow, the devastations which it causes to be committed, far from recalling the voice of nature, far from testifying the least sentiments of grief, it inebriates it with joy. Courage, say they to themselves; more blood, some other heads more, and they will not dare to think otherwise than we do. The present generation must have the generosity to sacrifice themselves, to sacrifice everything which is imperfect, in order to assure posterity a population entirely angelical.

Unhappy wretch! If thou art not an atrocious villain, where does thy madness lead thee? Will the past ages never be a lesson for their posterity? Will not thy barbarity rather sow the seeds of an implacable hatred? Thou art preparing subjects of re-crimination for future ages, with which my soul is so much the more penetrated as thou hast the least foreseen it. Nothing ought to be done by a sudden emotion, in the social order; observe nature in her least effects: Everything has its infancy, its adolescence, before its virility. Thou callest thyself a philosopher! Wast thou born a philosopher? How many years have been necessary before thou could'st conceive a simple idea, before thou could'st combine it? Before thou could'st produce it even to the will of thy self-love, which seeks the applause of thy age, by telling it that thou pretendest only to that of posterity? Thou wilt, unhappy feverish man, live for posterity; learn then, first to live for thy contemporaries, who nourish thee, assist thee in all thy wants, and do not murder them. If thou succeedest in learning to live for the instant of thy transient existence upon this earth; go, thou shalt have then truly lived for the ages which are to come, and principally fear to transmit to them a remembrance worse than that of the foolish man of Ephesus.

IV. It is actually necessary to agree upon the mode in which children are to be admitted in the said establishment. It is here particularly necessary to call to mind the representations which we have made, the pressing reasons which we have represented in order to be occupied in increasing the population of the country as much as possible; to extract from those of the cities all what can be returned there in a solid and useful manner: but those persons who are of age are not susceptible of it, but only children; and yet in order to fix them there, it is necessary that they have not opened their eyes in the cities. Let them also call to mind that I have also announced that the social institutions in a wise government ought to be of an inviting character and not that of commanding of the laws. After this succinct rememoration, this is what I propose, and humanity solicits it with great clamors, independently of the interests of the United States of America.

1.  That there be in every city an office, under the daily and continual watch of the municipal officers, where shall be established a turning-box for the deposit of foundlings, bastards, or others. (If I would disclose all my reasons for everything, this would become a voluminous work, would make me digress from my object; especially it would delay its publication; let it suffice, then, that I only say here that the birth of bastards commands more than the secret and the mystery, and many indigent people in the cities demand this help. The fathers and especially the mothers of bastards, and what I here call by the general name of *others,* have need of the cloak of mystery.) There ought to be kept an exact register of all notes and signs which should be deposited with such children. It is proper to have in these houses of trust some nurses for the first days of the children's existence. And there ought to be a register of the inhabitants of the country who should demand some of these children, in order to educate them in their own families, equal to their own children; in observing to attach them to agriculture as their age and strength will permit. Till the age of eighteen years these inhabitants of the country shall owe nothing to these children but subsistence and maintenance, but from 21 to 25 years of age

these children shall be forced to remain attached to the rural labors of these same inhabitants, who shall then give them the wages which all others would have for the same labor.

This requests a correspondence well established near one another, of the inhabitants of countries which are farthest from the cities. This correspondence ought to be established by the inhabitants of every province to their respective municipal officers, and from these to their colleagues in the great cities. And more, the municipal officers in the respective provinces ought to watch and take care that these foundlings be suitably kept.

Besides what we have just announced for the profit and indemnification of these inhabitants of the country by the labor of the foundlings, as it is said, till the majority of 25 years, this inhabitant shall have as many children of his own educated gratis, in the house of the institution, till the age of 18 years, as he shall bring up as many foundlings, in the bosom of his family, to the labor of agriculture and that of the same sex of those that he shall educate.

Those foundlings at the age of 25 years shall be married between themselves according to their wills, and shall for their portion be furnished with a little household and shall receive instruments and other objects necessary for a farm of one plough in order to enable them to attend to the station of farmer. The little economy which every couple shall have made from 18 to 25 years upon their wages joined to this portion will put them in a condition of becoming farmers with means to prosper.

What has just been said and what will still be said concerning the inhabitants of the country comprehends the inhabitant proprietor as well as the inhabitant farmer.

2. Every inhabitant of the country shall have a right to have his children educated in the national house, though he does not bring up any foundling in his family, but then he shall pay for each of his children in the said house, half board. They shall there be educated till the age of 18 years.

3. Every child of inhabitants of the country who shall have lost father and mother shall be educated in the national house and shall be assimilated to the orphans employed in this house at the time of their decease.

4. Every child of a countryman who shall have lost his father will be educated in the house of the institution according to the 3rd article.

5. Every child of a countryman who shall have lost his mother, but whose father shall not have in his family any foundling, shall be educated in the national house, only paying a quarter of the board till the age of 18 years.

6. Every inhabitant of cities, proprietor of productive lands upon which he shall cause foundlings to be brought up to agriculture, shall have his children educated in the national house till the age of 18; to wit, if he has an equal number of foundlings in his charge, he shall have his own educated for half the board, and if he has a double number of foundlings, gratis.

7. Every inhabitant of cities, proprietor of arable lands, though he does not cause any foundling to be educated thereon, shall have his children educated in the national house till the age of 18 years, paying three quarters of the board.

8. Every inhabitant of the city, proprietor or not, who shall educate in his house orphans of the city or other children according to his profession or to the apprenticeship of trades on the same conditions as the inhabitant of the country ought to educate, according to the article 6th shall have an equal number of his own children educated at the national house till the age of 18 years, paying for each two thirds of the board.

9. Every child of an inhabitant of a city who shall have lost father and mother shall be educated in the national house and likened to the orphans of persons employed in that house, if it is proved that his parents have not left him any means, but if they have left him means, he will only remain there on that footing till the age of 18 years.

10. Every child of an inhabitant of a city who shall have lost his father shall be considered in the case of article 9th.

11. Every child of an inhabitant of a city who shall have lost his mother and whose father shall not have any foundlings or orphans upon his possessions nor in his house in the city shall be educated in the national house, paying a third of the board, till the age of 18 years.

12. Every inhabitant of cities who shall not be a proprietor of arable lands and who shall not have any foundling or orphan at his charge shall have his children educated in the national house, paying the board.

Here it is proper, I believe, to determine upon the price of the board, which ought to be three hundred dollars. The children shall be educated, instructed, lodged, and dressed, in a word, maintained in every point, both in health and sickness; both for their physical needs and for all that shall be useful to their education and instruction; as also for all which shall be judged useful both for their reward and recompenses, and their amusements in their recreation, in order to habituate them, to enjoy these with the amiable gaiety of their age and the decency which characterizes a good education.

13. But as the arts and sciences are friends to humanity, and not to any particular society or nation, it is their nature to love to extend themselves, and form, union between every people which are dispersed upon the globe. This character of the arts and sciences is not undoubtedly a stranger to the republican genius, and I think it proper to every good man, who enjoys with so much the more satisfaction that the objects of his enjoyment are the more extensive, for he may then be in correspondence with a great number. One likes to be heard or always improve by listening. I propose therefore in the last place that children who do not belong to the United States, that is to say, those whose father belongs to another country may be admitted into this house, which, I think, may be called a *Superb Institution,* by paying one quarter above the price of board, that is four hundred dollars. The continent of America presents a vast space without the limits circumscribed to the United States; correspondences which would tend to bring the

people of the different parts of this vast continent nearer could only produce a happy effect. The West Indies, which surround America like the satellites of planets, have their inclination and rotations in an orbit dependent on the United States. The wants of the inhabitants of all these isles place them in a continual correspondence with the continent. Everything announces that nature has created them to unite with the United States. May therefore the institution hasten the moment of so desirable a union.

14. The children of each sex ought to be admitted in the national house, from 5 till 7 years, those who shall have father and mother—Those who shall have lost their mother from 5 till 8; those who shall have lost their father from 5 till 9; those who shall have lost both father and mother from 5 till 10 years.

15. The children of all persons who shall have died in the service of the Republic in any kind whatever shall be in the class of the children of professors or other officers in the national house who shall have died in their offices.

16. The children of persons who are proprietors or attached to manufactures established in the interior shall be considered as those of the countrymen.

As to the rules for the policy of this house, the distribution and succession of classes, etc., I engage to furnish them when they shall be requested.

# FOUNDATION

If the utility of a national institution such as I have proposed is acknowledged, I do not think that there can be found any great obstacles in forming the funds necessary for its creation. I think, in order to succeed in it, it would be proper:

I. That in consideration of a register of the real population of the states, each one should furnish once only a sum which from an hundred thousand dollars for the weakest state should go in arithmetical progression to the most considerable, admitting the ratio of this progression should be twenty thousand dollars. This sum for the foundation should be in the hands of the treasury of every state, and its collection should be made by the gratuitive cares of the members of the Assembly of the States, aided in the same patriotic manner in the particular places by the municipal officers that are under the same jurisdiction.

II. This first foundation being finished, to create a lottery, in imitation of that of the royal military school of Paris, whose inspection and administration should be done gratis, by the commissaries of Congress, for the administration of the national establishment. The general offices held at the place of the Congress meeting, and the particular offices divided in the different states, by the cares and under the immediate inspection of the members of Congress assembled from each state, aided by the municipal officers under their respective jurisdiction.

III. To establish a small collection upon the colonial commodities, such as sugar, coffee, cocoanuts, tea. If they answer that these objects have become wants of the first necessity, I shall answer that they are not so in the order of nature. I shall neither discuss this question nor that of knowing if they are advantageous to health. But I shall observe, and I affirm it, that their great use is the reason which causes native cultivation to be neglected, the perfection of which more consonant to good health. They are generally proper for islanders such as the inhabitants of England and of Holland, which on account of the narrowness of their soil, not being sufficient to supply the great number of their population, nourish them both on the land and sea with foreign productions, and accustom infancy to needs which carry it to exterior commerce, and placing by that means their population as much upon the sea as the land, their territory only being in some sort the seat of their government, the cradle of their children, and the laboratory of their women; the men keeping much more without, where they travel incessantly.

IV. A collection upon the particular arms, liveries, and carriages of the city.

Such are the principal sources where I think the means of the foundation of this establishment may be had. But I shall not expatiate any more upon this object; it belongs to the representatives of the country: it specially belongs to Congress to know how to fix such collections. Certainly these are not taxes upon the people, and the destination of these collections is for the relief of every particular family and at the same time for the prosperity of their country.

In proportion as population shall increase and cause augmentations in the annual expenses, if the administration of the house has been well conducted, it will always be found to have revenues sufficient to defray its annual expenses. She must produce manufactures, navigations, favorable for exportation and for commerce in the interior, routes, etc., all things which will augment its annual revenues and conduct it more and more to an agreeable and useful interior culture, there to extend an agreeable ease and show with luster a numerous people in this happy country, sprung, as it were, from the earth, with the plants with which it was nourished. I shall furnish the plan of administration which must be followed in order to produce this effect.

I shall finish by wishing that this establishment may soon snatch from idleness and all the evils which are its attendants that quantity of individuals which are found in every city; and there will be occupation of every kind, consequently, for everyone, from the first steps of the creation of a national Institution in the United States.

# POSTSCRIPT

I heard that the President, at the opening of the present session, has solicited the attention of the legislature and the cares of government for the national institutions.[6] Being retired in the country, I have not yet been able to procure the President's speech, which would have given me great light upon the matter I have treated in this little writing, and the objects on which I ought more particularly to carry my plan. I deliver it then such as it is, and when I shall be acquainted with this speech, with the intentions of government more particularly, I shall betake myself to work if any is required from me.

In July 1796, I came for the first time in the United States. I then saw the southern and northern parts, during more than ten months which I passed on the continent. I returned here the 25th of last January. It is at that epoch that I have observed the houses of education with more attention. In April, I embraced the career of institutor, and my observations have acquired a more determined consistency. They have inspired me with the desire of ratifying what should be in my power, in a house of Institution, that I should hold. I have made my prospectus; it has been dispersed since last fall, both on the continent and West Indies. But through the advice of some American citizens, I have contracted it to the most simple representations.

By putting this prospectus on paper, my ideas have taken a character of extension which will be perceived in the writing I now publish. I have matured it in my reflexion. For want of time to put it in writing, I have kept it within myself till this day; but I have conversed of it with many well-instructed persons in order to enrich myself with their observations.

Being always occupied with the instruction of children, I have but a very little time to apply myself to other business. On account of finding all the elementary books defective and especially very insufficient for children, I am obliged at the beginning of every pupil to employ myself in making books, as well for the principles of the language as for all the other objects I teach. It is only in the silence of the night that I am able to lose a few hours of sleep in order to furnish my pupils with books on those several elements. And I am obliged to deprive them of some of these to lay down my ideas with haste. After this faithful account of my time, I dare hope some indulgence from the public, both for the plan which I here present them with and for all what I shall take the liberty of offering to them.

I am myself penetrated with the imperfection of my work. Perhaps it is above my abilities; the uprightness of my intentions determines me to deliver it to be printed and causes me to make the very sacrifice of my self-love. I present myself without the cares of a polish which perhaps would spare me criticisms, as severe as judicious.

Nothing remains now for me to do but to thank beforehand those who should honor me with their criticism, supposing my work worthy of their attention; and I hope they will do it with that politeness which well-intentioned persons and men of letters owe to one another. The flambeau of criticism ought to cast forth a pure and agreeable light and not to resemble those mirrors, the ardent flame of which wounds and devours.

# 8

# SAMUEL KNOX

*An Essay on the Best System of Liberal Education,
Adapted to the Genius of the Government of the
United States. Comprehending also, an Uniform
General Plan for Instituting and Conducting
Public Schools, in This Country, on Principles of
the Most Extensive Utility. To Which Is Prefixed,
an Address to the Legislature of Maryland on
That Subject (Philadelphia, 1799)*

[Samuel Knox (1756-1832) was born in Ireland and came to the
United States about 1795, after having graduated from the University of Glasgow. He settled at Bladensburg, Maryland, as a
Presbyterian minister. During a career as clergyman and educator,
he also mixed actively in politics; in 1800 he issued a pamphlet
supporting the religious ideas of Thomas Jefferson. For many years
he was principal of an academy at Frederick, Maryland. He shared
with Samuel Harrison Smith the prize offered by the American
Philosophical Society in 1797 for the best essay on a national system
of education. More detailed in his suggestions than most of the
essayists here collected, Smith with this essay probably influenced
Thomas Jefferson's planning of the University of Virginia. The
essay was published at Baltimore in 1799 by Warner and Hanna.]

# To the Critics

---

THE author begs leave to inform the public that in the writing as well as the publishing of the subsequent sentiments on an uniform plan of national education, nothing but the most solicitous desire to contribute even a mite to the interest or success of what so highly concerns the happiness and credit of the *United States* could have induced him to submit his observations on any subject to the eye of the learned and judicious critic, under the many disadvantages he had to encounter.

When he assures SUCH that, in writing, the unremitting labors of professional attendance prevented him from more than a few minutes attention to the subject at one time, and that by the same cause he has been prevented from superintending the *press,* he trusts the ingenuous and liberal will adopt the following sentiment of one whose taste and accuracy in composition have been long estimated as the standard of excellence.

> . . . Non ego paucis
> Offendar maculis, quas aut incuria fudit
> Aut humana parum cavit natura.       HOR.[1]

To the HONORABLE the LEGISLATORS of the STATE of MARYLAND, for the Session of 1798—the following observations, introductory to an uniform plan of national education, are most respectfully submitted by the author.

GENTLEMEN,

THE thorough conviction of your being to the utmost extent of your inclinations as well as of your delegated trust and power the zealous patrons of public improvement is the only apology your addresser conceives necessary for his presumption in laying before you the following considerations on the most interesting of all subjects to the happiness of MARYLAND in particular and that great civil community of which she forms so respectable a part in general.

There is no individual in society whom you may not hear ACKNOWLEDGING the great importance of education. Even those who are most ignorant of its advantages are heard to express the highest encomiums on its inestimable value to the state, to the interests of human happiness, social or individual. The learned and unlearned seem equally agreed on this subject. No party spirit breathes its jealous and pestilential influence in opposition to its general encouragement, patronage, and support. This is that subject on which, in a peculiar degree, the smiles and approbation of heaven may be expected to co-operate with the exertions of men. Seeing, then, it has obtained so universal an approbation in the minds of all, is it not, in some respects, paradoxical that all the members of the same community do not conspire in bringing into effect some well-digested plan for organizing and establishing that which seems to be the common object of their wishes, the most desirable attainment for the promotion of public happiness?

Should this interrogatory observation be applied to the STATE, which has chosen you, GENTLEMEN, to be its legislators, it will be found that, though much has been done in behalf of PUBLIC EDUCATION and though many excellent characters among us have lately given ample testimony of their liberality, philanthropy, and patriotism, in contributing to the state colleges and other seminaries, yet, as it is still too easy to observe, all that might reasonably be done in so *good a cause* has not yet been effected.

In every corner or portion of the state, how many hundreds of our youth are deprived of the means of any instruction suitable to the offspring of free and independent citizens? How much ignorance of literature do we everywhere meet with, even in those whose fortune and circumstances might have enabled them to have secured the means of proper improvement?

In a state like this, especially when considered as a distinguished department of a great united republican government, one or two pompous edifices and expensively endowed seminaries may give a partial and ostensible dignity to the literary character of our portion of the union, but in truth, without the means of establishing and providing proper subordinate nurseries of students, prepared for entering and attending such dignified seminaries, they may tend to absorb or swallow up the greater proportion of public patronage, but cannot, with any truth or propriety, be considered as the most effectual provision for diffusing the blessings of general knowledge or scientific improvement throughout the STATE.

Under such a government as ours and especially in a country where the inhabitants are so widely scattered over the surface of the soil, it would certainly be most suitable to have those means of *education* which are derived from the industry and exertions of the people disposed of in such a manner as would most effectually and generally promote the improvement and happiness of the people. There is no impartial or candid mind can dissent from this truth. If so, it consequently follows that the present mode of promoting the interests of public education in this state has not been with sufficient efficacy dictated by the influence of this consideration.

Were we to contrast what has yet been done in this state with that of our sister STATES throughout the union, it would be found that though MARYLAND has some share of *credit* for her exertions in behalf of public literary improvement, yet she has by no means been as generally liberal in this respect as the progressive state of her prosperity and the dignified situation she possesses should *dictate*.

In Pennsylvania, as your addresser has been credibly informed, no seminary subordinate to her university or college that has looked up to her for her fostering aid has been refused. In Virginia an excellent act has been passed during the last session of her state assembly for establishing three literary schools in each county and, consequently, for extending the blessing of education to those of her citizens who are most in want of it.

This ought ever to constitute the leading or favorite object of the legislature of a free state.

In all ages it has been the policy of those governments that existed by the slavish ignorance of the people to establish one or two sumptuously endowed schools for the sons of fortune and affluence, the expecting brood of despotical succession, leaving the canaille, the ignorant herd, to live and die, the *profanum vulgus*, the despised, enslaved, and stupid multitude.

In proportion, then, as our government is superior in its nature and constitution, in its principles and practice, to the systems of those which have been instituted for enslaving the minds as well as the bodies of their ignorant vassals, so should the most general means of diffusing and promoting knowledge be adopted, patronized, and supported in this and every other portion of the union.

It is not, gentlemen, the object of your addresser on this subject to censure what has already been done in behalf of education in that state of which you are the legislators. What is, or ought to be, of the highest importance with all who have any regard for the public good is to endeavor to call forth a proper attention to the present state of literary instruction, examine wherein it is defective, and try to point out such means as may have a tendency to render Maryland as respectable in a literary point of view as the situation and other dignified circumstances in her local and political existence should direct.

This it becomes all to consider as highly essential to the best interests of the community. We ought to be convinced by experience that no external advantage arising from situation, intercourse, or any other superficial means of improvement can be substituted for that solid instruction which the human mind can acquire only by the regular discipline of the school and the well-directed labors of literary study and application. The literary character of our state, it is true, may assume the tin-

seled outside of a superficial polish, but that dignity of understanding, that manliness of sentiment, that elegance of taste
and criticism, and that scientific illumination which ought to
constitute its most striking features we may look for in vain
without the public patronage of some general, well-digested
system of education.

The question, then, is, are we, or are we not, in possession of
such a system? No. The general complaint of the community
as well as a candid inquiry into the state of our public schools
must show, with incontrovertible evidence, that in this respect
MARYLAND is inferior to several portions of the UNION
whose resources for supporting such seminaries are not superior
to what we possess.

Such observations cannot be justly considered as derogatory
to the credit of the state college or any other seminary already
instituted in any part of the state.[2] For, allowing that all the
advantages reasonably to be expected from the state college
were fully realized—on the supposition that from the respectable attention and zeal of its *trustees*, the abilities of its *professors*, and the excellence of its discipline and regulations, it
held out the most flattering encouragement for the improvement of our youth—still it would be highly preposterous, repugnant to its interests as well as obnoxious to the genius of
our government and the spirit of the national constitution, to
allow it to supersede the necessity of patronizing subordinate
seminaries or to absorb all public liberality in support of literary instruction.

It would, thus, be repugnant to its own interest, inasmuch
as it must be on the preparatory nurseries of students throughout the state that its advancing prosperity and success must
depend. It would be, thus, repugnant to the genius or spirit of
our government, inasmuch as it could not be considered as
affording equal advantages to all who equally contributed to
its support.

Were there no more than one or two such seminaries or colleges established in the United States, then might ours attain

a dignified consequence, without much dependence on the particular state by which it was endowed. But, since every state in the union has been equally liberal in endowing or making proper provision for an institution of the same nature, the support of each, as well as the subjects of its *utility* and improvement, must be derived from that state alone to which it belongs.

Hence appears the necessity or importance, even with a view to the interest of the STATE COLLEGE, of proper nurseries, in order to supply it with a competent number and constant succession of students, as well as for promoting and extending the blessings of literary knowledge and improvement to the general body of the community.

This view of the subject is earnestly recommended to the attention of the legislature and all who have it in any degree in their power to become the patrons of scientific instruction.

On candidly examining into the present state of *education* in Maryland, it is impossible not to observe, and it is done with much regret, that some remnant of a former spirit of religious prejudice and partiality still prevails. It is true that, agreeably to the spirit or genius of our government, every particular religious denomination has a well founded right to erect such particular, private seminaries as they may consider most consonant with the spirit of that particular religious system they profess.

It should, however, become a free and enlightened people as much as possible to separate the pursuits of science and literary knowledge from that narrow restriction and contracted influence of peculiar religious opinions or ecclesiastical policies, by which they have been too long and too generally obstructed. Perhaps there is no circumstance can be brought into view in the history of scientific improvement that has more retarded its progress or tended to enslave the human mind than that of admitting any combination to exist between the interests of academical instruction and the too often partial interests of particular religious bodies. This combination every free republican state ought to break. On its dissolution the cause of *genuine federalism* as much as the cause of science ultimately depends. Disregarded in our publicly endowed systems of education it must more or less tend to cherish those civil broils, national prejudices, and religious feuds and jealousies that, hitherto, have stained the historic page of the otherwise most enlightened nations on earth.

Let it, then, be an established principle in all our patriotic exertions in promoting academical instruction that no publicly endowed seminary in this state shall ever be characterised as the NURSLING or even distinguished by the *appellation* of any particular party of religious professors.

So far would this, however, be from proving inimical to *liberty* of *conscience* or *religious privilege* that it would rather be directing them to their own proper and exalted sphere. It would be freeing from the partial restraints of religious system that which ought to be uncircumscribed from all connection with peculiar tenets or such habits and modes of thinking as have been imbibed without study or premeditation. As one great object of education should be to inculcate *independence* of *mind* and, consequently, an aversion to the embracing of any species of knowledge, moral, physical, or religious, without examination and consequent conviction.

So, in order to provide for these valuable attainments, every public seminary ought to be absolutely independent of all that would militate against these important objects. No public literary institution can, then, be suited to the genius of the constitution of this state that would tend either to dissolve or to establish any peculiar religious principles which may have been impressed on the minds of youth by their parents or the religious instructors of that particular society or denomination to which they might belong.

In nations where peculiar systems of religion are established, it is with consistency that the clergy of those national churches are generally preferred as the guardians, directors, and teachers of their national systems of education. But, under our happy constitution, the very great variety of religious denominations which in this respect its diversified citizens profess must render it exceedingly improper, partial, and unjust.

Besides, it should be considered that such a partial principle must be often ruinous in its tendency, by discouraging true merit and genius as well as in exciting and cherishing such selfish prejudices and invidious jealousies as public education ought rather to be calculated to eradicate than encourage or promote.

Let, then, the governor, the legislators, and the enlightened sons of science, whether of the clergy or the laity, of every description or denomination, be the only patrons, directors, and guardians of whatever seminaries have been or hereafter may be publicly patronized in the state of Maryland. The peculiar propriety of attending to this consideration, especially as it regards a *National University*, has been still farther considered and recommended in the subsequent essay on that part of the subject.

Another object of equal magnitude and importance to the state on the subject of education is the extent of the plan on which it ought to be conducted. With respect to this it may be observed, in the first place, that it is very common to find speculative theories abound where any field for innovation or encouragement presents itself. A safe guide in determining the merit or demerit of all such theories may be to examine them by such systems as have accomplished the greatest proficients in literature that the world hath yet produced. It will be found that ancient or modern times have furnished very few indeed who arrived at the zenith of literary merit in all its various departments by any other plan than a persevering submission to the well directed discipline and progressive improvement of academical instruction.*

---

* Multa tulit fecitque puer, sudavit et alsit,
abstinuit Venere et vino; qui Pythia cantat
tibicen, didicit prius extimuitque magistrum.
                                        HOR.

["He has borne much and done much as a boy, has sweated and shivered, has kept aloof from wine and women. The flautist who plays at the Pythian

Though it be true that some who were possessed of distinguished parts and genius may have acquired the most comprehensive literary knowledge, even on a very deficient or empirical plan of education, yet in so important an object to the state as public instruction, that which has been well tried and approved by experience ought not to be rashly abandoned. It is, surely, entitled to a decided preference to mere speculative theory.

A remark, too well founded with regard to the present taste for education apparently most prevalent in this state, is that a very superficial and contracted plan seems to be gaining ground. The dictates of interest or avarice on the one hand and the soft suggestions of ease, indulgence, and voluptuousness on the other appear to incline many to abridge, as much as possible, that path by which alone youth can be conducted to virtue and science. But is it not to be feared that this abridgment may prevent many from ever enjoying these inestimable acquisitions? Everything most valuable to the mental or corporeal constitution and happiness of man must be the attainment of long, steady, and persevering attention.

To the prevalance of a vitiated taste, in education, opposite to this observation, it is owing that classical erudition a few years since so liberally patronized by many in the most polished places in Maryland begins to be exploded.

In the minds of many who consider themselves capable of judging on this subject, it has been forced to relinquish its solid and invaluable advantages for a smattering in French and the accomplishments preparatory for the counting room. With many it begins to be an object of higher importance to have young master initiated in the science of a smart or graceful air and all the little arcana of social pertness and confidence than in the beauties of classical elegance; or the having formed a proper taste for literary and scientific accomplishments. In an

---

games, has first learned his lessons and been in awe of a master." H. Rushton Fairclough, trans., *Horace: Satires, Epistles and Ars Poetica*, lines 413-415 (Loeb Classical Library), pp. 484-485.]

enlightened and free state the *Graces* and *Muses* should ever go hand in hand. Wherever the former have been honored with the preference, there we may trace that superficial and tinseled national character which, in the eye of the ignorant, may assume a false and temporary splendor but must ever appear contemptible in presence of that sound and lasting polish which a comprehensive course of well directed education can alone confer.

The former may be decorated with such meretricious charms as may engage the attention of the superficial or the dissolute. The latter commands that respect which is lasting, and the more it is examined will be the more estimated and admired.

There is another mistake in education into which there is reason to apprehend some even of the most enlightened have fallen. Having before them the bright example of some transcendent genius who, untaught by any habits of literary discipline, unacquainted with the forms or systems of the schools, has by the dictates of his own vigorous mind directed chiefly to some favorite study been enabled to attain to a higher sphere of excellence in some departments of scientific knowledge than those who had been trained up in the most celebrated nurseries of scholastic education, such have been led to consider this as derogatory from the merit of academical instruction. Calculating on one or two instances of this kind, they have commenced the enthusiastic vindications of a new system or plan of literary education—such a plan as would immediately lead the scholar into the knowledge or study of the sciences, without the usual attention either to the classics and ancient languages, or even to that elementary preparation on the due attainment of which the thorough acquisition of any science must depend.

Such theorists, however, take but a very partial view of the subject. They do not consider the vast difference there is in the natural endowments of the human mind, especially in youth. They do not reflect that the course of education suited to a great or uncommon genius would be extremely improper for youth in general. They forget that some proceed with a rapidity of progress that appears directed by something like inspiration, while others are obliged to advance by such slow and almost imperceptible steps that their proficiency is scarcely apparent, and whom it is necessary to lead, as it were by the hand, examining every inch of the course from the simplest principles to the most difficult and abstruse.

From these considerations it would certainly appear most proper, in establishing or extensively patronising a liberal system of education, that it should be generally adapted to the various natural endowments and genius of those who are to be trained up by its discipline.

While such a system, instead of imposing restraint, should tend to encourage the ardor of extraordinary genius and application, it should, at same time, provide for the most suitable nurture of those of slower growth, yet equally rising to some maturity in improvement and knowledge.

Much, it is true, on every plan of literary instruction, depends on directing genius to the proper object of attainment. But it is certain that a highly distinguished genius will generally find out that subject which is most adapted to its own powers and can scarcely be confined to any other. It will therefore, in general, rise superior to that more restricting discipline which may be absolutely necessary for those of weaker endowments; and, consequently, proves that a general system of education ought rather to be adapted to those whose parts may be more properly assigned to mediocrity than to excellence.

Some are found to have taken up the opinion that the acquisition of the Greek and Latin languages, the minutiæ of their grammars, and a well-formed taste for the beauties of the ancient classical writers has a tendency to damp natural genius, pervert its powers, and misapply its attention.† It is, however, to be apprehended that this opinion arises chiefly from the

† See Doctor Rush's eloquent eulogium on David Rittenhouse. [Benjamin Rush, *An Eulogium, Intended To Perpetuate the Memory of David Rittenhouse* . . . (Philadelphia: for J. Ormrod by Ormrod and Conrad, 1796). Rittenhouse (1732-1796) was a prominent American instrument maker, astronomer, and mathematician.]

cause already assigned, together with the ill-judged modes on which education of that kind has been too generally conducted —as also from that variety of obstructions which the student of general literature is frequently obliged to encounter from the want of proper opportunities of improvement and, not seldom, from the negligence or indulgence of parents or guardians.

It may safely be presumed that no extraordinary genius has ever been injured by the acquisition of any part of knowledge or literature, provided it has been properly conducted or inculcated on the mind. Misdirected in its object it may have been, but, amidst the various departments of literary acquisition and that diversity of subjects it opens on the mind, such misdirection tends frequently to promote the general interests of science. It is thus that each subject of human knowledge becomes, in its turn, the favorite object of study and attainment. It may probably prevent an individual from attaining to distinguished eminence in some particular branch or department, yet, admitting a general system of education be adopted, true genius will be found to select and give a preference to that subject to which it is best adapted and in which it is most likely to become conspicuous.

Since, to a generally enlightened community, it is of importance that every part of human knowledge, whether of the useful or ornamental kind, should be patronised with the fostering hand of liberality and care, it would appear to be the most promising mean to promote this that the field for intellectual improvement or the efforts of genius should be left as wide and as varigated as possible. It is only on such a foundation that it could be calculated to afford ample scope and suitable discipline to the exceedingly diversified endowments to be found in the mental constitution of the youth of a whole state or nation. To this important consideration on the subject, as well as to the more distinguished walks of science, should the attention be turned in providing, publicly, for the means, but especially, in the direction, of a liberal system of literary education.

In certain stages or periods of human society, as well as in certain local situations, one method of establishing the means of public instruction may be preferable to another, merely on account of being more peculiarly adapted to that particular period or situation in which the state or community may be then placed.

The peculiar circumstances and present situation of the state of Maryland with regard to education, as in other respects, whether in a social or local point of view, must be best known to its government and legislature. It may, however, be observed that in every new country similarly circumstanced it should be no more than just policy, when any plan of public patronage for promoting public improvement is contemplated and to which the people are generally called upon to contribute, that the common interest should take the lead.

In providing the means of public education, if this principle prevail, it ought to excite the state legislature to attend particularly to those who are most likely to be deprived of the advantage of such an institution. This view of the subject also strongly corroborates what has been observed in behalf of the propriety of laying the foundation of the system, in the establishment of proper or suitable introductory seminaries, rather than in converting the greater part of the public support to the temporary advancement of one or two schools or colleges.

The highest advantage to be derived by the state from these must be only of a partial nature and consequently must fall far short of extending the means of proper literary information to the great body of the citizens. But, as has been already observed, the interest, dignity, and importance, as well as the utility or advantage of such seminaries, must depend, in a great degree, on well directed subordinate schools or academies. In introducing youth to a competent knowledge of the sciences, it has ever been found necessary to proceed from elementary principles. Perhaps, in the establishment of a proper system of schools for the acquisition of these sciences, a similar method is equally necessary. Let proper initiating seminaries be first patronised and instituted, and the necessity of liberally supporting the state college or university will not only be obviated but in some essential respects provided for and secured.

It is a just subject for public regret that for these few years past the cause of education throughout this state has not progressed equally with its prosperity and rising prospects. In some of the most opulent situations, to whatever cause it may be owing, the institution of well conducted seminaries appears to be less attended to than when they had less means of being liberal. It is true, some laudable attempts have been made by particular religious bodies, which have had a partial success, but even supposing such to be free from the dictates of that deference which all such bodies must ever pay to themselves and whatever is under their direction, it by no means can manifest any proof of the liberality of our state in patronising education that such particular bodies of her citizens have been most zealous and munificent in this respect.

The tendency of the influential partiality naturally inseparable from such bodies has already been noticed and is again brought into view, only to enforce the propriety of assigning the patronage and establishment of public instruction only to the province of the highest civil or legislative authority in the state, as the alone constituted guardian of whatever may promote its general prosperity and improvement.

In the prosecution of the subsequent essay, the different seminaries calculated to provide for the support of education on a liberal and extensive plan, it is presumed, may with equal propriety be suited to one state as to many. The equal distribution of the means of improvement is certainly a most desirable object. Primary or township schools and county academies appear to be best calculated for this purpose, and were the minds of the community as well convinced of the importance of a uniform established system of national education as they ought to be, it would not be considered an insurmountable expense to introduce and establish such in every county of Maryland.

Could the public mind be fully impressed with this truth,

that their interest, their character, their freedom, and their happiness depend on the state of the education of their youth, surely we should witness no patriotic exertions more zealously or generally called forth or more munificently supported than a well digested system of *public education.*

Were such schools and academies instituted in each county in the state agreeably to the plan laid down in the essay, the state college would soon be placed on the most respectable foundation, at least, with respect to the number of its students. This state alone would produce as many as might afford full employment to the most respectable body of professors. It might probably require the lapse of a few years ere such a system could be fully completed, yet if the foundation were well laid either in the institution of primary schools or county academies, though its progress on account of the other exigencies of the state would be slow, it might, by proper attention, be progressing to still higher and higher maturity and perfection.

Such a foundation most of the neighboring states have already laid; and shall MARYLAND that has ever been among the foremost in whatever concerned the public happiness or interest of the union be among the *last* in the divine work of public instruction? No—it is on the best authority we are warranted in the expectation that this subject is about to receive that respectable attention to which it so justly lays claim, that there is none the government or legislature have more at heart, and that an improved extension of its advantages has been and now is contemplated.

It has been owing to this information that I have presumed to address your Honorable Body on this occasion and should consider it as the most satisfactory circumstance in my life should any observations drawn from my long professional experience be well received and have any, even the smallest, tendency to turn your attention to this most important of all subjects to the happiness of any people.

Various are the considerations which should influence you, gentlemen, to an early and effectual attention to this business.

It has, in every age, been the genuine characteristic of civil liberty that under its cherishing auspices the most general, if not the most munificent, encouragement has been given to the improvement of the human mind. Perhaps, in the possession and under the happy administration even of such a government as that of the UNITED STATES, it would be no bad criterion for trying the various sense of their civil rights and political advantages which may be manifested in different local situations of the Union, to ascertain the degree of attention paid to the interests of education. Ignorance, more especially literary ignorance, has ever been the parent and stupid nurse of civil slavery —and in proportion as this ignorance prevails or is dissipated, so are men in every situation more or less disposed to support the interests of civil liberty or political happiness. Hence it has happened and ever will happen that despots either in religion or in politics have uniformly sought to maintain their tyrannical systems over the minds of men, by keeping those minds in the gloom of a stupid, uninformed, state of ignorance and insensibility.

Wherever we have an opportunity of observing any state, legislature, or commonwealth, or even any distinguished characters unsolicitous about the means of disseminating public instruction, there, we may be assured, the principles of despotism and ambitious encroachment have taken root.

In this place, I cannot resist the suggestion that from this view of the subject [there] presents itself to my mind [a sense] of the propriety and justice of observing that, throughout the history of that public and most illustrious living character which America or the world can now boast, there has been no trait or feature in it that has afforded a more convincing proof of his pure regard for civil liberty and its lasting or immortal existence among his fellow citizens, than his uniform patronage and liberal encouragement of public education.

To the mind whose highest and most exquisite enjoyment is constituted by the prospect of the ameliorating state of the improvement and happiness of his country and the human race, the laurels of the HERO or the triumphs of the Warrior are but secondary recommendations amidst those noble and disinterested exertions which a WASHINGTON has proposed, supported, and recommended to his country for the establishment of national literature and science.[3]

In the eye of philosophy—in the eye of all the excellent ones of the earth, these testimonies of a pure, uncorrupted spirit of patriotism and republican virtue will live to breathe their fragrant influence over the memory of that truly *great man*, when the trophies of the field, together with the monument that recorded them, through the lapse of ages, shall have lost their luster or become the mouldering victims of natural dissolution.

The illustrious example of such a character is one of the greatest blessings heaven can bestow on any people, more especially in the infantine state of their national government. Is it not then seriously to be regretted that this most amiable part of such an example and such a character should be the least honored, applauded, or imitated by a free and enlightened people? Is it not a too manifest proof that the predominant principle in our public or national taste, as well as in our civil policy, has not been always directed to its most excellent or praiseworthy object? Does it not afford an undeniable evidence that there exist other objects more influential in calling forth national munificence and patriotic exertions than the interests of intellectual improvement and the general diffusion of knowledge.

By some it may be considered as indulging too much in Utopian ideas to look for such perfection in any state as that which would influence it to consider no possible necessity under which it may be laid, either in peace or war, more powerful or energetic in its operation than the claims on that national munificence which would provide for the liberal and judicious establishment of the *general means* of intellectual improvement.

There appears, however, to be no absolute or natural impossibility in providing for such means, so as to prevent such public zeal and spirit being called forth in the cause of virtue, knowledge, and happiness. No free country, surely, ought to despair of seeing the existence of such a national spirit, and much less should it be negligent in exciting and calling it forth on all proper occasions. That this is a state which yet exists among us only in the flattering regions of hope, that it is a state to which we are not sufficiently ambitious to attain, were there not other proofs everywhere exhibited, the manner in which the subject of instituting a *National University* passed through the great legislative council of the nation may abundantly testify.

Is it to the honor of the freest country on earth—of the vindicators of that national independence which never could have originated, much less existed, but from the enlightened independence of the public mind, that the wisdom, philanthropy, and patriotism of that man, *"Who Unites All Hearts,"* has never been treated even with the appearance of disrespect, save in his liberal endeavors to cherish into maturity and perfection the all important object of a uniform national education?

But to return to what is more particularly applicable to the state of education in Maryland—some considerations still remain which may merit the attention of her legislators.

In the first place—it might be useful if the legislature would, periodically, at the end of every two years, adopt some method of enquiring into the state of such seminaries as are already instituted—either by some person appointed to inspect them or by a returned report from their trustees or visitors, which report should be published for the inspection of the state.

Such a measure would be salutary on many accounts. The legislature would thus ascertain in what respects they chiefly required their patronage or aid and consequently be prepared for supplying them in what they were deficient or encouraging them if liberally founded and conducted.

A proper investigation should also be made into the state of literary education in each district or county, in order to ascertain where it might be most proper to form some institutions, provided no *general system* could be yet adopted over all the state.

It is highly worthy of the most mature deliberation of the legislature whether it would not be better to dispose of whatever pecuniary aids or endowments they are enabled to grant in affixing certain salaries for teachers or professors of approved merit in such situations as required them, than to expend those grants in providing buildings and accommodations. It is presumed that the adjoining inhabitants of the township or county might provide a proper house suited to their circumstances or resources and that it would be found to terminate highly to the interest of education, if the legislature would confer their grants on such teachers, *and such only,* as should be certified to have merited them by persevering usefulness in their profession.

Without attending to this, considerable sums may be expended by the state in erecting proper buildings for schools and academies, and afterwards these remain as useless piles for want of proper teachers to occupy them. But were certain, fixed salaries to be paid by the legislature, tutors of approved merit would be easily procured, and there are few situations in the state where they would not be able to raise a suitable house for the education of their children, so being they had, afterwards, some public aid and encouragement in procuring and supporting a tutor of abilities and reputation.

It is not to be inferred from what has been here observed that the legislature should provide an adequate salary or support for the teacher or teachers in each of the county seminaries or primary schools. It is contemplated that such a sum only should be granted by the assembly as, together with a moderate price for the annual tuition of each student, would enable the county or township to procure and employ instructors of the first reputation. This, the legislature may assure themselves, is an object of the highest moment to the interests of public instruction—even superior to the providing of suitable buildings and accomodations, however conveniently situated or judiciously and liberally designed or executed.

It too often happens that tutors or professors are not only approved by prejudice, interest, or caprice, but also corrupted by placing their emolument on such a foundation as to render them in a great measure independent of their professional industry and exertions. Every institution so circumstanced, with respect to its professors, is defective. But a moderate patronage from the public, so as not to place the teachers independent on professional character, would have a happy effect. It would relieve their minds from those anxieties which arise from pecuniary embarrassment and at the same time could afford no effectual check to application and diligence.

In order to reduce these observations to some more practicable form, it may be necessary at present to add only the following particulars.

Should the legislature find themselves enabled to afford general and effectual aid, let, in the first place, some suitable annual salary be offered to each county or district *that may have certified to them* that they have erected a proper building for a county school or academy, should the assembly think such seminaries sufficient for the present—or if they prefer two or three township schools in each county, a suitable salary for the teachers of those schools. It would, however, be proper that the legislature should require from those to whom they made such grants that they should provide those buildings, whether for a county academy or township schools, on a plan to be directed by the committee of the assembly on the subject of education.

When it has been *certified* to the legislature that such houses or buildings have been completed agreeably to their act for that purpose—let a competent number of trustees or visitors be incorporated by act of assembly for each of those academies or schools. The business of those visitors should be to superintend diligently and regularly the conduct and progress of the institution—and to be the receivers of the annual salary from the legislature in behalf of such tutors or masters, and such only, as under their particular inspection had steadily, ably, and faithfully discharged the important trust reposed in them.

It should also be provided by the same act that the master or rector of the county academy be, ex officio, a trustee during incumbency—and it would be found no less necessary, if *practicable*, that the assembly should require some penal responsibility from all such trustees or visitors, when found deficient in so important and sacred a trust, through carelessness or neglect.

To ensure success and prosperity to any general plan the public mind ought to be prepared for its favorable reception; otherwise, however correct in theory, difficulties will embarrass its advancement. Heretofore any attempts at such a plan have failed, owing probably to a wish of having such a system as would diffuse the same advantages to all the counties in the state at the same time, even though few of them had discovered an equally laudable zeal to be among the first in promoting the interest of literature. It must surely be the duty of every enlightened legislature to cherish and call forth the emulation of the public to whatever may promote the happiness of the state.

On this principle, then, should the assembly patronize such seminaries as have been already established and commit themselves by a public notification that whenever the inhabitants of any county should erect suitable buildings for a school or academy, on a liberal foundation, the government should lend the public aid to the promotion of its prosperity and support. This could not fail to excite a spirit of emulation among the literary of each county, and the state might soon have the happiness of seeing education generally encouraged without any of those murmurs which are commonly the consequence of compulsory plans.

Should it still be asked, why ought one county to draw money, through the medium of patronage, from the public treasury in preference to another? On this principle it might be justly replied, in order that they, too, should be entitled to all the advantages of the same preference as soon as it had been merited by similar liberality and exertions.

In the establishment of any system for the public good, it must partake of some share of culpability not to provide, as far as possible, for that which may prove a reparation to the greatest deficiency. To this it is hoped the legislature so soon as they take up this subject will pay that attention which it merits. For this reason it has been here repeatedly urged as of the first importance. To such as allow themselves to examine into the present state of education in Maryland, I think there hardly can exist a doubt but that the great desideratum is the procuring of a competent number of well-qualified instructors. As already observed, there are few, if any, counties in the state incompetent to the expense of erecting suitable buildings, provided they are once properly impressed with the advantage and necessity of such institutions; but a powerful incentive to this impression would certainly be the aid of the legislature in procuring, encouraging, and supporting well-qualified teachers. The mere fame or reputation of such liberality in our legislature would induce professors of reputation to resort to Maryland as the literary patroness of science, virtue, and talents.

Should the legislature prefer offering their support on such voluntary terms to the several counties that should apply for it, it is presumed that proper and seasonable aid afforded to the forward, together with the manifest advantages derived from it, might more effectually operate in exciting such as were tardy in the business, than any pecuniary grant conferred previous to their being fully impressed with the necessity or importance of such an institution, so as to make, in its behalf, equally liberal exertions with their neighbors.

It might be enjoined on the justices of the several county courts, where any endowed school or seminary was established, to give in charge to the grand jury such parts of that law which imposed a penalty on any person or persons who refused or neglected to pursue the directions of the same, and that highly important trust, for the faithful execution of which they had been incorporated.

The legislature must be best able to judge whether it be most suitable to the genius of the constitution of the state and its present circumstances in every point of view to dispose of any contemplated aid on the above voluntary terms on the part of the different counties or to provide for an establishment by an obligatory act upon all.

It appears that the assembly of the state of Virginia, by their late provisionary act, in behalf of public *education*, have not left it to the option of the counties to erect the proper buildings for carrying their plan into effect. Each county is thereby obligated to have them prepared in a given time.[4]

Though there be every reason to believe that the general body of the citizens of this state may be as sensibly impressed with the necessity and importance of some public exertions being made by them in behalf of education as those of any other part of the Union, yet it is obvious that obligatory acts are too often necessary, in order to provide against that procrastinating disposition which frequently retards many from exerting themselves in behalf even of that which they may have much at *heart*.

Legislative aid on this plan, whether the county academies or the primary schools be first preferred, would not interfere or be inconsistent with the system of public education laid down in the subsequent essay, should it or any similar uniform national institution be at a more favorable future period established by the UNITED STATES.

There is, indeed, but too little ground for being so sanguine as to expect such a system can completely be adopted before we arrive at a more general, as well as more advanced, stage of progressive improvement than we can boast at present. Any advances,[5] however, towards it, should be considered not only highly conducive to the honor, interest, and happiness of this or any particular state that patronized them but also to the general welfare and prosperity of the union.

Such, gentlemen, are the few introductory observations I have presumed, with due deference, to lay before your honorable body in particular and the public in general—though consciousness of their great imperfection and deficiency should, perhaps, have dictated the prudence and propriety of leaving a subject of so much importance to greater and more respectable abilities. Yet, in a cause like this, I trust even a mite will be well received, as it is conceived to be the duty of every man who is in possession of even a mite to pay it into the public stock of information on whatever concerns the advancement of the prosperity or improvement of that community in which he exists.

It has not been attempted, either in this address or the subsequent essay, to introduce any lengthened declamation on the past, present, or future advantages of public education to any community. This, it is true, might have presented a more spacious and flowery field. Had it been the design of the writer to dwell upon such views of the subject it might, it is true, have exhibited scenes that would have entertained those who read from no other motive than the momentary enjoyment of gratifying their fancy or their taste. Such must be highly disappointed, then, who have expected any such amusement amidst the dry arrangement of didactic systems.

To you, gentlemen, and the enlightened part of the public, this might justly have been conceived as little superior to a species of insult. To have dwelt on the national advantages of national education, in the present enlightened age of the world, would appear like an eulogium on the benefits of the light of the sun to the solar system. It would only be recalling to your view and memory all the most eloquent and splendid encomiums of the ablest writers, most sublime geniuses, and enlightened philosophers who have diffused the rays of literary illumination over the ancient or modern world.

In the present eventful period in the history of governments and nations—while, on the one hand, powerful combinations have been formed to lay the axe to the root of the tree of *civil liberty*, by its old and hereditary enemies; and on the other, while some of those revolutionary nations who avowed themselves its champions and advocates, in behalf of themselves and others, appear to be assuming it only as a cloak for encroachment, plunder, and self aggrandizement; while the free and independent genius of our government has been alternately threatened by those convulsive assailants—be it the glory of the legislators of Maryland and united Columbia to be equally employed in defending her against the menacing shafts of foreign despotism or wild ambition and in patronizing whatever internal regulations or discipline may be conducive to the improvement, prosperity, happiness, and security of all her citizens.

Under the direction and all-powerful protection of that BEING who is the ineffable source of all knowledge, excellence, and happiness, attainable by man, in the present progressive stage of his improvement, that all your deliberations, in that exemplary sphere to which they have been raised, may tend to promote all that can render your country highly dignified amidst the most free, happy, and enlightened nations of the earth, is, gentlemen, the sincere and fervent prayer of your most devoted, most obedient, and very humble

Servant,

SAMUEL KNOX.

*Fredericktown,*
*Nov. 30th,* 1798.

To the attention of the AMERICAN PHILOSOPHICAL SOCIETY, the enlightened, impartial, and patriotic patrons of literature and science, the following essay is most respectfully submitted—founding its chief claim to their notice, not on any section or part of it, separately considered, but on the whole as an entire, general, uniform, national plan—accommodated not only to future improvement in the sciences but also preserving what hath already been so liberally done in behalf of public education by the UNITED STATES OF AMERICA.

# ESSAY

## ON

# EDUCATION

### Section First

*. . . Argumentum quod in pueris elucet spes plurimorum, quæ cum emoritur ætate manifestum est, non naturam defecisse sed curam . . .*

Quint. Inst.[6]

EDUCATION is the training up of the human mind by the acquisition of sciences calculated to extend its knowledge and promote its improvement. According to the attention paid to it and the plan on which it is conducted, it becomes more or less useful to society but seldom fails to improve and elevate the powers of the mind above their natural state.

Though we have been eminently endowed by the great Author of our existence with a structure of body and soul superior to all other animals, yet experience evidently manifests that, without the aid of education communicated by some means or other, mankind, instead of improving their mental faculties, too soon degenerate to a state of deplorable ignorance and evidently below that degree of dignity assigned them in the scale of existence amidst the works of God.

For a confirmation of this truth, were any necessary, we have only to observe the uninstructed conduct of human life where gross ignorance and barbarism prevail. As the diamond in the mine contracts an incrustation of dross, so doth the mind of man, when unenlightened by instruction or arts of refinement. It would require considerable progress in education to be able even to describe the difference between the mind of an Eskimo Indian and the late Benjamin Franklin's or between that of an Hottentot and Sir Isaac Newton's.

It may not require, however, much explanation to delineate its advantages to mankind in general; the most ignorant are in some degree sensible of these and are often heard to regret the want of means of education or improvement.

The nature of our constitution of mind appears to be such that our progress in knowledge or science depends, in a great measure, on our exertions for that purpose. Our improvement commences when the first principles of education are impressed upon the mind, and the progressive proficiency we make affords the most refined happiness we can possibly enjoy in our present state. The necessary application and industry which a proper course of education requires are no diminution of this happiness, more especially when we consider that the degree of our knowledge and literary acquisitions so much depends on diligence and exertion.

From considering the various faculties of the human mind, it would appear that its great Author had formed it for a progressive course of improvement. Even in the infantine state curiosity prompts, and that earnestly, to inquiry and knowledge. The external senses are so many inlets to the treasures of the mind and are in every respect suited to its most ardent researches, its most industrious application.

The several faculties of the mind, apprehension, perception, reason, judgment, and memory, are all invigorated and improved by exercise. Indeed it is only by habits of application and exertion that their strength or value can be rendered eminently conspicuous or serviceable. Such education or discipline as may be most conducive to this effect should be most highly esteemed and diligently cultivated. To neglect the cultivation of these powers is to neglect what constitutes man's highest dignity, and to enlarge or empower them is to promote not only his best interests but also his highest happiness as a rational and intelligent being.

On the subject of literary improvement the enlargement of the powers of the mind is often too little regarded as an object of importance. The acquisition of a few useful or ornamental arts and sciences is considered as indispensable, while at the same time little account is made, by many, of the high advantage the mind receives from enlarging the stock of its ideas, from acquiring habits of attention, and being constantly exercised in invention, reasoning, memory, and reflection.

It is then the design of a liberal course of education to call forth all the latent powers of the human mind, to give exertion to natural genius, to direct the powers of taste and criticism, and to refine and polish, as well as to exercise, strengthen, and direct the whole economy of the mental system.

But the various operations of the mind, however well arranged, combined, and directed, would lose the most important part of their efficacy or utility but for the organs and powers of expression, by which they are communicated and by which they, reciprocally, receive and convey additional augmentations of knowledge through various channels of information.

Hence the importance of studying language, not only as it is the great bond of human society, but more especially as the vehicle of instruction and mutual communication.

Had there never been more than one uniform language among men, it might possibly have much facilitated the means of acquiring knowledge; yet it may be doubted whether in that case the stock of human knowledge would have been as extensive as it is at present. It is true that were the attention confined to one language, it would acquire a more complete knowledge of it than of one derived from a plurality of languages, but it may be readily conceived that the copiousness of any modern language has been owing to a diversity of languages, and consequently the more comprehensive, copious, and enriched any language hath become, so much the better is its acquisition calculated to enlarge our stock of ideas and our knowledge of various kinds.

As an introduction to the arts and sciences, the most approved literary discipline hath prescribed, with great propriety, an early attention to the grammatical and critical knowledge of those languages to which the vernacular is most indebted and in which also the most renowned philosophers, historians, poets, and men of letters have written and recorded the fruits of their studies.

An attention to the proper acquisition even of any one language is of itself no inconsiderable course of progressive improvement in knowledge, and during the years of childhood is, certainly, the best system of literary instruction, whether we view it with respect to the enlargement of the mental powers or the attainment of such knowledge as is suited to the tender age that could possibly be cultivated.

During the childhood of life the faculties of the mind have not attained sufficient vigor or maturity for the acquisition of the higher departments of literature or a close investigation of the more abstruse sciences. During this period, therefore, the study of speech or language is not only the best suited to this state but is also most proper as a preparation for scientific improvement.

The study and thorough knowledge of the native language ought to be the leading consideration, and to those whose views or professions are not to be dependent on the highest degree of literary erudition, that language well acquired may serve every necessary purpose.

But without a proper knowledge of the learned languages, from which so considerable a share of ours is derived, it is impossible [that] it can be acquired in the highest degree of perfection. The mere comparing or contrasting of two languages together must afford considerable improvement to the mind. But the chief advantage, perhaps, which it derives therefrom consists in the exercise of its various powers in translating from one language to another and consequently in selecting and applying the most proper and suitable words and phrases for expressing the meaning or spirit of the author. Taste, memory, and reflection are all employed in this exercise, which from its nature cannot fail, if properly directed, to acquire the most general and extensive knowledge of the language.

It is a hackneyed argument by many against a classical education that all the authors in the dead languages of any eminence have been translated into English and consequently that the scholar's time has been ill applied in translating what has been already done to his hand. Such, however, must neither have attended to these considerations, nor duly weighed the advantages which the tender mind receives by such exercises, as well with regard to things as words, and that too at an age not well adapted to more arduous literary studies.

Indeed in the very pronunciation and phraseology of our language the ingenious mind, prone to literary acquisitions and researches, could not be satisfied without some knowledge of the original languages. Let a youth, never introduced to any knowledge of Latin, be asked why his collection of books is styled a *library*, and the answer, it is presumed, will amply justify this observation.

Considerations, however, of much higher importance may manifest the impropriety of excluding the study of the Latin and Greek languages from a system of liberal and polite education. It is only from the study of these and other languages that the improvement of our own language can be promoted by attending to the principles of universal grammar and the consequent enlargement of the mind from such literary views.

In painting and statuary, it has been considered an advantage of the highest consequence with all those who have a view to excellence to have studied the most exquisite models of the ancient schools. In the structure and various compositions in our language, must it not also be equally advantageous and important to have laid before us the most finished productions of antiquity, whether of rhetoricians and orators or philosophers, historians, and poets? From this view, then, it is not merely language that is to be taken into account, but also the various information the mind receives and the refinement of our powers of taste and criticism in every various species of composition.

A mind exercised and improved by such learning must be much better qualified and prepared for the study of the arts and sciences than that whose powers have never been called forth by habits of exertion or strengthened by assiduity and application. As most of the sciences and especially their elements were originally written in the Greek or Roman languages, it must certainly tend to assist and enlighten the mind of the learner to be acquainted radically with the technical terms of that art or the principles of that science which is the subject of his study.

Could the indulgence of parents permit them to confine the attention of youth at an age sufficiently early, there could not be so much objection made as there commonly is against the acquisition of the Greek and Latin classics.

In many parts of this country, owing either to want of proper seminaries of instruction, to the mistaken fond indulgence of parents, or to both, youth have the greatest part of their education to acquire when it ought to be nearly completed. Under such circumstances little solid improvement of any kind can be gained. A few useful gleanings may be collected from the fields of science, but the great and important purposes of a liberal and extensive course of education must, in a great measure, be defeated. Indeed nothing can be more hostile in any country to the interests of the education of youth than the pampered treatment and imprudent fondness of luxurious and indulgent parents. A public, patriotic, or general sense of the importance of education may lead to the establishment of proper seminaries and suggest plans or systems of instruction, but unless these laudable institutions be seconded by the wise and well-directed authority of parents and guardians much of their real and general advantage must be lost to the community.

---

# Section Second

## ON THE QUESTION WHETHER PUBLIC BE PREFERABLE TO PRIVATE EDUCATION.

. . . Mens in secretis aut languescit; aut contra tumescit inani persuasione . . .

Quint. Inst.[7]

CONVINCED of the great advantage and importance of education, in proportion as any nation or society of which we have any knowledge from historical records improved in the arts of civilization and refinement, so have they been forward in encouraging and patronizing seminaries of learning and systems of literary instruction. The enlightened part of the ancient world were no less sensible of the great advantages of public education than those of the same description in the modern. And though they sometimes encouraged private tuition, yet we find from the reputation of the famous academy at Athens that public education was most approved. Many are the illustrious characters of antiquity that bear witness to the truth of this observation. Most of those, indeed, who at any period of the world have made a figure in literature acquired their knowledge under the direction of some academical institution. The justly celebrated Cicero was so conscious of the advantage to be acquired at Athens that he sent his son there to complete his studies, though it is probable that, at that time, Rome was not deficient in the means of private literary instruction.

In modern times, also, we find few of those who have distinguished themselves in the higher walks of science but have been educated on some similar plan. Indeed, the superior advantages of academical education are sufficiently obvious. As they bid fairest for being furnished with tutors or professors of the most general approved merit and in whose abilities and character the greatest confidence may be reposed, they, thus, prevent the student from being exposed to the pedantic caprice of any tutor whom chance, favor, or necessity may have thrown in his way.

In such institutions, also, the means and apparatus for acquiring a competent knowledge of the arts and sciences may be supposed to be more liberal and extensive than could be expected or indeed obtained in a domestic or private situation.

Education would diffuse its happy influence to a very contracted extent, indeed, were there no public schools or universities established by national or public encouragement.

Independent of these important considerations, *emulation*, which hath so powerful an influence on the human mind, especially in the season of youth, would lose its effects in promoting improvement and the love of excellence on any other plan than that of the academical. Indeed this consideration alone ought to be sufficiently decisive in its favor.

Love of excellence predominates in every uncorrupted youthful breast, and where this principle is under the conduct of impartial and skillful directors, it is observed to have the happiest effects in promoting that intensity of application and persevering industry which the more abstruse and arduous departments of science necessarily require.

Granting that something resembling emulation may be excited even on a private plan of education, yet it is manifest that the great variety of abilities and genius which the university or academy exhibits must afford a much greater field for competition, as well as such public and flattering prospects of reward as are the principal incitements to a laudable emulation and love of excellence.

It is commonly observed, and perhaps, with some share of justice, that the man of the world has in many respects the advantage of the mere scholar, and that though a long and close attention to books and study may render him master of arts and sciences, yet he may still remain ignorant of many accomplishments, without which it is scarce possible to pass through the world with safety, satisfaction, or advantage. This is obviously the effect of the scholar's having his mind or ideas habitually applied to the same objects, and it is undeniable that this consequence of a close application to literary acquisition may be much more effectually checked or prevented by a course of public, than private, education. That diversity of character and variety of manners and conduct, together with other observations which the former affords, tends in a high degree to wear off that studious and awkward air which is apt to be rather confirmed than diminished by the latter.

Another argument in favor of an academical education is that such as are tutored in private are apt to form too high an opinion of their own attainments or abilities. Owing to the want of an opportunity of observing the abilities or exertions of others, it is easy to conceive that such may most probably be the consequence of that mode of instruction. It is but just to observe that to this cause we may assign that arrogance, pedantry, dogmatism, and conceit that too often disgrace the scholar who, without rivalship or competition, hath been accustomed to listen only to his own praise.

The academic school has, also, the peculiar means of affording youth an opportunity of forming such friendships and connections as often in a literary and interested view contribute eminently to their future prosperity and happiness. In that season, the youthful breast glowing with every generous, friendly, and benevolent feeling is generally most attached to those who discover the same amiable qualities and disposition. Hence friendships have been formed and cemented which no circumstance or accident during their future lives could entirely dissolve. The story of the two Westminster scholars in the civil war between Charles the First of England and the Parliament is well known.[8]

It is true that many object to public plans of education, because that, from their situation in populous towns and the various complexion of the many students who attend, opportunities are thereby given for corruption, by scenes of vice and examples of debauchery.

It may with equal truth, however, be replied to this that there are few domestic situations so private as not to admit of ground for the same objections. The first of these, as far as situation is concerned, might be easily remedied, but it requires no very elaborate proof to manifest that the most dangerous temptations to vice more effectually succeed in the private and retired shades of bad example and domestic indulgence than in the social scene, bustling crowd, or public assembly.

Another objection to an academical plan of education has been suggested on account of the division that must necessarily take place in the attention of the tutors or professors, from the great number of students that may be under their care. But it has been already shown that in faithful and skillful hands this may rather tend to forward their proficiency than otherwise. The partial abuse of any system by one or more individuals ought certainly to bring no discredit to the plan or institution; neither ought it, in justice, to furnish any argument against its merit or even excellence.

The celebrated Locke himself not excepted, we find very few who have attempted to offer any plausible objections to a public education, or, in preference to a private, any argument in its favor, who were not themselves indebted to some academical institution even for being qualified to reason upon the subject. The good effects of the one they had experienced, of which Locke, in particular, affords an illustrious testimony, those they would ascribe to the other could be but little better than mere theory or fanciful speculation.

Upon the whole, it appears that there are many and various arguments in favor of an academical, as preferable to a private, education, and that any objections that can be offered against the former are almost all, in an equal degree, applicable to the latter. One conclusive argument, however, in favor of public education arises from its becoming an object of national patronage and encouragement on some uniform and approved plan or institution. It is from this view that education might be made to assume a still higher degree of importance in its influence on human happiness in those advantages which it holds out to individuals or the nation in general. It is hence too that the best means would be furnished for distinguishing literary genius and merit and consequently pointing out to public view such talents as are best fitted to fill the various stations and offices which the different exigencies of the state and the many departments of society require.

---

## Section Third

### THE IMPORTANCE OF ESTABLISHING A SYSTEM OF NATIONAL EDUCATION.

Kalliston esti ktema paideia brotois.[9]

WHEN we take into consideration the many great exertions and laudable institutions which various commonwealths or nations have devised and adopted for the general benefit, in framing and maintaining wholesome laws and government, it would appear, in some degree, unaccountable that little hath yet been done in promoting some general plan of education equally suitable and salutary to the various citizens of the same state or community.

It is true that in the history of some of the most celebrated commonwealths of antiquity we find some such plans were adopted for the improvement of youth, but so circumscribed was the state of literature in those times and such the circumstances of those commonwealths that their plans of education were rather military schools preparing them for the camp, either for self-defense or for butchering the human species, than seminaries suited to literary acquisition, the conduct of life, or the improvement of the human mind.

This observation, however, extends no farther than as it applies to institutions of national education and is by no means considered as applicable to the schools of the philosophers or of many celebrated orators, grammarians, and rhetoricians of the ancient world. If some of the states or nations of antiquity had been possessed of the means which we enjoy since the invention of printing of diffusing literary knowledge, it is more than probable, from what they have done, that they would have availed themselves of them in a manner superior to what we have yet accomplished.

In our own times and language, we have been favored by ingenious men with several excellent treatises on the subject of education. The greater part of these, however, are rather speculative theories, adapted to the conduct of life and manners than applicable to the practical diffusion of literary knowledge. What has lately been done in France excepted, I know of no plan devised by individuals or attempted by any commonwealth in modern times that effectually tends to the establishment of any uniform, regular system of national education. Universities or colleges hitherto instituted by the pride or patronage of princes or other individuals are in general too partial either in their situation or their regulations to extend the necessary advantages of literature to the more remote parts of the community for which they were intended.

Immense revenues and donations have, indeed, been applied to the founding of such seminaries, while the poor and such as most wanted literary instruction or the means of acquiring it have been left almost totally neglected. A few, indeed, whom wealth and leisure enabled, might drink deep of the Pierian spring, while the diffusion of its salutary streams through every department of the commonwealth, has been either neglected or considered as of inferior importance.

It must be allowed that these remarks may, in some measure, apply to any plan of public education that can possibly be formed. It is not, perhaps, possible to establish any system that can render education equally convenient and equally attainable by every individual of a nation in all their various situations and circumstances.

This observation must be particularly applicable to the condition of the *United States* of America and the widely dispersed situations of their citizens. In undertakings, however, of the first national importance, difficulties ought not to discourage. It does not appear more impracticable to establish an uniform system of national education than a system of legislation or civil government, provided such a system could be digested as might justly merit and meet with general approbation.

The good effects of such a system are almost self-evident. In the present state of education, however ably and successfully conducted in particular local situations, the nation is in a great measure incapable of judging its condition or effects. Diversity of modes of education also tend not only to confound and obstruct its operation and improvement but also give occasion to many other inconveniences and disagreeable consequences that commonly arise in the various departments of civil society or even the polished enjoyments of social intercourse. But were an approved system of national education to be established, all these imperfections of its present state would, in a great measure, be remedied and at the same time accompanied with many peculiar advantages hitherto unexperienced in the instruction and improvement of the human mind.

Great, surely, must be the difference between two communities, in the one of which good laws are executed only in some particular situations, while in others they are almost totally neglected; and in the other are universally established with equal and impartial authority. Such, surely, must be the difference between the effects of education when abandoned to the precarious uncertainty of casual, partial, or local encouragement, and of that which has been established uniformly and generally by the united wisdom and exertions of a whole nation. In such a state it is elevated to no more than that importance to which it is justly entitled, and it is to be hoped that the close of the eighteenth century will be so enlightened as to see education encouraged and established, as well by this as other nations, in such a manner as to be considered next to the administration of just and wholesome laws, the first great object of national patronage and attention.

The history of human society informs us what have been the effects of nations uniting their zealous exertions for the accomplishment of any great object to which they were directed. The happiest effects, then, might surely be expected from the united public exertions of this country in the combined cause of public virtue and literary improvement. The patronage or encouragement of the one has certainly a very intimate connection with that of the other, more especially if it be allowed that in the same system may be comprehended the institutes of morals and the principles of civil liberty.

In a country circumstanced and situated as the United States of America, a considerable local diversity in improvement, whether with respect to morals or literature, must be the consequence of such a wide extent of territory inhabited by citizens blending together almost all the various manners and customs of every country in Europe. Nothing, then, surely, might be supposed to have a better effect towards harmonizing the whole in these important views than an *uniform system of national education.*

The late much celebrated Doctor Price, in a discourse delivered before the trustees of the academy at Hackney, on the evidences of a future period of improvement in the state of mankind, earnestly urges an improvement in the state of education.[10] He observes that it is a subject with which the world is not yet sufficiently acquainted and believes there may remain a secret in it to be discovered which will contribute more than anything to the amendment of mankind and adds that he who would advance one step towards making this discovery would deserve better of the world than all the learned scholars and professors who have hitherto existed.

It requires, then, little demonstration, I think, to prove that if a justly approved plan of national education constitute not the secret alluded to by the Doctor, it is at least the most important step towards it that hath ever yet been taken. National exertions directed to this important object could not fail to have the happiest effects on society. The rays of knowledge and instruction would then be enabled to dissipate every partial and intervening cloud from our literary hemisphere and the whole community receive a more equal distribution, as well as a more effectual and salutary display of their enlightening influence.

---

# Section Fourth

## THE EXTENT OF A PLAN OF NATIONAL EDUCATION CONSIDERED.

Plurima pars Juvenum solam ostentare speciem, quam solidam
    præstare Eruditionem, malit.
                                                MORHOF.[11]

I N a course or system of national education, there ought to be two and, I think, but two great leading objects to which it should be adapted, *the improvement of the mind and the attainment of those arts on which the welfare, prosperity, and happiness of society depend.*

Education ought to comprehend every science or branch of knowledge that is indispensably necessary to these important objects. To confine it to a system that comprises only the knowledge of mechanical, commercial, or lucrative arts; or even a knowledge of the world as far as it can be attained by literary accomplishments, would be to view its advantages in a very narrow and illiberal light. The nation that would conceive such a system as sufficiently entitled to its patronage could neither be considered as enlightened in itself nor as meriting the refined improvement of a liberal and cultivated course of education. In proportion, then, as a nation hath formed a just sense of its own dignity and importance, in proportion, also, as it hath formed just conceptions of the importance of virtue and science, founded on the enlightened improvement of the human mind, so must that nation be influenced to patronize or establish such a system of literary instruction as may bid fairest for the acquisition of these important ends.

It is certainly laudable to pay due regard to those sciences that tend to enlarge the sphere of worldly interest and prosperity and without which the various and complicated business of human life cannot be transacted. This, however, by no means ought to check the exertion of that refined and sublime knowledge on which the improvement of genius, science, and taste, rather than worldly circumstances, chiefly depends. Indeed, it might be justly observed that a narrow or illiberal system of education from lucrative views would not ultimately tend to the prosperity or happiness of any nation. Were the human soul taught to cultivate only the sordid dictates of avarice or the knowledge of lucrative speculations, soon must that community lose a taste for whatever is most excellent in science or best calculated to refine and improve the faculties of the mind. Where such a taste hath become prevalent in any state, it is rather an evidence of its degeneracy than reformation and is commonly the forerunner of whatever may tend to enervate the patriotism, corrupt the virtue, or contaminate the morals of the community. There is reason to believe that the history even of some modern states, as far as education is concerned, would show that this observation is not altogether unfounded.

It is remarked, with concern, that in this country, at least in some considerable share of it, such a false taste in education becomes more and more prevalent. The study of the English language only by those means it affords of itself, a smattering of French, arithmetic, and those branches connected with it, are considered by many as an abundant competence of literary acquisition. And so they may to such as attend to education merely as the handmaid to industry or what is called *fortune,* but surely [they] cannot by any means prove satisfactory to those who, independent of interested calculations, aim at the highest improvement of the mind and the acquisition of all knowledge or science to which it is properly competent.

A nation so unfortunately situated as to be forced to scrape a scanty sustenance either from a barren soil or a too confined territory might plausibly be disposed to encourage or establish public education only as far as it was subservient to business or industry, but this, surely, could, by no means be suited to the genius of a country where independence in worldly circumstances, exemption from manual labor, and an abundantly fertile territory afford such leisure and encouragement to literary improvement as are so generally enjoyed by the inhabitants of these states.

In establishing, then, a system of national education, this consideration ought to have its due weight; and that while it should comprehend every species of literary instruction *useful* to human life, the ornamental also ought to receive that patronage to which it is justly entitled. Seminaries of learning are the salutary springs of society, and their streams ought to flow not only to an extent but also with a copiousness proportioned to the circumstances and situation of those to whom their course is directed. On the manner in which such a system is established, in a great measure, would depend not only the happiness but also the dignity and character of the nation and consequently ought to be founded on the most comprehensive and liberal plan.

The course of education instituted in the public seminaries should be adapted to youth in general, whether they be intended for civil or commercial life or for the learned professions, that of theology alone excepted, at least after a certain degree of preparation for that study.

Under this view it would comprehend a classical knowledge

of the English, French, Latin, and Greek languages, Greek and Roman antiquities, ancient and modern geography, universal grammar, *belles-lettres*, rhetoric, and composition, chronology and history, the principles of ethics, law, and government, the various branches of the mathematics and the sciences founded on them, astronomy, natural and experimental philosophy in all their various departments. To which course also, at proper stages of it, ought to be added the ornamental accomplishments —drawing, painting, fencing, and music.

In treating of the various seminaries necessary for conducting this course, a more extensive view may be given of it; what is here introduced is to be considered only as showing how far a plan of national education ought to be liberal and comprehensive.

It is a happy circumstance peculiarly favorable to an uniform plan of public education that this country hath excluded ecclesiastical from civil policy and emancipated the human mind from the tyranny of church authority and church establishments. It is in consequence of this principle of our happy civil constitution that theology, as far as the study of it is connected with particular forms of faith, ought to be excluded from a liberal system of national instruction, especially where there exist so many various denominations among the professors of the Christian religion.

The establishment of education on some national or public plan would not prevent the several religious denominations from instituting, under proper instructors, theological schools for such as were intended for the ministry after their academical course had been completed at the public seminaries. One institution of this kind in each state, for each particular denomination that held it necessary for the ministry to be instructed in *Hebrew*, a critical knowledge of the scriptures, ecclesiastical history, and theology, might be considered sufficient. Such studies would be perhaps best conducted under the inspection or charge of some particular clergymen in each denomination properly qualified for that purpose.

Instead of this measure being degrading to the study of theology, the most sublime of all sciences, it would, on the contrary, if properly managed, exhibit in the most respectable view and at the same time render it more effectual and consequently more salutary to society. It would prevent that jealousy of partial treatment that would arise if conducted by professors of different religious principles in the public seminaries. It would also afford students of theology intended for the ministry an opportunity of cultivating those habits of sobriety and principles of private and public virtue so essential to their character —better than could be attained in the promiscuous colleges of youth, impressed with more licentious habits and under the influence of domestic indulgences but little suited to the pious examples and virtuous dignity of the sacred function.

This observation by no means implies that there ought to be any laxity of discipline with regard to morals in public seminaries, unsuitable even to the ministerial character. It would, however, be an improvement in education as it is conducted in most universities at present, if, as soon as students are prepared by a literary and philosophical course and designed for the office of the ministry, their theological studies should be conducted in such a manner and in such a situation as would best furnish them only with examples and habits of real virtue and practical piety. Not only the professors of theology, but, if possible, even the place of instruction should possess such a solemnity of character as would impress them with a just sense of their having set themselves apart to be the sacred instructors and pious example of society. Not that it should be considered their duty to acquire any pharisaic solemnity or monkish moroseness in their manners or conduct. No, the time spent at the public seminaries previous to the study of theology would, it is presumed, enable them to see the absurdity of such manners, while their change of situation and removal to the place of sacred instruction, if properly conducted, might tend to inspire them with sentiments suited to the dignity of that profession in which they were about to engage.

Upon the whole, it need only be farther observed on this part of the subject that whether a plan of national education be directed with a view to qualify youth for any of the learned professions, or transacting the various negotiations or business of society, or merely for mental improvement, it certainly, in all of these whether considered singly or collectively, ought to be conducted on the most liberal and effectual plan. Whatever is superficial can never, in that state, become solid, and whatever is not perfectly solid is incapable of receiving that polish which may justly lay any claim to merit or perfection. That system, then, of education which would deserve the patronage of this country ought to be solid and extensive. Instead of circumscribing the powers of genius or improvement, it ought to lay open the widest as well as the fairest field for still higher and higher degrees of future progress and exertion. As it would be highly unjustifiable to set bounds to the advancement of human knowledge or science, so would it be equally so to contract or circumscribe the means of acquiring it.

## Section Fifth

On the establishment of the various schools necessary to complete a system of national education.

Quam bene cum Republica ageretur, si lentis illis modestisque
  gradibus primum ad Academias et ab illis ad cathedras, tribunalia et subsellia procederemus.
  Morhof.[12]

PROVISIONARY laws being obtained for establishing an uniform system of literary instruction, under the proper sanction and authority of the nation, the first important object would appear to be the founding and organization of proper schools or seminaries.

These should be arranged and situated in such a manner as

most impartially to diffuse their advantages to the greatest possible extent and also to afford the means of enabling all the attending youth to rise gradually from the first rudiments to the highest departments of knowledge and science.

In a liberal course of public education, no one stage of it ought to be better provided for than another in whatever may best contribute to its success. From the elementary or grammar school up to the university, though in various situations and different departments, it should be considered, supported, and encouraged as constituting one entire system, no one part of which could be neglected without injuring materially the whole fabric or institution. Everyone knows that if the first principles of science be imperfectly communicated, it is seldom that any solid or lasting improvement can be attained. This, certainly, may be sufficient to point out the importance of having the elementary parts of education as well conducted as the most advanced.

For the first stage, then, of a system of public instruction suited to the United States, let parish schools in each county of every state be established at a suitable distance from each other and endowed with a few acres of land and a proper house sufficiently large to accommodate the teacher and the taught.

Secondly, let the next stage consist of country schools or academies endowed also and furnished as the parish schools, but on a much more extensive plan hereafter to be explained.

Thirdly, let this stage of instruction consist of state colleges as already instituted and endowed in the several states of the union but so regulated and organized as to fall in with the general uniform system.

Lastly, let the literary establishment be completed by the institution of a national university, situated in the best manner with regard to health and convenience and furnishing at the same time the best opportunities of information and instruction.

These various seminaries properly endowed, furnished, and conducted in such a manner as to complete one uniform course, afterwards more fully to be explained, will be found, it is presumed, well adapted to the acquisition of the most enlarged proficiency in scientific knowledge. The greatest difficulty in a country so thinly inhabited in many places as this would be in dividing the counties in each state into parishes or townships, so as to render the situation of the schools convenient to all the inhabitants. Each state in the union being already laid out into counties, less difficulty would arise concerning the situation of the county academies. And with regard to the state colleges and university, it is a favorable circumstance towards carrying this plan into effect that many of the former have already been founded and that the idea of the latter also seems to meet with the public approbation.

Hitherto, however, this country, one or two states excepted, seems to have fallen in with the error of many even of the most enlightened countries in the world, and that is in providing or endowing most liberally a few seminaries for the completion of education while the elementary, which most required the fostering hand of public bounty, has been left to support itself as chance or circumstances, sometimes the most adverse, might dictate.

Of the inhabitants of a country so wide and extensive as this, but few, comparatively speaking, can ever attend colleges or a university—and hence the importance of paying due attention to the parish and county schools, both as nurseries for the college and university and also the instruction of such as cannot extend their education to a more advanced stage of the system.

In order to found, lay out, and carry into effect the several seminaries, let *a board of education* be incorporated under the sanction of the united authority of the states. These gentlemen should be nominated and appointed in every state, either by the united government or by the respective state assemblies: one or two in each state might be sufficient. Their office should not only be to preside over the general interests of literary instruction, to digest, direct, and arrange an uniform system in all its parts and to correspond in such a manner as to support the general and united interests of education, but more especially, in their individual capacity, to preside with regard to it in those states in which they were resident.

Hence they might very properly be styled "Presidents of literary instruction and Members of the board of national education." As they ought to be chosen or appointed either on account of their distinguished literary merit or other qualifications for the office, little other inducement to accept of it than what the honor of being chosen to such an office by an enlightened society ought to hold out might be necessary. Indeed one member to serve for some proper stated time might be sufficient in each state, and therefore the price of his services, even supposing a salary would be required, could add but little to the public expense.

One leading department of his office should be to ascertain, by the best possible information, the annual state of all the primary or parish schools, county academies, and also the college, in that state in which he presided, in order to lay it before the board at their stated time of meeting, which might properly take place once a year. His situation and connection or correspondence with the other presidents of the several states would also enable him to assist in procuring such teachers or professors as might be occasionally wanted in the various schools under his inspection: he ought also to assist and preside at the public examination of the state college.

The attention, however, of one president would be inadequate to the superintendence of all the seminaries in one state. As more immediate visitation would then be requisite, there ought to be a rector appointed for each county in the state. The duty of those rectors should be to assist in procuring proper tutors, to visit every school in the respective counties, and at least twice a year to make a just report of their state and proficiency, and the number of the students or scholars, to the state president, or whatever other information he might require. The county rector should also attend quarterly the public examination of the primary schools, or at least twice a year, with such other local trustees or visitors as might be thought necessary. On those occasions there ought to be a catalogue of the youth produced by the master of each school, specifying their time of entrance and proficiency, leaving a vacant column to mark their progress between each successive examination, marking also such as discovered any extraordinary genius or even attention.

In order faithfully to discharge this office, it is obvious it would require a gentleman of the first erudition who would devote to it the whole of his attention and consequently should have a liberal salary paid by the county. His ordinary visits to the several schools should be at least once a quarter and ought not to be stated but, as it were, accidental. But on occasions of public examinations they ought to be accompanied with all the ceremony and dignity possible. It would be a favorable circumstance if those rectors would also be the conductors of the county academies. And it does not appear but that, by the assistance of proper under-masters, they might be also adequate to this charge.

The different rectors in each county having made a faithful return of the state of the primary or parish schools under their superintendence to the state president, these returns should be carefully preserved by him, either for the inspection of the board of education, the federal government, or the state assemblies, as they might be disposed to call for them.

The board of education, and consequently the whole community, by the assistance of such rectors, would be thus enabled to see the true state of literary instruction in every part of the union, at least every six months, and whether there existed any obstruction to its prosperity, either through a deficiency of proper teachers or any other cause, they would have the advantage at least of knowing where the defect lay.

The greatest apparent obstruction to the establishment of an uniform plan of national education consists in the difficulty of procuring proper tutors, well qualified and disposed to carry into effect the system laid down to them by the board. As much as possible, then, to remove this obstruction, the salaries of the various teachers ought to be liberal and fully equal to what men of their qualifications could make in any other department of business suited to their circumstances. The commodiousness and comfortable state of the houses built for both the primary schools and the county academies, endowed also with a suitable tract of land, would be a very great inducement, and the price of tuition for each scholar, or the fixed salary, whichever of these two modes of payment the board might approve, would thus be rendered more moderate, at least to posterity.

The constant and uniform communication between the county rectors, the state presidents, the board of education, and, when necessary, the government, it may reasonably be presumed would have the best effect in exciting a spirit of emulation amongst the professors and tutors of the various seminaries. To keep up and cherish this laudable spirit, it might be salutary to promote such of the masters of the primary schools as distinguished themselves by diligence and abilities to more lucrative situations in the county academies, as often as vacancies happened by death or otherwise. This, however, ought never to be done till a successor to the promoted teacher was first provided.

Various regulations of this nature would of course fall under the consideration of the learned board. It may, here, be only observed farther that in the appointment of professors or tutors, or even county rectors, it ought to be so regulated that none of them should resign their appointment with less than six-months' notice given to the state president by the masters of the county academies and by the masters of the primary schools to the county rectors.

# Section Sixth

On the advantage of introducing the same uniform system
of schoolbooks into a plan of public education.

. . . Nam et Græci licenter multa et Horatium in quibusdam
nolim Interpretari.

QUINTIL.[13]

O NE great inconvenience attending even the present mode
of education consists in the scanty supply of the best editions of the various schoolbooks that is to be met with in many
parts of the United States. The great diversity, also, especially
of the elementary books in education, serves much to distract
and retard its success. Every teacher has his favorite system, and
consequently the books best adapted to it are only those which
he recommends. But in the present state of literary instruction,
as there are few tutors who complete the scholar even on their
own system, he is often not only under the disagreeable and
injurious necessity of studying over again what he has learned
on a different mode but also perplexed with the diversified editions or translations of the same author.

To remedy and indeed entirely remove these obstructions,
in establishing a course of public education suited to the various citizens and local situations of the United States, there
ought to be a printer in each state for the express purpose of
supplying the various seminaries, in their respective states, with
such schoolbooks and other literary publications as should be
recommended or directed by the board of education. Throughout the United States the same uniform system of the most
approved schoolbooks would be thus established and consequently all the difficulties, hitherto in this respect experienced,
entirely removed.

This might justly be conceived as one of the greatest advantages arising from the adoption of a system of public instruc-

tion, not only in its tendency to facilitate its progress, but also in rendering it more agreeable to the learner, as well as in diffusing more generally the various benefits of an uniform plan.

Nothing would come under the direction of the literary board of greater importance than the selection of the best schoolbooks for each department of science. It would constitute from time to time a considerable share of their office to examine the merits of such as might be publicly recommended to their acceptance.

Throughout all the primary schools, county academies, and even state colleges the same uniform system of books should be taught, and it would be requisite that the several printers should be obligated to follow the instruction of the literary board with regard to the type, paper, binding, and even outward uniform appearance of all the schoolbooks for supplying the public seminaries of the United States.

It might not, probably, be found necessary to extend these regulations to the National University, at least in their strictest terms.

The president and professors of that distinguished seminary would constitute a faculty to which might very properly be referred the discretionary power of adhering to this, and perhaps some other regulations, necessary for the other seminaries —only as far as might be suited to the nature of that more dignified institution.

Indeed it would be necessary for the faculty of that University to have a printer under their own immediate direction, under such restrictions, however, as not to interfere with or counteract such as concerned the other seminaries.

But, as much good might result, especially in exciting a spirit of emulation, from the general uniformity, not only of education, but also of the means of acquiring it throughout the United States, there is no measure which could possibly tend more to this effect than a constant and well-chosen supply of the most proper books in all the various departments of instruction.

Schoolbooks are at present, in general, very inaccurately printed and often in such a manner, both with regard to type and paper, as much to obstruct the proficiency of the learner. Besides, many of them, particularly the Latin classics, are not fit, in their present state, to be put into the hands of youth without wounding that delicacy and purity of sentiment which education ought rather to cherish than violate.

Every person acquainted with the difficulties or obstructions which attend the present mode of education must have observed how often youth are retarded in their studies for want of having the proper authors to put into their hands as soon as they have finished the preceding. In public seminaries, where the youth are classed according to their proficiency, an irregular or deficient supply of the same books is often very embarrassing to the tutors and discouraging to the taught. To remove this obstruction, the state printer should be obligated to keep a constant supply, adequate to the demand of every seminary in the state; and the prices being fixed, the master of each school should keep a sufficient number of copies of every author his pupils might require, agreeably to the system and regulations recommended and prescribed by the board of education. In the farther prosecution of this essay, notice shall be taken of some of the most proper and suitable books for each stage of the literary course, agreeably to the view of it here laid down. What has been observed is to be considered as chiefly regarding the advantages of introducing an uniform system throughout the United States.

# Section Seventh

ON THE ESTABLISHMENT AND CONDUCT OF THE PARISH OR PRIMARY
SCHOOLS.

His igitur rudimentis puer in prima imbutus schola, deinde bonis
avibus ad ALTIORES DISCIPLINAS conferat sese.

ERASMUS.[14]

IN order to conduct education on the best plan, it is necessary
that the community be so convinced of its importance as
cheerfully to furnish every accommodation. On the supposition,
then, that the preceding plan be practicable, the houses for the
parish schools in each county should be sufficiently spacious for
the use of the teacher's family and also to accommodate one
hundred scholars. To suit these two purposes, it should be
built on such a plan as to have the schoolroom separate from the
part assigned to the master's use. Much also would depend on
having the rooms properly provided with desks, seats, and places
for keeping their books, etc., secure.

The best method for seating a room for this purpose is to
have it laid out into small single pews, somewhat similar to
those common in churches, one rising a little higher than another, so that the lowest be next to the open area where the
teacher sits, and the highest, the most remote, but so as that the
pupils would all sit with their faces to the teacher, having
before them a desk suited either for the purpose of reading on
or writing. One of these pews might accommodate a distinct
class, and being numbered, each class would, without confusion,
regularly place themselves in their own pew.

In a room large enough to contain one hundred scholars,
there ought to be three orders of such pews, with large areas
or double pews for the teachers' seats. One of these might be
properly placed at each end of the room and another in the

center upon the one side, having the single pews for the pupils made, as already shown, to face their respective teachers.

Every such primary school should be supplied with a teacher for every thirty, or at most, thirty-five pupils, and if it were found necessary that they should consist of both sexes, the pews would be found useful in helping to preserve that delicacy and reserve which they should be early taught to preserve towards each other. Where, however, it can be done, it will constantly be found eligible to have girls educated separately under a mistress.

In such schools as are here alluded to, it would constitute a very essential improvement if the teacher's wife could assist in the charge and education of such girls as attended, and particular encouragement ought to be held out to such teachers of the primary schools as could be so qualified. Indeed it should be almost indispensable that the headmaster of every school be a married man. His assistant or assistants should be chosen by himself, but as the prices of instruction would be fixed to him, so ought also the salary to be nominated which he should pay the assistants, in order that such as were properly qualified might offer.

In the primary schools the course of instruction should be confined to a proper knowledge of the English language, writing, arithmetic, and practical mathematics, completed by some approved compend of history and geography.

From these seminaries should be excluded not only Latin, but also the French language, excepting for those whose education was not to be extended to a higher stage of the course, from the consideration that the next stage of public instruction, namely the county academies, would accommodate all who were designed for a more comprehensive system of education.

To assign to each stage its own particular parts would also tend to support a due encouragement to the whole, while at the same time it rendered the attention less divided.

In the primary school the first rudiments should be taught with care. First, it should be provided with some large alphabets, printed on small sheets, each letter at least one inch in length. One of these sheets put on a piece of pasteboard, and properly placed, is the easiest mode of teaching the letters to young children in a public school. Having procured a frame and a stand similar to a fire screen, let the alphabet be placed, with all the children in the letters arranged before it. If the first in order miss the letter, ask the second, and so on to the last—by which means their attention is kept up and an emulation excited, which, if properly managed, has the happiest effects. After the letters and points are thus acquired, let spelling tables on a large scale be fixed up and managed in the same manner, and after them easy lessons of reading, the type being gradually diminished, till brought to the largest common size.

Initiating books for children should abound with easy reading lessons, and both paper and print calculated to entice and facilitate their progress. It is common with many teachers to employ their pupils much at spelling tables, but it will be found that children will make much more progress by first teaching them to read, and after having read their lesson to spell words out of it suited to their capacity, than by confining their attention to long dry lists or arrangements of words and syllables, however skillfully digested.

For this reason, though *Webster's Institutes* be excellent of its kind, yet it would be best put into children's hands after they had made tolerable proficiency in reading, on the plan which has been here mentioned.[15] The first lessons should consist of monosyllables, and as they became proficients in these, introduced to such as are still more and more difficult. By adhering to this plan, and carefully classing such as are of equal proficiency, causing them, for emulation's sake, to check each other throughout the various classes, the teacher may instruct a class of six or even ten with as much facility and more advantage than he could a single scholar.

Soon as the pupils can read with tolerable ease and readiness, *Webster's Institutes* might be properly introduced; after which they ought to be supplied with a vocabulary or pocket dictionary and at least twice a day get a lesson of spelling, at the same time giving the meaning of the words they spell without the book. If this be done previous to dismissing the school, by the whole pupils under each teacher whose proficiency may admit of it, standing up in order and alternately spelling and giving the meaning of the words, observing to make such as err give up their place to those who are correct, it will be found an agreeable and very profitable exercise.

For the most advanced reading classes proper books should be prepared. There are now extant several good collections in prose and verse taken from the best English authors, but there are none of them but what might admit of a more judicious arrangement for the use of reading scholars.

The first part of such collections would be best without any verse pieces, and to consist entirely of fragments from the best historians, and papers from the *Rambler, Guardian,* and *Spectator,* arranged so as that the easiest should come first, proceeding from the simple through all the various species of style, concluding with some pieces of the most difficult pronunciation.[16]

The last part of the collection should consist entirely of poetry, both rhyme and blank verse. The pieces should be so arranged that the scholar might be able to distinguish the different species of poetry and also of versification.

The first pieces might be all of the pastoral kind; the second elegiac; the third didactic; and the last heroic or epic: the nature of these several species of poetry should be carefully explained by the teachers.

In the instruction of such classes, when the lesson is given out, it ought to be read over by the teacher in the best manner in his power, not only with regard to the mere pronunciation, but also the management of the voice with gracefulness and propriety. Particular beauties in the style and sentiment should be pointed out, and some account of this required when the class came to read the lesson. It would greatly add to the order and regularity of the school, if the pews were so made and situated that each class when called upon to give an account of their lessons could stand up in their own pew without traveling through the room to get to their teacher.

Soon as the pupils were capable of reading with tolerable accuracy, English grammar should be introduced, and writing, and after considerable progress in these, arithmetic. In acquiring a proper knowledge of English grammar, let the scholar, after having committed the rules to memory, write exercises and parse in the same manner as is practiced in learning Latin. Ashe's *Introduction to Lowth's Grammar* is well calculated for this purpose; but as is it does not afford a sufficient number of examples for exercises of false grammar, *Buchanan's English Syntax* should be next introduced.[17] After a competent knowledge of English grammar, the pupils should be exercised in copying some approved specimens of letters and occasionally write some of their own composition. They ought also to copy deeds, bills, bonds, wills, and indentures, or any other species of writing the knowledge of which would be useful to them in life.

In teaching arithmetic and some of the practical branches of the mathematics, the master of the primary school would find it of great advantage to make his pupils carefully commit to memory the rules in the various branches, from some well-chosen system for that purpose, and rehearse these rules once a week. He ought to be provided with a frame on the plan mentioned in teaching children the letters, and having classed the arithmetical scholars, let each class alternately stand up before the frame, after having committed to memory their rule. Let the teacher, having a blackened board fixed upon the frame, give them examples written with chalk, and having asked the first to do the example, should he be found incapable, proceed to the next, and so on, till each pupil in the class work an example in this manner. After which, when prepared for more difficult examples on the rule, the question may be wrought out at full length by the teacher in their presence, and afterwards rubbed off the board, and the class set down to work it in the usual manner, giving particular commendations to the one who does it soonest and with the greatest accuracy.

There is every reason to believe that this method would much facilitate the acquisition of arithmetic and at the same time be less irksome to the teacher than that commonly practiced.

It is too much the custom with many teachers to keep their pupils puzzling over a question, perhaps for half a day, without giving them any assistance. But, though it be proper as they advance in the knowledge of any science to habituate them to call forth their own exertions, yet this requires to be managed in such a manner as not to discourage or check the ardor of their pursuit. To cherish and keep up this ardor constitutes no small share of the merit of a good teacher.

By the use of the frame or blackboard by the teacher and of the slate occasionally by the scholars, they will be enabled to keep their books, into which they copy their work, in the fairest and neatest manner, and it would be well, as much as possible, to excite an emulation among them in this respect.

As the minds of youth must flag by long attention to any one species of study at one time, it would be best to introduce, at this stage of their proficiency, a knowledge of history and geography. Some well-digested compend of ancient history should be studied first and well impressed upon the mind by examination. After which *Guthrie's General Geography* and *Morse's Geography* of this country, if judiciously taught by maps and globes, might not only instruct them in a proper knowledge of geography but also as much of modern history as is necessary to be acquired at school.[18]

Lessons of this nature introduced by way of relaxation from severer studies, at proper intervals each day, would be found of the highest importance. In these the teacher ought to assist them in forming a proper judgment of what they read, particularly in geography; in contrasting the various forms of government, manners, and customs; the causes of the arts and sciences flourishing under one system and being lost under another; as also how to estimate whatever is most conducive to the improvement and happiness of man.

What has been here observed, though it be in many respects deficient, yet may suffice to afford an idea of the manner in which the literary course of the primary schools may be conducted. If other, or better, regulations be found necessary, they will properly come under the consideration and direction of the board of education.

With regard to impressing youth early with the principles of religion and morality: however important this may be, yet, on account of preserving that liberty of conscience in religious matters which various denominations of Christians in these states justly claim, due regard ought to be paid to this in a course of public instruction.

It would, however, appear to be no infringement of this liberty in its widest extent for the public teacher to begin and end the business of the day with a short and suitable prayer and address to the great source of all knowledge and instruction.

It might, also, be highly advantageous to youth, and in no respect interfere with the different religious sentiments of the community, to make use of a well-digested, concise moral catechism. In the first part of this catechism should be inculcated natural theology or the proofs of the existence of the Deity from his works. It might on this head even extend so far as to show the insufficiency of the light of nature in communicating the knowledge of God and consequently the necessity of a more express revelation.

The second part might properly consist of the first principles of ethics, the nature and consequence of virtue and vice, and also a concise view of economics and the relative duties.

The third and last part should inculcate, concisely, the principles of jurisprudence; the nature of civil government, containing a short historical view of the rise and progress of its various species and particularly that of the federal government of these states.

It may be supposed that this would be rather too elevated for the capacities of pupils in the primary school; but it may be replied that this would depend on the manner in which such a collection was executed, which ought to be in the most concise and at the same time most simple and perspicuous style and of a length suited to their capacities, whether considered with regard to the particular responses or the extent of the whole system. It is certainly of the highest importance in a country like this that even the poorest or most uninstructed of its citizens be early impressed with a knowledge of the benefits of that happy constitution under which they live and of the enormity of their being corrupted in their right of suffrage—and there is certainly no more plausible way of communicating this knowledge, with any lasting effects, than by having it interwoven with the most early and general principles of education.

In order to impress on the tender mind a reverence of the Deity, a sense of His government of the world, and a regard for morals, it might be proper, previous to the commencement of their daily studies, for each pupil who had made proficiency for that purpose, to be constituted alternately orator for the day and to read from the rostrum a short essay on some subject of that nature. There have been published, in three volumes, *Reflections* by a Mr. Sturm, a German, and lately translated into English, one for every day in the year, which might with great propriety be read in this manner.[19]

In these *Reflections* almost everything interesting in the philosophy of nature is brought into view, adapted to the most common capacity, while at the same time they are calculated to present the most sublime ideas of the Deity and to excite to the love and study of science.

As these may have yet fallen into but few hands, in order to show how well they are adapted to the purpose here recommended, let the following serve as a specimen:

—JANUARY II—

The blessings granted to us by God in winter, and to which we pay too little attention.

If we were to examine the works of God more attentively than

we generally do, we should find at this season many reasons to rejoice in his goodness, and to praise the wonders of his wisdom.—
Few, without doubt, are so insensible as not to feel emotions of
pleasure and gratitude when beauteous nature displays the rich
blessings of God in spring, summer, and autumn; but even hearts
the fullest of sensibility, are rarely excited to the sensation of warm
gratitude when they behold the trees stripped of their fruit and the
fields without verdure, when the bleak wind whistles round their
dwelling, when a chilling cold comes to freeze the earth and its
inhabitants. But is it certain that this season is so deprived of the
blessings of heaven and of what is sufficient to kindle gratitude and
piety in the heart of man? No, certainly. Let us only accustom ourselves to be more attentive to the works of God, more touched with
the many proofs of his goodness towards us, and we shall find opportunities enough, even in winter, to praise our benefactor. Consider how unhappy we should be, if, during violent cold, we had
neither wood for fire, nor clothes to keep us warm. With what goodness the Lord prevents our wants and furnishes us (even in the
season the most void of resources) with the necessaries and conveniences of life. When at this moment, we may be enjoying the
comfortable warmth of a fire, shall we not return thanks to the
Lord, who gives us fuel with such profusion, that the very poorest
can be supplied with it.

If it was given to mortals to know the chain of everything in
nature, how great would be our admiration at the wisdom and
goodness of its author! But, however incapable we are of forming
to ourselves an idea of the whole of his works, the little we understand of it gives us sufficient reason to acknowledge that the government of God is infinitely wise and beneficent. Winter belongs to
the plan he has formed. If this season did not exist, the spring and
summer would not have so many charms for us, the fertility of our
lands would much diminish, commerce would be at an end in many
provinces, and part of the woods and forests would have been
created for no purpose. Considered in this light, winter is certainly
very useful, and supposing even that its advantages were not so
apparent, it would be sufficient for us to reflect that winter is the
work of the Creator, as well as spring and summer, and that all
which comes from God must be for the best.[20]

In some other of these *Reflections* the author accounts for
the change of the seasons and has omitted scarce anything
curious or interesting either in the planetary system or in the

structure of the earth or in the mineral, vegetable, and animal worlds, uniformly concluding with reflections and sentiments of adoration for the great first cause of all things.

The reading one of these reflections by the orator for each day, agreeably to the manner in which they are arranged for the days of the year, might not only be the means of communicating much knowledge but also leave the most happy impressions of piety and moral excellence.

On the subject of the primary schools and the manner in which they should be conducted, enough may have been suggested for an essay of this nature. There is, however, still remaining another consideration which would greatly tend to enlarge the extent of their advantages to the public.

In each of these schools at least three promising boys whose parents could not afford to educate them should be admitted at the expense of the parish or township to which the school belonged. The condition on which these boys should be received ought to be that their parents should agree to have them educated for the purpose of becoming teachers, so being they discovered, on trial, parts suited to that profession. A few of them who most distinguished themselves on public examination should be admitted in the county academies and afterwards to the state colleges and university. This, in the course of a few years, would train up a proper supply of tutors, both masters and assistants, for the different seminaries and at the same time extend the blessings of literary instruction to hundreds who would otherwise be deprived of it. Tutors so educated through the different stages of the literary course, on the same uniform national plan and under the direction of the same literary board or society, would, in every point of view, be rendered greatly preferable to strangers educated under different institutions.

# Section Eighth

## ON THE COUNTY ACADEMIES.

Scilicet ut possem curvo dignoscere rectum,
Atque inter Sylvas ACADEMI quaerere verum.

HOR.[21]

A s these academies, agreeably to the plan laid down, are to accommodate all the youth in the county intended for a more comprehensive course than what has been assigned for the primary schools, it is consequently necessary that in every respect they should be founded and conducted on a more extensive scale.

The plan of the academy houses and the manner in which they should be endowed under the sanction of the respective states might very properly be referred to the direction of the literary board. The houses, however, should be capacious, well designed, and accommodated to the purpose. Besides the apartments necessary for at least two masters and their families, there ought to be, at least, two halls for teaching, two diningrooms, and two dormitories, with an assistant's lodging room to open into each, one for the juniors and another for the seniors. Should it be found necessary or practicable that the county rectors should be the chief professors or masters in the academies, proper apartments should also be laid out in the building for their accommodation.

The teaching halls should be pewed after the manner of the primary schools. The one accommodated to the classical, the other to the mathematical students. In the extreme end of each there ought to be an exhibition room, elevated a few steps above the hall, and separated from it in front by a curtain, similarly to a theater. This room would be useful in common for the chief masters to teach in, affording a commanding view over the hall. It would also serve for a suitable library, and on occasions of public examinations would suit as a stage or rostrum, from which the youth would deliver their elocutionary exercises to the audience accommodated in the hall.

Without entering more minutely into the plan of a suitable academy house, it may only be observed farther, in general terms, that it should be sufficiently capacious to contain all the youth in the county whose parents or guardians inclined to give them a classical and thorough mathematical education. They should be built on a scale sufficiently large to contain at least two hundred or two hundred and fifty students. For, though it might be some years ere they should have occasion for accommodations for such a number, yet, as the population of the counties and the credit of the system increased, it is probable the number of students would increase in proportion.

Besides the county rectors, who, it is supposed, might preside in these seminaries, there ought also to be two principal masters, with one or two assistants according to the number of pupils.

In this country, owing chiefly to the precarious supply of schools and the scattered situations of the inhabitants, the childhood of life is too often passed ere parents think seriously of the education of their children. They are in too many places, on these accounts, sent to school only when the greatest part of the education intended for them ought to have been acquired. This is an error which, as far as possible, the establishment of an uniform system ought to correct. The time allotted to the primary schools should elapse at the twelfth year of their age, at least of all such as were intended for being admissible into the county academies; such as were not should be continued till the age of fourteen. At the age of eight, even in rural or scattered situations, it would be sufficiently late to enter the primary school, and the space of four years would be a competent term to complete the course assigned to that seminary. Such as had the advantage of a more contiguous situation might be prepared for the academy at a still earlier age.

Agreeably to the plan here recommended, no pupil should be

admitted into the county academy who had not been educated at the primary school or, if by the parents indulged with a private tutor, without having taken and completed the same course as taught in those schools and prescribed by the literary board. This should be ascertained by a strict and impartial examination on the pupil's being offered for entrance.

Were this uniformly and generally adhered to throughout all the county academies and were it also insisted on that no student should be admitted above twelve, or at most fourteen, years of age, it might surely have a powerful effect in enciting parents to turn their attention to the education of their offspring as soon as they were capable of receiving instruction. It would also have the effect, as has been elsewhere observed, of keeping separate the interests of the primary school and academy and consequently tend more effectually to promote and support the success of both.

The pupils on admittance to the academy would be properly prepared for commencing the classical course in Latin and Greek, and, after some knowledge of the former of these languages, in French and mathematics. A correct edition of the grammar taught in this country, under the denomination of the university Latin grammar, is as eligible upon the whole as any extant. The youth who commence Latin should be classed according to their proficiency, and as soon as any class had made such proficiency in grammar as to be able to decline nouns on the various declensions and decline verbs through the different moods and tenses, they ought to be set to reading and translating *Corderius*.[22] This, however, should be chiefly with a view to exemplify what part of grammar they had acquired, still continuing to advance daily in grammar till they had completed it in all its parts, prosody excepted. During this time they would have read *Corderius, Æsop's Fables,* and *Erasmus's Dialogues.*

Notwithstanding all that has been said by some writers on classical education against the use of translations, it would certainly much facilitate the progress of youth to read these three introductory little books with literal translations. If these be judiciously taught, the use of them should be afterwards laid aside, at which time they would be prepared for reading *Cornelius Nepos*.[23] In the reading of this excellent little book of biography, the teacher ought to explain to them the nature and advantages of that species of writing. Having by this time finished their grammar, as far as prosody, once or twice a day the class should read *Clark's* or *Mair's Introduction to Making Latin*,[24] beginning with the easiest lessons, reading the Latin as it should be rendered, each in the class alternately, the second in order observing to correct the first; the third the second, and so on throughout the whole class; the teacher not forgetting to applaud such as excelled.

After the book, or the easiest portion of examples in each rule had been read through in this manner, they might then begin to write it over in exercises, at least one each day. When the author had been finished a second time in this manner, they might next write such exercises as would require them to choose the Latin words themselves, and thereby be enabled to form a judgment when their choice of words and composition were classical or otherwise. To complete the course of writing exercises, let them, after these already mentioned, have some select sentences or passages from the prose author they are reading to translate into English and afterwards translated into Latin without any opportunity of consulting the author, and then let their Latin be contrasted by the teacher with that of their author. Some familiar Latin letters, ancient and modern, translated in this manner would be found highly useful.

It is only on account of observing at once all that is necessary on the subject of writing Latin exercises that the full course has been here brought into view. The first and second species of these exercises would only be suited to the class reading *Nepos's Biography*.[25] After this little author, *Cæsar's Commentaries* on his wars in Gaul and with his country might be next read with advantage, not only on account of the simplicity of the style but also that the teacher might enable them to mark with reprobation all the persevering ambition of that bold and too successful enslaver of his country.

It would not be too much to assign this progress of the class to the first year's attendance in the academy. This however would greatly depend on a proper division of their time and the order and number of the hours of instruction. For this purpose each academy ought to have a bell and the hours as punctually as the clock observed both by the teacher and the taught.

There ought to be two hours study before breakfast, three between breakfast and dinner, and three in the afternoon. These hours should be employed in such a manner as best tended to expedite the general plan.

After the first year, the classical students intended for the university should devote one lesson of each day to Greek. In order, however, to prevent this from embarrassing them or the teachers, one half of them should study Greek in the forenoon and the other in the afternoon, by which means the different tutors would be enabled to keep their respective pupils equally divided and employed.

When the proficiency above stated had been made, the Latin scholars not intended for the university might begin French and spend their morning hours in the study of that language and the remainder of the day equally between their Latin and mathematics, observing to accommodate the hours as above mentioned.

In acquiring a proper knowledge of Latin, they ought to read the books already mentioned, *Sallust* and a considerable part of *Livy*, with a little of *Tacitus*. It is a very absurd practice to set boys to reading Latin poetry till once they are able to translate any prose author with considerable facility.

In this stage of their course they ought to read, occasionally, *Rollin's Ancient History* and *Goldsmith's Abridgment of the History of the Grecian and Roman Republics*.[26] A certain portion of these ought to be assigned them for reading in their private chambers and at an appointed hour strictly examined on what they had previously perused. In the classical library of every academy there ought to be at least one copy of *Potter's Antiquities of Greece, Kennet's Roman Antiquities,* and *Tooke's Pantheon,* to which the students should be occasionally referred for a fuller explanation of many of the rites, cere-monies, institutions, manners, and customs of those distin-guished republics, than might be in the power of the teacher to communicate as often as they occurred in their reading of the various classics.[27]

At the termination of the first year of the course in the county academies, the student being so far master of Latin grammar as to change his application to it during the morning hours to the acquisition of Greek grammar, it would be an object highly worthy the attention of the literary board to select the most deservingly approved grammar of that language. It would, how-ever, be an improvement on every Greek grammar known to the writer of this essay if the rules were in English and rendered as concise as possible. Great ease and advantage have arisen to students of Latin since the grammar of that language, the examples excepted, have been taught in English, and there appears no reason why it would not in an equal degree facilitate the learning of Greek.

At the termination of the second year of this course, by the application of the morning hours alone to exercises and gram-mar, and one half of the day, either forenoon or afternoon session, to the Latin classics, the student might be qualified to read Latin prose with facility; translate, at least his author for making Latin, with considerable correctness, and also have acquired a competent knowledge of the Latin and Greek grammars.

On the commencement of the third year, such proficiency being made, those who were designed for the college or uni-versity might properly be introduced to the study of French for the morning session, one short lesson in Latin and another in Greek for the one half of the remaining day, and mathematics continued for the other, agreeably to the plan already suggested.

To such as are in a great measure unacquainted with the education of youth, so many different subjects of study on the same day may appear too embarrassing. But experience has not left this so long a subject of mere theory. It can be proved that by a proper division of the day different subjects of study, instead of embarrassing or retarding the pupil, tend both to expedite the literary course and at the same time to relieve from that irksomeness which cannot fail to arise from a long attention to one subject. It also has the effect of rendering the students, so educated, equally ready in every subject of literature to which they have applied. When conducted on a different plan, how often do we find youth losing considerably their knowledge of one language, branch, or science, ere they have acquired another.

During the third year's session at this seminary, the classical students should begin to read Latin and Greek poetry. In order to [do] this, the rules of prosody should be carefully committed to memory and the Greek and Latin authors read on the following plan. On the supposition that a competent skill has been acquired in Greek and Latin prose, let the various kinds or species of poetry and versification be attended to in the same manner as was recommended in reading English in the primary schools. Agreeably to this plan the *Bucolics of Virgil* should be read with the *Idylls of Theocritus*; part of the *Select Odes of Horace* with a few from *Anacreon* and *Pindar*; the *Georgics of Virgil* with *Hesiod*, and the *Æneid* with the *Iliad of Homer*.

In order also to be acquainted with the state of dramatic poetry among the ancients, one or two of the most celebrated performances in each language might be read, but it does not appear that a long attention to that species of composition would be either proper or improving.

As almost all the Latin poets were close imitators of the Grecian bards, it would certainly tend highly to the advantage of classical literature, since Greek and Latin are generally read together, to combine those of the same species of poetry and versification, and it would appear strange that this method of proceeding has not long ere now been adopted in reputable seminaries.

It would not only enable the pupil to understand both with greater ease, but also qualify him for making a critical estimation of their respective merits, and at the same time afford a more clear and competent knowledge of the state of the various species of poetry and composition in those languages.

In order that the scholar may be enabled to read a few of the ancient poets with a just taste, as well as understanding, his knowledge of the principal figures in rhetoric, first taught at the primary schools, should be revived, and a criticism on some of the most distinguished passages of each author occasionally prescribed as an exercise.

The mathematical department of the county academy should be conducted on the same plan as in the primary school. Those whose education was not to extend farther than the academy should be made thoroughly acquainted with all the practical branches; the use of the globes, geography, and as much of astronomy at least as is connected with that science. And those who were intended for the university should be perfectly taught the elementary parts, plain and spheric trigonometry, algebra, and conic sections, with their application to the higher mathematics.

For those who had acquired a tolerable knowledge of *Euclid's Elements* and also of Greek, it might be highly useful to demonstrate a few of the leading propositions of each book in the original. This would not only more thoroughly impress them on the mind but if properly directed, from the accuracy of the mathematical language, would serve the important purpose of instructing the Greek scholar in the correct use and application of the various prepositions and particles of that copious language.

As the students in the county academies would have made some progress in the primary school in mathematical studies, it may be rationally inferred that an attention to mathematics for one half of the day would, during the term of three years in the county academy, render their proficiency equal to what has been here stated. But as the classical students designed for the university would have mathematics to attend also in the state college, they would there have an opportunity of pursuing their improvement in the sciences founded on them still farther, and on this account, at the expiration of the third year, they would have finished their course at the academy and be properly prepared for entering the state college. Such as were not designed for that seminary might be continued a year or two longer.

The classical and mathematical teachers in the county academies should have the accommodation of the students with boarding, each to have an equal share. The prices to be fixed by the state president, county rector, and such other patrons and visitors as might be thought necessary.

The two headmasters should be obligated to keep assistants in proportion to their number of pupils subject to the regulations of the board of education.

The office of the county rector, who should also preside in the county academy, would be not only to visit the primary schools, on their public examinations, as has been already stated, but he should also, except when abroad on that business, examine once a week, or try the several classes, whether classical or mathematical, in the academy, on their proficiency, at the same time delivering them a suitable lecture on the importance of what was the object of their study, accompanied by such other admonitions and observations as would tend to their improvement both in literature and conduct.

A rector's hall in the academy, contiguous to his own apartments, would be necessary for this purpose, and it would certainly be a great incitement to industry if the students found that they had weekly to submit to such a revisal of their studies. The rector might also occasionally deliver them a course of lectures on natural, and afterwards on literary and civil, history, on ancient and modern manners, and the conduct of life, which in this stage of their course would contribute greatly to their improvement, not only in their knowledge of books, but of the world.

Public examination should be held thrice in the year. The first about the beginning of the new year; the second in May; and the third about the middle of August. On the two first, a week's vacation should be allowed, and in August two weeks, that being a season which requires a little indulgence.

Previous to these examinations, the youth should occasionally be prepared in proper exercises of elocution, and after their classical and mathematical examination during the day, deliver them in the evening, in presence of their parents, guardians, or such other company as should choose to attend on those occasions. Having been exercised in the same manner in the primary school on the easiest lessons in elocution, those for the county academy should be adapted to their abilities and proficiency, avoiding theatrical licentiousness and studying only gracefulness, energy, and accuracy of pronunciation. The county rector and the two headmasters would have to select such pieces as were best suited to the abilities of the several youth, whether natural or acquired.

Should one day be found insufficient to go through the business of those examinations, they ought to be continued for two or even three days, affording to every class in the academy an equal opportunity of exhibiting its progress. As in the primary school, so also in the academy, honorary prizes should be impartially conferred on such as excelled; and for this purpose regular catalogues should be kept by the masters of all the youth in the academy, having proper columns opposite their names, specifying the authors they were reading, or the progress they had made at the end of each examination, marking with an asterism such names as had obtained prizes or had given proofs of uncommon industry and application. These catalogues should be put up to public inspection at the next succeeding examination.

The prizes conferred might either consist of suitable books

provided for that purpose, or of a piece of green or blue ribbon to be worn on the breast, having stamped on them the name of the academy and having the words *"Merui Laudem"*[28] inscribed on them for the motto. They might also be numbered so as to exhibit different degrees of merit or industry.

In conferring such prizes in this or any other of the seminaries under the institution, it would be best to pay peculiar attention and respect to diligence and conduct. The youth possessed of the best natural genius and yet averse to application merits not public approbation, at least in the same degree as the proficient by means of extraordinary diligent exertions; though then some prizes might be properly conferred on such occasions for sudden and extraordinary efforts of genius, yet the general object of them should be understood by the students as a reward for that proficiency which arises from habits of perseverance and industry.

The proficiency of the students who had completed their three years' course at the academy as here laid down should consist, in addition to what they had acquired at the primary school, in a tolerable knowledge of the Latin and Greek languages, so as to translate with propriety and ease either prose or verse, to be able to write Latin, if not classically, at least grammatically; a like knowledge of the French language; a tolerable acquaintance with ancient and modern history, geography, with such a knowledge of prosody, Greek and Roman antiquities, rhetoric, criticism, and composition, as is necessary to read the classics with propriety and taste.

In addition to the rudiments of mathematics previously acquired, they should by this time have also attained a thorough knowledge of *Euclid's Elements*, at least of the first six and the eleventh and twelfth books; conic sections, algebra with its application to geometry, and plain and spheric trigonometry. Such students as were to be prepared for immediate business, and, as already suggested, not intended for the state college, might receive a less scientific course of mathematics, so that they could devote more of their studies to the useful or practical branches. It might be necessary that such continue a year longer at the county academy.

Through the whole of the term allotted to this seminary, it would be proper, occasionally, to give the students a view of what constituted the complete scholar and man of science. It is often found very discouraging to youth that they have labored for months at some of the most abstruse elements of scientific instruction without being able to judge of their utility to their future acquisition. This office would with great propriety belong to the rector, who, in his weekly lectures, as already suggested, should occasionally exhibit that connection which subsists between the several departments of knowledge and the dependence which the highest or most useful arts have on the elementary branches of science.

Such a view, it may be reasonably presumed, would prompt the student to proceed with greater alacrity, while at the same time it would serve to throw light on the darkest and most disagreeable parts of his literary course.

Of the three boys admitted into each of the primary schools at the expense of the public on completing their course, each county academy should receive at least five of such as discovered the best genius and disposition for literary instruction, on the conditions formerly specified. But it would be best to have it entirely unknown to the students in general or even to these youths themselves, at least in this stage of their progress, what were the terms of their admittance or that they were on any other foundation than their fellow students. Five of such pupils admitted into each county academy in the state and selected from those who discovered the best abilities and most amiable dispositions throughout the different parish schools would, as has been already hinted, train up an adequate number of teachers to supply every vacancy in the whole system.

Even such as could not be admitted into the county academies would have acquired as much at the primary schools as would render them highly useful to society and to themselves, and by admitting such as discovered the brightest genius into the state college and National University, an ample field would be offered even the poorest in society for exertion in literary improvement and the attainment of whatever can tend to call forth the most distinguished merit, equally conducive to their own happiness and that of the community.

---

# Section Ninth

ON EXERCISES OF AMUSEMENT DURING THE TERMS OF RELAXATION FROM STUDY.

. . . Sunt etiam nonnulli acuendis puerorum ingeniis non inutiles Lusus.

QUINTIL.[29]

PREVIOUS to entering on the subject of the state colleges, it may be proper to make a few observations on the manner in which the youth should conduct themselves in the hours of relaxation.

During these hours they are indeed seldom at a loss for subjects or exercises of entertainment—some of these, however, are certainly more eligible than others and have a greater or less tendency to give the mind a frivolous or effeminate bias on the one hand, or if well chosen, a manly and vigorous resolution on the other. All playful exercises of the latter cast, if moderately indulged, are salutary to youth. Swimming is an almost indispensable qualification, and the situation which affords a safe opportunity of their acquiring it is insofar entitled to a preference. It is a duty not unworthy the careful tutor to point out to youth from time to time as they advance in years the proper diversions, exercises, and amusements suited to those of their years and views in life. On every species of gambling they should be taught to look with not only contempt but abhorrence and to view all exercises perverted by that spirit as the seminaries of corruption, as calculated to blast the fairest features of the human mind.

Their recreations, however, should be laid under no restraint, until their understandings be convinced that it is salutary, because their amusements cease to be such if they are not free and voluntary. Exercise and temperance are necessary both for the vigor of body and mind and to these important ends ought even their recreations to be directed. With such they ought to have sufficient time to satisfy themselves even to fatigue and such muscular exertions as should tend to promote the growth, hardiness, and strength of the body.

Although, in general, it might be most proper to leave youth to the choice of such diversions as were most agreeable to them, especially while at the primary school, yet on their advancing in years, and after having entered the county academy, it might be suggested to them that even their amusements should discover some marks of their improvement and progress in knowledge.

At this stage of their proficiency, then, it would certainly constitute a very essential part of instruction if, during their recreative hours, they should be taught the manual military exercise with all the marchings and maneuvers in the practice of that art. This extended to every county academy in the United States, while it occasionally afforded a very agreeable exercise and amusement to the youth, would also train them up to the capacity of being serviceable to their country. The very exercise would inspire them, at that age, with such patriotic sentiments and accomplish them with such military adroitness as might be one day of the highest advantage to the nation.

It is only from the idea of the establishment of a general uniform plan of literary instruction throughout the United States that this mode of directing the amusements of the youth can lay claim to general approbation. Considered, however, in this view, it would at least be entitled to the attention of the board of education who by the direction of government might extend it to what degree should be thought most salutary, both for the youth as individuals and the interests of the community.

It perhaps would not be most advisable to put arms into the hands of the youth for the purpose of learning the manual exercise. Sham guns with tin barrels and ramrods so made as *to tell*, when they exercised, would be cheap and answer the purpose so far as well as real ones. On occasions of public examinations, there might also be a review of their military maneuvers, which, were no other advantage to be the consequence, would at least teach them habits of moving and walking upright and with graceful ease and dignity. It might not, probably, be difficult to procure a person in the vicinity of each academy capable of instructing them in such discipline; it would be most eligible, however, could it be done by some one of the assistant tutors in the seminary.

---

# Section Tenth

## ON THE STATE COLLEGES.

. . . Et ætas altioribus iam discipulis debita in schola minore subsidat.

QUINTIL.[30]

As has been elsewhere observed, it is a favorable circumstance for the establishment of an uniform plan of national education that in almost every state of the Union, a college has been instituted on a liberal scale. Such states as have not yet been able to found such seminaries, it is to be hoped, may also be soon in a condition to follow the excellent example of their brethren.

It does not appear that it could operate contrary to the interests of those colleges to adopt an uniform plan of education under the direction of a literary board. Should some such plan, as has been here partly sketched, be adopted, a competent number of students ought to attend the colleges from their own respective states. But whether it would be best to restrict the youth of each state to their own college, or to allow them to attend wherever they might prefer in a different state, so as to have a change of air and climate, would require the mature deliberation of the government and the board of education.

The privilege however of attending any state college the parents might prefer could not, consistently with the claims of natural liberty, be denied; and it does not appear that it could militate against the general plan, in as far as concerned the mode of education, as that and also the terms of admittance, both with regard to the proficiency of the pupils and the prices of boarding and tuition, should be perfectly the same throughout the different colleges.

It ought, however, to be an important object of attention with every state legislature to patronize and encourage, by all proper means, the colleges and seminaries of their respective states; and were this done, could they be once brought to be as jealous of their literary as of their national character, it would be seldom, except on account of health, that parents would incline to place their sons at the seminary of a different state.

Those colleges being properly endowed, provided with a principal and professors, and in every respect prepared for the reception of students from the county academies, they ought to be admitted only on the following considerations:

First, That they should have previously gone through the course of education prescribed by the primary school and county academy; or if instructed by private tuition, that their progress should be equal to and on the same plan with such as were taught at those seminaries.

Secondly, That none, educated either publicly or privately, should be admitted but such as on public examination should give satisfaction both in their classical and mathematical proficiency.

Thirdly, That all students in the state colleges should at least be intended for a triennial course, which, as nearly as possible, ought to be from the close of the fifteenth till the expiration of the eighteenth year of their age.

This course of literary instruction should be suitably and progressively adapted to the time or number of years. During the first year's session the studies of each day should be divided between the Greek, Latin, and French languages, and mathematics. But the plan of reading these classics should be, in some respects, different from what was pursued in the academies. It might be necessary for the professor to read only a small portion of each author, and that rather from a view to criticism on that species of composition than the acquisition of the language, in which by this time the student ought to be a tolerable proficient.

Exercises from this view ought to be frequently prescribed in all these languages and critical essays on particular passages occasionally required from every student without exception. One half of the hours assigned to study each day should, during this session, be spent in these exercises of classical criticism and the remaining devoted to the completion of the mathematical course in such a manner as should be prescribed by the literary board. The elementary parts of mathematics being acquired at the academy, during this session the students should be introduced to the most useful practical branches, comprehending mensuration of various kinds, surveying and navigation, gunnery and fortification.

On one day in each week, which might probably be most suitable on Saturday, the principal, having all the students assembled in the common or most spacious hall of the college, should deliver to them a suitable lecture on morals and conduct, illustrating the effects which education ought to have on them; demanding also, from such of the students as he might choose, an account of their proficiency through the whole week. Though it would be impossible to interrogate the whole in this manner, yet were a few different individuals so catechised each public hall day, everyone would be led to expect that it might possibly fall to his lot and consequently would be led to make the necessary preparation.

Either the principal or professor of classical learning or *belles-lettres* should occasionally, on stated days during this session, deliver a course of lectures on the history of literature, the manners and customs of the Greeks and Romans, and toward the end of the session, on taste, criticism, and composition.

A lecture of an hour's length would be sufficient every second day; the students should take notes, and, on the day on which there was no lecture, that hour should be spent by the professor in examing them on the subject of the last lecture.

The mathematical professor, in like manner, should have, each week, some hours allotted for recapitulation. It is essentially necessary, in order to impress literary and especially mathematical subjects on the minds of youth with lasting advantage, that their memories be frequently exercised in the repetition of what they have already attained.

In order that the students in the state colleges should have time to mix a little in society, see their friends, and know something of the world as well as books, the vacation between each session should be extended to a longer duration than in the primary school or county academy. They might from these views properly open the first of September and close the last of June each session, allowing also a short vacation of two weeks always at the beginning of the new year.

In the second session of this course, the students in their morning hours should complete their course of classical reading and criticism during the first half of the session, and in the other half be introduced to a concise view of rhetoric, logic, and moral philosophy during the forenoon studies; and continue through the whole of their course in the evening hours the complete attainment of mathematics, and particularly in this session geography by the use of the globes, the laws of motion, the mechanical powers, and principles of astronomy. During this session also, on the same plan as in the preceding, lectures both by the principal and professors adapted to the several subjects of study would become still more necessary, would afford the students some kind of relaxation from the intensity of close and retired application, and tend also to animate them to proceed with greater alacrity and emulation.

As rhetoric to a certain degree had been introduced at an earlier stage of the literary course, it would now require only a brief attention. Logic would only be necessary in as far as it explained the several powers and operations of the human mind; and for this purpose along with a compend of logic should be read Locke's admirable *Essay on the Human Understanding* and Bacon's *Novum Organum*. It might be sufficient to give the student a view of the ancient modes of Socratic and scholastic reasoning, but his time ought to be considered as too precious to be spent in acquiring a knowledge of all the logical laws or forms of the syllogism. *A thorough knowledge of "Euclid's Elements"* is preferable to the best system of Logic that ever was taught.

Moral philosophy, under the several views of natural theology, economics, and jurisprudence, would afford much entertainment and instruction, but it does not appear that in a seminary of literary education any farther attention to it is necessary than what should inculcate a scientific view of it in all its parts. The study of the various most approved systems of moral philosophy may be more properly assigned to the shades of domestic reading and retirement. From this consideration it is presumed that in the last five months of this session the student may have acquired a competent view of logic and moral philosophy during the morning hours of each day.

Throughout every part of this course, and on every leading or most important subject, the students should be required to write and produce essays which at proper seasons should be partly read and criticized by the principal and professors, as well with regard to the matter as the manner of composition.

As youth in pursuit of literary knowledge cannot be too

much exercised in composing essays, such exercises should be prescribed as prize essays to be determined or adjusted at the close of each session. Such as obtained the prize might be spoken or read before the literary characters of the state, the patrons of the college, and what other audience might be assembled on those occasions.

The prize essays or dissertations should, in a public seminary, be as various as the different subjects of study, so that an ample field for excellence and emulation should be afforded to those of every description of genius and proficiency in classical, critical, mathematical, and philosophical reading.

On the opening of the third and last session of the course of this seminary, the students would be prepared for turning the chief part of their attention to natural philosophy. A concise system of it, in all its parts, should be taught experimentally during this session, at least for two hours each day, and a suitable apparatus should be provided for this purpose. Each state college should also have an observatory and a proper apparatus for making astronomical observations.

Occasionally during this session the proper professors should continue lectures on the various branches formerly acquired, and each student designed for the National University should be prepared for taking a Bachelor of Arts degree.

Though natural philosophy ought principally to engage the attention during this year, yet the student ought carefully to attend, at the proper hours, on the professor of classical learning and *belles-lettres*, and also on the professor of mathematics, in order to be perfected in the higher branches especially as they are subservient to the more useful, as well as the more sublime, sciences.

At the end of the course, such as intended to stand candidates for a diploma or degree should give in their names to the principal, who, after an impartial and strict examination in the classics and various sciences, should confer on them their degrees according to the usual forms. But in order to promote the interests of and give the greater dignity to the National

University, no degree higher than that of Bachelor of Arts should be conferred at any of the state colleges.

As youth advance in years, their amusements should proportionably become more manly and dignified, so that while at this seminary I would have the recreative hours of their first session spent in learning to dance and in acquiring a polished address in conversation and manners. It would appear that the profession of teaching dancing might be extended to a much more important degree of dignity as well as advantage at a seminary of public instruction than it commonly is in the domestic scenes of society.

This is not to be understood as insinuating that the dancing master should be more respected than any other teacher or professor. This is already what the flippant airs and forward address of the greater part of these gentry too generally secure them from such as are disposed to be more captivated with external appearances than inward merit. But what is here designed to be inculcated is that it would be a great acquisition to a place of public instruction could such tutors be procured as would teach dancing, a polished address in conversation, and also the proper attitudes, gestures, and actions in elocution.

On the second session at this seminary, the students' hours of amusement, which from the course here laid down could not be many, might be properly spent in learning music, and on the third session, music and fencing. Were proper masters in teaching these several ornamental accomplishments constantly procured and patronized, it is presumed that the student would at the expiration of this course be properly qualified either for pursuing his literary course to the very highest stage of improvement at the National University or to commence his intercourse with the world as a scholar, a man of business, or a gentleman.

# Section Eleventh

## On the national university.

Qued enim munus REIPUBLICAE asserre maius meliusve possumus, quam si docemus atque erudimus IUVENTUTEM.

CICERO.[31]

THERE appears to be no object on which a great, extensive, and enlightened commonwealth could with more propriety and justice exhibit, even to some degree of excess, its munificence, than in founding, endowing, and supporting a suitable seat of national improvement in literature and erudition. Objects of public prosperity in manufactures, commerce, and inland navigation have a great claim to public and private patronage and encouragement, but even these are surely of no more than secondary importance when compared with what is essential in elevating, enlightening, and dignifying the human mind. As far as the mental powers of man and the means necessary to strengthen, increase, and invigorate those powers are superior to mere bodily endowments and the means of pampering these, so far ought institutions for mental improvement to be encouraged as superior to every other consideration or subject of public advantage.

To found, however, a National University on any other plan than as the consummation of some such system as the preceding would be in a great measure to circumscribe its advantages to the community.

Such a university could with propriety be only calculated for instruction in the higher departments of literature, and vain would be the effects of sending youth to such a seminary without due preparation.

It is owing to this neglect that so many of the universities in Europe have been so ineffectual and fruitless in their general operation, as they have hitherto proved. Such as attend after a proper preparatory course have reaped all that advantage from them they have expected, while such as were admitted when destitute of due qualifications have passed through the systems of instruction and remained nearly as ignorant as when they commenced.

But a National University, placed at the head of the foregoing plan and connected with every branch or seminary of the general system, would tend not only to finish or consummate the whole literary course but also to confer upon it that national dignity and importance which such a combination of public patronage and interest would justly expect and merit. It would thus constitute the fountainhead of science, that center to which all the literary genius of the commonwealth would tend and from which, when matured by its instructive influence, would diffuse the rays of knowledge and science to the remotest situations of the United government.

Considered in this point of view, and the different seminaries connected with it, it would resemble that great source and center of light to the natural world which, together with the primary and secondary bodies enlightened and preserved by its influence, form that wonderful, that harmonious system, which justly excites our adoration of him who is the great source of all knowledge.

The local situation of the National University ought to be centrical and well chosen with regard to healthiness and convenience. It might be of advantage in some respects to it to be contiguous to the seat of government, in order that the youth, having an opportunity of occasionally seeing the grand council of the nation, should be animated by that patriotism which they in their turn might on a future day be called upon to exercise for their country.

Their contiguity also to the collected wisdom and respectability of the legislative body might, when considering themselves as almost situated under their inspection, be the means of inciting them to that laudable emulation which is so conducive to literary improvement.

But though it might be most eligible that the situation of

such a seminary be contiguous to the seat of government, it does not appear that it ought to be within the confines of a great or populous city. In these in general, there abound too many scenes of seduction, too many examples of profligacy, and too many opportunities of vicious corruption. A few miles distance from such a city and also from the seat of government might occasionally afford all the advantages *both* offered, without subjecting the youth to any danger of acquiring disrespect for the one or being seduced by the temptations of the other.

The university buildings, in magnitude and style of architecture, ought to be suitable in every respect to the important purposes for which they were designed and also to the character and dignity of the nation. The suitable plan and extent of these buildings would properly come under the direction of the general government and board of education. It may not, however, be inconsistent with the design of this essay to throw out a few hints even with regard to these accommodations.

The following are the principal buildings that should be comprised under the general plan: proper apartments for the president and vice-president of the university, and contiguous to these a great room or hall for the faculty of professors to assemble in on the business of the university, in which also the students should be matriculated and the several degrees conferred after the proper examination by the faculty.

There ought to be also a very large and spacious public hall, sufficiently capacious to contain, on proper occasions, all the students of the university, the faculty of professors, and also any respectable assemblage of spectators or audience that might occasionally be introduced.

A commodious, well-designed, and fitted-out classroom for the professor of each particular art or science would be necessary, furnished with suitable pews, properly arranged and numbered, and also with a respectable desk or pulpit for the professor, together with such presses or other receptacles for books and such other apparatus as would be necessary for him during the hours of instruction.

Convenient houses or apartments should also be provided for all the various professors in the arts and sciences, and it might be most eligible that each of their classrooms should be contiguous to or adjoining their private apartments. A steward's house would also be necessary, in which department of the buildings it would be requisite to have a competent number of kitchens and spacious diningrooms and, over these, lodging rooms for the students. Under the direction of the steward, but subject to the authority and government of the faculty, the students should be accommodated with boarding and lodgings. Under the steward there ought also to be a chamberlain whose office it should be, by the aid of his servants, to keep all the halls, classrooms, and lodging rooms clean, in good order, and supplied in the winter with fire, candles, or whatever else should be necessary.

The buildings should also comprehend a house for a public library, a museum, and also proper apartments for those who taught the ornamental arts, especially a hall for painting, another for music, and a third for statuary. It might also, in a seminary of this kind, be useful to introduce some of the most ingenious of the mechanical arts. A printer of the very first abilities and reputation could not be dispensed with, who should be furnished with proper accommodations for carrying on that business and who should keep a book shop well supplied with such books and stationery as would be necessary for the students attending the university.

The front or elevation of the university buildings would from this view be properly designed for accommodating the president and vice-president, the large hall or room for the faculty to meet in on the business of the university, and also for the great public or common hall for accommodating occasionally the whole university.

The several professors' houses with their respective classrooms should, in the manner of wings, extend rearwards, so as that, being at right angles with the front building, on each end they together with it would form three sides of a square of

KNOX: LIBERAL EDUCATION 361

buildings. They should however be set at a distance so remote that the inner area formed by them should be sufficiently capacious for the following plan of buildings:

At the breadth of one hundred feet from each range of that square in the area, another should be built for the accommodation of the steward and chamberlain, the necessary kitchens, diningrooms, and lodging rooms for the students.

Within this square, at a proper distance should be a third, which would necessarily be diminished in its dimensions, for the accommodation of the teachers of the ornamental arts, with their respective halls, and also for the printing office and book shop. On the most central part of the buildings a magnificent steeple should be erected with a proper bell. On the top should be a cupola or dome fit for an observatory and sufficiently large to admit of an astronomical apparatus in the first style of improvement.

The smoke, however, arising from the surrounding buildings might be found an obstruction to this part of the plan. In this case the steeple might terminate with a spire and an observatory would have to be erected somewhere contiguous to the university.

On the fourth side of the external square allotted to the various professors of the sciences, being opposite to the front, might be erected buildings for the library, museum, etc. Exactly in the middle of each side of each of these three squares of building should be a public or common entrance, arched over so as not to intercept the range, and on each an iron gate to be shut precisely at a certain fixed hour at night. That on the front should be ornamented in a magnificent style, having on the upper part of the gate on each side, in *basso-relievo*, the arms of the United States.

The reason that the various professors' houses have, on this sketch of a plan, been assigned to the outside square is that they would find themselves, with respect to gardens and other conveniences most advantageously and comfortably situated in that manner and would also thus form an enclosure round the youth lodged in the inner squares of the buildings, so that when proper order and regulations were maintained, there should be no egress or ingress after a fixed hour at night, without the knowledge of some of the professors. The censor general ought also to visit each room at a certain hour and report the absent.

In the rear of the building should be an ample enclosure for walks and place of recreation for the students. Here also should be a botanical garden, containing a house for the gardener and a summerhouse hall for the purpose of lecturing upon that science. A building for a chemical laboratory and lecturing hall should be also erected in this enclosure, as being better secured against accidents than if connected with the university buildings.

In some celebrated universities, it is allowed the professors to board a few students each, generally the sons of persons of distinction who can afford to pay an extraordinary price for that privilege. Such students, building upon their intimacy and interest with the professors, commonly assume to themselves a supercilious conduct to their fellow students and consequently excite, and too often justly, a spirit of jealousy, especially in every general competition for literary prizes or distinction.

In order effectually to remove every jealousy of this nature, all students at the National University of the United States should be, with respect to public accommodations, on a footing of impartial equality, and the several professors prohibited from boarding or lodging any in their families. Any professor detected in acts of partiality from pecuniary or corrupt motives, or indeed on any consideration, should be immediately divested of his office, and accusations of this nature should be attended to by the board of education.

The faculty of the National University should be an incorporated body, invested with proper authority to make laws and regulations respecting the government of the university and for preserving peace and order through all its departments. It would, however, seem advisable that this learned body, as well as the professors in all the other seminaries, should be amenable to the board of education.

A principal of the highest literary character and well disposed to the office of instruction and also a vice-principal or chancellor of the same description should be placed at the head of this university, supported by such salaries as were suited to the dignity of their office.

There ought to be a professor of classical learning or *belles-lettres* and composition, a professor of Latin and Roman antiquities, a professor of Greek and Grecian antiquities, a professor of Hebrew and Oriental languages, a professor of rhetoric, logic, and moral philosophy, a professor and assistant professor of natural philosophy, a professor of mathematics, a professor of astronomy, a professor of history and chronology, a professor of law and the principles of government, and a professor of elocution and oratory. Besides these, the various professors in the medical department and also the professors of the various ornamental arts would compose that respectable faculty to whom the important charge of this seminary should be entrusted under the direction of the literary board.

All these different professors should have fixed salaries, so that their support should not depend on the precarious attendance of many or few students in the respective sciences or arts which they professed.

The principal of the university should have proper and regular accounts kept of the money received from all the different students for their boarding and instruction, which should be added annually to the funds raised for supporting the institution. These and all other regulations of the same nature under the sanction of government should fall to the direction of the board of education.

If the admission only of properly prepared students into the state colleges has with propriety been recommended on this plan, still more strictly ought this to be attended to in the National University.

In order to maintain the interest of the state colleges, as well as the university, no student should be admitted into the latter but such as brought a diploma or degree from the former, so being they were citizens of the United States; and if foreigners, without a proficiency on strict examination in classical and mathematical learning equal to those who had gone through their course at the state colleges.

On the entrance of every student, on the conditions above stated, it should be the business of the principal or vice-principal to receive, from their parents, guardians, or themselves, some information of their professional views in life, and agreeably to such information to direct the course of their studies at the university. The useful sciences should occupy the most serious hours of study, and the ornamental be attended for the purpose of relaxation.

It would probably be found necessary that an exception should be made with regard to the above terms of admittance, in favor of the medical students. Their literary proficiency and other preparatory knowledge ought, with great propriety, to be prescribed and required of them on entering the university, but it does not appear necessary or indispensable that they should have passed through such a comprehensive and scientific course of both mathematical and classical learning as has been assigned to students of another description, whose views were not directed to any particular profession but merely to the highest attainment in literary knowledge.

By this, however, it is by no means to be understood that the medical students should be in any degree deficient in useful or polite literature; it only suggests that most of them having to attend some practicing physician previous to entering the university, it would not appear reasonable to require it as a condition of their entrance that they should produce a degree from the state college.

The literary or scientific improvement of all the students, whatever were their views, would much depend upon a proper division of their hours of study, and it ought to be the peculiar province of the vice-principal to direct them in this respect.

On every Saturday there ought to be a general meeting of the faculty and all the students in the public hall and a catalogue of the names of all the students called by the censor general for the week. This office the students, agreeably to the alphabetical order of their names, should discharge alternately weekly, the censor at the time of calling the catalogue noting carefully such as were absent.

Each professor should also keep the same order in his class, having a weekly censor who should call the catalogue and note the absent. These catalogues should be laid before the principal and faculty every Saturday, and the delinquents in absenting themselves without a proper apology laid under a suitable penalty.

It would appear to be most eligible that none of the faculty of the National University, whether principals or professors, should be clergymen of any denomination; or if they were, that they should suspend every clerical function during their being members of that body and devote themselves solely to their office.

On every Saturday, after the examination of the catalogue with regard to conduct through the week, three of the students who had been in their turn nominated orators for the day should deliver alternately, from the rostrum, an oration, not exceeding twenty minutes in length each, on some literary or philosophical subject of their own choosing. The manuscripts of these orations should be kept by the faculty, at least till the end of the session, and prizes conferred on such as excelled. After the orations they may be dismissed by the principal with an exhortation to good behavior and with prayer.

On the Sabbaths there ought to be divine service in the public hall, and as, agreeably to this plan, none of the professors should act as clergymen, two university chaplains should be annually chosen to officiate alternately. To prevent any idea of religious partiality, these chaplains ought to be of different denominations of Protestants, as is commonly observed in choosing chaplains for the house of Congress. It would be most commendable also that they should be young clergymen, without any parochial charge, who might wish, on account of improvement, to reside in the university a session or two, even after being admitted to the ministry. Unprovided-for young clergymen thus chosen alternately by the faculty, especially such as had been educated on this plan, should be preferred; and in thus receiving a suitable salary would be greatly served thereby as individuals, and it would also be serving the religious interests of the community.

The whole faculty should, with the utmost solemnity, attend on divine service, in a body; and an elevated and respectable pew should be provided for them in the hall, as well for their accommodation on this as on other public occasions.

A few of the youth educated at the public expense who had taken a degree at the state college should also be admitted, on the same foundation, to the National University. Their course of study should also be directed by the principal, agreeably to the plans or conditions already specified.

At the end of a triennial course at the university, students properly qualified should obtain a Master of Arts degree. No fee whatever should be demanded by the faculty for any degree whatever, more than merely paid the expense of having the diploma made out in a proper manner. From a university of such dignity every cause of suspicion should be removed that any degrees were conferred from any other motive than real merit.

A degree of Doctor of Physic or Doctor of Laws might be conferred by the faculty, but it does not appear proper that it should confer a degree of Doctor of Divinity, more especially if, as previously observed on the foregoing plan, it should be considered most eligible that theological students, after their philosophical course, should not be taught in the University of the United States. Clergymen of any denomination ought surely to receive that honorary distinction with more propriety from the higher judicatures of their own body than from one, many members of which might be probably little acquainted with theological merit or subjects of divinity.

Agreeably to the uniform plan here laid down, students entering the university at the expiration of the eighteenth year of their age would have finished their course at the end of the twenty-first and thus at the age of maturity would be prepared for acting their part on the theater of the world.

If the various stages of proficiency throughout the other seminaries be attended to, it can be considered no objection to this that it is not completed till so late a period. The state college should prepare youth for any profession or business in life, but the great end of the National University should be to accommodate such as wished to indulge their literary genius to the greatest possible extent, and who were in such circumstances as to account no part of their life spent more agreeably or to better advantage than in receiving the highest possible improvement in arts and sciences.

# Conclusion

SHOULD the foregoing outlines of a plan of national education be suited to the local situation or extent of the United States of America, it is presumed that, under proper patronage and the direction of *a well chosen literary board*, it would amply provide for the proper instruction of youth in every possible circumstance of life and also for any particular business or profession. Much however has been here omitted that might be found necessary in filling up the system when reduced to practice.

The great end and design of education is the improvement of the human mind in virtuous, useful, and ornamental knowledge, and in the progress of a plan of public instruction much would occur from time to time to promote that invaluable purpose which without great prolixity could not be introduced in an essay of this nature. Indeed it is only just to allow such an ample field for progressive improvement, in this respect, as it would be illiberal to have circumscribed it by any fixed or exclusive practical system.

In this view of the subject, as well as in many others, appears the great importance of *an incorporated board of presidents of education*. Their abilities, literary knowledge, extensive information, and correspondence with the learned world would enable them occasionally to enrich such a plan as the foregoing with whatever might best tend to promote its success. One great deficiency in education as conducted in even the most enlightened countries is the want of such a respectable body of well qualified guardians as should constantly watch over its interests and add dignity to it by their virtue and talents. Public instruction has been too much and generally committed to the trust and direction of those only who were actual tutors, or if placed under the authority of some dignified patron, has been generally owing rather to the pecuniary endowments of the opulent dunce than to qualifications entitled to the highest respectability of character on account of literary merit.

Let it then be particularly observed that by the introduction of such a learned body for the purposes already specified, the foregoing essay is to lay, in the first place, some claim to the public attention, as in that respect superior to any system of instruction known to the writer of this essay. But, in the second place, the *uniformity* of this plan of public instruction would, it is presumed, contribute highly to its success and, at the same time, conduce much both to the improvement and embellishment of society. It might also, in no small degree, be productive of not only harmony of sentiments, unity of taste and manners, but also the patriotic principles of genuine federalism amongst the scattered and variegated citizens of this extensive republic.

Every person tolerably acquainted with the present state of education in this country, and the great obstruction and discouragement students meet with by not being constantly supplied with the necessary books, and also from the various editions of the same authors, must be disposed to allow that it would be necessary to establish or encourage a printer in each state for supplying the seminaries with the proper authors in each science. This regulation, it is presumed, would in no small degree contribute to the success of the plan.

The youth educated at the public expense might also, if properly conducted and disposed of, tend highly to the interests of literature, especially in keeping up a supply of proper tutors for all the different departments of the course.

Under such a system, properly founded and organized, it does not appear that the expense of education would be much greater to the community than it is at present, especially as it respects the two first introductory seminaries. On account of trusting to unsettled or itinerant teachers of the first rudiments of instruction, most of the youth sit for the primary school lose at one time what they gain at another, and, thus, not only misspend one half of the season for instruction but also occasion double expense for the same degree of proficiency.

It cannot be properly objected to the preceding plan that it requires too much time to complete the scientific course, while it provides for those of every possible circumstance, profession, or view in life. It may suit very many of the youth in the community to be satisfied with what literary instruction they receive in even the primary school, and should it be conducted on the plan specified in the consideration of that seminary, it must be sufficient for all the common concerns, business, or even happiness of life.

The higher stages of the system, it is presumed, may be adapted to all the different views or designs of the public, so that while an ample field of improvement is held out and provided for the most exalted genius or the most liberal professions, each subordinate degree also may be accommodated to its satisfaction.

Indeed it is only a system of this nature that can be worthy the adoption of an enlightened nation, disposed impartially to provide for the improvement of all its citizens agreeably to their views and circumstances.

In England, enlightened in literary improvement as they conceive themselves to be, has it not been owing to so much being expended on founding and endowing two pompous universities, without taking care to found proper preparatory seminaries connected with them, that a few only have become eminent in science, while the bulk of the community in that country continue to be so illiterate.

In every country possessed of genuine freedom and impressed with a just sense of its value, nothing can be more worthy of public attention than an improvement in the means of public instruction. Wherever scientific knowledge is generally cultivated, there must the dignity and rights of man be best known and, consequently, not only most highly valued, but also best secured from corruption and most ably maintained and vindicated from encroachment and usurpation.

But in order to [do] this it is necessary that the system of education should be generally suited to the citizens, that it should comprehend every description of situation and circumstance, uncircumscribed by partial endowments, local prejudices, or personal attachments.

Habits of attention to science are generally fraught with knowledge and virtue. It is impossible that the mind which has undergone, from the first dawnings of reason to maturity, that discipline which such an uniform and extensive system of instruction would inculcate and require can have imbibed any strong bias in favor of vice or immorality.

The principles of morals, however, and of public and private virtue would not, on the preceding plan, be left to the mere effect of scientific discipline. They would require the diligent, fostering hand of care, as well as all the influence of dignified example. And such, and such only, should be the examples exhibited in the characters and conduct of all the various tutors throughout their respective seminaries, at least in suitable proportion to the eminence of their situation.

One great deficiency in modern education, it must be allowed, is that as the sciences have been enlarged and improved, especially such as depend on mathematical knowledge, a proportionable attention to a preparatory introduction by mathematics has been, too generally, either dispensed with altogether or at best inculcated in a very superficial manner.

From this consideration, ample time has been allowed in every department of this course for acquiring a thorough knowledge of mathematical learning in all its various branches. No part of instruction so much merits public patronage as this, whether we view it as regarding all the useful purposes, arts, and occupations of life or as elevating the human mind, enlarging the capacity of its powers, and enabling it to extend its scientific comprehension from the most humble to the most sublime and exalted of the works of God.

In the pursuit of literary knowledge some may have a genius for mathematics and the sciences founded on them, who might discover little taste or abilities for understanding the elegancies of classical composition, the acquisition of ancient languages, or enriching their own by their copiousness and dignified beauties. A general or national system of instruction ought therefore to be well accommodated to every different genius whether classical or mathematical; and it is only by being so accommodated that it could merit general or public encouragement. It will be found, however, that there are few who have good natural abilities for one species of literature who may not also make competent proficiency to whatever part of it the mind may be directed. All, then, who should be considered as liberally educated ought to be well instructed in the mathematical sciences. There is, perhaps, no nation of the modern world that hath yet adopted any uniform system of public patronage for the general diffusion of this part of education, but its various advantages are perhaps impossible to be calculated, could it be generally extended to the greatest part of the youth in any community.

On an impartial review of the course here laid down, it does not appear that any known science, really useful or ornamental, or the means of acquiring it, hath been omitted. Should any such omission, however, appear, it ought not to discredit the plan, the principal object of which hath been, not only the consideration of the public establishment of the best means of promoting the highest degree of literary improvement but, more especially, its establishment on a general, uniform, national foundation, leaving, in some measure, the practical part to be filled up, as the progressive improvement in the sciences and in the means of acquiring them may, under proper patronage, encouragement, and direction, from time to time, inculcate.

. . . quibus hæc, sint qualiacumque, Adridere velim: doliturus, si placeant spe Deterius nostra.

HOR.[32]

# NOTES

## RUSH: ESTABLISHMENT OF PUBLIC SCHOOLS

1. Cesare Bonesana, Marchese di Beccaria, *An Essay on Crimes and Punishments* (London: J. Almon, 1767), p. 167. Quoted with insignificant changes.

2. In the original: "learned youth in the languages." Surely an unintended transposition.

3. Like most early American educational planners, Rush was often a dreamer uninhibited by reality. In 1787 the funds of the University were so inadequate that tutors' salaries were in arrears; in 1788 a trustee committee reported annual income from all sources at £2,200 and the annual deficit at £600. Edward Potts Cheyney, *History of the University of Pennsylvania 1740-1940* (Philadelphia: University of Pennsylvania Press, 1940), pp. 65-66, 144-146.

4. Dickinson College at Carlisle was founded in 1783 by the Presbyterians with the energetic encouragement of Rush.

5. As a result of a settlement of outstanding grievances between the Commonwealth of Pennsylvania and the Indian tribes of the Six Nations, treaties in 1784 and 1788 extinguished Indian rights within the charter bounds of Pennsylvania and in the area known as the "Lake Erie triangle." These treaties opened up to sale the vast lands north and west of the Ohio and Allegheny Rivers in Pennsylvania. Lewis S. Shimmell, *Border Warfare in Pennsylvania* (Harrisburg: R. L. Myers, 1901), pp. 145-150.

6. *The Carlisle Gazette, and the Western Repository of Knowledge,* published at Carlisle, Pennsylvania, 1785-1817.

7. This sentiment, in various forms, is attributed to Henry IV in the standard reference works. Rush, being an American, appears to have substituted turkey for chicken.

8. Antipater (c. 397-319 B.C.), Macedonian general and regent of Macedonia from 334 to 323 B.C. and of the Macedonian empire from 321 to 319 B.C.

9. The national, ethnic, and religious origins of the people of Pennsylvania were more diverse than anywhere else in the English colonies.

10. Edward Moore and Henry Brooke, *Fables for the Female Sex* (London, 1744); Samuel Croxall, ed., *The Fables of Aesop and Others* (Philadelphia: Robert Bell, 1777). See also the first American publication of Moore's *Fables for the Ladies* . . . (Philadelphia: Thomas Dobson, 1787).

11. Maximilien de B. Sully, *Memoires du Duc de Sully,* 6 vols. (Paris: Etienne LeDoux, 1827), I, 431-432. Sully reports himself as having expressed this sentiment in 1592, when he decided to persuade Henry IV of France to turn Catholic, rather than in 1597, when he was made minister of finance.

## RUSH: FEMALE EDUCATION

1. The quotations are based on the opening lines in *Hamlet*, act III, sc. 2.

2. Charlotte and Werter are the heroine and hero of Goethe's sentimental romance, *The Sorrows of Werter*, first published in English translation at London in 1780 by J. Dodsley.

3. Rush's choice of the word "banished" is problematic. No Philadelphia or Pennsylvania statutes of the period banished or regulated Bible reading in the schools. Perhaps under the influence of Deism or denominational rivalry, schools neglected the Bible, but neglect is not banishment.

4. Rush has apparently freely paraphrased from Jean-Jacques Rousseau, *Emile ou de L'Education*, 3 vols. (Leipzig: M. G. Weidmann & Reich, 1762), I, 191: "Oserais-je exposer ici la plus grande, la plus importante, la plus utile règle de toute l'éducation? Ce n'est pas de gagner du temps, c'est d'en perdre." In the English translation, *Emilius; or, An Essay on Education*, 2 vols. (London: J. Nourse and P. Vaillant, 1763), p. 100, the passage reads: "Shall I venture now to lay down a rule of education, of all others the most important and most useful? It is, not to gain time, but to lose it." Frederick Charles Green, *Jean-Jacques Rousseau: A Critical Study of His Life and Writings* (Cambridge: Cambridge University Press, 1955), p. 232, discusses this passage.

5. Voltaire and Henry St. John Bolingbroke were enemies of all kinds of orthodoxy.

6. Proverbs 31:28.

7. A version of this sentiment appears in Andrew Fletcher, *An Account of a Conversation Concerning a Right Regulation of Governments for the Common Good of Mankind. In a Letter to the Marquis of Montrose* . . . (Edinburgh, 1704), p. 10. Although often attributed to Confucius, it does not appear in his works.

## WEBSTER: EDUCATION OF YOUTH

1. Benjamin Franklin recounts his own difficulties in establishing an English school in conjunction with an existing Latin school in Philadelphia in "Observations Relative to the Intentions of the Original Founders of the Academy in Philadelphia. June, 1789," in Jared Sparks, ed., *The Works of Benjamin Franklin*, II, 133-159 (Boston: Hilliard, Gray, 1836). His plans for the English academy are in Leonard W. Labaree, ed., *The Papers of Benjamin Franklin* (New Haven: Yale University Press, 1959–), IV, 101-108.

2. Alexander Pope, *An Essay on Criticism* (London: W. Lewis, 1711), p. 14.

3. "If parts allure thee, think how Bacon shined,
    The wisest, brightest, meanest of mankind."
Alexander Pope, *An Essay on Man: In Four Epistles*, epistle IV, line 281.

4. Alexander Pope, *An Essay on Man: In Four Epistles: Together with*

*the Notes* (Hartford: Nathaniel Patten, 1787), epistle II, lines 217-220, p. 23.

5. *Ibid.*, p. 48.

6. Richard Price (1723-1791), British moral philosopher and supporter of the American Revolution, and Anne Robert Jacques Turgot (1727-1781), French statesman and economist, both "absurdly" considered the role of state governments in the future of the new republic in Price, *Observations on the Importance of the American Revolution, and the Means of Making it a Benefit to the World* (Boston: Powars and Willis, 1784). Turgot's observations are included in a letter to Price, pp. 71-87.

## CORAM: POLITICAL INQUIRIES

1. Guillaume Thomas François Raynal, *The Revolution of America* (London: Lockyer, Davis, Holborn, 1781), p. 181. Raynal (1713-1796) was a leading ornament of the Enlightenment in France, both as author and politician.

2. In 1642 an act of the General Court of Massachusetts held parents responsible for the ability of their children to "read and understand the principles of religion and the capital laws of the country." In 1647 another act required each town of fifty householders to hire a schoolmaster for teaching reading and writing; each town of one hundred householders was required to operate a Latin grammar school to prepare young men for Harvard. Similar legislation was enacted in the other New England colonies, with the exception of Rhode Island.

3. Guillaume Thomas François Raynal, *A Philosophical and Political History of the Settlements and Trade of the Europeans in the East and West Indies*, 8 vols. (London: W. Strahan and T. Cadell, 1783), VII, 156-157.

4. Georges Louis Leclerc, *comte* de Buffon (1707-1788), in his *Histoire naturelle générale et particulière, avec la description du Cabinet du Roi*, which he edited and which was published in 44 volumes in Paris between 1749 and 1804 by the royal printer. For Raynal, see his *Revolution of America* and *A Philosophical and Political History*. For a consideration of Raynal's and Buffon's views, see Edwin T. Martin, *Thomas Jefferson: Scientist* (New York: Henry Schuman, 1952), pp. 148-211; Daniel J. Boorstin, *The Lost World of Thomas Jefferson* (New York: Henry Holt, 1948); Gilbert Chinard, "Eighteenth Century Theories on America as a Human Habitat," *Proceedings of the American Philosophical Society*, Vol. 91, no. 1 (Feb. 25, 1947), 27-57.

5. Francisco Javier Clavijero, *The History of Mexico*, 2 vols. (London: G. G. and J. Robinson, 1787); Thomas Jefferson, *Notes on the State of Virginia* (Philadelphia: Prichard and Hall, 1788); Jonathan Carver, *Three Years Travels, Through the Interior Parts of North America, For More Than Five Thousand Miles . . .* (Philadelphia: Joseph Crukshank, 1784); Cadwallader Colden, *The History of the Five Indian Nations Depending on the Province of New-York in America* (New York: William Bradford,

1727); Edward Bancroft, *An Essay on the Natural History of Guiana, in South America* (London: T. Becket and P. A. De Hondt, 1769).

6. Miguel Venegas, *A Natural and Civil History of California . . .* , 2 vols. (London: James Rivington and James Fletcher, 1759), I, 64.

7. Corneille de Pauw, *Recherches philosophiques sur les Américains,* 2 vols. (Berlin: G. J. Decker, 1768-69). See Henry Ward Church, "Corneille de Pauw, and the Controversy over his *Recherches philosophiques sur les Américains," Publications of the Modern Language Association of America,* vol. LI, no. 1 (March, 1936), pp. 178-206.

8. Venegas, *A Natural and Civil History of California . . .* , I, 68, 79.

9. *Ibid.,* 79-80. Father Sigismundo Taraval (1700-1763) was rector at a Jesuit mission in lower California.

10. Alexander McGillivray (1759-1793), chief of the Creek Indians.

11. On June 27, 1790, two friendly Seneca Indian chiefs were murdered by four white men on Pine Creek, Lycoming County, Pennsylvania. C. Hale Sipe, *The Indian Wars of Pennsylvania* (2d ed.; Harrisburg: The Telegraph Press, 1931), pp. 692-693.

*The Delaware Gazette* was published at Wilmington, 1785-1799.

12. Carver, *Three Years Travels . . .* , p. 107.

13. Diogenes Laertius, *Socrates* II.xxvii, in *Diogenes Laertius: Lives of Eminent Philosophers,* trans. R. D. Hicks (Loeb Classical Library), I, 156-157, says of Socrates: "He used to say that he most enjoyed the food which was least in need of condiment, and the drink which made him feel the least hankering for some other drink; and that he was nearest to the gods in that he had the fewest wants." The same sentiment also appears in Xenophon, *Memorabilia* I.vi.10, in *Xenophon: Memorabilia and Oeconomicus,* trans. E. C. Marchant (Loeb Classical Library), pp. 70-73, in which Socrates says: "You seem, Antiphon, to imagine that happiness consists in luxury and extravagance. But my belief is that to have no wants is divine; to have as few as possible comes next to the divine . . ."

14. Bancroft, *Natural History of Guiana,* pp. 337-341.

15. "O happy husbandmen! too happy, should they come to know their blessings!" *The Georgics* ii.458, in *Virgil,* trans. H. Rushton Fairclough, 2 vols. (Loeb Classical Library), I, 148-149.

16. William Blackstone, *Commentaries on the Laws of England,* 4 vols. (Philadelphia: Robert Bell, 1771-72), is the first American edition. Editorial notes are based on the 4th English edition (Oxford: Clarendon Press, 1770), the set of Thomas Jefferson now in the Library of Congress.

17. *Ibid.,* II, 2.

18. *Ibid.,* I, 6.

19. *Ibid.,* II, 2.

20. *Ibid.*

21. *Ibid.,* 3.

22. *Ibid.*

23. *Ibid.*

24. "But all things were common and undivided to all, even as one inheritance might be to all." Justin, *De historiis Philippicis et totius mundi orginibus* XLIII.i.11-12 (London: R. Clavel, 1701), p. 22. Quoted in Blackstone, *Commentaries*, II, 3.

25. *Ibid.*, 3-4.
26. *Ibid.*, 4.
27. *Ibid.*
28. *Ibid.*
29. *Ibid.*
30. Carver, *Three Years Travel*, p. 107.
31. Blackstone, *Commentaries*, II, 5.
32. *Ibid.*, 4.
33. *Ibid.*, 5.
34. *Ibid.*, 7.
35. Antoine Yves Goguet, *The Origin of Laws, Arts, and Sciences, and Their Progress among the Most Ancient Nations*, 3 vols. (Edinburgh: Alex. Donaldson and John Reid, 1761), I, 16-17. Goguet (1716-1758) was a French legal historian.
36. Martino Martini, *Histoire de la Chine*, 2 vols. (Paris: C. Babin and A. Seneuze, 1692), I, 18. The quoted sentence is from Goguet, I, 31.
37. Le P. José de Acosta, *Histoire naturelle et moralle des Indes tant orientalles qu' occidentalles* . . . (Paris: M. Orry, 1598), pp. 295-296. The quoted sentence is from Goguet, I, 31.
38. Goguet, *The Origin of Laws*, I, 32.
39. *Ibid.*, 4.
40. Vincent le Blanc, *Les Voyages fameux due sievr Vincent le Blanc* . . . (Paris: G. Clovsier, 1648), pp. 144-145, 157; *Histoire naturelle de l'Islande, du Groenland* . . . (Paris: S. Jorry, 1750), II, 21, 236, 244, 252, 266; Charles Gobien, *Histoire des Isles Marianes* . . . (Paris: N. Pepie, 1700), pp. 44, 51, 53; *Lettres édifiantes et curieuses, écrites des missions étrangères par quelques missionnaires de la Compagnie de Jesus*, 34 vols. (Paris, 1707-1773), II, 177; V, 278; X, 193; XXV, 3-4, 8, 77, 201; *Nouvelle relation de la France equinoxiale* (Paris, 1743), p. 235; Antoine François Prévost, ed., Histoire générale des voyages . . . , 20 vols. (Paris: Didot, 1746-1770), I, 170, 197; II, 308; Amédée-François Frézier, *Relation du voyage de la Mer du Sud aux côtes du Chily et du Perou, Fait pendant les années 1712, 1713 et 1714* (Paris: J. -C. Nyon, 1716), pp. 54, 66; *Recueil des voyages au Nord* (Amsterdam, 1731), VIII, 403.
41. Goguet, *The Origin of Laws*, I, 5.
42. The *Encyclopédie*, prepared under the direction of Diderot and D'Alembert and eventuating in a work of 35 folio volumes (1751-1780), is a landmark in French philosophy and a major document of the Enlightenment. The first American edition "greatly improved" appeared as the *Encyclopaedia*, 18 vols. (Philadelphia: Thomas Dobson), issued in parts between 1790 and 1797, the title pages bearing the year 1798. See I, 243-325, for Agriculture. The quoted remark appears on p. 244.

43. Goguet, *The Origin of Laws*, I, 31.

44. Blackstone, *Commentaries*, II, 7.

45. *Ibid.*, 7-8.

46. Hugo Grotius (1583-1645), Dutch jurist and statesman, pioneer in the formulation of international law; Samuel von Pufendorf (1632-1694), German publicist and jurist, author of a pioneer treatise on natural law and international law; Jean Barbeyrac (1677-1744), French jurist who translated and edited the major work of Pufendorf and Grotius; Theophile Gerard Titius (1661-1714), jurisconsult and commentator on German public law; John Locke (1632-1704), English philosopher, influential in shaping Enlightenment thought in England and France.

47. Blackstone, *Commentaries*, II, 8-9.

48. *Ibid.*, 5.

49. *Ibid.*, 14.

50. Joseph Priestley (1733-1804), English theologian and scientist, and Philip Furneaux (1726-1783), English theologian and nonconformist, carried on a public correspondence with Sir William Blackstone on religious liberty. The correspondence is contained in *An Interesting Appendix to Sir William Blackstone's Commentaries on the Laws of England* (Philadelphia: Robert Bell, 1772).

51. Blackstone, *Commentaries*, I, 47.

52. Cesare Bonesana, marchese di Beccaria, *An Essay on Crimes and Punishments* (London: J. Almon, 1767), p. 83. Beccaria was an influential Italian criminologist and economist.

53. William Harrison, "The Description and Historie of England," in Raphael Holinshed, compiler, *The Chronicles of England, Scotland and Ireland*, 3 vols. in 2 (London, 1587), I, 186.

54. *The Maryland Gazette; or, The Baltimore Advertiser*, published at Baltimore, 1783-1791.

55. Raynal, *A Philosophical and Political History*, VII, 157.

56. For Henry Fielding's classic treatment of crime in London see *An Enquiry into the Causes of the Late Increase of Robbers, etc. with Some Proposals for Remedying This Growing Evil* (London: A. Millar, 1751), pp. 75-94, as well as his novels.

Oliver Goldsmith's history of the poor soldier appears in *The Citizen of the World; or Letters from a Chinese Philosopher, Residing in London, to His Friends in the East*, 2 vols. (London: The Author, 1762), II, 216-222.

57. Raynal, *A Philosophical and Political History*, VII, 158.

58. *Ibid.*, VIII, 17.

59. Catharine Sawbridge Macauley, *The History of England, From the Revolution to the Present Time, In a Series of Letters to the Reverend Doctor Wilson* . . . (Bath: R. Cruttwell, 1778), 369-370.

60. Blackstone, *Commentaries*, IV, 349.

61. Jonathan Swift, *Travels into Several Remote Nations of the World, by Lemuel Gulliver*, 2 vols. (London: Benjamin Motte, 1726), in which the legendary flying island of Laputa was populated by scientific quacks.

62. *The Spectator,* No. 200 (October 19, 1711), p. 1.

63. Joshua Gee, *The Trade and Navigation of Great-Britain Considered* . . . , (2d ed.; London: Sam Buckley, 1730), p. 90. Actually, Gee says: "It is a common Opinion, that we have above a Million of People in the three Nations destitute of Work . . ."

64. Paul de Rapin-Thoyras, *The History of England, As Well Ecclesiastical as Civil,* 15 vols. (London: James and John Knapton, 1728-1732), VIII, 55-57.

65. See Herbert Davis, ed., *The Prose Works of Jonathan Swift,* 13 vols. (Oxford: Shakespeare Head Press for Basil Blackwell, 1939-1959), especially the sermon "Causes of the Wretched Condition of Ireland" in *Irish Tracts 1720-1723 and Sermons,* IX, 199-210 (1948) and "A Modest Proposal" (1729) in *Irish Tracts 1728-1733,* XII, 109-118 (1955).

66. Erasmus Philips, *The State of the Nation, In Respect to Her Commerce, Debts, and Money* (London: J. Woodman and D. Lyon, 1725), pp. 7-8, 46-48.

67. Jacob Vanderlint, *Money Answers All Things* . . . (London: T. Cox, 1734), pp. 76-77.

68. Sir Samuel Garth (1661-1719), English physician and poet, published in 1691 the long mock-heroic poem, *The Dispensary.* The lines quoted here do not appear in the first edition, but the first and second are in the 7th London edition (Jacob Tonson, 1714), p. 15. The third and fourth have eluded the editor.

69. Charles Marguerite Jean Baptiste Mercier Dupaty, *Travels through Italy in a Series of Letters* (London: G. G. J. and J. Robinson, 1788), pp. 30-33.

70. Daniel Shays (1747-1825), leader of debtor rebellion in western Massachusetts 1786-1787; Lord George Gordon (1751-1793), tried and acquitted for treason in 1781 for his role in riots protesting Catholic relief legislation passed by Parliament.

71. Noah Webster, "On the Education of Youth in America," in *A Collection of Essays and Fugitiv Writings* (Boston: I. Thomas and E. T. Andrews for the Author, 1790), pp. 22-23. See pp. 65-68 of the present volume. Coram's occasional trifling errors in transcription and omissions of italics have been corrected.

72. *Ibid.,* pp. 23-24.

73. *Ibid.,* pp. 24-25.

74. Coram here apparently is referring to England. The context suggests that some part of Coram's original text was mistakenly omitted by the typesetter.

75. Raynal, *The Revolution of America* pp. 21-22.

76. *Ibid.,* p. 22.

77. Oliver Goldsmith, "Essay VII," *The Miscellaneous Works of Dr. Goldsmith* (Boston: Thomas and Andrews, 1793), pp. 44-45.

78. William Cowper, *The Task: A Poem in Six Books,* book II, lines 771-779 (Philadelphia: Thomas Dobson, 1787), pp. 55-56.

79. Jonathan Carver, *Three Years Travels,* p. 107.

## DOGGETT: DISCOURSE ON EDUCATION

1. Line 149 of "Epistle I" of *Moral Essays* in *The Works of Alexander Pope*, 5 vols. (Edinburgh: J. Balfour, 1764), II, 83.
2. Ephesians vi, 4.
3. II Timothy i, 10.
4. I Corinthians ii, 9.
5. William Paley, *The Principles of Moral and Political Philosophy* (Philadelphia: Thomas Dobson, 1788), pp. 224-225. An insignificant error in the quotation has been corrected.
6. Proverbs xxii, 6.

## SMITH: REMARKS ON EDUCATION

1. John Locke, "Of the Conduct of the Understanding" (Section 18), in *Posthumous Works of Mr. John Locke* (London: A. and J. Churchill, 1706), p. 58.
2. Cincinnatus (519?-439? B.C.), statesman and general, dictator of Rome.
3. Smith has paraphrased Jean-Jacques Rousseau, *Discours sur l'origine & les fondements de l'inegalite parmi les hommes* (Amsterdam: Marc Michel Rey, 1755), p. 25: "Si elle [la nature] nous a destinés à être sains, j'ose presque assurer que l'état de réflexion est un état contre nature, et que l'homme qui médite est un animal dépravé." In the English translation, *A Discourse upon the Origin and Foundation of the Inequality among Mankind* (London: R. and J. Dodsley, 1761), p. 27, the passage reads: "Allowing that Nature intended we should always enjoy good Health, I dare almost affirm that a State of Reflection is a State against Nature, and that the Man who meditates is a depraved Animal." Frederick Charles Green, *Jean-Jacques Rousseau: A Critical Study of His Life and Writings* (Cambridge: Cambridge University Press, 1955), p. 123, considers this passage.
4. Samuel Clarke (1675-1729), English theologian and philosopher, friend and disciple of Newton.
5. Sullivan, *A View of Nature . . .* , VI, 278.
6. *The Institutio Oratorio of Quintilian* I.i.15-19, trans. H. E. Butler, 4 vols. (Loeb Classical Library), I, 26-29. Smith has here paraphrased the original.
7. Charles Louis de Secondat, baron de la Brède et de Montesquieu, *The Spirit of Laws*, 2 vols. (London: J. Nourse and P. Vaillant, 1750), I, 48.
8. *Institutio*, trans. Butler, I, 38-55; Allan Abbott, ed., "Of Education" (1673) in Frank Allen Patterson, gen. ed., *The Works of John Milton*, 18 vols. in 21 (New York: Columbia University Press, 1931-1938), IV, 275-292; R. H. Quick, ed., John Locke, *Some Thoughts Concerning Education* (Cambridge: Cambridge University Press, 1880), pp. 45-51.
9. Montesquieu, *Spirit of Laws*, I, 50.
10. *Lucretius: De rerum natura*, trans. W. H. D. Rouse (Loeb Classical

Library), pp. 84-85. Smith has paraphrased the opening prologue to book II, lines 1-13.

## LAFITTE: A NATIONAL INSTITUTION

1. "Unless the vessel is clean, whatever you pour in turns sour." *Epistles* I.ii.54 in *Horace: Satires, Epistles and Ars Poetica,* trans. H. Rushton Fairclough (Loeb Classical Library), pp. 266-267.

2. Guillaume Thomas François Raynal, *A Philosophical and Political History of the Settlements and Trade of the Europeans in the East and West Indies,* 8 vols. (London: W. Strahan and T. Cadell, 1783), VII, 422-426.

3. Lafitte here is referring to the massacre of French colonists in Haiti during the slave revolt of 1791.

4. Claude Louis, comte de Saint-Germain, French general, appointed minister of war by Louis XVI in 1775.

5. In Roman mythology Bellona, the wife of Mars, was the goddess of war.

6. John Adams, in his first annual message to Congress, urged support for a national university.

## KNOX: LIBERAL EDUCATION

1. "I shall not take offense at a few blots which a careless hand has let drop, or human frailty has failed to avert." *Ars Poetica,* lines 351-353, in *Horace: Satires, Epistles and Ars Poetica,* trans. H. Rushton Fairclough (Loeb Classical Library), pp. 478-479.

2. Washington College at Chestertown was chartered by the Maryland legislature in 1782, St. Johns at Annapolis in 1784. By the law of 1784 chartering St. John's both of these institutions were to constitute the University of Maryland. The law achieved its purpose only nominally; in 1805 the legislature withdrew its support and in 1812 a new University of Maryland was chartered. Bernard C. Steiner, *History of Education in Maryland* (Washington: Government Printing Office, 1894), pp. 69-71.

3. George Washington's support of a national university is considered in Edgar Bruce Wesley, *Proposed: The University of the United States* (Minneapolis: University of Minnesota Press, 1936), pp. 3-10.

4. Thomas Jefferson's difficulties in gaining legislative support for his detailed system of education for Virginia is recounted in his "Autobiography," which appears as a "Memoir" in Thomas Jefferson Randolph, ed., *Memoir, Correspondence, and Miscellanies from the Papers of Thomas Jefferson,* 4 vols. (Charlottesville: F. Carr and Co., 1829), I, 1-89.

5. The original reads "academies," but "advances" is surely intended.

6. "A proof of what I say is to be found in the fact that boys commonly show promise of many accomplishments, and when such promise dies away as they grow up, this is plainly due not to the failure of natural gifts, but to lack of the requisite care." *The Institutio Oratorio of Quintilian* I.i.2, trans. H. E. Butler, 4 vols. (Loeb Classical Library), I, 20-21.

7. Knox abbreviated a longer passage which, translated, runs: "His mind requires constant stimulus and excitement, whereas retirement such as has just been mentioned induces languor and the mind becomes mildewed like things that are left in the dark, or else flies to the opposite extreme and becomes puffed up with empty conceit." Quintilian, *Institutio* I.ii. 18, trans. Butler, I, 48-49.

8. This no longer very "well known" story appears in *Spectator* No. 313 (Feb. 28, 1712). It recounts at length how an act of brave generosity by one Westminster schoolboy toward another was repaid years later when, during a royalist rebellion that broke out against the Protectorate in 1655, the two old schoolboys found themselves on opposing sides. The befriended of years before was now a Protectorate judge; the friend, a prisoner. The prisoner's life was saved.

9. "Education is the best possession for mortals." Attributed to Menander (343?-291? B.C.), Greek comic poet and playright, in Augustus Meineke, *Fragmenta Comicorum Graecorum*, 5 vols. (Berlin: G. Reimer, 1839), IV, 347.

10. Richard Price, *A Sermon, Delivered to a Congregation of Protestant Dissenters, at Hackney, on the 10th of February Last, Being the Day Appointed for a General Fast* (London: T. Cadell, 1779). Price (1723-1791) was an English moral philosopher.

11. "The greater part of our youth prefer to exhibit only a surface knowledge rather than to manifest solid erudition." Daniel Georg Morhof, *Polyhistor, Literarius, Philosophicus et Practicus . . .* , 2 vols. (Lubeck: Peter Boeckmanni, 1732), I, 457 (book II, ch. x, line 46). Morhof (1639-1691) was a German philosopher and historian.

12. "How much better would it be for the State, if we were to proceed by those slow and modest steps first to the Academies, and then from these to Professorial chairs, tribunals, and law courts." Morhof, *Polyhistor*, I, 457 (book II, ch. x, line 46). Inaccuracies in the quotation have been corrected.

13. "For the Greek lyric poets are often licentious and even in Horace there are passages which I should be unwilling to explain to a class." Quintilian, *Institutio* I.viii.6, trans. Butler, I, 148-149.

14. "When a boy has therefore been imbued with these rudiments in elementary school, then with good omens let him apply himself to the higher disciplines." From the *De ratione studii* of Erasmus in E. V. Scheidius, ed., *Ioachimi Fortii Rengelbergii, Desiderii Erasmi, M. A. Mureti, G. J. Vossii, & C. Barlaei commentationes de ratione studii* (Leiden: Sam. et John. Luchtmans, 1792), p. 108.

15. Noah Webster, *A Grammatical Institute, of the English Language, Comprising, an Easy, Concise, and Systematic Method of Education, Designed for the Use of English Schools in America . . .* (Hartford: Hudson and Goodwin, 1783).

16. Of the three eighteenth-century English journals here mentioned by Knox, the *Rambler* was started by Samuel Johnson in 1750. The *Guardian*,

started in 1713, and the *Spectator*, in 1711, published the essays of Joseph Addison and Richard Steele.

17. John Ash, *Grammatical Institutes; or, an Easy Introduction to Dr. Lowth's English Grammar, Designed for the Use of Schools, and To Lead Young Gentlemen and Ladies, into the Knowledge of the First Principles of the English Language* (New York: Hugh Gaine, 1792); James Buchanan, *A Regular English Syntax* . . . (Philadelphia: Styner and Cist, 1780).

18. William Guthrie, *A New System of Modern Geography* (Philadelphia: Mathew Carey, 1793); Jedidiah Morse: *The American Geography* . . . (Elizabethtown: Shepard Kollock for the author, 1789).

19. Christoph Christian Sturm, *Reflections on the Works of God, and of His Providence, Throughout All Nature, for Every Day of the Year* . . . , 3 vols. (3rd ed., Dublin: William Jones, 1790). Sturm (1740-1786) was a German philosopher.

20. *Ibid.*, I, 4-6.

21. "So that, you know, I was able to distinguish the straight from the crooked, and to hunt for truth in the groves of Academe." *Epistles* II.ii.44-45 in *Horace: Satires*, trans. Fairclough (Loeb Classical Library), pp. 426-427.

22. Mathurin Cordier (1479-1564), French author of early schoolbooks for Latin instruction, preceptor of John Calvin.

23. Cornelius Nepos (99-24 B.C.), Roman historian who wrote biographies of eminent Romans and foreigners.

24. John Clarke, *An Introduction to the Making of Latin* . . . (Worcester: Isaiah Thomas, 1786); John Mair, *An Introduction to Latin Syntax* . . . (Philadelphia: Campbell, Conrad, & Co., by J. Bioren, 1799).

25. The surviving portion of the library of Thomas Jefferson preserved at the Library of Congress includes *Cornelii Nepotis, vitae excellentium imperatorum* (Amsterdam: P. and J. Blaeu, 1687) and (Glasgow: Robertus and Andreas Foulis, 1761).

26. Charles Rollin, *The Ancient History of the Egyptians, Carthaginians, Assyrians, Babylonians, Medes & Persians, Macedonians, and Grecians*, 13 vols. in 14 (London: James, John, and Paul Knapton, 1734-1739); Oliver Goldsmith, *Dr. Goldsmith's Roman History. Abridged by Himself. For the Use of Schools* (Philadelphia: Robert Campbell, 1795). *The Grecian History* . . . *Two Volumes in One* . . . did not appear in an American edition until Mathew Carey published it in Philadelphia in 1800, but it was certainly available in America in the English editions.

27. John Potter, *Archaeologica Graeca*, 2 vols. (Oxford: A. Swall, 1697-1699); Basil Kennett, *Romae antiquae notitiae; or, The Antiquities of Rome* (London: A. Swall and T. Child, 1696); Andrew Tooke, ed., François Antoine Pomey: *The Pantheon* . . . (London: ?, 1698).

28. "I have merited praise."

29. "There are moreover certain games which have an educational value for boys." Quintilian, *Institutio* I.iii.11, trans. Butler, I, 58-59.

30. *Ibid.* II.iii.1, trans. Butler, I, 205.

31. "For what better or greater service can I render to the commonwealth than to instruct and train the youth." *De divinatione* II.ii.4, in *Cicero: De senectute, De amicitia, De divinatione*, trans. William Armistead Falconer (Loeb Classical Library), pp. 374-375.

32. "In their eyes I should like these verses, such as they are, to find favor, and I should be grieved if their pleasure were to fall short of my hopes." *Satires* I.x.88-90, in *Horace: Satires*, trans. Fairclough, pp. 122-123.

# INDEX

# THE JOHN HARVARD LIBRARY

*The intent of
Waldron Phoenix Belknap, Jr.,
as expressed in an early will, was for
Harvard College to use the income from a
permanent trust fund he set up, for "editing and
publishing rare, inaccessible, or hitherto unpublished
source material of interest in connection with the
history, literature, art (including minor and useful
art), commerce, customs, and manners or way of
life of the Colonial and Federal Periods of the United
States . . . In all cases the emphasis shall be on the
presentation of the basic material." A later testament
broadened this statement, but Mr. Belknap's interests remained constant until his death.*

*In linking the name of the first benefactor of
Harvard College with the purpose of this later,
generous-minded believer in American culture the
John Harvard Library seeks to emphasize the importance of Mr. Belknap's purpose. The John Harvard
Library of the Belknap Press of Harvard University
Press exists to make books and documents
about the American past more readily
available to scholars and the
general reader.*